SPOILING FOR A FIGHT

SPOILING
FOR A FIGHT

THE RISE OF
ELIOT SPITZER

BROOKE A. MASTERS

TIMES BOOKS

HENRY HOLT AND COMPANY | NEW YORK

Times Books
Henry Holt and Company, LLC
Publishers since 1866
175 Fifth Avenue
New York, New York 10010
www.henryholt.com

Distributed in Canada by H. B. Fenn and Company Ltd.

Library of Congress Cataloging-in-Publication Data

Masters, Brooke A.
   Spoiling for a fight : the rise of Eliot Spitzer / Brooke A. Masters
     p. cm.
   Includes index.
   ISBN-13: 978-0-8050-7961-6
   ISBN-10: 0-8050-7961-0
   1. Spitzer, Eliot.   2. Attorneys general—New York (State)—Biography.
3. New York (State). Dept. of Law—Biography.   4. Antitrust law—
New York (State)—Biography.   I. Title.

KF373.S65M37   2006
340.092—dc22
[B]   2006040495

Henry Holt books are available for special promotions
and premiums. For details contact: Director, Special Markets.

First Edition 2006

Designed by Victoria Hartman

Printed in the United States of America

1   3   5   7   9   10   8   6   4   2

For John,
who always reminds me
to see the other side

CONTENTS

SPOILING FOR A FIGHT

1

WHEN MARKETS NEED TO BE TAMED

ELIOT SPITZER HAD HAD ENOUGH.

It was October 2004. For six months, the hard-charging New York State attorney general and his staff had been following a tip that the huge corporate insurance broker Marsh Inc. was taking secret payments to steer clients to particular insurance companies. And for six months the company's corporate parent, Marsh & McLennan, had been effectively stonewalling, contending that there had been no underhandedness—that Marsh's clients had known about the payments and that the money hadn't affected the recommendations of the firm's brokers. Months of combing through e-mails and company documents had shown just the opposite, and worse. Some Marsh brokers had solicited false bids and told insurance companies what fees to charge so that they could steer business to favored firms. That was price-fixing, which was not only fraudulent behavior but a crime. Several insurance executives involved had already confessed and agreed to plead guilty.

But when Spitzer and his lawyers met with Marsh & McLennan's general counsel, William Rosoff, on October 12, they didn't get the mea culpa they had expected. Instead, they got the brush-off. Rosoff insisted that his company didn't understand what all the fuss was about. It wasn't really clear what had happened. No clients had been hurt by the arrangements. This was just the way things worked. And finally he said dismissively, "You just don't understand the insurance business."

It was time to go public. Spitzer wasn't about to let an insurance broker push him around, even if it was the world's largest. As New York attorney general, Spitzer had spent much of the past six years mounting legal attacks on a variety of wrongs, which in his estimation included everything from Wall Street corruption to President George W. Bush's environmental policies. His balding pate, jutting chin, and pointing finger were ubiquitous on television news shows and in the pages of the country's top newspapers. When he ventured outside his downtown Manhattan office, he couldn't walk two blocks without being stopped by well-wishers who praised him for standing up to Big Business. Tipsters jammed his office phone lines with tales of woe and financial malfeasance. What's more, his investigations got results. Spitzer had faced down all kinds of giant firms, from the investment banks Citigroup and Merrill Lynch to the drug maker GlaxoSmithKline to the Food Emporium supermarket chain. He had exacted reforms and huge penalties: more than $1.5 billion from a dozen Wall Street investment banks for issuing biased research; more than $3.5 billion from mutual funds and brokers for improper short-term trading. And he was still only forty-five years old. All of this made him a rising star in the Democratic Party.

But in the Marsh case, Spitzer wanted to do more. He had decided to send a strong message to corporate America that his investigations were about more than money. From now on, top executives who presided over bad behavior couldn't simply claim they had had no idea what was happening, pay a fine, and expect to walk away unscathed. "We've been trying, through these cases, to make the larger point that some core ethical behavior is necessary," Spitzer reflected. "At some point you have to say, wait a minute, fellows. That's it. It's only when you hold the CEO accountable that you show people that something must change. The question is how to do that."

Dogged lawyers in Spitzer's office had already spent sleepless nights crafting a detailed and dramatic legal complaint that laid out the bid-rigging and contract-steering allegations against Marsh. But there was no evidence that the company's chief executive, Jeffrey Greenberg, had known about or condoned the scheme, which had started before his arrival at the company. Nor was it entirely clear that Greenberg had authorized Rosoff's stiff-arm defense. But even though the attorney general's investigators had never talked to the CEO directly, Spitzer was convinced the problems flowed from the executive suite. The bid-rigging case wasn't his first run-in with Marsh & McLennan. Its Putnam Investments subsidiary had been embroiled in the mutual fund trading scandal that had started the previous year. And its Mercer Consulting arm had paid a settlement as part of Spitzer's high-profile battle with New York Stock Exchange chairman Richard A. Grasso over Grasso's $140 million pay package. Marsh & McLennan "had three main businesses and no apparent controls in any of them. At some point you suspect the laxness is coming from the top. . . . It was at best a completely passive management," remembered David D. Brown IV, the assistant attorney general who spearheaded both the mutual fund and insurance probes for Spitzer. Bringing charges against Greenberg personally would be unfair, Spitzer knew. But there must be something else he could do.

On the morning of October 14, Spitzer gathered with his senior staff in his twenty-fifth-floor office in downtown Manhattan to prepare for that day's press conference about the Marsh case. Television cameras and newspaper reporters were already assembling in a room down the hall, and stock traders were hovering by their televisions, ready to dump their shares of whatever company turned out to be Spitzer's unlucky target. In Spitzer's office, his top deputies clustered beside his desk and peppered their boss with questions, pretending to be reporters. As the mock session broke up, Spitzer made an announcement. "I'm going to refuse to negotiate with this management," he said. Spitzer's lieutenants stared at him in silence.

Spitzer was proposing something unprecedented, at least in the recent annals of white-collar crime. In a free-market economy, boards of directors were supposed to have the freedom to choose company executives without government interference. By announcing that he would not negotiate with the firm's current leadership, Spitzer was imposing a Hobson's choice on Marsh & McLennan's board of directors—they could fire Jeffrey Greenberg or face possible criminal charges against the company. Recent history had shown that it was virtually impossible for a public company to withstand a criminal indictment. Just two years earlier, the accounting giant Arthur Andersen had all but vanished after being charged in federal court with obstruction of justice. And Merrill Lynch's stock had lost about 20 percent of its value in three weeks when Spitzer publicly refused to rule out corporate criminal charges. In the past, some prosecutors had asked for leadership changes as part of a settlement, but they had done it quietly, indirectly—the government might say to company lawyers with a knowing look, "You might find this case easier to settle if you had a different chief executive." No one could remember a case where a prosecutor went public with such a demand. "Are you sure you really want to do that?" asked First Deputy Attorney General Michele Hirshman, Spitzer's number two.

Hirshman and the others knew that Spitzer was already being roasted in the corporate world as a headline-hunting bully with no respect for market forces or due process of law. The *Wall Street Journal* editorial page, often seen as the voice of the business community's conservative wing, had made him its top enemy, editorializing against him weekly (and sometimes daily) as an ambitious meddler. The Forbes.com website was offering readers a printer-ready Halloween mask of Spitzer. Even some people who supported Spitzer's efforts to uncover fraud and change industries were perturbed by some of his tactics: the constant publicity, the rhetorical attacks on fellow regulators, and a perceived fondness for using the threat of criminal sanctions to pressure individuals and companies into cooperating with his probes. Forcing out Marsh's chief executive would only fan the flames.

To Spitzer, however, unusual times called for unusual measures. The collapse of the 1990s technology bubble had wiped out the college and retirement savings of millions of Americans. He believed that the country's business leaders had lost their moral compass. Some corporate giants, such as Enron and WorldCom, were so riddled with wrongdoing that they had collapsed when the fraud was revealed. Others, including some investment banks and mutual funds, had exploited their customers' trust in the name of higher profits. "How could we live in a society where we have so many smart people at the tops of these institutions and things have gone so terribly wrong?" Spitzer asked. "Have we forgotten our ethics?" Someone had to take action to protect the vulnerable, he believed, if only to restore the country's faith in its financial and political system. "The market does not survive without transparency, fair dealing and fair play," Spitzer explained. "We have persuaded tens of millions of Americans to invest in the market. If those new entrants to the market began to lose faith . . . they could withdraw from the market and put their money someplace else."

Spitzer believed that government officials should look back a century to another period when the country was coping with rapid economic change that created great wealth while impoverishing millions. Back in the 1890s, a small group of visionary but ruthless businessmen profited immensely from rapid industrialization and new economies of scale. Known collectively as the robber barons, titans such as John D. Rockefeller, J. Pierpont Morgan, and Edward H. Harriman built multimillion-dollar conglomerates and drove competition out of entire sectors of the economy. They dominated industry, finance, and commerce and tried to control the political process as well. But their success had a dark side. Factory workers lived and worked in appalling conditions. Poor harvests and rising indebtedness put many rural Americans at risk of losing their homes and livelihoods. Fraudsters abounded in the fledgling financial services sector, tricking innocent people out of their savings with promises that they too could make fistfuls of money.

The firebrand politician William Jennings Bryan tapped the rising anger of those who were losing out in the new industrial economy. He and his followers, the Populists, blamed Eastern banks and businesses for the high tariffs, expensive credit, and low agricultural prices that were impoverishing untold thousands of small farmers. The Populists wanted to flood the country's tight, gold-based monetary system with unlimited silver coins, a policy that would have made it easier for debtors to pay off their obligations but would also have sparked inflation. Dividing the world into "producers" against "elites," Bryan terrified the country's business and political establishment with his anticapitalist rhetoric. When the Democratic Party nominated Bryan for president in 1896, conservatives feared he would spark a bloody revolution. The nation's largest businesses ponied up millions of dollars to help elect William McKinley, dubbed by Republicans the "Advance Agent of Prosperity."

To some contemporary observers, Eliot Spitzer seemed to be a dangerous populist in the Bryan mold. In 2002, at a time when small investors were looking for someone or something—other than their own greed—to blame for their stock market losses, Spitzer supplied them with a ready target: the stock analysts who had blanketed the airwaves with rosy predictions for technology companies that later went bust. Wall Street and federal securities regulators had been talking for years about biased stock ratings and the conflict inherent in having investment banks rate the stocks of the companies they brought public. But they had taken little concrete action. In April 2002, Spitzer blew the issue wide open: he accused Merrill Lynch of fraud and released internal e-mails in which a star analyst called companies "dogs" even as he publicly rated those firms a "buy."

Spitzer's hyperactive manner, steely eyes, and burning sense of moral outrage played directly to investors' anger and charmed congressional committees and television audiences alike. He made the cover of *Fortune* and was named Crusader of the Year by *Time*. His flair for dramatic accusations and his willingness to use the media appalled executives accustomed to dealing with more discreet and less confrontational regulators. Many business leaders responded much as the old robber barons had done, by rallying around Spitzer's Republican opponents and using their influence within the political sphere to try to curb his power. U.S. Chamber of Commerce president Thomas J. Donohue took the unusual step of singling out Spitzer for criticism, calling his investigations "the most egregious and unacceptable form of intimidation that we have seen in this country in modern time."

But Spitzer explicitly rejected the populist label. Yes, some of his biggest cases touched on populist themes: he had gone after Wall Street and frightened supermarkets and restaurants into extending minimum-wage protections to some of New York's most vulnerable immigrant workers. He had also taken aim at gun manufacturers' sales practices, forced midwestern power plants to cut emissions, and challenged the Bush administration's efforts to gut the Clean Air Act. But none of that meant he wanted to destroy the market economy that had made his own family and the country rich. "The issues we've raised clearly have a populist air to them because they're designed to guarantee that there is equity and fairness regardless of who you are, the small investor, the low-wage worker," he acknowledged. "But the resolutions aren't designed to tear down the institutions. The effort was to make them work properly. A populist would have indicted the institutions."

Instead, Spitzer argued, his historical role models were Theodore Roosevelt and the Progressives, the less radical, and in many ways more successful, reform movement that grew out of the corporate excesses of the late nineteenth century. Spitzer kept a framed photo of TR on the wall of his Manhattan office, considering it a call to action rather than just another decoration. "I invoke him for the notion that capitalists understand when the market needs to be tamed," he explained. Spitzer also cited the Progressive influence in major speeches. "We are heirs to one of the most august, powerful political traditions in the world—New York's proud progressive tradition, embodied by Teddy Roosevelt, Al Smith and FDR," he said in late 2004. "Their politics of inclusion, opportunity and hope blazed the way for a capitalist system that went beyond favoritism and cronyism, a system that gave every person an opportunity to succeed. . . . During these last several years, their example inspired me. Our efforts in fighting fraud were meant to level the playing field, restore the integrity of the markets and give small investors and all others who participate in the markets the same opportunity as enjoyed by others."

Like the Populists, the Progressives sought to restore power and prosperity to the lower rungs of American society and tame what they saw as out-of-control capitalism. They agreed that ordinary people had lost their voice in government. But the Progressive solution was reform, not revolution. The Progressives believed that if politics and the financial markets could be cleansed of corruption and if power were given back to the people, the capitalist system could work well for all Americans, not just the rich. These reformers first sought to expose the country's ills through newspaper articles and civic investigations and then turned to sympathetic politicians to enact reforms, often at the state level first. Whenever the proposals proved effective and the Progressives could gather the votes, they sought legislation and regulation on the national level as well. New York was a hotbed for such crusaders, spawning not only Theodore Roosevelt, Alfred E. Smith, and later FDR, but also Charles Evans Hughes, who investigated the insurance industry, and Frances Perkins, the future labor secretary who did so much to establish worker-protection rules. Often derided at the time as traitors to their class and threats to America's prosperity, these reformist politicians and lawyers pushed through many of the laws and won many of the court cases that we now regard as cornerstones of our society. Among their accomplishments were minimum-wage laws, food and drug purity statutes, investor-protection laws, and limits on business consolidation.

Spitzer's interest in the Progressives was more than rhetorical. Many of his most famous cases relied on largely forgotten statutes and court decisions from the period: the Marsh bid-rigging case was based on violations of New York's first-in-the-nation 1893 antitrust law; his much-vaunted Wall Street investigations relied heavily on a largely forgotten 1921 antifraud statute known as the Martin Act; his efforts to crack down on illegal guns and out-of-state pollution both relied on the definition of a public nuisance that had solidified during the period. Months before the Marsh showdown, Spitzer and a former aide, Andrew Celli, Jr., wrote in *The New Republic* that the future of the Democratic Party depended on its ability to "promote government as a supporter of free markets, not simply a check on them" and to evoke "a vision consistent with trust-busting and other progressive market measures first enunciated early in the last century by Theodore Roosevelt." Nor was that article an isolated incident, Celli remembered. "He gets a perverse joy from pointing out to people that Teddy Roosevelt, the great trust-buster, was a Republican. He invokes TR almost to say you don't have to be a lefty Democrat to care about fairness in the market," Celli said. In political debates, Spitzer often described himself as a "pragmatic liberal" or "progressive." "What many people ascribe to the word *liberal* is a rejection of the market as a critical piece of what creates wealth," Spitzer said. "People understand *progressivism* as an effort to create opportunity within the market environment. . . . It has traction right now. Having seen a boom and bust, people feel that they've been taken. They understand that the rampant love we had for anything that had to do with the market was misplaced."

Though Theodore Roosevelt is remembered fondly today mostly for his groundbreaking efforts to protect investors, workers, consumers, and the environment, his attempts to rein in large companies and powerful businessmen—first in New York State as an assemblyman and governor and later as president—drew sharp criticism at the time. When Roosevelt made his first significant appearance on the political stage, as a New York assemblyman in 1882, he was widely ridiculed for his efforts to attack the state's entrenched culture of financial double-dealing. Colleagues dubbed him the "Cyclone Assemblyman" for his energy and lack of accomplishment and mocked him for his nasal tones—"Mister Spee-kar, Mister Spee-kar," he would call when he wanted attention on the Assembly floor.

Like Spitzer, Roosevelt first won attention for trying to protect ordinary shareholders. But his efforts to investigate whether a state court judge had taken bribes to help a financier take control of the giant Manhattan Elevated Railway company fell short. His fellow legislators, whose palms had been duly greased by the railroad, voted against impeaching the judge. Roosevelt was undaunted. When he was elected governor years later, he launched a series of reform efforts that so irritated New York business interests that they maneuvered to have him nominated in 1900 for the vice presidency as a way of getting him out of the state. National party bosses thought the move was foolish. One of them, Mark Hanna, scolded the delegates, "Everybody's gone crazy. . . . Don't any of you realize there's only one life between that madman and the presidency?" Hanna's fears were realized when an anarchist shot and killed President William McKinley in September 1901, propelling the forty-two-year-old Roosevelt into the highest office in the land.

As president, Roosevelt viewed regulation and gradual change as the best way to protect the capitalist system and stave off social upheaval. In a 1903 speech to the New York State Fair, he argued that a just society offered equal opportunity and equal protection to all people: "We must treat each man on his worth and merits as a man. We must see that each is given a square deal, because he is entitled to no more and should receive no less. . . . The welfare of each of us is dependent fundamentally upon the welfare of all of us." Unlike some of his fellow reformers, Roosevelt had nothing against bigness per se—he recognized that large-scale manufacturing could cut costs for consumers and that increased productivity could improve living standards for all. "In the long run, we all of us tend to go up or go down together," he said.

But Roosevelt was denounced as a dangerous radical when he decided in 1902 to take on the Northern Securities Company, a mammoth railroad holding company that had been formed a year earlier. The brainchild of J. P. Morgan, the firm dominated rail passenger and freight traffic between Chicago and the Pacific. It had an extraordinary market capitalization of $400 million but was considered to be overvalued by as much as 25 percent. Several states started antitrust investigations, but no one expected the federal government to act. The national regulators had sat on their hands while Morgan helped create a series of other enormous combinations—U.S. Steel, General Electric, and International Harvester—and the U.S. Supreme Court had largely neutered the federal Sherman Antitrust Act only a few years before. Roosevelt threw expectations out the window, ordering his staff to file an antitrust lawsuit against the holding company. "Government must now interfere to protect labor, to subordinate the big corporation to the public welfare, and to shackle cunning and fraud exactly as centuries before it had interfered to shackle the physical force which does wrong by violence," he explained. The stock market tanked on the news. "Wall Street is paralyzed at the thought that a President . . . would sink so low as to try to enforce the law," said the *Detroit Free Press*. Morgan and his peers were not only furious but frightened. How far was Roosevelt planning to go? Were all large corporations at risk? Morgan quickly reached out to Republican Party bosses and arranged a White House meeting with Roosevelt. "Are you going to attack my other interests, the steel trust and the others?" Morgan asked anxiously. Roosevelt was emphatic: "Certainly not, unless we find out that they have done something that we regard as wrong."

Five years later, Roosevelt enraged his business critics again, this time taking on the Standard Oil cartel that had been built by John D.

Rockefeller. The company's president, John D. Archbold, complained that Roosevelt had treated his firm with less respect than he would have given an African colony, and said, "Darkest Abyssinia never saw anything like the course of treatment we received." The philanthropist and Rockefeller protégé Frederick T. Gates predicted in a 1907 letter that the case would prove to be Roosevelt's undoing: "This amazing and reckless robbery and plunder under the forms of law may awake the business interests in the country and thoughtful men to the perils into which we have drifted." In the end, though, Roosevelt's view prevailed, and the Supreme Court ordered the breakup of Standard Oil in 1911.

To Spitzer, Roosevelt's goals and the criticism he encountered felt extremely familiar. Both men were Harvard-educated sons of privilege who believed that government had a duty to even the balance of power between individuals and corporations and to make sure that capitalism worked as well for small investors, workers, and consumers as it did for business executives and big investors. Spitzer was the son of an immigrant Jewish family that rose from a Lower East Side tenement to fabulous wealth in a single generation. He believed in hard work and smart investments and saw his labor and financial services cases as a way of making those same opportunities available to others. As a young man, Spitzer had made a concerted effort to see every side of this country's economic equation. He spent one summer in college doing backbreaking day labor—picking vegetables, stacking insulation, and digging ditches; in law school, he interned for the New York State Attorney General's Office and for the consumer advocate Ralph Nader. As a young prosecutor he stood out in the Manhattan District Attorney's Office for his reading material over lunch—while his coworkers scanned the *New York Post* and *Daily News* for news of their organized crime targets and investigations, Spitzer read *The Wall Street Journal*. Later he worked for white-shoe law firms and helped manage his family's investments. Like Roosevelt before him, Spitzer knew the world of his corporate targets well, which made him a particularly effective enforcer. "He understood Wall Street. All his friends worked there and he knew where the bodies were buried," said his Harvard Law School mentor, Alan Dershowitz.

Though Spitzer played up the Roosevelt parallels, he lacked the powers and bully pulpit of the presidency. He had to find other ways to force change. His chosen methods were simple: use old laws to attack new problems; do meticulous research; and share his findings with the media to maximize public pressure. He was a master of the accusatory press conference and the selective leak. His office's legal complaints were pointed, well written, and chock full of dramatic details. When his targets and other regulators complained that he was more interested in headlines than in real change, Spitzer often turned to the words of another icon of the Progressive era to defend and explain his approach: Louis D. Brandeis. "Publicity is justly commended as a remedy for social and industrial diseases. Sunlight is said to be the best of disinfectants; electric light the most efficient policeman," Brandeis wrote in 1913, a quotation that Spitzer repeatedly cited.

The two men shared more than a passion for using the media. Though Brandeis is best remembered as a Supreme Court justice, he got his start attacking many of the same targets that would draw Spitzer's ire a century later: Wall Street bankers, insurance firms, and companies that provided essential services such as public transportation and gas. Spitzer's critique of the financial services sector drew heavily from Brandeis's views a century earlier. Spitzer believed that the problems he uncovered in mutual funds, stock research, and insurance all stemmed from the same source: giant financial conglomerates that emphasized their bottom line and stock price at the expense of customer service. "We have seen larger and larger companies dealing with more and more atomized investors. These companies view customers as fee generators rather than individuals to whom they owe a fiduciary duty," Spitzer observed in 2004. Brandeis said much the same thing in 1905 as he argued that small customers were being overcharged for life insurance: "The extraordinary wastefulness of the present system of insurance is due in a large part to the fact that the business . . . is carried on for the benefit of others than the policyholders. The needs and financial inexperience of the wage-earners are exploited for the benefit of stockholders." By 1907, Brandeis had convinced the Massachusetts legislature to increase competition by allowing savings banks to issue small life insurance policies. Other states soon did the same. Brandeis followed up in 1913 with an attack on the securities industry that was perhaps the most effective critique of Wall Street ever issued. First published as a series in *Harper's Weekly*, "Other People's Money and How the Bankers Use It" was a clarion call for antitrust reform. In it, Brandeis displayed a talent for boiling complex abuses into catchy slogans, such as "The Endless Chain: Interlocking Directorates" and "A Curse of Bigness." Although Brandeis's economic theory was simplistic, his articles stirred public support for banking reform and the creation of the Federal Reserve and led President Woodrow Wilson to tap Brandeis to help establish the Federal Trade Commission in 1914.

As a lawyer, Spitzer knew that muckraking wasn't Brandeis's only tool. Brandeis had also used the courts effectively, pioneering a new kind of legal argument that revolutionized American litigation. Until Brandeis came along, the courts had largely been hostile to Progressive causes such as worker-protection statutes, ruling that they violated an elusive constitutional right to "freedom of contract." But then Brandeis took up the case of an Oregon law that set maximum hours for female laundry workers. Legal precedents were against him—in 1905 the Supreme Court had struck down a New York state law limiting bakers to ten hours of work a day, ruling, five to four, that it was "mere meddlesome interference with the rights of individuals." So Brandeis tried something new. He turned in a brief full of sociological, statistical, economic, and even medical data showing that overworked women were less healthy and less effective mothers. The filing revolutionized the practice of law—similar arguments are now known as "Brandeis briefs"—and achieved exactly what Brandeis had hoped. Concerned about "the strength and vigor of the race," the Supreme Court voted unanimously in 1908 to uphold the Oregon statute.

Brandeis's methods—both in court and in the media—won him widespread praise. Newspapers dubbed him "the People's Lawyer," a moniker Spitzer later adopted to explain the public advocacy side of his role as the New York State attorney general. But Brandeis was also deeply controversial. When Wilson nominated him to the Supreme Court in 1916, Brandeis found himself under unprecedented attack by the business and social interests whose dominance he threatened. Two U.S. Steel lawyers were seen in Boston just five days after the nomination was announced, trying to round up "a little knot of men" to speak out against the nominee. Eventually fifty-five prominent Bostonians, including Harvard president Abbott Lawrence Lowell, sent a petition to the Senate, saying, "We do not believe that Mr. Brandeis has the temperament and capacity which should be required in a judge of the Supreme Court. . . . He has not the confidence of the people." The opposition fell short, but it served as a reminder how divisive Brandeis and his methods had been.

Spitzer also turned to Brandeis for another kind of inspiration. As a Supreme Court justice, Brandeis became a vocal advocate of allowing states broad leeway to try new ways of protecting consumers, investors, and workers. Most famously, he wrote in 1932, "It is one of the happy incidents of the federal system that a single courageous State may, if its citizens choose, serve as a laboratory; and try novel social and economic experiments without risk to the rest of the country." Brandeis was often a lone voice, issuing dissents as his conservative colleagues struck down Progressive state statutes in the name of unfettered national commerce. But the justice's eloquent defense of federalism gained new relevance some seventy years later, when modern-day progressives such as Eliot Spitzer began seeking new ways to protect investors, workers, and the environment.

The country underwent not one but two sea changes in between Brandeis and Spitzer. First, the advocates of government regulation scored an extraordinary victory on a national scale. Rampant financial fraud and the devastating 1929 stock market crash made reformers believe that the states alone could not protect American society from the excesses of big business. As part of the New Deal, Congress enacted new national worker-protection rules, strengthened the Food and Drug Administration, and created the Securities and Exchange Commission, laying down rules that still hold sway over Wall Street. By 1938, even an initially skeptical Supreme Court had signed on by adopting the view that Congress's power over interstate commerce gave it the right to regulate business in areas that had once been the exclusive province of the states. The lasting impact of the New Deal reformers on our own times cannot be overstated: until 1934, for example, public companies did not have to submit to annual audits or make annual reports to either the government or their own shareholders. Until 1938, the FDA could not punish companies for making false therapeutic claims. With the addition of civil rights legislation and the creation of the Environmental Protection Agency in the 1960s and 1970s, the transformation was complete. The national government had become the main protector of consumers and investors, and the doctrine of states' rights was associated primarily with southern racists who had used it to try to fend off desegregation.

But by the time Spitzer ran for office in the 1990s, the balance of responsibilities between the states and the federal government was shifting back again. In the 1970s, federal officials, acknowledging that they couldn't do everything, gave grants to the states to beef up consumer and investor protection. Ten years later, President Ronald Reagan spearheaded a conservative revolution and launched what may be the greatest pullback of federal power in this country's history. Espousing a doctrine they called "federalism," economic libertarians and business interests began trying systematically to dismantle the federal government, arguing that power and programs rightfully belonged with the states. Reagan and his supporters cut back—or tried to cut back— federal regulation in areas ranging from consumer protection to civil rights to environmental safety. Cooperation with industry, rather than criminal enforcement, became the watchword of the day.

But the progressive impulse to use government to rein in business didn't wither away and die. Rather, it reemerged on the state level, particularly—but not exclusively—in areas where Democrats still held sway. In 1984, six northeastern states sued to force Reagan's Environmental Protection Agency to order pollution cuts, and twenty-one states teamed up to challenge a proposed settlement in a federal class-action securities fraud case in 1985. "They didn't really expect the states to step in, but we did," said Lloyd Constantine, who spearheaded antitrust issues for then New York State attorney general Robert Abrams's office. "Sometimes three states, sometimes five, sometimes all fifty sued at the same time on the same day." Led by Abrams, all fifty states worked together to combat price-fixing in the sneaker industry, and a coalition of forty-five states opened up the field for consumer satellite television by forcing seven of the largest cable operators to make more television programming available to consumer satellite broadcasters.

There was a brief pause in the 1990s, when Bill Clinton, a Democrat, became president and his administration began bringing more federal environmental and antitrust actions. Most liberal state attorneys general backed off or coordinated their actions with the federal government. But the 1994 Republican capture of Congress limited what Clinton and his appointees felt they could do in areas such as environmental protection and securities regulation. Arthur Levitt, the chairman of the Securities and Exchange Commission, wrote that fear of Congress had forced him to tone down his reform proposals on several occasions. He cited a 1994 decision to drop a proposal to change the way companies accounted for stock options. He called that decision "the single biggest mistake during my years of service." The federal pullback also picked up steam in the courts as judges appointed by Reagan and George H. W. Bush regularly reined in federal enforcers. In 1995, the Supreme Court ruled for the first time since the 1930s that there were limits to Congress's power to regulate interstate commerce—the part of the Constitution that authorizes most federal protection of investors, consumers, and the environment. In the next nine years, the high court would strike down nearly three dozen federal laws, circumscribing the federal government's ability to act in areas as diverse as stopping domestic violence and protecting rights of the disabled.

George W. Bush's election in 2000 completed the conservative sweep of federal power. Many of his appointees to key federal agencies had spent years working for or representing the industries they were going to regulate—Food and Drug Administration general counsel Daniel Troy and SEC chairman Harvey Pitt were prime early examples. The few obvious exceptions, such as Christine Todd Whitman, the moderate New Jersey governor named to head the Environmental Protection Agency, did not survive Bush's first term. Many of the regulatory agencies were also understaffed as the new century dawned. Thousands of skilled senior employees were nearing retirement, and competition from the private sector in the booming 1990s economy had made it all but impossible to replace them. By the time Spitzer turned his attention to the financial services industry, three-quarters of the SEC's front-line staff—the inspectors responsible for making sure brokers and mutual funds played by the rules—had been on the job fewer than three years. The combination of chronic overwork and Bush's political appointees left many federal agencies not only sympathetic to complaints about the high cost of complying with federal regulations but also too demoralized to fight hard when abuses were uncovered.

The Democrats concluded that they had to find a new strategy. Without control of the White House or Congress, efforts to control corporate interests would have to come from the states, using laws already on the books. State cooperation during the 1980s served as a blueprint, but in the 1990s and 2000s, key Democratic state officials were emboldened to take on far more. The epic 1998 tobacco settlement was one of the first and most dramatic successes. Forty-six states won billions of dollars for Medicaid and smoking cessation programs at a time when the federal courts were thwarting a national effort by the FDA to impose new regulations on nicotine products. "I doubt we could have done it if we were just one state," said Maryland attorney general Joseph Curran, Jr. "Collectively we are a much stronger adversary." The tobacco suits also introduced some state officials to a new resource: plaintiffs' law firms that added expertise and manpower and were willing to work on a contingency fee basis. At the same time, consolidation in the retail and health care sectors changed the nature of the consumer-protection work that has long been the bread and butter of many state attorneys general. "Twenty years ago, I did a bunch of cases against local drugstores," said James E. Tierney, a former Maine attorney general. "Today, what RiteAid does in Lisbon Falls, Maine, RiteAid does in San Francisco. . . . So it makes sense to pick up the phone and call California."

Eliot Spitzer took the practice to a completely different level. Progressive by instinct, prosecutorial by training, he had no compunction about diving headlong into areas that had previously been forbidden territory. If the federal government wasn't going to do it, he reasoned, New York State would. Just as Theodore Roosevelt and Louis Brandeis had ridden middle-class outrage at corrupt financiers and monopolists to national fame in the early twentieth century, Spitzer would become the avenging angel for millions of small investors who were angry that their dreams of easy wealth had vanished along with the 1990s bubble. "The timing was perfect, especially the issues involving the securities market," said Lloyd Constantine, who became a close friend of Spitzer's. "Once the stock market declined, people wanted to understand that everyone had played fairly, and they hadn't. There was a historical moment where the Bush administration wasn't going to do anything. . . . Eliot seizes the moment. He's fearless. He doesn't care that nobody's done this before. He doesn't care about offending the powers that be."

That willingness to overturn established norms also left Spitzer open to charges that he was an interfering hothead, convinced of his own righteousness and more interested in headlines than in forging compromises that would bring substantive change. Rather than hailing Spitzer as a hero, much of corporate America saw him as simply the most recent and most dangerous example of a pernicious problem they had been battling for years. Politically ambitious prosecutors had long viewed the financial services industry as an attractive target. As early as 1928, New York attorney general Albert Ottinger tried to ride his reputation as the hammer of Wall Street to the governor's mansion. He shut down one of the fledgling stock exchanges, investigated "investment trusts"—as mutual funds were known back then—and calculated that his prosecutions had saved investors $500 million a year. More recently, in 1993, Rudolph W. Giuliani parlayed a flamboyant career as a tough-as-nails federal prosecutor of white-collar crime in the 1980s into a successful run for mayor of New York. His high-profile cases had led the evening news—Wall Street executives were dragged out of their offices in handcuffs; the giant brokerage firm Drexel Burnham Lambert Group was forced to plead guilty to criminal charges and pay $650 million to settle a stock trading investigation; and Michael Milken, the "junk bond king," went to jail. But many of Giuliani's successes had a dark side—Drexel collapsed under the weight of the criminal case, costing thousands of jobs; Giuliani's office couldn't prove its case against several of the traders who had been so prominently arrested; and several of Giuliani's other high-profile corporate cases were overturned on appeal. "There should be a law passed that precludes any prosecutor from running for office for three or five years [after he leaves office]," said Robert G. Morvillo, a former prosecutor and a prominent white-collar defense attorney who tangled several times with Spitzer. "You really don't want your chief law enforcement officer running the office based on what's going to be politically popular. . . . It takes away the appearance of fairness."

Many on Wall Street still bore the scars of Giuliani's enforcement efforts, and to them, Spitzer, in his crusade against white-collar crime, seemed to be making all the same mistakes. In seeking to change entire industries, these critics charged, Spitzer ran roughshod over individuals and corporations. His office was famously dismissive of the ordinary regulatory process—setting tighter deadlines and demanding quicker decisions than the defense bar had seen in years. His emphasis on litigation and public shaming produced headlines and forced many firms to settle, but it sometimes caused collateral damage. Many of the companies Spitzer targeted were major employers whose shares were held by millions of small investors. When their share prices tumbled, the pain ran deeper than the executive suite. "The industry and the economy of New York City were done great harm, a needless harm" by the Marsh investigation, said New York insurance superintendent Howard Mills, a Republican former legislator. "A surgeon tries to take out the cancer and leave the healthy tissue behind. A lot of healthy tissue was sacrificed here. Small people who had nothing to do with this were hurt: investors, employees, an entire industry was shaken. . . . He wasn't using a scalpel; he was using a machete."

Spitzer's success also spawned imitators around the country, raising the specter of regulatory chaos. Securities regulators in California, New Jersey, Massachusetts, and elsewhere brought their own investigations of the investment banks and the mutual fund industry. Oklahoma filed criminal charges against the leadership of WorldCom, and Connecticut sued to force the federal government to pay for the educational testing required by the federal No Child Left Behind Act. And a host of attorneys general banded together to challenge all manner of federal environmental decisions. But this flowering of regulatory competition produced a backlash. Some of Spitzer's emulators lacked his skills. Business groups complained—rightly in some instances—that their members were wasting millions responding to dozens of duplicative subpoenas and defending themselves against weak cases brought by politically ambitious state officials. This trend toward state regulation also meant that some citizens—those in New York and California, for example—got more protection than others. There was a good reason why the first Progressives fought to pass national standards. "A proliferation of conflicting state rules can create inefficiency and inflexibility in our national economy," said John D. Graham, head of the federal Office of Management and Budget's Office of Information and Regulatory Affairs. Registered Rep Online, a Web site for the securities industry, put it more succinctly: "Imagine 50 Eliot Spitzers."

Even Spitzer has conceded that the flurry of state activism could cause problems, though he challenged his critics to point to a current example. "The most intellectually consistent view is the one I held in law school: Let the feds do it—but do it," he said. A strong federal regulator beats a clutch of activist states "hands down," he said. "Then the question of Balkanization doesn't come up." But Spitzer rejected the charge that he was overreaching or bringing marginal cases in order to boost his own political career. "There will always be apologists for the powerful and politically connected who commit crime," he said. "What is amazing to me about these cases that we have made is that nobody was willing to make them before. No one was willing to stand up and say this is wrong."

When Spitzer strode to the microphones on October 14, 2004, to announce his case against Marsh & McLennan, he was as wired and pumped up as his staff had ever seen him. Describing his insurance investigation as "broad, deep and disappointing for what it reveals," Spitzer told the media that he had uncovered "classic cartel behavior," "collusion," and "price-fixing." "It will be prosecuted," he said. Then, visibly angry, he paused and said he had a message for the board of directors of Marsh & McLennan. "You should look long and hard" at the company's top executives, he said. "The leadership of that company is not a leadership I will talk with. It is not a leadership I will negotiate with." Asked to elaborate, he hammered the point home: "We were misled by the very highest levels of that company."

2

A MAN IN A HURRY

TO GET A SENSE OF HOW FAR AND HOW FAST THE FAMILY OF ELIOT LAURENCE
Spitzer has risen through American society, just look at the places
where they have lived. Spitzer's paternal grandfather, Morris, who arrived in New York after World War I after a stint in the Austrian army
as a communications officer, lived above his printing shop on Manhattan's Lower East Side. Eliot's father, Bernard, grew up on East Fifth
Street near Avenue B in that neighborhood, in a series of walk-up railroad flats without hot water. Eliot's maternal grandfather, Joseph Goldhaber, lived nearby but was slightly better off. A teacher who had
emigrated from Palestine, he lived in a cooperative with a guard and an
elevator. Eliot's parents moved in and out of a series of tiny apartments
during the early years of their marriage, but by the time Eliot was
born, on June 10, 1959, they had purchased a modest town house just
off the Henry Hudson Parkway in the Riverdale section of the Bronx.
The end unit of four, it was perched on a hillside and made up for its
lack of lawn by being across the street from a city playground. Three
years later, the Spitzers moved across the highway into the wealthy
Fieldston community, just blocks from the exclusive Horace Mann
School, where both Eliot and his older brother would attend middle
and high school. Built in 1928, their sprawling but gracious Tudor

home had not only a backyard but also a front field, where the children could play soccer, and a paved area by the garage for basketball. By the time he became attorney general, Eliot Spitzer was living in a luxury Manhattan apartment building that was built by his father on Fifth Avenue, just south of the Metropolitan Museum of Art. His parents split time between their own Fifth Avenue apartment and a home in the tony Westchester County suburb of Rye.

The family lived an accelerated version of the classic Eastern European Jewish success story, albeit with a few bumps in the road. Though Morris had studied medicine in Vienna, he survived in America by opening a small print shop that churned out wedding invitations, synagogue bulletins, and advertising leaflets. He did well enough to bring his wife and oldest son, Harry, to the United States from Austria in the early 1920s. Bernard (1924) and Ralph (1929) were born in New York. The Great Depression hit the family hard. According to Spitzer family lore, Morris once went nearly a year without receiving a single printing order. Rather than climb the walls, he passed the time by printing fancy borders on his paper stock—that way, when business returned, he would be able to offer customers fancy paper at little or no additional cost. Morris was ruthlessly practical. He squelched Harry's dreams of being a concert pianist and insisted he study accounting instead. Bernard rocketed through high school and college, earning an engineering degree at City College by age eighteen, even though he had a lifelong love of political philosophy and an interest in studying law. Bernard met Anne Goldhaber at a down-at-the-heels resort in the Catskills, where he was playing saxophone in the band and she was working as a counselor planning activities for guest children. She was just fourteen, and they hit it off immediately, even though she already had a beau—the future actor Jerry Stiller used to carry her books home from school. Anne and Bernard married in 1945, while she was still in her teens, but World War II was on, and he shipped out almost immediately to Europe, as a naval intelligence officer. She stayed home and finished her bachelor's degree at Brooklyn College.

Bernard briefly tried his hand at engineering and almost immediately decided to go into construction. "The practice of engineering as engineering is deadly dull," Bernard said. "What I do, which is to create buildings, is more challenging." After a brief stint in Syracuse, where Anne got the first of two master's degrees, Bernard began building what would become one of New York's premier real estate development businesses, with a specialty in luxury high rises. Anne taught English literature, ending up at Marymount Manhattan College, where, as recently as the fall of 2005, she taught an extension school course on twentieth-century literature. The Spitzers set high standards for their three children—Emily, born in 1954, Daniel, born three years later, and Eliot. All three children went to Riverdale Country School, a well-known local private school, for the elementary grades. Emily then carpooled into Manhattan to attend The Brearley School, a top-notch girls' school, while the boys walked to Horace Mann. All three sailed into Ivy League colleges—Harvard for Emily, and Princeton for Daniel and Eliot. The values Bernard sought to pass on were simple: "Curiosity, commitment to an undertaking, and virtue. If you're going to do it, do it," he explained. The whole family skied and played tennis with a passion. At the age of four, Eliot was dropped off for ski school with his siblings even though he was officially still too young to participate. His parents instructed him to play dumb rather than lie if asked his age. Even well into their forties, Eliot and Daniel continued to scare their mother by bombing down the double-black-diamond runs on the annual family ski trip to Colorado. According to his parents, Eliot was determined from the start. As a toddler, he loved the playground across the street and would absolutely refuse to leave. "It would take two people to pick him up. He kept himself so stiff that he was rooted," Anne remembered.

The Spitzers also played board games to win. Scrabble routinely sparked friendly but intense squabbles—family members still joke about Emily's impassioned attempt to use *rehaze* despite its absence from the family dictionary. In one often-repeated tale, Bernard reduced Eliot, then about seven or eight, to tears during a game of Monopoly when the boy landed on a property heavily loaded with houses and was unable to pay the rent. "He said, you're going to learn what happens when you borrow and you don't repay," Eliot remembered. What gets told less often is that this was not the message Bernard was trying to convey. When the game started, Eliot, not Bernard, held the crucial piece of property and Bernard was able to buy and build on it only because he had ordered his son to sell him the square. "He didn't realize his own rights," Bernard said, adding that he believed that the experience "convinced Eliot, never defer to authority." The famous foreclosure was also far from the only time that Bernard subjected his children to the same hard-core wheeling and dealing that he used at the office. Not content simply to buy, sell, and swap properties, as the Monopoly rules called for, Bernard Spitzer negotiated for partial interests, shared rent payments, and free passage deals that often left his offspring eating his dust. "His eyes would gleam. . . . I don't know that he ever lost a game," said Daniel Spitzer, now a neurosurgeon.

The Spitzers were culturally Jewish rather than religiously observant. Though the family gathered for the major Jewish holidays, Eliot did not have a bar mitzvah and Bernard and Anne did not join a temple until they had grandchildren. The family lived well—they had a live-in housekeeper, belonged to an exclusive beach club, and took interesting vacations—but shied away from spending money on cars, clothing, and other showy things. Bernard and Anne cared deeply about politics and progressive causes—they supported Eugene McCarthy for president in 1968—and they wanted their children to make an impact on the world, to leave it a better place than when they arrived. They found a variety of ways to drive that point home. Once, when Eliot and Daniel were small, probably seven and nine, Bernard took them to his current highrise project and left them there to try their hand at construction work. The two boys spent the entire morning using ice chippers almost as tall as they were to scrape construction dust and other flaws off recently hardened concrete. The Italian foreman who had been left in charge of the boys repeatedly advised them through his thick accent, "Go to school. Don't do what I do. Use your brain."

The family ate breakfast together every morning, but it was their dinners that really made them stand out. Never ones for small talk, and addicted to fierce intellectual arguments, Bernard and Anne insisted that the adolescent children take turns coming up with a nightly discussion topic. Emily often chose feminist issues, challenging her father's views on the proper roles and behavior of women; Daniel, a budding scientist, would lecture on the definition of a desert or the inner workings of a steam boiler, clearing the way for a less serious discussion of baseball; Eliot opted to spark debate on political topics: the death penalty or the need to balance safety needs with civil liberties. By high school, Daniel was reading *Scientific American*, and Eliot was paging through *Foreign Affairs* in preparation for the nightly meal. "I don't think Eliot's B.S.'d in his life," Daniel said. "The idea of him walking into a discussion and winging it is so foreign. He's not going to claim a fact unless he has determined it." The verbal jousting was so intense that the family often intimidated dinner guests. "I used to study harder for a Saturday night dinner at the Spitzers than I ever did for an exam at Princeton," said Bill Taylor, Eliot's college roommate, who later founded the magazine *Fast Company*.

Despite the high-toned content, family gatherings were also full of laughter. Anne and Bernard took as much pleasure in teasing each other and the children as they did in intellectual combat. Snappy comebacks were valuable currency, and the only real enemy was pomposity. The children routinely made fun of Anne's lack of interest in cooking—"If it takes more than thirty minutes to make it, my mom won't make it," they would warn their friends. And on one occasion, when Anne announced that she and Bernard were going out to the movies, their teenagers rolled their eyes and replied, "Mom, you and Dad are going to see a *film!*"

Life at the Spitzers made Eliot unusual even within the rarified world of Horace Mann. His classmate and lifelong friend Jason Brown (whose friendship with Eliot followed a series of vicious arguments about rent control in the seventh grade—Brown was for, Spitzer against) can still quote a line from a story Spitzer wrote for the in-house literary magazine about a poor man looking up at a skyscraper. "'His visage described discountenance.' Translation: he was unhappy," Brown said. "Eliot's vocabulary was always more sophisticated than the rest of us." At Horace Mann, Spitzer was liked and well rounded—he played on the tennis and soccer teams, narrowly lost out on being editor of the school newspaper, and excelled in academics. His nickname, "Toile Reztips," was simply his name backward, but the *toil* part also captured his classmates' sense of him as something of a grind. Friends joked that he would be secretary of state someday. But he wasn't wildly popular—when the school yearbook, the *Mannikin*, published its list of bests, "most likely to" and favorites, Eliot didn't appear in a single one. Self-conscious about his tree trunk–like legs and angular chin, Eliot also didn't stand out in the looks department and did not have a serious girlfriend during high school. It didn't help that Horace Mann was all male for most of his career there and didn't hold a prom.

It was on the tennis team that Eliot had his first brush with celebrity. One afternoon, Horace Mann got completely destroyed by Trinity, its rival on the Upper West Side of Manhattan. Eliot went home and told his parents, "I just saw the fellow who's going to be the number one player in the world." He later recounted what followed: "My parents looked at me, and they said, 'Just 'cause he beat your team doesn't mean he's going to be the number one player in the world.' And I said, 'No, no. He really is. . . . He's a phenomenon.'" The player was John McEnroe. Eliot used to joke to Jason Brown that he was responsible for McEnroe's tennis career because the two also faced each other on the soccer field and Eliot refrained from breaking his opponent's legs.

In 1976, Eliot and Emily volunteered for the congressional campaign of Edward Meyer, a liberal Democrat who was seeking to represent their home district. Meyer assigned Eliot to door-knocking and literature drops, because he wanted the already charismatic and personable teenager to come in contact with and impress voters. Emily and Eliot also convinced their parents to host a fund-raising reception. Meyer won the primary but lost the general election. A few months later, Eliot had to choose quotations for his senior yearbook page. "The worst thing about political jokes is that some of them get elected," he wrote.

A year later, Spitzer graduated and went on to Princeton, where he opted to study at the Woodrow Wilson School, perhaps the premier institution in the country for budding policy wonks. He studied politics, philosophy, and economics, listened to the Grateful Dead, and developed a lifelong love of rocker Bruce Springsteen. Like most college students in the late 1970s, he tried marijuana and drank some alcohol. But friends from that time, such as Elena Kagan, now the dean of Harvard Law School, recall him as "earnest" and "a very serious guy," more interested in intellectual debate than partying. The young Spitzer was assigned to the Economics 101 class taught by Princeton president William G. Bowen, whom he impressed as a "superb" student who asked challenging questions and really listened to the answers. He was also intensely competitive—when he and his classmate Carl Mayer got into a spaghetti-eating contest at a local restaurant, they didn't stop until each had consumed nearly seven pounds of pasta. Spitzer also took up running, lost his baby fat, and developed the phenomenally disciplined approach to exercise and diet that has kept him trim even on the rubber chicken fund-raiser circuit. "We'd go to the salad bar and he'd say 'good roughage,'" remembered Jason Brown, who went with Spitzer to Princeton.

One night, at the end of Eliot's sophomore year, Bernard and Anne Spitzer got a very late night call from a jubilant Eliot. He had just become the first sophomore in recent memory to win the presidency of the student government. "I didn't even know he was running," Anne remembered. "He didn't want us to worry." Or know that he had tried and lost. Spitzer had beaten a field of juniors with a tireless campaign and a popular issue: pushing the deadline for switching from a letter grade to the pass/fail option further back into the semester so that students would be able to avoid damage to their GPA after a disastrous midterm. Once in office, he also tried to get the student government to address hot political issues of the late 1970s, such as apartheid in South Africa and the poor treatment of the university's clerical and technical workers.

Spitzer was clearly an "organization person," in President Bowen's words, focused on working within the system rather than using guerrilla tactics. Carl Mayer, who shared Spitzer's library carrel, staged a two-day sit-in at the main administrative building to protest the university's refusal to divest from companies that did business in South Africa, while other activists picketed the building daily. Rather than participate in direct action, Spitzer introduced a resolution in the student government on the subject. However, Spitzer also impressed his roommate Bill Taylor, who fancied himself a rabble-rouser, by talking tough about the issues directly to President Bowen and the deans. "I remember being woken up out of a sound sleep, and Eliot was reading the riot act on the phone to some administrator. Eliot was willing to be combative one on one with the administration. He was willing to take it right to the person who was on the other side of the table," Taylor said.

For most of his college career, Spitzer spent his summers like the policy maker he hoped to be. He interned for Ralph Nader's Public Citizen, and on Capitol Hill for Congressman Bruce Caputo, the Republican who had beaten Edward Meyer for the Riverdale seat. But one year, inspired by a classmate who had taken a year off to wander the country, Spitzer did something a bit more unusual. He worked day labor jobs in Atlanta, in New Orleans, and on a farm in upstate New York, rising at 5:00 A.M. each day and accepting whatever work was available. The assignments were often lonely, dirty, and backbreaking—he did heavy construction work in a hotel kitchen, picked tomatoes on the farm, and stacked fiberglass insulation in a warehouse, by far the worst job of all. At night, he slept at YMCAs and in single-room-occupancy flophouses, some of them crawling with cockroaches, and tried unsuccessfully to change people's lives. "He tried so hard to talk to the young men and induce them to go to school or learn some trade, and it didn't take," his mother remembered. His brother Daniel described that summer as the ultimate policy experiment: Eliot "wanted to see if you were uneducated in this country, did you have to be on welfare or could you support yourself and potentially a family. . . . He came away with a conclusion that this was still the land of opportunity but you had to want to work hard."

Spitzer's only serious academic crisis occurred in early 1981, during his senior year at Princeton. Required to write a thesis to graduate, he initially opted for a demanding theoretical topic: applying the philosopher John Rawls's theory of distributive justice to conflicts between generations. Rawls believed that social goods such as liberty, opportunity, and wealth should be evenly shared, but Spitzer reasoned that if one generation followed Rawls's admonition to maximize everyone's well-being at that moment, the next generation would be that much poorer because no one would save for the future. He wanted to find a fairer solution. Two months before the thesis's due date, he had nothing written. "It was a really tense time. He bit off way more than he could chew," Taylor said.

Finally, Spitzer realized something had to give and changed topics completely. "I thought, 'I've got to come up with an easy question.' So I said, 'Will the Soviets invade Poland [to quash the country's Solidarity labor movement, which was dominating the headlines at the time]? This is easy, I'll just read *The New York Times* every day,'" he remembered. There was one catch: what if he made a prediction and then was wrong? Spitzer decided to play the odds, concluding that if he predicted the Red Army tanks would not roll, he only had to sweat out the monthlong grading period. The resulting 147-page document, "Revolutions in Post-Stalin Eastern Europe: A Study of Soviet Reactions," helped earn him high honors and admission to the academic honor society Phi Beta Kappa. Spitzer's thesis adviser, Miles Kahler, was impressed. "To change topics midstream and still successfully complete a thesis—that's an accomplishment," said Kahler, now an international relations professor at the University of California–San Diego. "This was a young man who was ambitious for the right reasons and had the skills and talent to do it. He was clearly on his way to making his mark."

Spitzer's college days also brought a couple of romances with women who were as serious about academics as he was. During his junior year, Spitzer met Anne-Marie Slaughter, a senior who was passionately interested in policy-making and international affairs. He knocked her socks off. "I remember when I first met him, thinking 'Wow!' He just radiated this ferocious energy and commitment," said Slaughter, who is now dean of the Woodrow Wilson School. Slaughter and Spitzer dated briefly until she graduated and went off to Oxford. Slaughter remembered Spitzer as a man in a hurry. "He had just a tremendous sense of being able to make things happen," she said. "He was ambitious . . . [but] this was not about the cult of Eliot. It was more about getting things done." Spitzer also had a more serious romantic relationship with another Woodrow Wilson School student, Runa Alam. During their more than a year together, she said, Spitzer was "very steady, very caring, very honorable, somebody who was a bit of a Rock of Gibraltar." In his thesis he thanked her for helping to "create an environment in which we could all write theses or J.P.s [junior papers] without sacrificing our sanity." They broke up at graduation because she was going to New York to work for Morgan Stanley, a major investment bank (she now runs three private equity funds that invest in Africa), and he was headed off to Harvard Law School.

In Cambridge, Spitzer did quite well academically, surviving the cutthroat competition to make the staff of the *Harvard Law Review*. When Anne and Bernard heard the news, "we showed our glee," Anne said, but couldn't resist the customary family dig, this time at Eliot's terrible handwriting. "There's only one reason you made law review. They didn't know what you were writing," Anne teased. Eliot was ready with a comeback: "Mom, I don't write my exams. I type them." While in school, Eliot found ways to stay connected to politics and the outside world. He wrote his note—the published article required of all *Harvard Law Review* editors—on the constitutional implications of the proposed Balanced Budget Amendment then being considered by Congress. He was against it, arguing that the Constitution should be amended to protect minority rights or improve the lawmaking process, not simply to advocate a particular policy. Spitzer also worked with the famed arms-control lawyer Abram Chayes on an article about the international laws governing weapons in space.

Spitzer and his good friend Cliff Sloan also worked as research assistants for Professor Alan Dershowitz on a variety of issues, including the successful appeal of socialite Claus von Bulow's murder conviction. Dubbed "Cliff Eliot" for their close relationship and habit of working together, the two students took pride in their fast turnaround, often working late into the night in order to have a memo on Dershowitz's desk by morning. Nor was their work confined to library research. During the von Bulow appeal, Dershowitz sent Spitzer into a series of dicey situations to reinterview seedy witnesses to uncover new evidence. "It was Sleazeville, USA," Dershowitz remembered. "I was worried, but he loved it. We uncovered every rock and looked under every stone. . . . He was just so determined to get things right."

Back then, Sloan stood out as the politically ambitious one, while Spitzer seemed destined to be a policy wonk. "Cliff was clearly going to run for elective office, but Eliot was . . . clearly going to work in a back room somewhere as the brains behind someone. We were shocked when he emerged," Dershowitz said. "He was the quiet one, the behind-the-scenes guy, the library guy. It's amazing how he's blossomed." In fact, during their second year, Sloan ran for president of the *Law Review* and Spitzer supported his unsuccessful candidacy.

Still, Spitzer struck other friends and teachers as combative, cocky, and fiercely determined, albeit in a rather friendly way. When Dershowitz gave Cliff Eliot his tickets to a Celtics-Knicks game, the seats were behind the Boston Celtics bench. Spitzer showed up in full New York regalia and rooted so loudly for the visiting team that other ticket holders complained. And during a summer internship at the New York Attorney General's Office between his first and second years of law school, Spitzer challenged his boss, Lloyd Constantine, to a tennis match within days of his arrival. "He was very polite. He said, 'I'm Eliot Spitzer and I'm your intern,' but the subtext was 'I can lick you,'" said Constantine, who realized he had found a kindred soul and would become one of Spitzer's closest friends and backers. When Sloan, Spitzer, and a third friend decided on a whim to run in the New York City Marathon, only a few months away, two of them got tired of the training almost immediately. Spitzer stuck it out and not only ran in the race but finished it.

While at Harvard, Spitzer also had his first introduction to the Federalist Society, the conservative group founded in 1982 to fight what its members saw as activist judges and liberal law professors imposing their values on the rest of the country. Federalist Society members were advocates of limited government and the free market, and they revived the principle of states' rights as a way to curb the power of Congress and the federal judiciary. Back then, Spitzer said, he was completely opposed to federalism theory, seeing it as an attempt to revive a discredited philosophy that had been used to justify segregation, pollution, and the oppression of minority groups. Federalism also struck him as economically impractical—companies that did business in many states would find it difficult to cope with multiple regulators.

For most of his first two years of law school, Spitzer dated Nadine Muskatel, a fellow Princeton graduate then attending Harvard Medical School. Set up by mutual friends, they were both Jewish and from New York, though his family was far wealthier than hers. "He was such a brilliant guy. He had such a wonderful way of debating and listening to people," she remembered. "He lets you talk. He'll take it all in. He grants you all the points you have made, and then he'll gently show you the other way." Though some friends thought they might get married,

Nadine broke up with Spitzer after meeting the man who would eventually become her husband. Even so, Spitzer let her brother borrow his Cambridge apartment for the summer.

Then, in January of his third year, Spitzer met Silda Wall, a self-possessed woman from North Carolina who had recently returned to the law school after a one-year leave of absence. Spitzer had rented a condo near Mount Snow, in Vermont, and offered its use to a group of friends for the weekend. This being graduate school, the friends brought more friends, and the house was full to the gills by the time the host got there. Spitzer arrived a day late, having stayed behind in Cambridge to finish up his January term work. It was perhaps five in the morning. Wall, who had insomnia, was awake in the living room when Spitzer let himself in. "Who are you?" she demanded. ("I thought he was a burglar," she said later by way of explanation.) "Who the hell are you? This is my house," he replied. She was wearing what Spitzer remembered as "piggy pajamas," fuzzy flannel nightwear that would have been appropriate on a little kid.

Spitzer was intrigued. But when he got back to Harvard, he realized that he had somehow misheard or mangled her name and he had no idea how to get back in touch with her. So he paged through the entire face book—all the way to the *W*s—to find her. Cliff Sloan, his research buddy, told him he didn't have a chance. Indeed, Spitzer almost blew it, calling Wall at midnight on a Wednesday to ask her out for that Friday. She turned him down. He tried again in February, after running into her on Valentine's Day with her arms full of flowers. This time she agreed to go out on a date. When Spitzer arrived to pick her up in his beat-up red Chevy Cavalier, she asked where they were going. He had no plan in mind, so Wall decided to teach him a lesson. She picked the Peacock, an upscale Cambridge restaurant that students tended to save for parental visits and other special occasions. "I learned something there," remembered Spitzer.

Silda Wall was from an entirely different world. Born and raised in a small town in North Carolina, she was an accomplished artist. Protestant to his Jewish, spiritual to his secular, she was also, he said fondly, "too much of a southern belle" to ever call him for a date. She was coming out of an intense but unhappy relationship and not looking for anything serious. But she intrigued him immensely. She was passionate about international affairs and could more than hold her own intellectually, a necessity if she was going to survive in the Spitzer clan. Told that Bernard's first comment about her had been "nice teeth," she gave as good as she got. When Spitzer asked for her opinion of his father, she replied, "He has very nice legs." Wall turned out to be nearly as unostentatious as her new boyfriend. After law school, they moved to separate apartments in New York and soon were both working so hard that they had little time for romance. Wall was billing more than three thousand hours a year at the high-powered firm of Skadden, Arps, Slate, Meagher & Flom, so many of their dates were for takeout food in the law firm's conference rooms—Wall marked up documents while Spitzer read the newspaper. They also met regularly at the Silver Star Diner on Second Avenue, a Manhattan coffee shop with laminated menus, greasy spoon décor, and a reputation for surprisingly good seafood.

Spitzer initially clerked for U.S. district judge Robert Sweet, a liberal Republican whom Spitzer credits with teaching him "what the law is for [and] how it can be used to make sure people who need help can get it." In Sweet's chambers, Spitzer developed a taste for organizing his work in three-ring binders and an abiding belief that the law is a dynamic thing that, in Sweet's words, "should be an effective instrument for change." The young clerk impressed the judge with his diligence. "When he's working, he's like a steam engine," Sweet said, noting that while Spitzer was around, the office had no backlog of hearings or rulings to speak of. "He was not unassuming. Even then you noticed when Eliot came into the room, but he was not showy. . . . I knew his father was in real estate, but that was the end of it." It was only when Spitzer invited the judge out to his folks' house in Rye for a sharply competitive game of tennis that Sweet realized the size of his protégé's bankroll and the strength of his ambition. Sweet later performed Eliot and Silda's civil ceremony at the Central Park Boathouse in 1987, and he would swear in Spitzer for his second term as attorney general in 2003.

Shortly after moving to New York, Spitzer played a trick on his big sister, Emily, that remains one of the family's best remembered practical jokes. It also reinforced the family ethos that no one—with the possible exception of Bernard Spitzer—was so smart or important that they couldn't be challenged. A relatively young lawyer for the National Organization for Women, Emily had been invited to participate in a panel on women's issues on a local radio station with a couple of well-known political figures, including Carol Bellamy, the president of the City Council. But when the show reached the audience participation section, all the calls were for Emily. Even stranger, she knew all the answers. Then suddenly, she heard Eliot's voice. He was asking some kind of bar-exam-type brainteaser about the relationship between the Fourteenth Amendment and the right to an abortion. He and his friends had set her up. "All I really wanted to say was, 'I'm going to kill you, Eliot,' but I answered the question somehow," she remembered. To this day, Emily said, whenever she hears Eliot doing a call-in show, she fantasizes about returning the favor.

After his clerkship ended, Spitzer did a brief stint at the top-ranked law firm Paul, Weiss, Rifkind, Wharton & Garrison, but he remained a serious policy wonk with an interest in criminal justice. In December 1985, he, Carl Mayer, and Bill Taylor reunited in Cambridge for a weekend bachelor party. Spitzer arrived early, and when Taylor showed up to let him into the apartment he found Spitzer getting into the mood for the party by reading a RAND Corporation study on juvenile recidivism. When the trio decided to rent *Animal House* and *Caddyshack* for their evening's entertainment, the clerk at the video store was so outraged by their lame stag night plans that he threw in a complimentary copy of *Debbie Does Dallas*. The trio never took advantage of the clerk's generosity—a porn flick "seemed even more lame than watching *Animal House*," Taylor said.

About that time, Spitzer took a new job working for the longtime Manhattan district attorney Robert M. Morgenthau, who was already building a reputation for barging into securities fraud and other white-collar cases when he felt federal authorities weren't being aggressive enough. Spitzer benefited from a program that allowed top recruits to skip the customary break-in period prosecuting run-of-the-mill street crimes. He soon caught the eye of Michael G. Cherkasky, the investigations division chief charged with reviving the DA's moribund rackets bureau and building new cases against organized crime. Cherkasky had the pick of the office, and Eliot Spitzer was at the top of his list. "Eliot was the star and he was the star from the beginning. He's hardworking and has good judgment," Cherkasky said. "He's smart and innovative and he gets along with people. Nobody carries Eliot's bag. He's gonna get in there and do windows."

Morgenthau had promised to attack mob elements that were dragging down the city's economy, and Spitzer argued in a 1988 memo that the garment industry was a great place to start. Concerned about what he referred to as the "white-collarization" of the mob, Spitzer had his eye on Thomas and Joseph Gambino, two college-educated sons of a Mafia don. They claimed to be legitimate businessmen, yet their trucking companies appeared to have a stranglehold on the routes between the clothing manufacturers on Manhattan's Seventh Avenue and the Chinatown subcontractors who actually sewed the clothes. Spitzer hoped to find evidence that the Gambinos were colluding with other firms to extort unfair payments from the clothing manufacturers. It wasn't just a hunch—Spitzer knew from his law school girlfriend Nadine Muskatel that her father had quit the industry out of disgust at the growing corruption.

Using a theory developed by a state Mafia expert, Ronald Goldstock, Spitzer and the rackets bureau chief, Robert A. Mass, reasoned that they needed to figure out where the corrupt deals were being struck and then capture the bargaining on tape. So they persuaded Cherkasky to set up a fake sewing shop called Chrystie Fashions on Chrystie Street in Chinatown, where they waited for the Mafia to come calling. Spitzer quickly became immersed in his new business. At first the sewing work was awful, but Spitzer soon began bringing samples of his new employees' handiwork—buttonholes, seams, and zippers—to show Cherkasky, as he begged each week for more money to keep the sting alive. "He's the *schmatte* salesman," Cherkasky remembered fondly, using a Yiddish term for a ragged garment. "He's now bringing garments to me, to show me how well they sew buttons, trying to tell me they can resell it and recoup some of our money."

Sadly, the sting wasn't accomplishing what the prosecutors had hoped. They had taped thousands of hours of conversations between the Gambino truckers and the undercover police officer who was posing as head of Chrystie and now had clear evidence that the trucking firms had divided up the market and steered clear of each other's routes. But they had virtually no evidence of actual extortion. So police investigators broke into the Gambinos' West Thirty-fifth Street headquarters, past thirteen locks and a secret motion detector, to install a listening device. Even those conversations provided relatively weak evidence. Though there was evidence that garment shops that went outside the system and used a "gypsy trucker" still had to pay their assigned trucker for shipping that was never provided, the tapes never captured explicit threats of violence, only an overriding sense of fear.

So Spitzer and Mass took a step that would become one of Spitzer's hallmarks—they came up with a novel use of an old state law, indicting Thomas and Joseph Gambino for violating nineteenth-century antitrust laws in addition to the extortion and enterprise corruption charges more typically used in mob cases. The February 1992 trial marked Spitzer's first real brush with the media. The case drew wide coverage from the New York press, and as lead prosecutor, Spitzer served as the face of the government. He talked tough, telling the jury in his three-hour opening statement that the two men were "organized crime members motivated by greed," who extracted a "mob tax" from garment manufacturers on the strength of their reputation. "These defendants don't go in with guns drawn. They go in with reputation, the Gambino name. And they take that reputation to the bank," Spitzer said.

Defense lawyer Gerald Shargel initially disliked Spitzer, particularly after the prosecutor tried to get him disqualified from the case. "He presented as a young Eliot Ness, a straight-ahead kind of guy, head down and determined. . . . He was stern and humorless," said Shargel, who represented Joseph Gambino shortly after having defended the mob boss John Gotti. But the prosecutor loosened up during the trial, showing a taste for ironic humor even as Shargel poked a key government witness full of holes. "I realized he was a good guy," Shargel remembered.

By week three, Shargel and Spitzer were talking on the sidelines about how the case was going and who had scored points during which witness's testimony. Both sides were worried—Spitzer and, back at the office, Cherkasky knew they had only a slim chance of winning an extortion conviction without overt threats, and they feared a skeptical jury would also vote not guilty on the antitrust counts because those sounded less serious. Shargel and Thomas Gambino's lawyer, Michael Rosen, knew their clients faced likely conviction on the antitrust counts and worried that they might lose on extortion as well. In that case their clients would be looking at years in state prison. Within days, the two sides had hammered out a highly unusual mid-trial deal. The defendants would plead guilty, pay a $12 million fine, and give up their stranglehold on garment industry trucking. A former New York City police commissioner would oversee the sale of three Gambino trucking companies and ensure that new competitors entered the market.

The bargain drew all kinds of public criticism: one former federal prosecutor sniped to *The American Lawyer,* "I come from the old school. You know, the one that says that when you're a prosecutor and you're in a trial, you try to put these guys in jail. . . . Jesus. Aren't the wiseguys laughing at this?" But the prosecutors defended it as the city's best chance of loosening the mob's grip on a deeply troubled but vital industry. "Yes, we gave up jail," Morgenthau said as he announced the deal, but he added that the one-hundred-thousand-dollar five-year probe had accomplished a goal that law enforcement had been seeking since the 1930s. "This takes them out in one fell swoop." Said Mass, "We might have gotten a bigger headline if we had sent them away for a long time, but the goal was a consent decree to change the industry."

In 1992, Spitzer left the District Attorney's Office for private practice. He joked that he had a choice between trading on his own reputation by going back to Paul, Weiss or trading on Silda's by going to Skadden, Arps. Naturally, he said, he chose the latter. He and Silda also had two children—Elyssa, born in 1989, and Sarabeth, born in 1992—and were thinking of having a third. But he was soon bored and began looking for a way back into public service. Then, in late 1993, the Attorney General's Office came open for only the second time in nearly four decades. Robert Abrams resigned after an unsuccessful run for the U.S. Senate, and his appointed replacement, G. Oliver Koppell, would be in office for less than a year by the time the 1994 election rolled around. Spitzer heard the news while vacationing with his family in North Carolina and began thinking about throwing his hat into the ring. Initially, Silda didn't think he would do it. When he asked for her views, she didn't immediately answer. No fan of public speaking, she wasn't thrilled at the prospect of being a political wife. But the next morning, she left him a note saying that if he really wanted to run, she would support him. "I didn't want to be the one who told him no. If this is truly a dream of his, who am I?" she remembered thinking. Everyone close to him knew it was a long shot. "You're not going to win, Eliot. Nobody knows you," Constantine said when Spitzer broached the idea over breakfast after one of their early-morning tennis games. Spitzer replied, "I know, but I've got to start somewhere. It gets my name out." Even Spitzer's father was skeptical, until he heard his younger son take the floor at a small fund-raiser. "I had no sense how articulate he was until that moment," he said.

Spitzer joined the race late—by the time he declared his candidacy, in May 1994, Koppell and two other candidates were already running for the Democratic nomination. Basically unknown, he lacked the time and connections to do any serious fund-raising. So he took a bank loan secured by some Manhattan real estate he owned and then used the proceeds to lend more than four million dollars to his campaign. On the advice of Bill Clinton's political consultant, Dick Morris—a friend of Bernard's—Eliot started buying air time for commercials and hired a public relations consultant, Steven Alschuler, to introduce him to the media. Alschuler, who had spent years in state politics, was immediately impressed. "I remember sitting with him for the first time and in about fifteen minutes being blown away by his knowledge of the issues," Alschuler said. "It was really dazzling." Spitzer had ideas for revamping the juvenile justice system, improving environmental protection, and protecting consumers. He also wanted to return New York to its role as a leader for the country. "One of his big themes was 'Why is the New York State attorney general always tagging along with other states in litigation? It's always someone else's idea. . . . New York is an add-on,'" Alschuler said.

The consultant knew that the New York media would be immediately skeptical of a political newcomer with family money to burn, but

Alschuler figured that if he could just get the Albany press corps to sit down with Spitzer, they would be as impressed as he was. By and large, the strategy worked. Newspapers that had started off describing Spitzer as an afterthought began running pieces about his command and passion for the issues. But in a year when crime was a top voter concern, Spitzer really gained traction when he positioned himself as tough on crime, running television commercials promising to "change totally the failed justice system" and touting his plan to engrave serial numbers on bullets. He was the only Democratic candidate to support the death penalty, and he argued that the Attorney General's Office should take a larger role in fighting crime.

Spitzer's opponents attacked him as a rich kid who was trying to buy the race and argued that the former prosecutor was improperly glossing over the attorney general's relatively limited role in handling criminal cases. Koppell complained that Spitzer was "almost contemptuous of the traditional and very important role of the Attorney General's office," and Karen Burstein, who was seeking to become the first lesbian to hold statewide office, said Spitzer was pandering to voter fears. His support of the death penalty helped Spitzer win endorsements from both the *New York Post* and the *Daily News*, but it wasn't enough. When the votes were counted in the Democratic primary, Spitzer had come in fourth out of four candidates, with just 19 percent of the vote, well below the 31 percent garnered by Burstein, the ultimate winner.

Right after the primary, Silda and Eliot took the kids, including the newest addition, Jenna, apple-picking upstate. Eliot didn't want to sit at home moping, and Silda thought the mini-vacation would help ease the sting of the loss. When they checked into the Beekman Arms, an historic inn in Rhinebeck, the desk clerk recognized Spitzer's name and said, "Mr. Spitzer, I voted for you." Spitzer's whole demeanor changed after that encounter, Silda remembered. "That made it all okay," she said. "He knew he had actually reached someone." The November general election also reinforced Spitzer's sense that his focus on the criminal justice system had not been misplaced. Burstein lost to the Republican nominee, Dennis Vacco, 50 to 47 percent, after a campaign in which Vacco promised to be tough on crime and help reinstate the death penalty.

The mid-1990s were also a time when Eliot and Silda, who had stopped work in 1994, were deciding how they wanted to raise their three girls. Though his parents had held traditional roles within their marriage, Eliot encouraged Silda's career and outside interests and wanted to help out with his kids. The incessant political meetings made it hard for him to be available for after-school or evening activities, but—a perpetual early bird—he could help out in the morning. After getting up at five and going for a run and reading the papers, Eliot would take primary responsibility for getting the girls breakfast and—in the early years—dressed for school. At first, he served a lot of frosted donuts and "we had to get used to some very interesting clothing combinations," Silda remembered. "At the nursery school, they would say, 'Oh, did Eliot dress the girls today?' I realized that I couldn't say anything [to him] because you can't give something over and retain control." As the girls grew bigger, they began dressing themselves, but when they followed in Eliot's footsteps to Horace Mann, he took on the job of walking them to the corner to catch the bus to the Bronx campus. His girls also expected him to produce a hot breakfast on the days he was at home. "I can do scrambled eggs in ten minutes," he bragged. Silda and Eliot also made a conscious effort to ensure that their girls saw the world beyond their wealthy Manhattan enclave. They regularly took the kids to visit Silda's family in North Carolina, and when they bought a second home, they opted for an upstate farming community in Columbia County, rather than the Hamptons. In 1996, Silda and Eliot founded Children for Children, a charity that seeks to help children provide volunteer service to their communities. The first program focused on convincing parents and children to scale back birthday parties and gifts and give the money saved to charity.

At work, Spitzer joined forces with his former boss Lloyd Constantine to start a new law firm, where he specialized in antitrust issues, but both men knew this wasn't a long-term arrangement. Spitzer had his eye on the next attorney general's race, in 1998. For the first couple of years, Constantine said, Spitzer put in long hours at the office. He handled disputes with Time Warner and Cablevision on behalf of a smaller cable operator and brought a lawsuit on behalf of light-heavyweight boxer William Guthrie, a case which Spitzer has since cited as one of his favorites. The complaint alleged that the International Boxing Federation had denied Guthrie a shot at the title because he refused to hire boxing promoter Don King. When Guthrie won both the court case and the ensuing bout, he thanked Spitzer from the ring. Spitzer also helped found a chapter of the American Alliance for Rights and Responsibilities, which sought to balance community safety with individual rights. The group defended "Megan's Law"—which notifies neighbors when a convicted sex offender moves in—and fought to give judges the authority to commit out-of-control mental patients. He also spent an ever-increasing amount of time on raising his public profile, making dozens of appearances on television news and talk shows as a legal pundit on everything from the O. J. Simpson case to Monica Lewinsky. Perhaps more important, Spitzer also won over hundreds of Democratic loyalists by driving the family's purple minivan all over the state to political meetings, both large and small. Spitzer "knew when the 1994 race was over what he had to do to win in 1998. He had to spend time in upstate New York showing that he cared," said his friend George Fox, who helped Spitzer introduce himself to voters at subway stops during the early campaigns. "Nineteen ninety-four was the opening salvo: 'I had one year and I got almost twenty percent. If I have four years, I can win this thing.' "

One wintry evening in early 1996, Spitzer showed up in Middletown, a community of twenty-five thousand located some seventy miles north of Manhattan, for a meeting of Orange County's leading Democrats. About five of them gathered in the back room of a bar owned by the town mayor, Joseph DeStefano. Despite the falling snow, Spitzer wore a suit, and he spent ninety minutes listening respectfully to a group that was accustomed to being overlooked. "Most people come in and tell you that they're running and how their campaign is going," said Rich Baum, who was then minority leader of the county legislature. "He spent most of the time asking questions. He was talking like he was truly interested." Two years later, Baum, who was at loose ends after losing a race for county executive, became Spitzer's campaign manager.

By the time Spitzer formally declared he was running in 1998, he was more than ready. He had made friends all over the state and had greased the wheels by making donations to county Democratic organizations, a tactic that paid off when he won the race's first electoral test, a straw poll of upstate Democratic officials in March. Once again there were four candidates, and once again Spitzer sought to position himself as the electable moderate. He sought and won the nomination of New York's Liberal Party, which often endorses the major party candidate its leaders consider closest to the center. He called himself a "pragmatic liberal" and a "centrist" and again touted his support of the death penalty. But he also broadened his campaign beyond the tough-on-crime stance that had gotten him noticed in 1994. Shelling out more than four million dollars on the primary, Spitzer was on the air with commercials months before his rivals—Koppell again, former Cuomo adviser Evan Davis, and state senator Catherine Abate. Spitzer's ads highlighted his plans to fight pollution, make landlords pay interest on tenants' security deposits, and require AIDS testing of accused rapists. He touted endorsements from high-profile politicians he had spent years courting, including Buffalo mayor Anthony Masiello and former New York mayor Edward Koch. "He did his homework; he hit the bricks; he broke his back, all because he lost [in 1994] and the embarrassment of it," said Hank Sheinkopf, a political consultant who worked on Spitzer's first two campaigns. "I shot ninety-eight spots in that [1998] campaign. I'd never done anything like that for an attorney general."

Spitzer won the primary comfortably, with 42 percent of the vote. But even then, political experts were skeptical. Dennis Vacco was a Republican incumbent running on a ticket headed by another incumbent, the enormously popular governor, George E. Pataki. When the state's leading Democrat, Senator Daniel Patrick Moynihan, finally agreed to endorse Spitzer on October 22, the aging lawmaker walked away unimpressed. "Nice kid. He's gonna get killed," Moynihan murmured after the cameras were turned off. The general election was marked by a hail of increasingly nasty charges and countercharges. First Spitzer took aim at what he called Vacco's cronyism. He argued that the Republican had undermined the Attorney General's Office by forcing out 150 lawyers to make way for less experienced staff with Republican Party connections, and he complained that Vacco had taken $37,500 in campaign donations from the subsidiaries of a car leasing company after settling a lawsuit with the parent company. "Shame on you, Dennis, shame on you," Spitzer jeered during their first debate. "Don't you know that it is unethical and wrong to take money from the companies that your office is investigating?" (Vacco denied any wrongdoing.) Two days later, in their second and even nastier debate, Spitzer accused Vacco of ignoring the danger posed by violent antiabortion protestors and linked the issue to the slaying of a Buffalo area abortion provider a few days before. Then, just days before the election, Vacco was quoted by the newspaper *Jewish Week*—incorrectly, the incumbent claimed—as saying, "You don't stand outside the bodega and ask the bandito if he would have killed someone if there was no death penalty." Hispanic leaders were outraged by what they saw as a racial slur, and Spitzer joined several of them at a press conference outside a Manhattan bodega to blast Vacco for not putting enough emphasis on hate crimes and civil rights enforcement.

For his part, Vacco focused on Spitzer's money—the Democrat ended up outspending the incumbent, $9.7 million to $6.6 million—and on allegations of improper campaign financing, an issue that grew inflamed when Spitzer refused for months to come clean about exactly how he had paid for his 1994 race. "It was just brutal; attacks coming in every day. Every day was just another thing," remembered Rich Baum, the campaign manager. First Vacco's camp accused Bernard Spitzer of selling condominiums without a license, a charge the elder Spitzer denied. Then the Republican produced documents that appeared to contradict Eliot Spitzer's claim that he had financed both of his campaigns through bank loans using some Manhattan apartments as collateral. Accusing Spitzer of telling "falsehoods" to hide the millions his "millionaire landlord father" was pumping into the race, Vacco said to the debate audience, "How can we trust anything you say when you will say anything at all to get elected? . . . You have a tendency, Eliot, not to tell the truth."

The truth was this: In 1994, Spitzer took a personal bank loan from JPMorgan and used the money to lend his campaign $4.3 million. He then paid off the bank loan shortly after losing the primary, using money he had gotten from his father. The transactions were apparently legal but skirted the intention of a New York campaign finance law that limits contributions from family members. When he started to repeat the pattern in 1998, by taking out personal loans and then lending his campaign upward of eight million dollars, the press began asking questions about how the money would be repaid. Spitzer repeatedly insisted that he had paid off the 1994 loans without help from his family and would do the same in 1998, even though his tax returns showed he didn't have that kind of money.

When Spitzer finally admitted in the last week of the campaign that he had paid off the 1994 debt by taking a loan from his father on very favorable terms, the issue exploded. His primary rival, Oliver Koppell, withdrew his endorsement. "Your lack of candor and violation of the spirit, if not the letter, of the law makes you unfit to serve as the chief legal officer for New York state," Koppell wrote in a letter to Spitzer that he released to the media. Spitzer had no excuse for what he had done, telling the *Daily News* at the time, "It was stupid. . . . I should have said, 'Hey, this is what I did.' Proper response. And why didn't I? Because there are some personal financial relationships that I don't like to get into." For his part, Bernard said he was "flabbergasted" by the accusations that he and his son had broken the law. "It never occurred to me that if I were contributing funds to my son that it could somehow be against the law. It's not as though anyone was trying to buy his vote or anything," he said. The controversy nearly cost Spitzer the election. Vacco led in every pre-election poll, and most newspapers in the state endorsed the Republican. Even the staunchly Democratic *New York Times* editorial board wrote that "the temptation is to skip an endorsement. . . . Mr. Spitzer has misled the public. . . . We endorse Mr. Spitzer because Mr. Vacco's performance and his key policy positions make him an even worse choice." Spitzer eventually promised that he would pay off his 1998 loans rather than continue fund-raising to cover them. (He would eventually pay off the 1994 loan from his father in the fall of 2004, shortly after the *Daily News* asked about the debt.)

The election turned out to be a squeaker. At 1:00 A.M. on Election Night, Spitzer was leading by 33,000 of 3.6 million votes counted, but nearly 200,000 absentee ballots were outstanding. Spitzer stayed holed up in his campaign suite at the Waldorf-Astoria Hotel, and Vacco did the same at the New York Hilton. Spitzer's spokesman, Steve Goldstein, told the reporters to go home at 1:20 A.M., saying the results might not be known for a week. "I've been in politics since I was six years old, and I'm thirty-three now. This is the first time I've been so nervous that I threw up on my shirt," Goldstein said. Some analysts noted that Vacco might have cost himself the election by turning down the endorsement of the state's Right to Life Party, whose alternate candidate garnered 60,399 votes. Others pointed to Catherine Abate's decision to run on the Independence Party line after she lost the Democratic primary. She garnered 81,439 votes, nearly all of them siphoned from Spitzer.

What followed was a wild six-week recount that included one of the best *New York Post* headlines of the decade: "Aliens Stole My Election." Each side organized teams of lawyers to contest ballots in each of New York's sixty-two counties. Vacco's team made a variety of claims: dead people had voted; illegal immigrants had voted; thirty-seven thousand phantom votes had materialized in heavily Democratic New York City in the days after the election. None of it stood up to scrutiny. The Republicans tried to get the Board of Elections to order the New York City Police Department to go door to door verifying that those residents had really voted. When that failed, the Republican Party hired a team of private investigators to do the same thing. "Vacco just couldn't believe he had lost," said state senator Marty Connor, a Brooklyn Democrat and an election law expert who served as one of Spitzer's key advisers on the recount. "I've done a lot of recounts, and it's a really stressful thing for a candidate. They want it to be over. Eliot was cool and calm and professional about it." Finally, after a decisive court ruling in Spitzer's favor, Vacco conceded the race on December 14. "I believe it fell upon me as a leader in this state to put an end to it," he said. The official margin was 25,186 votes out of 4.3 million cast. Spitzer, who had worn the same, increasingly scuffed, dress shoes throughout his campaign, celebrated by going out and buying a new pair.

3

AN EXCITING TIME
TO BE A NEW YORKER

"TODAY IS PURE FUN. BUT WHAT I REALLY LOOK FORWARD TO IS MONDAY, when I can go back to being a lawyer," said Eliot Spitzer as he took the oath of office as New York State's sixty-third attorney general on Friday, January 1, 1999. Now that Spitzer had the job, he had to decide what to do with it. The new resources at his command were impressive. The New York Attorney General's Office was one of the largest of its kind in the country with 1,775 staff members, 538 of them lawyers, two main offices in Albany and Manhattan, a dozen other offices all over the state, and a budget of $152 million. Like almost all state attorneys general, Spitzer quickly found himself trying to wear multiple hats. He was the state's chief lawyer, charged with defending New York's government and its laws against everything from constitutional challenges to personal injury claims. This responsibility by itself was akin to running a large law firm, and it consumed more than half of the office's enormous resources. New York attorneys general also prosecuted organized crime and cases that didn't fit easily into a particular local district attorney's jurisdiction. The attorney general also served as the public's advocate, vested with significant civil and criminal enforcement powers to hold powerful people and businesses accountable when they wronged the citizens of New York.

Over the next few years, Spitzer would grow from political neophyte to legal powerhouse, willing and able to tackle misbehavior at the country's biggest and best-known institutions. He would repeatedly venture into areas that traditionally had been the domain of the federal government, from environmental protection to civil rights to gun control. Some of his efforts would be more successful than others, but taken together they would help him develop the confident and outspokenly progressive approach that he would later train on Wall Street.

Spitzer faced a rocky beginning. Outgoing staff members who had worked for Dennis Vacco had programmed the office fax machines to stamp all of its messages as being from the "$8 million man," a reference to the personal money Spitzer had spent on the 1998 campaign. A few Albany wags quickly dubbed Spitzer "the accidental attorney general" because of his narrow victory and the Vacco missteps that had helped him win. Even Spitzer's first effort to rid the Attorney General's Office of cronyism—a major issue during his campaign—drew skepticism. Though he won points for prohibiting his new staff from contributing to his campaign, skeptics noted that he also installed a high-ranking Democratic Party official to run the office's regional outposts. "He's off to a disappointing start," opined the *New York Post*.

At the other end of the spectrum, Spitzer's liberal supporters were distressed when he announced that he would take his role as state counsel seriously and defend the administration of Republican governor George Pataki from lawsuits, even when the two men disagreed ideologically. When Spitzer arrived, the state was in the middle of defending its school funding formula against a constitutional challenge filed by the nonprofit Campaign for Fiscal Equity (CFE) on behalf of poor New York City parents. Under Vacco, the state had hired an Atlanta law firm to spearhead its defense, at a cost of eleven million dollars. CFE supporters urged Spitzer to recuse himself and his office on ideological grounds, but the new attorney general refused. Instead, he brought the work in-house, and his staff argued that the state funding for the New York City educational system—under which the city received less money per pupil than other school districts around the state—met constitutional requirements. He even gave the appeals staff a congratulatory pep talk when they won a round in the intermediate court, saying that he felt "extremely proud that we had taken the case and won," according to David Axinn, one of the lawyers who assisted with the case. Eventually the state's highest court ruled for the parents. Spitzer responded by writing an op-ed in *The New York Times* urging all sides to work together to come up with a funding plan. But Pataki rejected his advice, and the case went back to court. Despite more pleas from the CFE, Spitzer continued to defend the state. "I had an obligation to represent the state. And I did that. That is my oath of office," Spitzer explained. "Deep down in my core, I may think, 'You know what? I wish this weren't my duty on this case.' But I've got to do it. That's the job." Critics contended that Spitzer lacked backbone. They noted that two of his predecessors, Robert Abrams and Louis J. Lefkowitz, had refused to defend policies with which they disagreed, such as the state's controversial "Westway" plan to develop the western shore of Manhattan. But Spitzer and his staff held firm. They insisted that they were trying to avoid "politicizing" the office, and were saving the state money by doing it themselves. Even CFE's chief lawyer, Michael Rebell, was impressed. "I find myself objecting violently to the position he is taking, but respecting him for seeing it through," Rebell said. "He's been steadfast; he's been consistent and unyielding, I think, for ethical reasons."

But the new attorney general felt no qualms about following his own beliefs when it came to the office's public advocacy role. New York had a proud tradition of activist attorneys general, from Ottinger, with his securities fraud prosecutions in the 1920s, to Lefkowitz and his groundbreaking decision in the 1950s to begin suing corporations on behalf of the people, to Abrams, with his multistate antitrust and environmental initiatives in the 1980s. Spitzer sought to draw all the threads together. "Eliot ended the false but time-honored tradition that an attorney general must choose between being the state counsel, the people's advocate, the criminal justice area, and exercising his civil law powers," said Pamela Jones Harbour, an antitrust lawyer who worked for four New York attorneys general and served on the small transition team that helped brief Spitzer on the office's functions and pending cases. "He knew how to make these powers reinforce and support each other."

Spitzer fostered that melding with his personnel selections. A couple of top picks turned him down because they did not want to risk going to an office that had been seen as a legal backwater, but others were excited at the prospect of having a base from which to launch progressive Democratic initiatives. Spitzer's transition team recruited a slew of current and former federal and state prosecutors and then put many of them in charge of areas that weren't focused on criminal cases. This meant that many of the people who ran his office—including Spitzer himself—were accustomed to making public allegations and then having to follow up by meeting the very high standard of proof (beyond a reasonable doubt) required for a criminal conviction. "As a former criminal prosecutor, you have a stronger appreciation for the burden of proof," said first assistant Michele Hirshman, a former federal prosecutor who signed on as Spitzer's top deputy. "The supervisors here are exceedingly demanding, and people rise to the occasion." She added that prosecutors are "also people who once they have evidence are not afraid to do battle." The change in attitude would shock some civil attorneys in private practice, who were used to dealing with a much more conciliatory foe.

One of those early prosecutorial hires was Eric Dinallo, a top white-collar-crime specialist from the Manhattan District Attorney's Office, where he had won convictions of the executives of A. R. Baron, a shady brokerage firm. A blunt-spoken Brooklyn resident, Dinallo had big plans, as he made clear during a job interview with a top Spitzer deputy, Dietrich Snell, known in the office as Dieter. Unlike the other applicants, Dinallo had actually read the entire text of New York's general business law, known as the Martin Act for its long-forgotten Republican sponsor, Louis M. Martin. Though that 1921 statute was considered weak when it was enacted, Dinallo focused on later amendments that had strengthened the act and given the state attorney general unusually broad power to investigate and crack down on those who commit financial fraud. While the Manhattan DA's Office had been limited to using the Martin Act's criminal side, the law gave the attorney general a whole range of civil powers: he could subpoena documents, haul brokers and investment bankers in for public questioning, and, unlike his federal counterparts at the SEC and the Justice

Department, he didn't have to specify up front whether he was going to seek criminal charges or file an easier-to-prove civil case. An equally obscure 1926 court case, *People v. Federated Radio Corp.*, had further strengthened the attorney general's hand by holding that the Martin Act did not require proof that securities sellers made a willful decision to commit misconduct. In most states and in federal cases, proving "intent to defraud" is often the most difficult part of building a white-collar case. With the Martin Act, New York prosecutors had a far easier hurdle to jump. They didn't even have to prove that securities had actually changed hands—making plans to rip people off was sufficient to trigger the act. With these powers, Dinallo argued, the attorney general could and should become a force for protecting small investors. Snell was impressed enough to recommend Dinallo's hiring. "This guy is great," Snell told Hirshman. "He's got some really creative ideas for using the Martin Act."

Even so, Spitzer's first attempt to hold financial institutions accountable did not come from Dinallo's bureau and it did not use the Martin Act. On Monday, January 18, less than three weeks after being sworn in, Spitzer read a *New York Times* article about Delta Funding, a Long Island home equity loan company. Black homeowners in Brooklyn claimed they were being victimized when the company issued them high-interest, high-fee loans and then foreclosed when they could not meet the payments. It was Martin Luther King, Jr., Day and Spitzer and the new head of his Civil Rights Bureau, Andrew Celli, Jr., were on their way to a black church. "Look at this, we've got to go after these guys," Spitzer said, showing Celli the article. The allegations pushed all of the new attorney general's buttons. A more traditional Democrat might have focused on employment discrimination or affirmative action; what Spitzer cared most about was economic opportunity and making sure that the capitalist system worked for everyone. Spitzer reminded Celli of their conversation a few weeks earlier, when he had offered Celli the civil rights job: "What I want us to focus on is economic discrimination. . . . These poor neighborhoods don't have access to capital."

The state banking department ordinarily had jurisdiction over banking rules and lending practices, but Celli and Spitzer found a way into the Delta Funding issue through a novel use of a civil rights law from the 1970s. Delta, the state's largest home equity firm, did virtually all of its New York City business in minority neighborhoods. "They were only doing loans in black neighborhoods," Celli remembered. "They had discovered a population they could victimize." This practice potentially put Delta in violation of the Equal Credit Opportunity Act, a law originally enacted to prevent redlining—refusing to lend in black neighborhoods. The law prohibited banks from favoring one neighborhood over another on the basis of race. During the investigation, the company denied wrongdoing. It argued that it simply made loans to people who couldn't get credit elsewhere. Weeks of settlement negotiations fell apart in mid-June when Delta's executives refused to change the practices that Celli found objectionable. So Celli went in to see Spitzer, outlined the case, and asked for permission to file suit. "Do these guys have it?" Spitzer asked Snell, the deputy attorney general in charge of public advocacy. Assured that they did, Spitzer approved the lawsuit: "If you've got it, do it," he was fond of saying.

Then they called *The New York Times* to offer the newspaper a scoop—a lawsuit would be filed the next day. Two hours later, Delta's lawyers called back. We want to settle, they said. That night the two sides hammered out a deal in principle: Delta would pay six million dollars in restitution, change its business practices, and agree to ongoing monitoring. The company denied wrongdoing but agreed to change its underwriting guidelines to make sure that borrowers were left enough money to live on after making their payments. Then things got complicated. Two months after the tentative deal with Spitzer, Delta Funding backed out, saying it had forged a different settlement with the state banking department over the same practices. This settlement called for a bigger payment—twelve million dollars—but had far fewer restrictions on what Delta could do in the future. Spitzer was on vacation in North Carolina when he heard about the other deal. Searching for words to describe his fury, his eye fell on the sandwich fixings lying on the kitchen counter. The settlement, he said, was "a Swiss cheese agreement where the exceptions to the rules overwhelm any relief that's supposed to be provided." His office filed its civil rights suit against Delta Funding the same day. The turf battle between Spitzer and the banking department—headed by an appointee of Governor George Pataki—continued for another month before the various sides hammered out a deal that satisfied both the banking regulators and Spitzer. Delta would pay twelve million dollars, but it would also make the changes to its lending practices that Spitzer had demanded, in all twenty-six states where it operated.

The new attorney general had cut his teeth on the Delta Funding case. To those who were watching, the case served as a harbinger of the methods he would use to extraordinary effect over the next seven years. From the novel use of old precedents to promote economic equity to the judicious media leaks and Spitzer's willingness to publicly criticize the work of other regulators, the Delta Funding case was "a microcosm" of much of what Spitzer stood for and a herald of bigger things to come, Celli remembered. For Spitzer had arrived in office with a far broader view of his domain than that of many of his peers and predecessors. Based partly on his experiences as an antitrust lawyer, Spitzer believed that the conservative "new federalism" theory had changed the legal landscape and that his office had an obligation to react. The theory, which was then gaining steam at the Supreme Court and elsewhere, held that the national government had overstepped its authority and that many regulatory functions properly belonged with state officials. Spitzer, like most progressives, had initially viewed the rise of the new federalism with skepticism and alarm, because they believed it masked a conservative effort to weaken or eliminate the national rules that protected consumers, workers, and the environment.

But now he and his first solicitor general, a former Supreme Court clerk named Preeta Bansal, were starting to formulate a more proactive response. If the U.S. Constitution really did reserve power to the states, Spitzer told his staff, there should be lots of new issues for the office to take on. "I started out talking about federalism on day one, and everyone here thought I was nuts. The whole staff started rolling their eyes," Spitzer remembered. He pressed on, firing what he considered to be his first public warning shot in June 1999, when he spoke at a national meeting of the Federalist Society. The organization by then had twenty-five thousand mostly conservative members speaking out in favor of states' rights. Spitzer was part of a panel discussing state lawsuits against tobacco companies and Microsoft. He told the crowd he agreed with conservatives that the Supreme Court had changed the legal landscape. "There has been this tremendous redistribution of legal power away from Washington, away from the federal government, away from Washington, D.C., back to the states," he noted. But then he added his own personal twist. "So, therefore, it is up to the states to step into that void. . . . Attorneys general across the country can—not only can, but must—step forward into a void to ensure that the rule of law is enforced, whether it relates to health, antitrust, or public integrity." As Spitzer has frequently told the tale, the conservatives in the audience were "aghast" or "ashen" at what he was suggesting.

In fact, it's not clear anyone was paying very much attention. Spitzer was just one of several state officials on the panel, and other speakers were far better known. There is no evidence in the transcript that anyone in the audience was interested enough in Spitzer to ask him to explain his ideas in detail. A few months later, Spitzer had even less success when he tried to make the intellectual case for a liberal version of federalism. He and his staff wrote an op-ed article arguing that the states now had the obligation to step up and promote progressive solutions through litigation and regulation. They submitted it to *The New York Times*, which turned it down. Bansal, the solicitor general who had crafted much of the language in the op-ed, suggested that there was another way. If Spitzer put his ideas into practice and invoked federalism theory to explain them, she said, the media would cover the results.

Federal officials, energy companies, and reporters certainly did sit up and take notice in the fall of 1999 when Spitzer made his first serious venture onto federal turf. His target was interstate air pollution, an area that in the past had largely been the province of the Environmental Protection Agency, and his methods would fray relations between the EPA and his newly hired environmental team. The year 1999 had started badly for the federal air-quality enforcers, then led by Clinton appointee Carol Browner. In May, a federal appeals court had tossed out the agency's big push to set tough new air-quality standards for smog and soot, declaring the regulations unconstitutional because Congress, not the EPA, should be writing new environmental rules. The same court, in the same month, also blocked the EPA's efforts to force twenty-two eastern and midwestern states to cut nitrogen oxide emissions, pending the outcome of a lawsuit challenging the rule. Newspapers from Buffalo to San Jose ran editorials calling the EPA "overzealous" and "arbitrary," and leading Republicans were out for blood. "By that time a majority of Congress hated us and would have done anything to take me and the agency down," Browner remembered.

If the EPA was going to make progress, it would have to find a different way. The air enforcement team was readying a bold new attack on the air pollution that contributed to smog and acid rain. If it worked, the legal strategy would force utilities to install new pollution controls on older coal-fired power plants that had previously escaped tight regulation. But the effort would almost certainly be controversial. To win, the EPA was going to have to persuade a federal judge to apply a provision of the Clean Air Act to power plants in a new and different way. So Bruce C. Buckheit, the director of the EPA's Air Enforcement Division, went looking for outside legal allies. Would any of the environmental groups and state officials who shared the EPA's concern about acid rain and smog be willing to join the agency's planned lawsuits? New York seemed like a good place to start because, under Abrams, the New York State Attorney General's Office had established a tradition of environmental enforcement. Furthermore, Buckheit was personally friendly with Peter Lehner, the head of Spitzer's environmental bureau. A former lawyer for both New York City and the Natural Resources Defense Council, Lehner said he had agreed to join Spitzer's office only because the new attorney general had promised he was "interested in pushing hard . . . [and] I could be as much of an advocate as I wanted to be."

In the spring of 1999, Buckheit and Lehner met for lunch at a restaurant near Spitzer's Manhattan office and discussed the EPA's litigation strategy. The premise was simple: EPA rules under the Clean Air Act set minimum health and safety standards for existing factories and power plants but required that new sources of pollution meet much higher standards. These rules assumed that the power plant industry would gradually replace their old, dirty plants with new, cleaner ones as the equipment wore out, but by the mid-1990s this didn't seem to be happening. Some EPA officials became convinced that the utilities were secretly overhauling and upgrading their older power plants, under the guise of routine maintenance. These federal enforcers believed that they could use a rule called "new source review" to force the utilities to install state-of-the-art scrubbers and other pollution controls on old plants if they could prove that the utilities had made major plant upgrades—called "modifications" in the rules—that significantly increased sulfur dioxide and nitrogen oxide emissions. So EPA investigators spent two years combing through a database of permits filed with the Federal Energy Regulatory Commission. They found more than two dozen plants, mostly in the Midwest and South, that had made major financial investments, were running their power plant generators for longer periods, and were emitting more pollution each year. But here was the novel and controversial part: the power companies had always argued that they should be judged by how much pollution their plants emitted per hour, and these cases would be based on increases in yearly emissions.

Lehner and Spitzer were immediately enthusiastic. The Empire State was tired of being on the receiving end of faraway pollution, and this new strategy seemed like the best way yet to clean up the one-thousand-foot midwestern smokestacks that protected the power plants' immediate neighbors at the expense of the eastern seaboard. Count us in, they said. But the months ticked away, and nothing seemed to happen. The EPA lawsuits were being reviewed by the Justice Department, as is customary for federal agency actions. Browner and other EPA officials kept saying they were building a comprehensive national enforcement plan that could withstand congressional criticism. "As the head of a regulatory agency, I had to be careful about announcing something before the *i*'s were dotted and the *t*'s were crossed," Browner remembered.

To Spitzer and some environmentalists, it looked as if Browner were stalling or paralyzed with fear, and they were growing impatient. "New York could park every car and close every factory, and our air still wouldn't be as clean as it should be," Lehner said. "We wanted to do more than just beg the federal government to do something about it." Lehner's experience years earlier as New York City's environmental enforcer provided a model. Back then, city officials thought New York State was failing to crack down on upstate sewage plants that fouled the city's reservoirs, so Lehner's team surprised everybody in the early 1990s by suing the plants directly under the citizen's suit provision of the federal Clean Water Act. A similar section of the Clean Air Act seemed to create the same opportunity when it came to the coal-fired midwestern power plants. "The parallels seemed powerful. All we had to do was get the evidence," Lehner said. Once his team did, Spitzer "was decisive enough to say, 'Let's do it.'"

One September morning, Bruce Buckheit got a call. It was Lehner. "I hate to tell you this but . . . ," he began. Spitzer had pulled the trigger and was holding a press conference to announce that he had notified the owners of seventeen midwestern power plants that New York State was going to sue. "Air pollution simply knows no boundaries," Spitzer said at the press conference. The suits were based on the EPA's theory that the power plants had violated the Clean Air Act by failing to install emissions scrubbers when they made other major upgrades, but they followed the citizen's suit model that Lehner had developed for clean water. The suits' purpose was twofold, Spitzer later explained— to clean up New York's air, but also to spur the EPA to broader action. "We needed to pull the EPA along a little bit. The EPA had been a little hesitant on these cases," Spitzer asserted.

Power industry officials were outraged that Spitzer was tackling issues that were ordinarily the province of the EPA and Congress. They viewed his lawsuits as unfair efforts to rewrite the rules regulating when they had to install multimillion-dollar pollution controls. "What we do has historically been considered maintenance, so naturally we disagree that these are upgrades and that they should be considered new emissions sources under the Clean Air Act," said Pat Hemlepp of American Electric Power of Columbus, Ohio. Steve Brash, spokesman for Cincinnati-based Cinergy, called the suits "another in the 25-year continuing effort in the Northeast to blame their problems with air quality on other areas of the country." Some EPA officials felt blindsided. Half a dozen of them dispute Spitzer's view that the agency was afraid to bring the power plant cases, and they interpreted his filing as an attempt to grab the headlines. "It was not nice playing inside the sandbox for us to invite them to join us and then have them jump us," Buckheit said.

But the lawsuit accomplished what Spitzer had hoped for. The EPA and the Justice Department filed their own lawsuit against the seventeen power plants on November 3, just six weeks after Spitzer's announcement. They also seized the initiative by taking administrative action against seven additional plants owned by the federal Tennessee Valley Authority. From then on, EPA officials found it easier to view Spitzer as an ally. Not only did he appear to understand the issues fully when he showed up at meetings and press conferences, but he also assigned a nation-leading forty lawyers to environmental enforcement and bolstered their work with ten staff scientists capable of doing their own studies. With the end of the Clinton administration fast approaching, the federal regulators also recognized that the newly elected Spitzer might outlast them. "I was constantly looking for ways [to make sure] that the things I cared about would continue even if there was a Republican administration," Browner remembered. "Having Eliot Spitzer in the mix was one way to do that."

In 1999, Wall Street enforcement was not at the top of the new attorney general's agenda. The stock market was booming, and violent crime, not white-collar misbehavior, had been the hot topic during the campaign. Investment Protection Bureau chief Eric Dinallo's hiring did not even merit its own announcement—he was mentioned at the bottom of the press release about the new head of environmental enforcement. The fiefdom Dinallo inherited was considered by outsiders to be something of a legal backwater. For decades, the bureau had concentrated on low-level schemers—larcenous stockbrokers and "boiler rooms" that pushed worthless penny stocks. The lions of Wall Street were the territory of the SEC and federal prosecutors. In the 1970s, for example, investigators working for Attorney General Lefkowitz used the Martin Act to turn up evidence that investment banks were pumping up the prices of initial public offerings (IPOs). But rather than launching a fraud case of their own, they turned over what they had uncovered to the SEC. "The SEC has plenty of power and we didn't want to duplicate efforts," Lefkowitz aide David Clurman remembered. "When it came to major problems, we felt it was our job to point it out and seek a national solution, not a New York solution." Even in Dinallo's big A. R. Baron case for the District Attorney's Office, the SEC had handled the lion's share of the case against the big-name Wall Street firm involved, imposing civil sanctions against Bear Stearns for clearing A. R. Baron's improper trades. Hirshman and Snell had both come to the Attorney General's Office from the U.S. Attorney's Office for the Southern District of New York and they believed that their former colleagues had a good handle on the criminal side of Wall Street misbehavior, such as insider trading. But upstate, where federal prosecutors weren't as vigilant or as knowledgeable about securities fraud, might be a different story. Hirshman and Snell told Dinallo and the dozen lawyers under his command to start digging around northern and western New York to see what they could find. "We sensed where there was a vacuum and we moved right in," Hirshman remembered.

In June 1999, Dinallo's team negotiated a one-million-dollar settlement for a group of dairy farmers who had unknowingly invested in a fraudulent financial plan offered by agents affiliated with the Mutual of New York insurance firm. "We were real desperate," the head of the farmers' group, Bob Dygert, told the Albany *Times Union*. "We were thrilled to have this offer." A few months later, Dinallo's bureau used the Martin Act to indict two former Metropolitan Life Insurance agents on charges of defrauding forty-five western New Yorkers, mostly senior citizens, of five million dollars, in what the office called one of the largest frauds ever perpetrated in that part of the state. To Dinallo, the cases were among the most satisfying he had ever done. "It was an amazing feeling to help these victims. We were handing real checks to real people," he remembered. But neither case made the downstate newspapers or television stations. Some of the local coverage barely mentioned Spitzer's name.

The bureau drew more news coverage—a clip of Spitzer even appeared on CNN—when it took on the hot topic of online trading. In the wake of several high-profile slowdowns and crashes at fledgling Internet brokers such as E*Trade and TD Waterhouse, Dinallo and his staff used their powers under the Martin Act to gather data from seven online brokers. Their two-hundred-page report detailed the pitfalls of Internet investing, including time lags between the placing of an order and the actual trade, fees that were poorly disclosed and hard to understand, and advertising that understated the risks and overstated the potential rewards. Dinallo prodded the online brokers into funding a five-hundred-thousand-dollar investor education program run by the Securities Industry Association that detailed both the advantages and the pitfalls of day trading and other online investing. But Spitzer kept his goals relatively modest. Rather than force change directly by filing a lawsuit, he urged the SEC and the brokerage industry to consider new disclosure rules and stricter oversight.

This caution was also reflected in the way the attorney general responded to another hot-button topic in 1999: allegations that New York City mayor Rudolph Giuliani's much-vaunted crackdown on crime was unfairly targeting minorities. Community leaders had grumbled for years that the New York City Police Department stopped and frisked a disproportionate number of black and Latino pedestrians. The cops argued that they were just trying to catch bad guys, but minority leaders saw discrimination at work. The quiet smoldering burst into a full-fledged racial conflagration in February, when four members of the elite Street Crimes Unit fired forty-one bullets at an unarmed African immigrant named Amadou Diallo, killing him in the doorway of his Bronx building. There were pickets outside City Hall, and the federal Justice Department started an investigation of the shooting.

After meeting with community leaders, Spitzer called together his senior staff to discuss whether he should get involved. As head of the Civil Rights Bureau, Celli took the lead, telling Spitzer he had two choices. He could "whistle past the graveyard and let this die down," or he could file a major civil rights lawsuit that would seek to prove that "this is systemic"—that the police routinely and unfairly targeted minorities.

Spitzer was cautious. "Imagine a scenario," he told Celli. "You've filed your case, you've pulled . . . a liberal judge and he says, 'You're right. They're illegally targeting minorities. You win. Now, tell me, how do we fix the problem?' What do you ask for?"

"Well, it's . . . uh . . . complicated," Celli confessed. "I'm not sure what we could get a court to do to really fix this."

"Courts are about remedies. I can't get on a train if I don't know where it is going," Spitzer said. So the new attorney general found a third way: his office would contribute hard facts to what had so far been an emotional debate about perceptions. Celli and his staff examined 175,000 "stop and frisk" forms—the piece of paper police were supposed to fill out each time they searched a civilian. In a report issued in December 1999, they concluded that, even accounting for higher crime rates in some minority neighborhoods, blacks and Latinos were twice as likely as whites to be stopped on suspicion of carrying a weapon. Minority stops were also less likely to lead to an arrest—the Street Crimes Unit stopped 16.3 blacks per arrest, but only 9.6 whites per arrest. Even with the evidence in hand, Spitzer still had practical objections to going to court. "We don't bring cases if we don't think there's a remedy," he explained.

Elsewhere in the attorney general's Manhattan office, labor lawyer Patricia Smith was watching her new boss carefully. She had been in the office for a decade, and she had seen the commitment to defending employees wax and wane. New York had a strong tradition of protecting workers—labor laws make up five volumes in the state code, including many dating back to the Progressive Era. For Smith, the Vacco years had been frustrating. Not only was the Republican ideologically unsympathetic to many labor cases, but he also appointed supervisors and line attorneys who knew little or nothing about employment law. The state Labor Department, also headed by Republicans, was emphasizing voluntary settlements with employers, leading to lighter fines and fewer cases for the Attorney General's Office to defend in court. By 1999, Smith was "looking to get out; we all were," she said.

Spitzer had said little about labor issues during his campaign, and he knew even less about New York employment law. But he promised Smith he would be different. "He came in with sympathy for immigrants and a sense that injustice was bad," Smith remembered. The new boss also said he subscribed to the century-old Progressive view that government had a duty to step in when vulnerable people—workers, in this case—were being exploited by those who should know better. Spitzer told Smith he wanted to breathe life into the old labor laws by having his office make its own cases, rather than waiting for the Pataki administration to see the light on worker protection. "Eliot said, go out and make those cases yourself. . . . He has a whole theory about how we have to make the marketplace work," said Smith, who kept a poster of FDR's pioneering labor secretary, Frances Perkins, on her wall. Spitzer named Smith head of the Labor Bureau and told her she could fire anyone she thought was incompetent. One lawyer she booted turned out to have Democratic political connections, but Spitzer backed the firing anyway.

Then, in the fall of 1999, a young man from Mali named Mamadou Camara decided to take a stand. He was a Manhattan supermarket deliveryman who provided the backbreaking but essential service of transporting customers' groceries and other purchases from the store to their apartments. These "walkers," who trundled their heavily laden metal carts through all kinds of weather, made large shopping purchases possible in a city where most residents lacked cars. But they were paid peanuts—often just $1.25 a delivery, plus tips—for working twelve-hour days, six days a week. Some deliverymen took home just fifteen dollars a day, after the store deducted rental fees for use of the carts. After five years on the job, with a baby on the way, Camara, a thirty-year-old former bank teller who spoke four languages, had advanced to the role of dispatcher, but he was fed up. So, he persuaded nearly one hundred fellow deliverymen to picket an Upper West Side grocery store, the Food Emporium at West Sixty-Eighth Street and Broadway, to protest the store's low wages and long hours. Unsure of the protocol and wary of retaliation, the picketers were subdued and unfailingly polite. WE ARE SLAVES. SET US FREE, one placard read. The strike fizzled when the subcontractor that officially employed the walkers threatened to fire everyone involved. "I guess we were naïve," said

Camara. "We thought people would be outraged by how exploited we are, and things would change."

Smith and Spitzer took notice. Spitzer's summer of day labor had made him more aware than most of his neighbors that their coddled Upper East Side existence was made possible by low-paid immigrant workers. To Smith, the deliveryman situation seemed to be an egregious example of a broader and growing problem: big, reputable companies, such as supermarket chains, were subcontracting out menial jobs and then looking the other way when the subcontractor allegedly paid less than the legal minimum. The issue wasn't new. In the 1930s and 1940s, clothing manufacturers seeking to evade Progressive Era worker-protection statutes had farmed out piecework and then claimed to have no responsibility for the resulting sweatshop conditions because the workers were independent contractors. The practice now seemed to be spreading to the service sector, agriculture, and construction, and Smith wanted to stop it. "Outsourcing was leading to really bad working conditions. It's straight out of the early garment industry," she said. Suing the subcontractor delivery services that directly employed Camara and his compatriots wouldn't be enough to change the industry, Smith and Spitzer believed. They were going to have to find a way to rope in the drugstore and supermarket chains. So Smith dredged up a 1946 U.S. Supreme Court case that held that a man who washed the windows at a Michigan factory was covered by the same federal overtime rules as the workers on the factory floor, even though he had been hired through a subcontractor. "Employees are not to be excluded from such coverage merely because their employment to do the same work was under independent contracts," the court held.

The precedent hadn't been used in decades, but Spitzer didn't care. He told the labor lawyer to "go for it," and about three months after the protest, in January 2000, Spitzer's office filed suit against the Food Emporium, its parent company, and the delivery service. The state court suit charged that the walkers had been paid just $1.25 to $1.75 an hour, well below the state-mandated minimum of $3.20 an hour plus tips. An advocacy group, the National Employment Law Project, which had been independently investigating the case, filed a parallel suit in federal court. Food Emporium's owner, A&P, wanted to settle, but a dispute broke out over the amount. Smith's auditors had estimated that the four hundred deliverymen were owed $3.2 million, but the advocates at the law project thought the workers deserved a payment closer to $20 million. Personally involved in the negotiations, Spitzer held firm. "He gave them a number and he stuck by that number even when there were pressures on him to raise that number," Smith said. "It gave [A&P] a certain amount of confidence that we weren't inflating" the back wages. In December 2000, A&P agreed to pay $3 million to an estimated four hundred deliverymen. Despite the disagreements about the size of the settlement, the litigation director of the National Employment Law Project, Catherine Ruckelshaus, had good things to say about Spitzer. "His office is really head and shoulders above any other state on labor and worker issues," she said. "The only thing I tell groups that are considering working with him is that you don't have complete control. If his office declares, 'Okay, we're done; this [settlement] is what is needed,' you can't stop that."

The tactic of bending old laws to cover new problems was one that Spitzer and his aides would turn to again and again. Even as Smith was building her deliveryman case, two other Spitzer aides were combing through the precedents looking for ways to tackle a completely different issue: the nexus between illegal guns and street crimes. Though homicide rates had been dropping for nearly a decade, many New Yorkers were still shell-shocked by the drug-fueled violence that tore through the city in the 1980s. The state's tough gun-control laws had done little to keep weapons out of the hands of criminals, and sentiment was running high against guns and gun manufacturers in the Empire State. The Republican-dominated Congress had made clear that it would not approve new national gun-control legislation, so Spitzer decided to see if there was anything he could do to force gun makers to sell safer guns and to keep closer tabs on who bought them.

As former prosecutors, Spitzer and his lieutenants believed that firearms manufacturers knew a lot more about what happened to their products than they sometimes let on. Moreover, the federal Bureau of Alcohol, Tobacco and Firearms (ATF) required recordkeeping each time a gun changed hands legally. Whenever a police officer or FBI agent recovered a gun in connection with a crime, investigators could call the manufacturer and find out where the gun had been bought. From there, the trace would go to the wholesaler and on to the dealer. So, gun-control advocates argued, it wouldn't be too hard for manufacturers to figure out which wholesalers and which dealers were selling guns that ended up in criminal hands. Indeed, in 2000, the ATF would release a study that found that 1 percent of the dealers who sold guns to the public were responsible for selling 57 percent of the guns used in crimes. The path from the dealers to the criminals was surprisingly short. In most states, private individuals could purchase and resell as many guns as they liked, without keeping any kind of records at all, a rule that created financial incentives for straw purchasers and other kinds of informal gun markets. While few statistics were available for New York, a Philadelphia-area study found that about half the handguns sold over a fifteen-month period were purchased by buyers who bought at least one other handgun, and nearly a fifth of all handguns were bought by people who also purchased at least four others. A lawyer named Elisa Barnes had filed a class-action lawsuit in Brooklyn on behalf of seven gunshot victims, arguing that gun makers had distributed their product in a negligent way that fostered violence and an illegal underground market for handguns. Both New Orleans and Chicago had filed their own suits in late 1998, and other communities were making plans to take similar action. But no state had taken the plunge.

Spitzer initially gave his old college friend Carl Mayer, now serving in the office as special counsel, the task of coming up with a legal theory that might work in New York State. Mayer argued for a broad-based assault that would hit a variety of issues, including antitrust violations, product liability, negligence, and public nuisance. But another Spitzer deputy, Peter Pope—who, like Spitzer, had clerked for Judge Sweet and had worked for the Manhattan DA—wanted to target a single promising argument. In his view, an antitrust case would fail because there didn't seem to be any illegal collusion. Product liability fell short because the guns weren't defective; they were working all too well. Elisa Barnes and the gun-violence victims she was representing had done well initially with a negligence argument, winning a jury verdict in February 1999, but Pope doubted that that victory would withstand appeal.

The answer seemed to be public nuisance theory, which allowed a state or city to sue to force a company to remedy a threat to public health and safety. Mayer sought help from David Kairys, a Temple University law professor who was working with Chicago and several other cities on their lawsuits. Kairys explained the advantages of the theory he had developed: the plaintiff in a nuisance suit was generally a government seeking to protect the general public health rather than to recover damages for a specific incident. That distinction minimized the problem of connecting particular manufacturers to particular crimes. Kairys thought a suit by Spitzer's office might have more force than those brought by various cities because the New York State attorney general had a specific legal duty to protect the public health and safety. "Factually the strongest case was in Chicago because they had done a study [showing where their illegal guns came from], but legally, in terms of which case would look the strongest, Eliot's was it," Kairys said. Spitzer was sold, particularly after Mindy Bockstein, a policy researcher in his office, discovered a 1907 law that specifically declared the carrying of an illegal gun to be a public nuisance.

But Spitzer knew the lawsuit wouldn't be a slam dunk. The gun industry had never lost this kind of case. "It was an aggressive theory. . . . We understood that it was sufficiently aggressive that we negotiated with the gun manufacturers for a year," Pope said. The first step was to try to split the well-established gun companies from the fly-by-night manufacturers of cheap nine-millimeter guns favored by gangs, known as "the ring of fire." Spitzer's people arranged a series of meetings with the industry to explain their planned lawsuit and offered to settle with companies that would agree to install safety locks, limit retail purchasers to one gun a month, and—most important—stop selling to dealers with a history of selling crime guns.

At the gun meetings, Spitzer came on strong. In a style that would become his trademark, he bluntly laid out the consequences of the manufacturers' not coming to a settlement. There would be hundreds and hundreds of expensive lawsuits filed by cities and states all over the country, he said. He even warned Glock vice president Paul Jannuzzo to expect "bankruptcy lawyers knocking at your door" if the company didn't sign on to what Spitzer was calling a "code of conduct." Spitzer's people were optimistic that he was making headway, particularly after a couple of manufacturers met secretly with Pope to discuss methods for identifying and freezing out crime-associated dealers. "They said, 'We really get this; it's time for you to bring in other cities and states,'" Pope said. "It felt like we were very very close." In late September 1999, gun industry representatives sat down in Washington with Spitzer, Connecticut attorney general Richard Blumenthal, and representatives of a number of cities that had filed or were filing lawsuits. Some manufacturer participants hailed the talks as historic.

In retrospect, industry representatives said, Spitzer and the gun-control advocates were kidding themselves about the prospects for a broad deal. "We met with them to explain how they were wrong," said Lawrence Keane, general counsel for the National Shooting Sports Foundation, the main trade association. "It was readily apparent that these people knew nothing about the industry. There were no settlement discussions." Many gun manufacturers were unimpressed by Spitzer's claims that he could broker a nationwide settlement of all the city and state claims. "He didn't have the juice to do it," Keane said. Still, the parties agreed to schedule another multistate meeting in Las Vegas, for January 2000, to coincide with the industry's annual Shooting, Hunting and Outdoor Trade (SHOT) Show.

When the Clinton administration got wind of the talks, it wanted in. Secretary of Housing and Urban Development Andrew Cuomo, who was eyeing a run for governor of New York, told *The New York Times* on December 7 that the White House was contemplating a federal gun lawsuit, and the next day he used a press conference to publicly invite the states and gun manufacturers to "put everyone at one table, in one room and see if we can come up with a global settlement. If we cannot, then we are prepared to go the litigation route." Spitzer learned about Cuomo's interest from the newspapers rather than from Cuomo directly, but Spitzer professed enthusiasm for federal participation. Cuomo then came to see Spitzer, and the two of them helped organize another Washington meeting with the city and state plaintiffs to come up with a united front. New problems developed when the White House wanted to participate in Spitzer's direct negotiations with the gun manufacturers. Industry representatives and their Washington allies put their foot down. Spitzer they would talk to; but they had hated Clinton for years and they weren't going to meet with his people. Cuomo and various White House aides upped the ante, telling Spitzer's office in essence, you can't go to the January 2000 SHOT Show meeting without us; you can't leave your president outside the room. Spitzer reluctantly pulled out of the Las Vegas meeting.

Three months later, Pope got a call from a gun industry source telling him that Cuomo had stabbed them and the other state and local governments in the back. (Cuomo did not respond to multiple requests for an interview.) The HUD secretary—without a heads-up to Spitzer—had secretly approached a couple of selected manufacturers with a proposal. Bob Morrison, the president of Taurus, was not interested, but after he refused the initial offer, he said, he got a personal call from Cuomo in which the HUD secretary offered a deal. "If we would come . . ." Morrison said, "he would absolutely make us favored with lush government contracts to buy more firearms from us." Morrison turned Cuomo down. But Ed Shultz, the chief executive of Smith & Wesson, was interested, if the deal included a promise by Spitzer and the cities to drop their planned and pending lawsuits. Pope and Spitzer rushed to Washington to get into the Smith & Wesson talks and decided to make public another idea Spitzer had been working on—using the government's purchasing power to reward manufacturers who were willing to make safer guns and limit where they sold them. On March 16, 2000, Spitzer announced that he was forming a coalition of state and local governments to boycott gun manufacturers who failed to adhere to his code of conduct.

The next day, Spitzer was part of the group that flanked President Clinton as he announced from the Oval Office that Smith & Wesson had become the first gun manufacturer ever to agree to change the way it designed and marketed its products in exchange for protection from state, local, and federal lawsuits. When Clinton got to the marketing part of the deal, Spitzer's main focus, and announced that "the company will cut off dealers who sell disproportionate numbers of guns that turn up in crimes," Spitzer and Pope, who was seated in the audience, caught each other's eyes and smiled.

Andrew Cuomo then latched on to Spitzer's purchasing coalition and took it national. On March 22, Spitzer was part of the press conference that Cuomo used to announce that twenty-eight cities and states had agreed to steer their police weapon purchases to Smith & Wesson or to any other manufacturer that adhered to the code of conduct. Spitzer spoke fifth. He stepped to the microphone and boldly predicted that the combined buying power would bring the other manufacturers to heel: "We have the capacity to squeeze them like a pincers and say to them, we will deny you of your most important market. They can sell all they want to the membership of the NRA, but we are bigger."

The gun industry and gun owners were outraged by the deal. Smith & Wesson found itself frozen out of industry meetings, and its sales plummeted. On March 30, Spitzer, Blumenthal, and the Federal Trade Commission announced that they were starting an antitrust investigation to see if the company was being improperly blackballed by leading distributors and retailers. The industry fired right back with an antitrust lawsuit of its own in April, alleging that the purchasing coalition brokered by Spitzer and Cuomo was "an illegal attempt by a number of self-appointed and self-important elected officials to violate the basic rights of a legitimate and a responsible industry." Within days, coalition members had begun backing down, saying that the purchasing preference was pure public relations and they had no plans to stop buying from the other gun companies. (The industry would voluntarily withdraw its lawsuit nine months later, in January 2001.)

By the time Spitzer filed his own gun lawsuit in June 2000, it was almost anticlimactic. Thirty-two cities had beaten the state to the punch, including New York City, which made a mockery of the HUD deal by including Smith & Wesson as a defendant. Spitzer's complaint was dry and narrow. It sought to link the 8,340 handguns confiscated by police in the state of New York in 1997 with the 1,234 gun deaths that occurred that year. Gun manufacturers were "on notice" from the ATF about the illegal uses of their products, the lawsuit said, yet they continued to design guns that appealed to criminals and continued to sell them to wholesalers and dealers who had a history of selling guns that ended up being used to kill people. "In sum, defendants know that a significant portion of their guns become crime guns, but turn a blind eye so as to increase their profits at the cost of many human lives and much human suffering," the complaint said.

The case went nowhere. The judge tossed it out at the first possible moment without granting Spitzer's team access to gun industry records or ATF data that might have helped them prove their claim that the manufacturers were contributing to the flood of illegal guns. "Defendants are engaged in manufacturing lawful non-defective products and are subjected to considerable regulation. They are also several steps removed from the unlawful use of handguns which constitutes the nuisance here. . . . To assert broad liability, plaintiffs must allege more facts which would demonstrate that defendants are somehow contributing to the handgun nuisance," the opinion said. The judge also dismissed the 1907 law that Spitzer's team had dug up, saying it merely restated that illegal guns were a public nuisance and did not prove that the industry was to blame for them.

No other state ever sued the gun industry, though Blumenthal considered it, before deciding that he had no case under Connecticut state laws. (Despite the flood of city lawsuits, as of early 2006, no court anywhere in the country had required gun manufacturers to change their marketing practices.) The antitrust investigation of the industry's alleged Smith & Wesson boycott petered out without bringing charges. "The fact of the matter is, we didn't have a case," said Blumenthal, whose office led the investigation and negotiations. The battle left gun industry representatives with nothing but disdain for Spitzer. "All he wants is a press conference [and] we'll never give him that satisfaction," said Lawrence Keane, the trade association lawyer. "We've been successful because the allegations were false. They underestimated the resolve of the executives to fight this."

The loss taught Spitzer and his team three important lessons. First, they now knew they had to watch their backs, even with fellow regulators and ideological allies. "We learned that you have to expect other regulators are going to get into the game and you can't predict how they are going to do it," Pope said. Second, they discovered that public shaming worked much better when their opponents were economically vulnerable. On Wall Street, Spitzer "goes in and he finds out all kinds of things and they all fold because you can't have that kind of adverse publicity," observed the gun-control lawyer Elisa Barnes. "He goes in with the gun makers . . . and they don't care what the New York attorney general thinks. He's just another pretty face that will come and go. They refused to even grant one inch." Third, and most important, the Spitzer team learned to make sure they had damning facts in hand before they tried to negotiate a settlement. "Now we're a lot more skilled at putting the lawsuit together first and talking later. Now we sit down after an exhaustive investigation, after turning over every stone, and we say, 'This is what we've got. What are you going to do about it?'" Hirshman said.

Spitzer, meanwhile, was refining his personal views on federalism based on his practical experiences and repeated discussions and arguments with his aides. He was practically fervent when he took up the topic again at New York's annual Law Day celebration in the spring of 2000. "Despite my initial skepticism, the day I awoke as attorney general of New York, I had an epiphany" about states' rights, Spitzer said. "I now see this change as a tremendous opportunity for legal ingenuity and innovation on the part of state actors. . . . The new federalism has, in effect, unbound the hands of state actors to be, once again, the center of creativity and initiative, just as the states were in the Progressive Era of the last century. . . . It is an exciting time to be a New Yorker."

In 2001, the Investment Protection Bureau grew bolder. Dinallo and the staff were bringing bigger and bigger cases—and creeping ever closer to Manhattan and the luminaries of Wall Street. In May, Spitzer took on his largest case yet, a twenty-five-million-dollar rare coin scam on Long Island. This time the office exploited the flexibility of the Martin Act by bringing criminal charges against twenty-six people and five interlocking companies for running a "boiler room"—a high-pressure sales operation that conned nearly a thousand people into sinking their savings into overpriced coins. Some victims lost as much as $750,000. It was a classic use of the Martin Act. Dinallo's two-year investigation showed that salespeople would offer the coins at inflated prices and promise investors they would be able to resell "at a significant profit." Skeptics who wanted a second appraisal were referred to "independent" dealers, who actually worked for the same operation. "The coins were real, but just about everything else about the operation was a lie," Spitzer told the media. "These defendants were the worst of the worst. They preyed on elderly victims, earning their trust and stealing their retirement nest eggs."

Patricia Smith's Labor Bureau was also knocking heads and taking names. In March 2001, the office won the first felony conviction of a sweatshop operator in nearly a decade, convicting Mary Yue Cheung of falsifying wage records and failing to pay wages at the Kimtex Fashion factory in the Garment District. The deliveryman issue expanded beyond Food Emporium to several other major supermarket and drugstore chains and gave Spitzer an early taste of what it would be like to take on the wealthy and well connected. Gristedes Foods chairman John A. Catsimatidis was one of the state's largest Democratic donors, and he wasn't pleased to find himself on the receiving end of a Spitzer investigation. "They went after us under an obscure law. We felt it was not fair because these deliverymen are not our employees," Catsimatidis said. "They were all illegal aliens and nobody said boo. Maybe they weren't making minimum wage, but they were making an average of five hundred dollars a week in cash tips, tax free." Catsimatidis asked for and got a number of face-to-face meetings with Spitzer, but each time, the attorney general invited Smith to attend, and each time, Spitzer refused to reduce the size of the penalty. Eventually, Gristedes agreed to a $3.25 million settlement. Catsimatidis contended he had been strong-armed: "You have to settle in these cases. Nobody wants to go through a full-blown trial. The trial costs as much in legal fees, and there's a chance you could lose."

By the end of 2001, affirmative cases—those developed independently by the Attorney General's Office—had more than tripled since 1998, Vacco's last year in office, to just over 150 a year. Immigrant groups and labor advocates were coming to see the office as a place that would take their tips seriously and act on them expeditiously. Denis Hughes, the president of the New York State AFL-CIO, said that

Spitzer "has redefined what attorney generals do—not only in our state but throughout the country—in enforcing worker rights." To Spitzer, the Labor Bureau cases embodied the purpose of progressive government. "These are the individuals who are least able to represent themselves. . . . They are vulnerable parties and easy prey," he said. "They speak to the notion of what equality under the law is all about. One of the things this office does is prove that nobody is above the law and nobody is below it. Vindicating the rights of those who are ignored is incredibly important."

4

A SHOCKING BETRAYAL OF TRUST

ON THE MORNING OF SEPTEMBER 11, 2001, ELIOT SPITZER WAS WORKING IN his twenty-fifth-floor office in Lower Manhattan when he heard a crash. American Airlines Flight 11 had just barreled into the North Tower of the World Trade Center, only one hundred yards away. He was staring at the billowing smoke sixteen minutes later when United Airlines Flight 175 smashed into the trade center's South Tower. "We saw this eruption coming right at us through the open air, and we didn't know if the windows would hold," he said at the time. When authorities began to evacuate Spitzer's building, 120 Broadway, he initially refused to leave because he wanted to stay until all his staff got out. He and Chief of Staff Rich Baum were still waiting for word from authorities when the South Tower began to rumble and slowly collapse. They headed immediately for the street and were walking away when the North Tower crumbled to the ground. The air went black. Spitzer and his aides stumbled through the clouds, making their way uptown on foot. "It was like what we've read about Pompeii. Everything buried in soot," Spitzer said. When they got to the governor's office, in midtown, George Pataki was so relieved to see the dust-covered attorney general that he gave him a hug.

The Attorney General's Office had gotten lucky. Although 120

Broadway suffered some damage and was closed for nearly two weeks, all nine hundred of the employees who worked there had survived the disaster. Within days, they were back at work from satellite offices around the city and state, issuing warnings to donors to be wary of scams when they opened their wallets for the attack victims. "Try to give to organizations that you know," Spitzer told the *Daily News*. "Try to give to organizations that are reputable." As the 9/11 donations rolled in—estimates put the eventual total above a billion dollars—Spitzer became deeply immersed in making sure that the outpouring would actually benefit the victims of the attack. His office's Charities Bureau was already charged with overseeing nonprofit organizations, and if ever there were a time to make sure charity worked well, this was it.

So, on September 26, Spitzer convened a meeting of more than two dozen major charities to urge them to work together. "We said, look, we have jurisdiction over charities. We don't want to tell you how to spend the money. I just want to make sure you talk to each other," he remembered. He then announced plans to create a central database of aid recipients, modeled on the one used after the Oklahoma City bombing, to streamline the application process and limit fraud. His involvement instantly raised hackles. Not only had he neglected to give the Federal Emergency Management Agency advance warning of his plans, but New York mayor Rudolph Giuliani countered that he, not Spitzer, should be in charge of any coordinated effort. To make matters worse, the American Red Cross, which had raised by far the largest sum, more than five hundred million dollars, refused to participate in the database. Its president, Bernadine Healy, told reporters she was "shocked" that Spitzer had suggested it. "People will not come to us if they think that we are going to put their names in some big database," she said.

Spitzer wouldn't take no for an answer. "The logic of the database was so simple. Oklahoma City had done it. . . . [But] without the Red Cross, getting the project off the ground would have been impossible," he said. He traveled to Washington to negotiate with the Red Cross's general counsel and recruited the consulting firm McKinsey & Company to design and run the project in a way that would address Healy's privacy concerns. He also kept up the public criticism, but privately he had some doubts. At one point, he asked his wife, "What am I doing? This is the Red Cross. They are the good guys." On October 24, the Red Cross reversed course and announced plans to join the database.

But Spitzer wasn't through. A couple of days later, he learned from the media that the Red Cross was considering diverting a large chunk of the money it had raised for 9/11 victims to cover overhead and funding for other causes, such as preparing for future terrorist attacks. He knew from his visit to Washington that the organization was in the middle of planning a lavish new headquarters, and he was instantly suspicious. So he threatened legal action. "Those who gave to the Red Cross intended unambiguously that their funds be used for the victims of September 11," Spitzer said. "You cannot as a charity raise funds for Purpose A and then spend them on Purpose B." The flap got Spitzer on the national news, and he was invited to testify before Congress, where he pulled no punches. "I am personally very discomforted by the inconsistent and conflicting statements from the Red Cross" about use of the money, he proclaimed, adding that the charity's proposal "amounts to a violation of the trust that the American public gave them." Within days, the Red Cross backed down and promised that every penny it had raised would go to the victims. Healy said later that Spitzer used "Jekyll-and-Hyde tactics" and alternated between "being utterly charming" and "manipulative and scary."

The fight with the Red Cross helped teach Spitzer several important things. The American people didn't like to be lied to, particularly when it came to the use of their money. They would support a public official against even the most beloved and well known institution, if that official had the facts on his side. Public shaming and the threat of legal action had worked wonders in forcing change. Those lessons would come into play again over the next few months as Spitzer tackled an even more powerful adversary: Wall Street.

In the early weeks of January 2002, Eric Dinallo, the chief of the tiny Investment Protection Bureau, asked for a meeting with his boss. For nearly a year now, lawyers on Dinallo's staff had been working on a potentially explosive case that could put the Attorney General's Office on a collision course with Merrill Lynch, one of Wall Street's biggest firms. They believed they had the goods to bring a fraud case involving one of Merrill's stock analysts, Henry Blodget—a Yale-educated media darling who had sprung to fame at a smaller outfit by predicting, correctly, that the online bookseller Amazon.com would hit four hundred dollars a share. Spitzer's investigators thought they could prove Blodget had published misleading research reports on an Internet company called GoTo.com. But their probe suggested that Merrill might have a broader problem, one that called into question the way all the major investment banks did business. Dinallo wanted guidance from Spitzer about just how far and how hard to push. After all, Merrill Lynch was an enormous employer, the firm had suffered losses during the attack on the World Trade Center, and the big Wall Street firms had traditionally been the responsibility of the Securities and Exchange Commission and the federal prosecutors in the Southern District of New York.

This was not the first time Spitzer had heard of the investigation. It had started more than a year earlier, when Dinallo and his deputy, Roger Waldman, were drawing up a priority list for 2001. After two years of doing boiler room cases and going after relatively small-scale fraud, the bureau was ready to think big. They knew that small investors who had poured money into technology stocks in the 1990s were losing their shirts. Given Spitzer's well-known views about making the markets fair, the Investment Protection Bureau lawyers expected the boss would be asking hard questions. Had some in the securities business played fast and loose with investors' trust? Waldman's interest had been piqued by a couple of *New York Times* articles, including one citing a study by Zacks Investment Research of eight thousand research reports written by stock analysts who worked for investment banks about the companies in the Standard & Poor's 500 Index. Only twenty-nine reports recommended that investors "sell." For his part, Dinallo thought back to a dinner-table conversation from the previous October about the cold calls his father was receiving from a big-name Wall Street firm in which the brokers pushed stocks based on the advice of in-house research analysts. Why hadn't prominent analysts such as Merrill's Blodget, Jack Grubman of Citigroup, and Morgan Stanley's Mary Meeker warned their own brokers that the market had begun to turn? Were they true believers in the Internet or had something compromised their judgment? "When analysts recommend these stocks, what is their interest in it?" Dinallo's father had asked. When Dinallo forwarded the bureau's 2001 action plan on to Spitzer, "Investigation of investment banking firm analysts" was number two on the list. Spitzer read the report but paid little attention to that one item. "It was just one of many investigations," he later recalled. "There was no premonition that this was a more important case. It was like everything else. You say, 'Let's see where it takes us.'"

Under Spitzer's leadership, the Attorney General's Office routinely tackled new topics by following the model pioneered decades earlier by organized crime expert Ronald Goldstock, which Spitzer had employed in his Garment District Mafia cases. Rather than randomly starting to interview people or subpoena documents, Spitzer's approach was to try to understand the structure of the industry the office was investigating. In this case, the Investment Protection Bureau sought to isolate conflicts of interest that might explain why Wall Street analysts were churning out such rosy reports. The bureau staff drew diagrams of the various relationships between the banks and the companies their analysts wrote about. Investment banks had been making money by helping technology firms raise money through stock and bond offerings. What kinds of quid pro quos might be occurring, and where in the bowels of the giant Wall Street firms should Spitzer's team focus their efforts?

Bruce Topman, a new hire assigned to the analyst issue, came up with the answer. Topman was one of the older attorneys in the office, a dapper former corporate lawyer who had turned to public service once his kids were grown. He seized on the idea of initial public offerings, known colloquially as IPOs. In these transactions, the investment bank made money by helping a private company offer shares to the public for the first time. The bank's researchers then wrote reports about the newly public company, and if the research was positive, it could help boost the share price. "It's the most obvious trade," Topman explained. "You give us the IPO, we'll give you coverage, and there's no history on the coverage so we don't have to reverse ourselves or reinvent the wheel. It's perfect."

Dinallo decided that the bureau should start with Merrill Lynch and Bear Stearns, two investment banks where he had contacts in their legal departments. The two institutions also had very different reputations. Merrill and its legions of retail brokers were considered top drawer, while Bear Stearns had previously faced regulatory scrutiny. The bureau chief checked in briefly with Spitzer before sending out the information requests, to make sure his boss had no objections to taking on such big-name Wall Street firms. Spitzer gave him the green light.

Then, in early summer, news reports helped focus their inquiry. First, while riding on the subway, Dinallo spotted a small item in *The Wall Street Journal.* Merrill Lynch had just paid four hundred thousand dollars to a Queens pediatrician named Debasis Kanjilal to settle allegations that he had been suckered into buying and holding stock in a sinking Internet company called InfoSpace by enthusiastic reports from Henry Blodget. That kind of settlement money meant Merrill was worried about something. The Bear Stearns inquiry was put on hold, and another member of Dinallo's bureau, Gary Connor, paid a call on the pediatrician's lawyer, Jacob Zamansky, who outlined the now-settled case.

In March 2000, Kanjilal had put $571,000—much of it cash he had put aside for his daughters' college education—into InfoSpace, an Internet platform then trading at about $122 a share. Over the next nine months he watched the stock plummet and worried as company insiders dumped their shares. But his Merrill broker talked him out of selling, citing enthusiastic research reports from Blodget. By the time Blodget downgraded the stock in December 2000, the share price had dropped to ten dollars. Zamansky believed he had discovered an explanation for Blodget's enthusiasm deep in corporate proxy reports. In July 2000, Merrill had been hired by another Internet firm, Go2Net, to sell itself to InfoSpace in a deal that involved a stock swap. The investment bank stood to make fees of seventeen million dollars if the deal went through. But that would happen only if InfoSpace's stock price stopped its precipitous fall. Blodget had stayed positive on the stock until after the Go2Net deal closed. Rather than turn over Blodget's documents on the company, Merrill offered Zamansky a confidential settlement. "I've been waiting for someone to call me," Zamansky said

he told Connor. "Serve me with a subpoena, and I'll give you everything I've got." About the same time, the investment protection team
also read a bunch of media coverage about GoTo.com, another, unre-
lated, California-based Internet search firm that Blodget had made the
subject of one of his rare downgrades in June 2001. Newspapers had
leaped on the fact that the downgrade came on the same day that the
Internet firm officially passed over Merrill to pick Credit Suisse First
Boston to handle its upcoming stock offering. Merrill denied there was
a connection, but Dinallo's investigators had their doubts. So Topman
sent Merrill a subpoena asking specifically for documents about Info-
Space and GoTo.com, including Blodget's e-mail correspondence.

The results were better than the bureau had hoped. Investigators
found they could reconstruct a tortured history between GoTo.com
and Merrill's analysts that dated back to September 2000, when the
cash-strapped firm had hired the investment bank to do a "private
placement," a method of raising money from large investors in Europe. At that time, Blodget and his assistants weren't issuing reports on
GoTo's stock, but the Merrill investment banker trying to win GoTo's
business promised that that would change if Merrill got the deal. Sure
enough, Merrill issued its first analysis of GoTo in January 2001, under
Blodget's name, a report that rated the stock a "3" out of 5 (neutral) for
its results in the next twelve months, and a "1" (buy) for its long-term
prospects. But when a mutual fund manager e-mailed Blodget about
the new report, asking, "What's so interesting about GoTo except
banking fees????" Blodget answered, "Nothin." The investigators also
found that those rating numbers had been the product of an angry
back-and-forth between the analysts and the investment bankers. The
bankers wanted the stock rated a "2-2," Merrill Lynch's code for "accumulate" as both a short- and long-term investment. But Kirsten Campbell, who worked for Blodget, complained in an e-mail that she did not
"want to be a whore for f-ing management." Campbell made it clear
that she was concerned about the effect her upbeat research was having
on ordinary investors, writing, "If 2-2 means that we are putting half
of merrill retail [the small investors who used Merrill brokers] into this
stock . . . then I don't think that's the right thing to do. We are losing
people money and i don't like it. john and mary smith are losing their

retirement because we don't want todd [Todd Tappin, the chief financial officer of GoTo] to be mad at us." After repeated conversations with the investment bankers and GoTo's management, the analysts issued a 3-1, but at their insistence, Campbell moved up her reported projections of when the company would become profitable from 2003 to 2002. "This whole idea that we are independent from banking is a big lie—without banking this would be a 3-2," Campbell wrote.

In April 2001, Blodget and Ed McCabe, another analyst who reported to Blodget, upgraded GoTo to 2-1 (short-term, accumulate; long-term, buy), and the next month Merrill began lobbying the company to put it in charge of another big stock offering. But on May 25, Todd Tappin and Ted Meisel, GoTo's chief executive, informed Merrill that they were leaning toward hiring Credit Suisse First Boston instead. That same day, McCabe e-mailed Blodget about plans to downgrade the stock based on "valuation"—in English that meant its price had doubled in the past month and it was now too expensive. "I don't think I've downgraded a stock on valuation since the mid-90s," McCabe observed. "Beautiful fuk em," Blodget replied. Spitzer's investigators noted that the timing was odd for a valuation-based downgrade—GoTo's closing price of $22.75 had not changed materially from its level two and three days earlier, when Blodget had issued positive research reports on the company. Even more suspicious, Blodget did not announce the downgrade immediately. Instead, he waited until June 6, just hours after GoTo.com officially announced an offering of 2.5 million shares of new stock with Credit Suisse First Boston as the lead banker. The new rating was 3-1 (neutral, buy). Merrill adamantly denied a link between the downgrade and the offering, but Topman said he and Dinallo knew they were on to something. "We really started to make the case on GoTo that the research wasn't objective," he said.

The InfoSpace e-mails were also revealing. The company was included in Merrill's "favored 15" list of top stocks to buy from August to December 2000—a period that included the entire time Merrill was helping Go2Net sell itself to InfoSpace. Yet Blodget had e-mailed a colleague in June of that year that he had "enormous skepticism" about the company. While issuing reports that rated the stock a 1-1 (a strong buy for both the near and long term), Blodget was also referring to it in e-mails as "a powder keg," complaining to a colleague, "I'm getting killed on this thing," and noting that better-informed institutional investors had commented on the stock's "bad smell." Dinallo started using a whiteboard in his office to keep track of the disconnect between the analysts' recommendations and their private e-mails.

In August 2001, Blodget came in for five days of depositions. The Merrill analyst was seen by Wall Street competitors as a lightweight because he had never taken courses in economics or accounting, but he impressed investigators as he spent hours explaining how he picked his price targets and why he had legitimate bases for his stock ratings. Sure, investment banking had a say in his compensation, but Merrill had strong policies that protected the independence of its stock analysts, he said. He often did not know about Merrill's efforts to win banking business from the companies he covered, and in any case, he had never allowed such knowledge to taint his ratings. "I thought that I would succeed or fail based on the credibility that I had," he told Topman. "I saw no other way early on of maintaining my credibility and integrity . . . other than by calling it like I saw it."

Yes, it was true that he had handed out lots of "buy" ratings and almost never rated a stock a "sell," but look at the period he was working in, Blodget argued. Under Merrill's system, a "1" or "buy" rating simply meant that the analyst thought the stock was going to go up 20 percent or more in the next year. The NASDAQ index had averaged that kind of growth for most of the 1990s, so even an average company was going to do that well. While it was now clear that the market had turned for the worse in March 2000, he couldn't have known that at the time. The sector had been volatile for years, he noted. "I remember in the summer of 1997 and then the summer of 1998 and then the summer of 1999, having the stocks drop something like 30 to 50 [percent] from their highs, having the press say all the Internet analysts are idiots, look it was a bubble. . . . Then only to have the stock come back . . . then resume their upward climb," Blodget said. "I should have downgraded at the top. . . . But it's a lot harder than it seems when one is actually looking forward and not looking at the rearview mirror."

Blodget also took pains to explain away the specific GoTo e-mails.

The June 2001 downgrade of GoTo.com, he said, was completely un-related to Merrill's efforts to win the stock offering deal and was "one of his best" calls. His "fuk em" e-mail had nothing to do with the company's decision to use Credit Suisse First Boston, even though it came just hours after the Merrill bankers had learned they were being passed over. "I was being somewhat tongue in cheek," Blodget said. The "em" in the e-mail did not refer to GoTo's management, Blodget said. Rather it showed his independence because he was referring to Merrill's big institutional clients—fund managers and the like—who had a history of complaining whenever he downgraded a stock they owned. As for the e-mail exchange in which Blodget wrote there was "nothin" interesting about the stock except banking fees, the analyst said he was "sort of poking fun" at the American Express fund manager who had asked the question.

By the time Dinallo came to Spitzer for guidance in early 2002, the Investment Protection Bureau knew they were sitting on dynamite. The analyst issue had hit the big time when Enron filed for bankruptcy on December 2, 2001, wiping out billions of dollars in market capital-ization. Small investors were furious that analysts at many of the major Wall Street firms had continued to recommend the energy company's stock until the bitter end. At their meeting in Spitzer's office, Dinallo explained his dilemma. He felt sure they could bring a narrow fraud case against Blodget that focused on the GoTo e-mails. But the dam-ages were likely to be small, and Blodget had accepted a buyout offer a few months earlier. Dinallo wasn't sure it was worth picking a fight with Merrill Lynch for such a small case. But there was another option. The e-mails and depositions suggested that Wall Street had a much broader problem with biased research.

Dinallo thought the investigators should comb through everything Blodget and his underlings had written to see if the independence and quality of their work had been compromised by pressure from Merrill investment bankers. Such a plan, however, would require an enormous amount of manpower. Blodget's technology team had been prolific and had covered dozens of companies that had later gone bust. Dinallo also knew that Spitzer generally preferred broad cases to little ones: "Cases ought to be brought where there are structural issues and there are smaller people in our world that need to be protected," Spitzer later explained. But did he really want to invest in that kind of all-out effort? After paging through some of the spiciest e-mails that the bureau chief had brought with him, Spitzer made his choice: "Get me the damn e-mails! All of them," he said.

As the boxes of e-mails kept rolling in, most of the Investment Protection Bureau joined the hunt. They were paging through files, hoping to find something good. Dinallo was staying late into the evening and taking folders home every night, and Beth Golden, the deputy attorney general whom Spitzer had asked to provide some top-level supervision, took a box with her on vacation in Palm Springs. It was a difficult slog. "You could spend a whole day going through a box and if you found one thing, that was great," remembered Gary Connor, who had been on the case since he had checked out Merrill's settlement of the Debasis Kanjilal case. And sometimes new discoveries would force the team to go back and review everything they had already looked at. For instance, an October 10, 2000, exchange between Blodget and research assistant Eve Glatt was a serious eye-opener. In it, the star analyst sent Glatt a cheat sheet of the abbreviations and acronyms he routinely used to speed up his e-mail. Some were basic Internet terms: "lol" = "laugh out loud," "gt" = "great," "imho" = "in my humble opinion," and "nfw" for an unprintable expletive. But the revelation that "pos" = "piece of shit" sent the investigators diving back into their boxes of discarded e-mails. Connor and others in the Investment Protection Bureau weren't heavy e-mail users and they had assumed that "pos" meant "positive," and had therefore paid little attention to the phrase. Now, they were learning, it meant just the opposite. This discovery made a December 4, 2000, e-mail exchange between Glatt and Blodget about an Internet advice firm called LifeMinders downright explosive. Noting that the stock had fallen to four dollars, Blodget wrote, "I can't believe what a POS that thing is. Shame on me/us for giving them any benefit of doubt." "Yeah, hard to believe," Glatt replied. "SO glad we don't have a 1-1, not that a 2-1 is all that much better."

Then the bureau's Elizabeth Block found the killer evidence. The longest-serving attorney in the bureau, Block had been with the office since the days of Louis Lefkowitz and was not the kind of lawyer who was expected to do the grunt work. But she, too, had been infected by Dinallo's enthusiasm and Spitzer's demand for speed. Look at this, she told Dinallo, waving a 2000 e-mail in which Blodget complained he was not getting enough guidance on how to reconcile management's demand for downgrades on falling stocks with the investment banking team's demands for good press for its clients. "If there are no new e-mail forthcoming from Andy [Melnick, Blodget's boss and the head of research] on how the instructions below should be applied to sensitive banking clients/relations, we are going to just start calling the stocks (stocks, not companies) . . . like we see them, no matter what the ancillary business consequences are."

"I've found the smoking gun," Block told Dinallo.

"No, you've found a Howitzer," Dinallo replied.

There was no way Merrill could claim that Blodget was being flip or tossing off a smart reply, they believed. His language showed that he believed his team had been allowing business concerns to affect their research reports. "I had been a defense attorney for thirty years," Roger Waldman said, "and I've spent a lot of time thinking of defenses. On this e-mail, there was nothing I thought anybody could say."

In fact, the situation was more complicated than it appeared. Despite Blodget's obvious frustration about investment banking pressure, in the three years 1999–2001, he had personally downgraded sixteen client companies a total of twenty-nine times. His lawyers would later contend in civil litigation that this particular e-mail, rather than being an admission of bias, was a spirited defense of his decision to issue downgrades based on the overall falling market. Blodget himself is prohibited from discussing his days at Merrill Lynch as part of a confidentiality agreement he signed in exchange for a severance package estimated at five million dollars. But a national regulator who has reviewed the full panoply of evidence against the analyst said there is some truth to Merrill's argument that the e-mails were taken out of context. "Even for the worst e-mails, there is an explanation that is not totally ludicrous," the regulator said. Blodget also noted, in a piece he wrote for the online magazine *Slate* in 2004, that he had personally invested seven hundred thousand dollars in Internet companies in February and March 2000 and essentially lost it all by failing to sell as the market sank. "My now-agonizing decision was based in part on promising fundamentals, in part on optimism fueled by years of mind-boggling stock performance, and in part on the perception that Internet companies might continue to steal value from traditional companies and that one way to hedge this was to invest in a basket of them," Blodget wrote. "I would love to say I lost this money because I was swindled. Alas, I lost it because, in hindsight, I was a moron."

In March, Merrill Lynch's legal team arrived in Spitzer's office for the first of several meetings to discuss the results of his investigation. To lead the charge, the bank had hired both the white-shoe firm of Skadden, Arps and Robert Morvillo, a pugnacious former federal prosecutor with decades of experience facing down federal regulators. The defense lawyers came in expecting to talk specifically about InfoSpace and GoTo.com because those two IPOs had been the subject of all the depositions. On those grounds, Morvillo believed that both the firm's and Blodget's conduct could be explained. Sure, the analyst had been dismissive about the companies in his private e-mails, but the reports themselves were accurate. As for the allegedly "secret" deals linking research coverage with investment banking business, the deals hadn't been secret at all. The SEC had known about them; the media had written about them; Congress had even held hearings on them in the summer of 2001.

Spitzer was having none of it. He wasn't looking only at InfoSpace and GoTo anymore, but at the second, more damaging round of e-mails that his team had just spent weeks frantically sorting through. "I'm here to talk about remedies, not liability," he said. "I've now read the e-mails. . . . What you have done is indefensible." The Merrill lawyers blanched. Already uncomfortable because they had been seated on Spitzer's soft blue couch—known to the staff for inducing the sensation that your knees were about to hit your ears—they could not believe what they were hearing. In many cases, they hadn't even read the e-mails that Spitzer was so exercised about. "He's way beyond where we are. We don't understand what he is talking about and why he's already focused on penalties," Morvillo remembered.

This was not the way the SEC did business. Before the federal regulators filed a civil fraud case, they always issued a so-called "Wells notice" inviting the targets to explain their conduct and make a formal argument as to why the SEC should not take action. The Merrill team assumed that Spitzer would engage in a similar give-and-take. "We have wonderful defenses . . . and we'd like the chance to explain them to you," Morvillo remembered saying. Spitzer cut Morvillo off. "We're past that now. We're talking about penalties," he said. The defense lawyer—well known to New York prosecutors for his hot temper and willingness to use colorful language—continued to argue. Eventually, he got Spitzer to agree to let the Merrill team come back and formally explain the bank's view of the case.

But the presentation focused primarily on InfoSpace and GoTo and only dug Merrill into a deeper hole. Spitzer and his chief deputies concluded that they were witnessing a moral breakdown at the top of investment banking society. "Their defense was, you are right but we are not as bad as our competitors," Spitzer said. "They knew what was going on, and rather than individually or collectively changing their behavior, they said, 'Unless my competitor changes, I won't either.' I said, 'It usually takes longer for people to start ratting out their colleagues.' The lesson I took from that was that any hesitancy that we had in intervening had been misplaced."

For his part, Morvillo concluded that Spitzer wasn't really listening. "He had clearly made up his mind, gave lip-service to our presence, and continued the negotiations as if we hadn't made a presentation," he recalled. One of Spitzer's top deputies, Dieter Snell, denied that, saying, "The meetings were real as far as we were concerned. Everyone from the top down was concerned that we understood what their position was." But events were moving past the investment bank. The night before Morvillo's presentation, Dinallo asked Topman to draft an outline that would begin to get the case in shape for presentation to a judge. Intent on finishing, Topman skipped the meeting to get the outline done.

By early April, Merrill's top leadership had realized that Spitzer would not be easily deterred, and they feared that he might actually file criminal charges against the firm. So they placed a nervous call to the SEC general counsel, David Becker, telling him that Spitzer was sitting on a pile of e-mails he had taken out of context and was considering filing a case. "They're far too sophisticated to say 'Come save us,' and it's safe to say I was too sophisticated to believe that it was just a bunch of e-mails," Becker remembered. "I certainly didn't take it as something we should help about."

The SEC was far from ignorant about the analyst issue. Back in 2000 and 2001, its Office of Compliance Inspections and Examinations had done inspections at eight major Wall Street firms. The SEC staff drafted a preliminary report in mid-2001 arguing that analysts risked becoming shills for the companies they covered because their compensation was tied to investment banking, they often owned stock in the subjects of their reports, and they considered themselves part of the deal team—essentially in a sales role. But the SEC's widely reported effort had focused on structural issues—reporting lines and compensation rules—and the commission had never looked at e-mails, so it lacked the explosive details that Spitzer's team had uncovered. Based on the results, the SEC's Enforcement Division staff began investigating three firms, but plans to issue a public report ran headlong into the newly installed SEC chairman, Harvey Pitt. A talented securities lawyer with years of defending the industry under his belt, Pitt had used his maiden speech to promise "a new era of respect and cooperation" between accountants and an SEC that had not been "kinder and gentler" in the past. Rather than issuing a public document that would have embarrassed the investment banks, Pitt ordered the report buried, over the objection of the examination staff. Instead, he convened a secret meeting of the top banks at the Wall Street Regent hotel in November 2001, telling them, "You have a huge problem. Either you solve it or we're going to." Pitt gave the two major self-regulatory bodies, the National Association of Securities Dealers (NASD) and the New York Stock Exchange (NYSE), six months to come up with new rules that would protect analyst independence from investment banking pressures. But that secret deadline hadn't expired when word came that Spitzer was sniffing around the issue.

Stephen M. Cutler, the head of the SEC's Enforcement Division, and his staff had also caught wind of the Merrill probe and were trying to find out what Spitzer was up to. Associate Enforcement director Bill Baker offered to give Eric Dinallo a call because they had worked together years before on a case when Dinallo was still at the Manhattan DA's Office.

"Are you about to do something on analysts at Merrill?" Baker remembered asking.

"Why are you interested in that?" Dinallo replied cagily.

"We'd like to work with you on it," Baker said, adding that the SEC was already looking at the analyst issue and wanted to combine forces.

"Let me talk to Eliot and I'll get back to you," Dinallo replied.

He never called back. The phone call left Baker and Cutler with the false belief that whatever Spitzer was up to, it wasn't going to be a big deal anytime soon. That was just fine with Dinallo and Spitzer. As state prosecutors, both of them had been shunted aside in the past by competitive federal enforcers, and they were not about to tip their hand this time.

The negotiations between Spitzer and Merrill Lynch had gone from bad to worse. Although the rank of Merrill's representatives had increased with every meeting, Spitzer and his staff still felt the bank wasn't taking them seriously. Merrill was willing to pay a fine—estimates ranged wildly, from as low as ten million dollars to several times that—and to take steps to insure the independence of their analysts. The real sticking point turned out to be the e-mails. As part of any settlement, Merrill wanted the missives kept quiet—why pay Spitzer money if he was going to air their dirty laundry in public anyway? It wasn't an outrageous demand. SEC settlements usually disclosed relatively little evidence, and civil settlements with plaintiffs' attorneys often included confidentiality agreements. "We wanted what you normally get in civil settlements. We wanted closure; we wanted finality," Merrill's attorney, Morvillo, remembered. "Spitzer didn't care whether it was normal or abnormal. He thought it was in the public interest" to make the e-mails public. Indeed, Spitzer was adamant. "I will not seal the evidence," he repeated each time the issue came up. In his view, insiders had known about biased research for years yet had done little. Only public shaming would produce the wholesale change Spitzer hoped to accomplish. "In a case of structural impact, where there is an underlying practice that needs to be reformed, the only way to do that is to lay out the evidence," he said.

The two sides continued wrangling in the first week of April, and once again the bank and the attorney general found themselves at cross purposes. "We always communicated on his terms, which always avoided the merits of the case and focused on the penalties," Morvillo said. On the Spitzer side, Beth Golden thought the Merrill team was deliberately glossing over the evidence, "defending themselves in every way except on the merits." Merrill officials brought up the firm's commitment to New York City—the firm had been the first major bank to return to its offices in Lower Manhattan after the devastation of the 9/11 attacks. Late in the negotiations, Spitzer and his staff remembered, Morvillo angered the attorney general by alluding to the firm's strong political ties, saying, "Merrill Lynch has a lot of powerful friends." Spitzer's stance hardened. "I had no choice but to file the lawsuit," he said later. "What was I going to do at that point? Should I back down and say, 'Oh, I didn't know you had powerful friends. Now you tell me. If only you had told me that last week, we wouldn't be here.'" (Morvillo acknowledged he made the remark, but placed it more than a week earlier, during his effort to convince Spitzer to let Merrill make a presentation of its defenses.)

Spitzer's final warning to the Merrill team came at the end of that week. On Thursday, April 4, he stopped by the office of one of the Skadden lawyers, David Zornow. "I said to David, 'I don't understand where you guys are going on the refusal to release the evidence. . . . There are two ways the facts come out—either as a [civil fraud] complaint or in a settlement where you are basically doing the right thing,'" Spitzer remembered. "I thought Merrill understood that. Then they called back and said no." By the end of that phone call on Friday afternoon, Skadden partner Ed Yodowitz believed that Spitzer had agreed to continue thinking about the issue over the weekend. In fact, Spitzer was done. "I want to file on Monday," he told Golden. He later recalled, "It was time to pull the trigger. When you are sitting on a wiretap, because it's fun and you can always keep listening, it can go on and on. E-mails are the same thing. . . . I always ask, is it possible we will find anything to prove us wrong? Do we have enough to make a clear and convincing case?"

The staff knew it was going to be a long weekend. Spitzer had given them no warning of his intentions. They didn't even have a complete first draft of the affidavit they would need to file to get the case rolling. Dinallo had written a detailed memo summarizing the evidence and the factual basis for a fraud allegation, but it needed legal reasoning and a serious rewrite before it could be filed in court. The Investment Protection Bureau chief had just spent the day at the hospital, where his wife was giving birth to their second child. But Spitzer wasn't about to sit around and wait. So the top lawyers in the office launched into a process that would become increasingly familiar as the years went by— everyone rallied around and worked all weekend to finish writing and editing the thirty-eight-page affidavit explaining the evidence so that Dinallo and Connor could file it on Monday. "We file nothing before it's time, but if it's time, we all pitch in to make it happen," explained top aide Michele Hirshman. Dinallo spent much of the weekend in cabs between the office and his wife's hospital room. Golden did yeoman's work editing and fine-tuning the sections Topman and others had already drafted. Waldman worked through the chart that would highlight the differences between Blodget's e-mails and his public ratings on particular stocks. In the end there would be more than forty versions of the graphic before Spitzer was satisfied. "I'm always worried we won't be right, so we have to be careful," Spitzer explained.

To guide them through the requirements of the Martin Act, the office turned to Connor, a veteran public servant with nearly two decades in the office. He was the only lawyer among them who had ever used the act's powers under section 354 of the General Business Law to seek an injunction against a securities firm "ex parte"—without the target's lawyers present. The same section would also allow a judge to grant Spitzer broad authority to conduct a public investigation and compel public testimony from Merrill officials. Connor had used such actions against corrupt real estate developers in the 1980s, and it was his job to make sure a judge would believe that the Merrill affidavit fit foursquare within historical precedents.

When Spitzer came in to the office on Sunday, he sent Dinallo home to photograph the homecoming of his newborn baby girl. Then the attorney general made one final set of decisions—as to which Merrill employees and which Internet firms and executives would be identified by name in the affidavit. He knew that the filing was likely to start a media storm and he wanted to make sure he had personally decided which individuals and companies would be named and therefore face tough questions from reporters. Spitzer also made one stab at rounding up allies for what he expected would be a brutal public relations battle with Merrill: he called New York's senior U.S. senator, Charles Schumer, who was a member of the Senate Finance Committee. Spitzer explained what he had found and invited the Democrat to stand with him as he announced the case. Schumer turned him down flat. Spitzer himself was worried. "This could be my end," he confided to Mike Cherkasky, his former boss at the District Attorney's Office, before the filing.

On Monday morning, Merrill Lynch pulled out its last card—it hired Rudolph Giuliani, who had just left the mayor's office to open a consulting firm, and asked him to intervene on their behalf. On paper, it must have sounded like a good idea. As a U.S. attorney in the 1980s, Giuliani had been the last crusading prosecutor to win fame for taking on Wall Street corruption, and he had seen the downside of precipitous action. He had put a major brokerage firm—Drexel Burnham Lambert—out of business by indicting it on corporate fraud charges; and he had watched one of his highest-profile cases—against three top traders at Goldman Sachs and Kidder Peabody for insider trading— fall apart. Only a few months after two of the traders were dragged out of their offices in handcuffs, Giuliani's office had to dismiss the charges against them. And in terms of public relations, the former mayor was now a national hero for his leadership after the attack on the World Trade Center.

Anyone who actually knew Spitzer well also knew that Giuliani was nearly the last person he wanted to hear from at this time. Not only were the two men from different political parties, but they had clashed repeatedly, first over Spitzer's 1999 probe of alleged racial profiling by the New York City Police Department and then, more briefly, over 9/11 charity coordination. When Spitzer's aides heard that Giuliani was on the line about the Merrill case, they joked that he must be returning a phone call from three years earlier. The conversation was polite and distant. Giuliani urged Spitzer to reconsider—"Is there a way to talk about this?"—and then tried to press Merrill's case. Spitzer made clear that he wasn't interested, but he neglected to tell Giuliani that Dinallo and Connor had already left for the courthouse. The judge assigned to handle ex parte requests, State Supreme Court justice Martin Schoenfeld, was on the bench hearing another case, and he kept the two lawyers waiting for several hours. Exhausted from the weekend, Dinallo nearly fell asleep. The judge was a bit concerned that Merrill's lawyers weren't present, but Connor and Dinallo assured him that the Martin Act specifically permitted ex parte orders.

By the time they got back to the office at 120 Broadway, the press conference room on the twenty-fifth floor was packed to the gills. The television cameras were assembled. The poster-size blowups of the most dramatic e-mails were ready. Dinallo and Connor had persuaded the judge to issue a court order instructing Merrill to tell its customers about conflicts of interest that could bias its research. Spitzer strode to the podium and began speaking quickly and gesticulating strongly, as he always did when excited with a righteous anger. "This was a shocking betrayal of trust by one of Wall Street's most trusted names," Spitzer told the assembled media. "This case must be a catalyst for reform throughout the entire industry." Pointing to his poster boards, Spitzer told the stories of GoTo and InfoSpace and of Blodget's threat "to just start calling the stocks . . . like we see them." But these weren't his only evidence. Waldman's chart told the story. Publicly, the Merrill team had said that Maryland-based Aether Systems was a long-term "buy." Privately they had written that the firm's "fundamentals [were] horrible." Excite@home was publicly a 2-1 (short-term, accumulate; long-term, buy), but privately it was "such a piece of crap." Privately, the analysts thought Internet Capital Group was dreadful—"there really is no floor to this stock," Blodget wrote. Publicly, they rated it a 2-1. The affidavit also alleged that Merrill's rosy public pronouncements had been profitable—both for the analysts and for Merrill Lynch. In the fall of 2000, Blodget's group told their superiors that they had been involved in fifty-two completed or pending investment banking transactions, with the completed deals worth $115 million to the company. Blodget's annual compensation package was then increased from $3 million for 1999 to $12 million for 2001.

When Merrill learned about the judge's order, its lawyers were dumbfounded and absolutely furious. Spitzer's willingness to use his little-known power under the Martin Act to act ex parte had come as a complete shock. "We were lulled into thinking we were still in negotiations. They basically snuck behind our backs into court," Morvillo said. Publicly, the firm was standing tall, insisting that Blodget's e-mails had been taken out of context and issuing a statement that "there is no basis for the allegations made today by the New York attorney general. His conclusions are just plain wrong. We are outraged that we were not given the opportunity to contest these allegations in court." Privately, they knew they were facing a public relations disaster. Thanks to the affidavit Dinallo had just filed, Blodget had become the poster child for everything that was wrong with investment banking research. Even worse, Schoenfeld's court order requiring Merrill to change its ways had triggered a little-known clause of the 1940 Investment Company Act that barred securities firms under court order from operating mutual funds. Unless someone or something intervened, Merrill's huge mutual fund business would have to shut down, jeopardizing billions of dollars in investments and hundreds of thousands of small investors. The firm called the SEC for help, and its lawyers appealed personally to Spitzer.

Down in Washington, the SEC had been caught by surprise. Dinallo had left Bill Baker a voice mail after getting the Martin Act order from Schoenfeld, but Chairman Pitt learned of the e-mails and allegations from the media. "I was shocked," Pitt remembered. Even though he had been urging the banks to reform their research, the allegations in Spitzer's case went far beyond anything Pitt had ever seen or suspected while working as a defense lawyer. "If anybody working for me had ever done anything like" what Spitzer was alleging those e-mails showed, "I would have strung them up." The SEC Investment

Management Division, which oversaw mutual funds, began scrambling to help keep Merrill's fund business alive.

Amid the chaos, the SEC's Steve Cutler's phone rang. It was Spitzer. Though the two men had never talked before, Spitzer knew the SEC Enforcement director by reputation as one of the smartest securities lawyers around, and Golden and Cutler were old friends. "I've got to ask you something: Merrill's lawyers are telling us that they're out of the money management business. Are they full of it?" Spitzer asked. "No, they're not," Cutler replied. He proceeded to explain the crucial section of the 1940 act, which no one on Spitzer's team had ever heard of. ("We were a state agency, so out of our league," one of them remembered.) "How do you guys ever bring a case?" Spitzer asked. Cutler explained that "we have an ability to give them an exemption" when the commission decided that it would be in the best interest of investors. But Cutler added that the SEC was unlikely to grant a similar exemption based on a state investigation that it knew nothing about. Spitzer sent Dinallo back to court accompanied by several top deputies. There they asked Schoenfeld, the judge, to stay the injunction part of his order pending settlement negotiations, which would allow Merrill to keep operating. This time the Merrill lawyers were present, but deeply angry. "This is irresponsible," Morvillo snarled at Snell. "We disagree," Snell responded.

Then the case took a turn Spitzer had not expected. Shortly before the filing, he had told a breakfast date that he would soon be "bringing out a case, something that'll be interesting for twenty-four hours," but not much longer. "I thought the SEC would take it over immediately. I thought Harvey Pitt would say, thank you very much, we will now do a full-throttle investigation," he remembered. Two days after the filing, he told an exhausted Dinallo something similar. "Well, Eric, it's been fun, but in two or three days the SEC will swoop in and take over." Since Spitzer had discovered the e-mails, he hoped and expected that the Feds would invite him to stay involved. That's what the EPA had done in 1999 when it followed his power plant cases with its own, even bigger, wave of lawsuits. He knew federal involvement dwarfed that of the states almost every time, and ultimately was more effective at prompting industry-wide change. Indeed, just a day after filing the

Merrill case, Spitzer told *The Wall Street Journal,* "At the end of the day, I'm hoping to resolve these issues through some global resolution that the industry will accept. . . . That will require participation from Congress, the SEC, and the industry."

Instead, everyone hung back. At the SEC, Cutler and general counsel David Becker urged Pitt to launch an industry-wide investigation or at least publicly offer to work with Spitzer. But the chairman had serious reservations. "We weren't racing to keep up with Eliot Spitzer. . . . We were already looking into the issue," Pitt said. "There was a certain amount of concern about having a piling-on approach." Spitzer didn't help his credibility with either the SEC or the industry's self-regulatory organizations, NASD and the NYSE, when he gave media interviews in which he refused to rule out filing criminal charges against Merrill Lynch. The other regulators considered such tactics a form of blackmail, particularly because the accounting firm Arthur Andersen was at that moment going belly-up under the weight of a federal indictment. Nor were industry insiders impressed when the news media reported that Spitzer had at one point proposed that Merrill spin off its research analysts into an independent business. "That speaks volumes to anybody who knows anything about Wall Street. Research has not been self-sustaining since Congress deregulated commissions in the 1970s," said Stuart Kaswell, the general counsel of the main industry lobbying group, the Securities Industry Association.

For days and then weeks, it seemed, Spitzer was all alone. He confessed to having a brief moment of doubt when he wondered, "Am I Don Quixote tilting at windmills or am I shattering the glass with one stroke?" But then he sent out subpoenas to more Wall Street firms and increased the pressure on Merrill Lynch to settle by threatening to haul top executives into court to testify publicly about the firm's research practices. And the isolation had a heady side benefit. The investigation was getting great play in newspapers across the country and around the world. Spitzer was no longer just one of fifty ambitious state attorneys general. He was "Wall Street's Inquisitor," said the *Financial Times,* and a "Prosecutor in the Spotlight," according to *The Washington Post.* The cable television shows invited him on; congressional Democrats asked him to come down to Washington to lobby for their version of a corporate responsibility bill. True, the famously conservative *Wall Street Journal* editorial page had flayed him as a publicity seeker and opined, "The market will do a better job of eventually sorting this out than Mr. Spitzer would." But being one of their targets wasn't all bad for an ambitious "pragmatic liberal" such as Spitzer. At least the communications staff was no longer having trouble getting reporters to include Spitzer's name when they wrote about the Attorney General's Office.

Privately, the national regulators were starting to get involved. Two top SEC officials—David Becker and Annette Nazareth, who was in charge of market regulation—flew to New York in the third week of April. They came not only to offer Spitzer encouragement for his fraud investigation but also to warn the New Yorker that "he was getting out a little bit too far in terms of where he should be in terms of remedy. From our standpoint there was one national securities market, and it would not be a good idea for each state AG to impose" his own set of regulations, Becker remembered. NASD vice chairman Mary L. Schapiro came along because her organization already had an active probe into whether analysts at Citigroup and elsewhere had a "reasonable basis" for their reports, as was required by industry rules. Spitzer and the national regulators brainstormed about possible ways to protect analyst independence, and Becker urged Spitzer to get to know Steve Cutler and to work with him. Becker and Spitzer clashed briefly over the limits of the New Yorker's authority. When Spitzer asserted that the Martin Act gave him the power to force structural changes, Becker countered with a list of federal court cases propounding an opposite view, which he had compiled in advance, just in case. To Becker, the meeting with Spitzer was largely friendly. "There was maybe thirty seconds of bristling in a half-hour conversation," Becker said. "It was there and gone in a flash."

Spitzer and his aides walked away from the meeting with a different impression. Instead of jumping enthusiastically on the reform bandwagon, the national regulators seemed to be emphasizing the potential problems. The issues were complicated; the structural reforms Spitzer wanted would be expensive, they said. According to Spitzer, Schapiro and the other national regulators threw cold water on his reform ideas, saying, "The banks won't go for it."

"My response was, so what, who cares? You're the ones who are supposed to tell them what to do," Spitzer said. "Regulatory folks had been cowed. They were afraid to stand up and say, 'That is wrong.'" Both Schapiro and Becker flatly contradicted Spitzer's interpretation of the meeting. "Any suggestion that we were there to urge Spitzer to go easy on the investment banks, or in some measure back off, is utterly false," Becker said. Schapiro was equally strong. "I didn't care if the banks liked it or not. That wasn't my concern—and it never is when it comes to an enforcement action," she said, adding, "My concern was about the operational feasibility of completely separating analyst pay from investment banking revenue, when all the employees of a firm are compensated based on the overall financial performance of the firm." Spitzer's dealings with the regulators over the next few months would be colored by his impressions of that first meeting, leading to complications and hard feelings on all sides.

After the meeting, Spitzer quickly worked out an arrangement with Merrill Lynch to replace the court order that had been withdrawn to keep the firm's mutual fund business alive. Merrill agreed to disclose potential conflicts of interest that might affect its analysts' reports and to keep talking about a larger settlement. Spitzer also helped persuade other state securities regulators to form a multistate task force—with Dinallo as co-chairman—to investigate the larger problems associated with investment banking research. Still, Spitzer hadn't given up on the idea of working with the SEC, and in Cutler he now had a sympathetic ally. Unlike some of his SEC colleagues, Cutler saw little point in trying to compete with Spitzer or push him off the stage. "It didn't make sense for us to go to Merrill Lynch and request the same sorts of things that Eliot had already requested," he remembered. "It wasn't good government and it wasn't efficient to all send the same requests for documents." So he and his old friend Beth Golden helped arrange a meeting in Washington to allow Pitt and Spitzer to size each other up and talk about the possibility of cooperation.

The day Spitzer, Dinallo, and Golden flew down to Washington was brutally hot, even though it was only April 24. When they arrived at the SEC, the security desk sent them up to a big conference room. The room was full, but there was no sign of Pitt, Cutler, or anyone else familiar. Spitzer, ever the politician, started to work the room. He approached the nearest person, stuck out his hand, saying, "Hi, I'm Eliot Spitzer. Who are you?" The blood rushed from the face of Spitzer's new acquaintance. "I'm with Merrill Lynch," he said. It was a whole room full of Merrill people. Spitzer and his staff had been sent to the wrong room. They beat a retreat back to the security desk and then on to Pitt's office. That meeting didn't go much better. Despite Pitt's plans to quietly take the measure of his new competitor, the SEC chairman's pugnacious manner was on display. Famously described by colleagues as "seldom wrong, never in doubt," Pitt made the New Yorkers think he viewed them as rinky-dink state enforcers with no business taking on major structural issues such as analyst conflicts. Pitt remembered that he "made clear the regulatory side of it was clearly our concern. . . . As important as New York is, it's only one of fifty. The SEC is one of one. You can't have fifty attorneys general trying to dictate what standards are." At one point the chairman told Spitzer he was disappointed that the New Yorkers had gone after Merrill unilaterally and had not consulted with the SEC beforehand. "We'd like to work with you. Here's how we're going to proceed," Pitt remembered saying. "Whatever gets done has to get done together." Spitzer bristled. He was an independently elected New York official, not one of Pitt's minions. But he kept the tone of the meeting light and said mildly that he did not know whom he should call. The SEC chairman responded in a similarly friendly fashion. He whipped out a piece of paper, scrawled out his private phone number, and handed it to Spitzer. "I was trying to be very very helpful. . . . I really wasn't interested in going to war," Pitt said.

The two men walked out of the meeting officially committed to working together but privately confirmed in their mutual suspicions. Pitt saw an ambitious politician with no respect for the SEC's preeminent role and a dangerous taste for headline grabbing. "He's not as smart as he thinks he is because nobody could be that smart," Pitt said.

Spitzer saw a brilliant defense lawyer who was miscast as SEC chairman. "He had internalized the defenses he had made for too many years on behalf of his Wall Street clients—technical defenses," Spitzer said. Spitzer thought that as chairman of the SEC, Pitt should have understood that his job "was to push back. . . . He should have said, I'll be reasonable but you've got to internalize a new set of ground rules."

On the same day he met with Pitt, Spitzer got his first real taste of what it meant to be a national media star when he attended a press conference touting a Democratic plan for corporate ethics reform. Hundreds of reporters crowded around him, hanging on his every word as he proclaimed that Merrill's research practices were "corrupt" and "may be criminal." He rose to the occasion, reviving his pet intellectual theory to jab at the SEC and the Republicans. "This is a consequence of federalism," Spitzer said. "The whole new federalism approach vaunted by the Bush administration and Reagan administration was designed to empower state securities regulators. That's what I'm doing." For his part, Harvey Pitt announced the next day, April 25, that the SEC had launched a "formal inquiry" into research practices, and pointed out that the commission would vote on adopting new rules for analysts in early May. On April 29, the SEC, NASD, and the NYSE then sent their first-ever coordinated request for documents to twelve investment banks.

Merrill Lynch wasn't inclined to sit around and wait for the federal regulators to do their own investigation. The firm's lawyers argued that they could defend Blodget's e-mails against a fraud complaint—if Spitzer ever got around to actually filing one, rather than just using the Martin Act to conduct a public inquisition. But chief executive David Komansky had had enough. Merrill's stock price was tanking. It had fallen nearly 20 percent since Spitzer's filing, and the SEC's announcement on April 25 of a formal inquiry had sent the entire financial services sector into a tizzy. At Merrill's annual meeting, held a day later, on April 26, Komansky told shareholders, "We regret" what Spitzer had uncovered. "The e-mails that have come to light are very distressing and disappointing to us. They fall far short of our professional standards and some are inconsistent with our policies," Komansky said. "We have failed to live up to the high standards that are our tradition." He made clear that he intended to do all he could to settle the case within the next few weeks. In public, Spitzer's spokespeople were politely encouraging, saying that their boss had called the apology "a good first step." In private, Spitzer was exultant. "It was game over at that point," he remembered.

Just then, an old problem resurfaced: Spitzer's unsuccessful effort to crack down on illegal gun sales came up for argument on appeal. Still enthusiastic about their argument that gun manufacturers were causing a public nuisance, Spitzer's office had appealed their defeat to the intermediate court known as the First Department, and Spitzer had promised to argue the case himself, the first and only time he would do so as attorney general. But as the date approached, both Spitzer and Golden, the deputy charged with preparing Spitzer for the appeal, were still wrapped up in the Merrill negotiations and Spitzer was still taking serious flak from Congress and the business community for having intruded on the SEC's turf. Moreover, Golden knew that the appeal's prospects were pretty grim. Much as she wanted Spitzer to argue the case, Golden decided she ought to make sure he understood the likely outcome. "Eliot, are you okay with being associated with a case we're going to lose?" she asked during the prep sessions. Spitzer decided not to back away. "Some small piece of me thought if I stood up and argued it, it might convince them that it was important to the state," he said.

The appeals panel was skeptical when Spitzer took the podium on May 10, 2002. Why, asked Justice Alfred D. Lerner, had the state decided to go after manufacturers and wholesalers, when retailers are much closer to the actual crime? Drunk drivers could be considered a nuisance, too, but in that case the state shut down pubs, not breweries, Lerner observed. Justice George D. Marlow wanted to know why the issue was in the courts rather than the legislature. Spitzer tried to get the justices focused on giving his lawyers access to evidence they believed would prove their case. "The single question which the court must answer is whether the state is entitled to discovery" to find out if there is evidence "to overcome the burden that the People have to meet at trial," Spitzer insisted. The gun industry, represented by Baltimore lawyer Lawrence S. Greenwald, did better. Greenwald mocked Spitzer's claims, describing the gun manufacturers as at the "North Pole," while the true nuisance, "the illegal acquisition and use of firearms," was at the South Pole. The argument proved to be a true predictor of the outcome. The panel voted three to one against Spitzer. "The legislative and executive branches are better suited to address the societal problems concerning the already heavily regulated commercial activity at issue," the majority opinion said, adding that Spitzer's efforts to force the gun manufacturers to change their marketing and distribution methods were "legally inappropriate, impractical and unrealistic." The state's highest court then refused to hear the case. Spitzer was philosophical. "In my gut, I always suspected we would lose. Nuisance law is incredibly elastic, and courts get uncomfortable. . . . The results hinge on the particular judge panel you get," he reflected. "There are some cases you bring knowing the probability of success is not great."

His staff was having far better luck with the Merrill matter. New York Stock Exchange chairman Richard Grasso, who had become something of a national folk hero for reopening the Big Board so quickly after the September 11 attacks, had interceded, offering to broker a meeting between Komansky and Spitzer. Grasso told the media he had lent his prestige to the settlement process because he feared that small investors were starting to believe that "Wall Street is totally corrupt. . . . America doesn't feel good about the securities business." The negotiations kept leaking to the media—at one point, the two sides were standing in Spitzer's foyer when a reporter called one of Merrill's representatives for comment on their progress. But both sides wanted a deal done, and on May 21, they got it. Merrill Lynch agreed to pay a one-hundred-million-dollar penalty, issue a statement of contrition, and take steps to insulate its analysts from banking pressures.

The settlement had its critics. Though Spitzer had talked about helping small investors, all one hundred million dollars went to the coffers of New York, the other forty-nine states, Puerto Rico, and the District of Columbia. Not a penny was earmarked for restitution.

Spitzer also backed off from an early proposal to separate completely research and banking. Instead, the firm's analysts would disclose their conflicts of interest, and their compensation would be insulated from most banking pressures "except to the extent such activities and services are intended to benefit investors." The size of the penalty also drew some criticism—*The New York Times* pointed out that Merrill Lynch spent three times that much on office supplies and postage alone in 2001. "You can't do that right, no matter what you do on money, either it looks too small or you drive them bankrupt," Spitzer said later. But none of the criticism could change one essential fact: Eliot Spitzer had his first big Wall Street settlement. "Merrill Lynch is setting a new standard for the rest of the industry to follow," he told a packed news conference. And Spitzer was just getting started.

5

GOING GLOBAL

NOW THAT SPITZER HAD WON A BIG VICTORY AGAINST MERRILL LYNCH, HE decided it was time to aim higher and seek a wholesale reform of Wall Street research and IPO practices that would make the capital markets fairer and more efficient. Though Spitzer had not acknowledged it during the Merrill Lynch negotiations, he had some sympathy with the bank's complaints that his investigation lacked "horizontal equity," that Merrill was being forced to make reforms while its competitors were conducting business as usual. Spitzer's solution, though, wasn't to give Merrill easy treatment but to extend his investigation to all of Wall Street and to drag the other state, national, and industry regulators along with him.

Right before Memorial Day, the Attorney General's Office hosted an enormous get-acquainted meeting to introduce the state regulators to their federal and industry counterparts. Eric Dinallo chaired the gathering; Steve Cutler and Lori Richards, who headed the SEC's Inspections Division, flew up from Washington; the industry regulators—the NASD and NYSE—sent top representatives; and more than a dozen other state securities officials attended. The meeting was a bath of cold water. Cutler urged the group to reduce the burden of overlapping and duplicative requests on the investment banks by sending out a single request for documents, much like the one the national regulators had issued in late April. Most of the state regulators turned him down flat. "We're sovereign states," one regulator protested, refusing to dilute state authority. Spitzer's team was interested in tapping the SEC's expertise and clout, but many of the other state regulators were embittered by what they saw as years of being treated as second-class citizens by the SEC. Now they were itching to return to favor. To some of the national regulators, some states seemed to have little interest in investigating the problem—they were already fighting over how to split up the money they expected the banks to fork over. While the SEC and industry regulators already had staff members plowing through boxes of e-mails, many of the states were still in the planning stages. Some had become obsessed with the idea of building an enormous computer database that would somehow scan all the banks' e-mails and highlight the key documents. Though the meeting broke up with everyone promising to hold weekly conference calls to keep one another informed, the reality was far less collegial. "Any thought of a coordinated investigation went out the window," Cutler remembered. "From that point until October third, it was as though we were little toddlers engaged in parallel play. The interactions with each other were very minimal."

The race to pull together another analyst case was on, and Spitzer made clear to his staff that he didn't want to get beaten. "We were in his office shortly, very shortly after Merrill, within a week of the settlement," Roger Waldman remembered. "Eliot laid down a very ambitious schedule for developing a case against whomever we were going to go after. I remember thinking, whoa." It wouldn't be easy. The SEC had manpower that Spitzer simply couldn't match. NASD had been looking at analyst reports for months before the Merrill case broke and was getting close to bringing a case against Jack Grubman, the superstar telecommunications analyst for Citigroup's Salomon Smith Barney unit. In a nod to his limited resources, Spitzer agreed to split up the targets with the other states that had joined the multistate task force that Dinallo now co-chaired, but he made sure to keep the first picks. Bruce Topman's team would tackle Grubman and Citigroup; Waldman got Morgan Stanley, the home of Mary Meeker, known on television as the Internet Queen and Henry Blodget's most visible competitor. Regretfully, Dinallo had to pass on the other obvious choice. Credit Suisse First Boston's high-profile tech banker Frank Quattrone and his army of analysts and bankers would be the responsibility of Massachusetts Secretary of the Commonwealth William Galvin. States as varied as Utah, Alabama, and Washington stepped in to pick up the other big banks.

The Merrill settlement had also drawn Spitzer unwelcome attention from another arm of the federal government. The Republican leadership in Washington professed on paper to believe in federalism and states' rights, but there was no room in their vision for uppity state enforcers such as Eliot Spitzer, who challenged not only the SEC's primacy but also the wisdom of congressional leaders. Representative Richard Baker, a powerful Louisiana Republican, had held hearings on analyst independence in 2001, but had then left it up to the industry and the SEC to come up with solutions to the problem. Spitzer's emergence as a media darling and his announced plans to impose new rules on the securities industry struck Baker as unforgivable gall. In late April, he wrote a letter to Pitt (and released it to the media), saying he had "grave concerns" about what he called Spitzer's "unprecedented efforts to propose and impose [his] own rules on the marketplace." Not only that, Baker wrote, the New Yorker was a Johnny-come-lately to the issue. "Throughout last year's entirely open and public process of congressional efforts toward reform, when the Capital Markets Subcommittee specifically invited input from anyone concerned, not a single substantive contribution to the dialogue was received from the NYAG," Baker wrote. Spitzer fired back that he had filed the Merrill action because serious reforms were needed and Baker's hearings had "failed to elicit any of the evidence necessary to bring about reforms."

The battle quickly got uglier. Morgan Stanley CEO Philip J. Purcell made the rounds on Capitol Hill in the weeks after the Merrill settlement, pushing legislation that would sharply limit the century-old ability of states to investigate securities fraud and use settlements to impose new rules on companies—like the investment banks—that were already regulated by the SEC. "We think that legislation at the federal level is a good way to restore investor trust and confidence," said

Raymond O'Rourke, a Morgan Stanley spokesman. But everyone involved—both for and against—knew that the bill was aimed at stopping Spitzer. Spitzer was furious. "This is a perversion of American law," he said. "The only good this does is that it helps Phil Purcell and Morgan Stanley because he wants to be excused from the scrutiny that he's subject to—and it won't work." Privately, he called Pitt, asking whether the chairman was going to take a position on these efforts to "preempt" state authority. Pitt was equivocal. "I said, 'Eliot, as long as you go after fraud, I'm perfectly happy, because it adds a lot to the mix. But when you try to affect the way people are regulated, you go too far,'" Pitt remembered. He added that he did not believe Purcell's bill was necessary—"I don't think we need preemption because we already have it." "Not good enough," Spitzer replied.

Days later, when Spitzer flew down to Washington to testify about the research scandal on June 26, he seemed to go out of his way to attack Pitt personally. "There has been a void, a vacuum, in leadership from federal regulators," he told a Senate subcommittee that was considering new corporate governance legislation. It would not be the last time he made comments that Pitt and others at the SEC found personally offensive. "I became for him, a whipping boy. For him it was all ad hominem. It was all one-upmanship," Pitt said later. Spitzer's staff urged him not to include Steve Cutler in the attacks because the SEC's Enforcement chief was someone they could work with. But Spitzer's view was that he was simply using strong language to make an important point. The SEC "had become lethargic, lazy, and inattentive," he said. "Unless you rattle the cage with some rhetoric that isn't the traditional inside-the-Beltway rhetoric, they won't change."

Spitzer also saw the preemption bill as part of a larger effort "to box us in on every front." Just two weeks earlier, the Bush administration had announced plans to revise the Clean Air Act in a way that would completely undercut the legal rationale for Spitzer's power plant cases. "Every American should be outraged," he said, as he promised to challenge the revisions in federal court. "The EPA is turning its back on environmental protection." His twin verbal assaults on the leaders of the SEC and the EPA, Spitzer said, shouldn't be seen as personal attacks but as a way of advancing his ideological agenda. "I'm trying to say when the federal agencies are failing the public, I will step in," he explained.

Then fate intervened. The morning Spitzer testified on Capitol Hill, the telecommunications giant WorldCom announced that it had uncovered a massive accounting fraud and would have to restate billions of dollars in profits. The firm soon declared bankruptcy, and its chief executive, Bernard J. Ebbers, was later sent to prison for twenty-five years. That scandal, on top of the Enron collapse, was too much for the American public. Momentum now built for strong corporate accountability legislation and for more antifraud enforcement, not less. After Congress held hearings on the close relationship between WorldCom and the analysts who covered it—particularly Jack Grubman—Morgan Stanley's preemption proposal was effectively dead, at least until the spotlight dimmed.

But Spitzer, who was running for reelection that fall, continued to use the SEC as a punching bag. In late July, as he accepted the AFL-CIO's endorsement, he lashed out at Pitt for having tried to raise his own salary and said that the commission's Market Regulation Division had "been asleep at the switch, thoroughly asleep at the switch" and should have issued new rules for analysts years before. He also made a serious effort to shore up his multistate coalition, addressing the North American Securities Administrators Association (NASAA) at a summer conference in New York to persuade them to sign on to the settlement he had negotiated with Merrill Lynch. "He struck me as bright, competent, and charming, what you would expect of a politician of his caliber," said Maine securities administrator Christine Bruenn. "It was a little bit intimidating for me. I'm not used to being around people like him."

In mid-September, NASD grabbed the headlines, and made clear that Spitzer had not cowed the national regulators, by bringing a case against analyst Jack Grubman for his glowing reports on Winstar Communications, which had gone bust in 2001. NASD's enforcers not only fined Citigroup's Salomon unit five million dollars but also became the first regulators to take on the superstar analyst personally, alleging that Grubman and his assistant had issued "misleading research" by setting and sticking with a public price target of fifty dollars for the broadband telecommunications firm while privately saying he had done inadequate research and thought the stock was worth less. Drawing a page from Spitzer's book, NASD quoted liberally from Grubman's private e-mails: "If anything, the record shows we support our banking clients too well and for too long," he had written after Winstar fell below one dollar a share. About the same time, word leaked to the media that Pitt had asked the SEC staff to research the possibility of requiring Wall Street firms to separate their research and investment banking operations into separate businesses, an idea that Spitzer had discussed earlier. "It really wasn't anything but a possibility we explored and rejected. It wasn't something I was eager to pursue," Pitt remembered.

Relations between Spitzer and the SEC appeared to be breaking down completely, but once again New York Stock Exchange chairman Dick Grasso stepped in. The Dow Jones Industrial Average had fallen by more than 10 percent in September, and Grasso feared that the escalating regulatory competition would exacerbate the slide. "You've got to come together for the benefit of the markets," the tough-talking NYSE chairman told Pitt in a phone call. He followed up by inviting Spitzer, Pitt, and NASD's top leadership to a private dinner in New York on October 1.

Before they met, however, Spitzer flung down another marker, to make sure the national regulators and the media understood that the Merrill Lynch case had not been a fluke. The day before the scheduled truce dinner, Spitzer filed a lawsuit that declared war on "spinning," another common Wall Street practice that had been under investigation by NASD and was the subject of congressional hearings. *Spinning* was Wall Street slang for the investment banks' practice of "allocating"—doling out—shares in hot IPOs to current and potential clients. Historically, the banks had a legitimate reason to make sure IPO shares got into the right hands because fledgling companies were more likely to prosper if their newly issued stock was held by supportive investors rather than by speculators. But during the tech boom of the 1990s, the allocation process, like many other things on Wall Street, had become distorted. Rather than being initially risky investments, IPO shares turned into such hot commodities that they routinely doubled and tripled in price within days of being issued. Getting an allocation at the opening price, therefore, became akin to being handed cash, and the investment banks began using the shares to reward and woo top corporate executives who could send them banking business. Other securities regulators were already looking at the issue: the Justice Department was probing the IPO process for criminal violations, and NASD had issued proposals in late July to limit IPO allocations to corporate executives. But Spitzer charged right in anyway. After pushing Dinallo to work all night for several days running, the office filed a lawsuit on September 30 against WorldCom's Bernard Ebbers and four other top executives of prominent technology companies, alleging they had violated the Martin Act by accepting IPO shares from investment banks with which their companies did business. "The spinning of hot IPO shares was not a harmless corporate perk," Spitzer said. "Instead, it was an integral part of a fraudulent scheme to win new investment-banking business."

Spitzer's demand that the executives return twenty-eight million dollars in profits outraged many on Wall Street, who thought it was fundamentally unfair to go after five people when hundreds and perhaps thousands of other executives had enjoyed similar benefits. Ebbers's lawyer, Reid Weingarten, called the lawsuit a "publicity stunt," and many legal experts predicted the lawsuits would ultimately fail. Spitzer's fellow regulators, meanwhile, saw the case as a naked grab for media coverage. Much of the information in Spitzer's complaint appeared to come either from Citigroup's own internal investigation or from the congressional probe, yet his office was the only one to file suit. SEC and industry regulators made a practice of coordinating their fraud investigations with the Justice Department, because they did not want their civil and administrative cases to mess up or preempt a more serious criminal probe. Since they shared overlapping responsibilities, frequent communication was the only way to avoid stepping on each other's toes. Steve Cutler and the SEC now expected Spitzer to show the same deference to the federal prosecutors. But the New York State attorney general was steeped in an entirely different tradition—state and federal prosecutors in New York had been crossing swords for decades. Spitzer himself, during his Morgenthau days, had engaged in several brutal turf battles with the U.S. Attorney's Office for the

Southern District of New York. (One confrontation with Michele Hirshman when she was a federal prosecutor almost cost Spitzer his future top deputy. In 1998, she still had such bitter memories about his behavior that she was reluctant even to interview for a job in the Attorney General's Office. She took the job only after mutual friends interceded and Spitzer apologized.)

Ever jealous of his rights as a state prosecutor, Spitzer was unmoved by complaints that his civil suit might cause problems for the federal criminal probes of IPO allocations in general and of executives from WorldCom and other technology firms in particular. In his view, spinning was part of what his staff jokingly referred to as "Spitzer's Unified Field Theory" of Wall Street corruption, and he had to attack it head on. As he saw it, investment bankers got business by promising positive research; analysts earned money and fame by hyping stocks; and the corporate executives, who hired the bankers, got IPO shares that were all but certain money-makers because of the same dishonest research. "Everybody was making money except the investors and the capital markets. There was enormous distortion of capital here," Spitzer explained. (Despite the public criticism, Spitzer eventually got settlements from three of the executives he had sued on September 30, although the form was controversial. The executives agreed to make charitable donations totaling $5.2 million, close to the $7.5 million in IPO profits that Spitzer had originally demanded, but none of the money went back to investors. Ebbers turned over almost all of his remaining wealth to WorldCom investors. When Clark McLeod, the former CEO of McLeod USA, elected to challenge Spitzer's charges in court, a Manhattan judge found him liable for improper trading. Litigation over the size of McLeod's penalty was still pending.)

Grasso's October 1 summit dinner took place at Tiro a Segno, an old Italian-American club in Manhattan. The Stock Exchange chairman broke the tension with a reference to a scene in *The Godfather* where the five big Mafia families broker a truce, and the meeting was surprisingly friendly. Both Spitzer and Pitt declared their interest in forging a single global settlement that would cover all the banks. No one had thought to invite a representative of the other state regulators to the gathering, but Cutler quickly tracked down Bruenn, the Maine regulator who had been sworn in that very day as president of the multi-state group NASAA. "We're going to get together and either you're in or you're out," she remembered Cutler saying. Bruenn was able to throw together a late-night conference call of state regulators, and together they placed a call to Dinallo's apartment. "So, how was the tiramisù?" asked Matt Nestor, the Massachusetts representative on the call. Despite their pique, the other states agreed to join the accord. On October 3, the regulators issued a joint statement promising to sit down with the investment banks "to bring to a speedy and coordinated conclusion the various investigations concerning analyst research and IPO allocations."

Despite the agreement, Spitzer was intent on driving both the timing and the shape of any "global settlement." The morning after the truce at the Italian-American club, he told his staff to draft a list of proposed reforms that should be part of any deal with the banks. "I want something tomorrow," he insisted. Spitzer's proposal was in the SEC's hands by the time the joint investigation was announced. That first draft focused mostly on structural issues—strengthening the "Chinese wall" that was supposed to limit contact between bankers and analysts and changing the reporting and compensation rules to insulate analysts from investment banking pressure. But Spitzer's animating principle remained the same: he wanted to find ways to even the playing field between average Americans and the institutional investors. One key difference he had noted was that the big players had access to better information. While institutional investors used the investment banks' analyses, they could also afford to commission their own untainted research. Prominent securities lawyers that Spitzer respected warned him that a total separation between investment banking and research might lead the Wall Street firms to drop published research entirely, leaving small investors with even less information than they had now. There clearly had to be a better way.

One day Spitzer had a brainstorm: if he could create a market for truly independent research, then small investors would have the same ability as big players to pick and choose among the analysts, and might have a better chance of avoiding improperly hyped stocks. "I did not know then and I do not know now whether the independent research is better or worse than the reformed internal research" by the banks,

Spitzer remembered. "At least investors would have more data points [and] have the capacity to say, why is it that you have a buy when all the independent analysts have a sell?" His first attempt to explain his idea—at a meeting of his own staff—did not go well. "That's got to be one of the most impractical ideas I've ever heard of," one attendee remembered thinking. "There was not a lot of enthusiasm in the room." Even after the banks insisted that there was no way to make independent research profitable, Spitzer remained undaunted and looked for new ways to make the idea work. At one point he explored a proposal from one of the financial magazines of having a government source of research, funded by a fee levied on each company that was registered on one of the stock exchanges. Then he got interested in a proposal being floated by several banks—that there should be an industry-funded consortium that would buy independent research from third-party sources and supply it to the public.

Several top SEC officials thought Spitzer was crazy. Such a consortium would be vulnerable to pressure from the banks that funded it, and it was only a small step from a government-sponsored monopoly. "I put my foot down," Pitt remembered. "As bad as research is, this will only make it worse." Another SEC commissioner, Harvey Goldschmid, tried a less confrontational approach. A Democratic appointee, Goldschmid shared Spitzer's view that it was the government's responsibility to step in to protect small investors from market excesses. He and Spitzer occasionally talked privately, and Goldschmid found the New York State attorney general receptive to his concerns about government-run research. "I remember telling him, we got rid of the Soviet Union in 1991, let's not go down the road to recreating it," Goldschmid said. "He was very willing to listen. He's very good at listening and trying to understand."

Steve Cutler ultimately came up with a way to foster independent research without creating a government bureaucracy. The banks would be required to spend a specific amount of money on independent research, but they wouldn't be allowed to pick and choose the providers, lest they exert too much pressure on them. Instead, each bank would hire independent consultants to buy and distribute research from outside companies that did not engage in investment banking business. "Since independent research was meant to compete with and act as something of a brake on the research published by established Wall Street firms, we couldn't have those firms choosing the research. That's why we went to the independent consultant approach," Cutler remembered.

Spitzer and the other regulators had agreed to talk regularly to hammer out the reforms they intended to extract from the banks, and Grasso seemed to have a sixth sense that helped keep the talks alive. Each time the truce seemed to be breaking down, Grasso would organize another dinner meeting, first at the Georgetown Club, in Washington on Columbus Day, and then a few weeks later at the New York Stock Exchange. But finding solutions sometimes proved contentious. Part of the problem stemmed from a basic philosophical difference. The SEC and NASD generally followed a disclosure-based system that gave investors as much information as possible and allowed them to pick and choose where to invest. Except in extreme cases, they preferred not to tell companies how to run their businesses. Instead, they tended to require companies to tell customers about problems, conflicts of interest, and other issues. Spitzer's approach was far more interventionist and based more on the merits of an issue. He wanted to ban what he saw as bad behavior and require what he saw as good behavior. Spitzer and the national regulators also clashed on matters of style: some of them found him unnecessarily confrontational and unwilling to consider alternatives to his own ideas. "He has a winners/losers mentality. Once he stakes out a position, he needs to win," one of them observed. Others felt he was accusing them of caving in to industry whenever they criticized his proposals. Spitzer acknowledged that he did sometimes charge his fellow regulators with bending to pressure. "Sometimes there's sheer frustration," he said. "But it's not as though I always react that way."

Both issues came into play when the regulators tried to tackle the issue of spinning. Because Spitzer viewed spinning as commercial bribery, he wanted a flat-out ban on the practice. But NASD chairman Robert Glauber and other regulators objected—sometimes banks had legitimate reasons to give IPO shares to a CEO. Instead, they wanted to require public companies to disclose that their top executives were benefiting from spinning and then allow investors to factor that information into their buying decisions. At the dinner meeting at the Stock Exchange, Spitzer initially agreed to accept a less-than-total ban. But in the morning, he organized a conference call and announced that he had changed his mind. "I know I said yes," Spitzer said, "but I slept on it. I just can't do it. We need a bright-line policy. Spinning has to be illegal." Glauber blew his top. With so many items on the table, he said, it was irresponsible for Spitzer to reopen an issue after an agreement had been reached. Besides, Glauber said, Spitzer was wrong. "We shouldn't make it a status crime to be a CEO," Glauber said. "Don't CEOs have rights?"

"I'm not here to protect fat cat CEOs," Spitzer shot back. The conference call broke up angrily, but within a few days, Glauber's annoyance subsided, and NASD enforcement officials decided they could support an absolute ban on spinning. Negotiations with the banks began in earnest in late October with a series of meetings, first at the SEC in Washington and then at the New York Stock Exchange. Never shy, Spitzer dominated the early discussions, and his manner alienated many of the participants. "It was a cram-down," one of the bank negotiators remembered. "He said, 'I have a new idea. You're going to do something and you're going to do it because I am telling you to do it: third-party research.'" Another participant, Maine securities regulator Christine Bruenn, who represented the other states, was more admiring. "What Eliot brought to the table was a determination and a sense that things were not right," she said. "This was the firms hearing for the first time what they were up against."

The sessions were marked by constant leaks to the media that many of the participants blamed on Spitzer. The SEC and NASD had historically prided themselves on carrying out investigations discreetly, lest they harm public companies or frighten investors before all the facts were known. Spitzer tended to go public much faster. When criticized, he would cite Louis Brandeis's adage that "Sunlight is said to be the best of disinfectants." His staffers also argued that they weren't the only ones talking to the media. Some of the most tantalizing information was coming from other sources. The other regulators weren't convinced—they saw Spitzer as a headline-hunting politician who failed to understand the distinction between telling investors about the final results of an investigation and selective leaks from an investigation in progress. The banks were shocked when they arrived for the meeting at the SEC in Washington on October 24 to find the financial press camped outside. By the time they met again, on October 31, at the NYSE, the bank lawyers were furious—an article in that morning's *Wall Street Journal* had included detailed descriptions of the negotiations leading up to the group's previous meeting. When Theodore Levine, a top lawyer for UBS Paine Webber who was serving as one of the banks' main spokespeople, tried to address the publicity issue, a huge confrontation developed. Levine spoke first. Citing the *Wall Street Journal* article, he told the regulators on the other side of the table, "Look, we're really concerned because there's a leak of information, and from the articles it looks like it's the regulators. It hurts our ability to negotiate or communicate with government when every time anyone opens his mouth, it ends up in the newspapers." Though Levine had carefully not singled out Spitzer or anyone else, the New York attorney general took it personally. He lashed out, blaming the banks themselves for the leaks. "This investigation is costing you billions of dollars in market cap," Spitzer said, referring to the banks' dropping stock prices. "If you want to continue to lose it, well, this can continue." Goldman Sachs's general counsel, Greg Palm, tried to defuse the tension, saying, "We're off to a good start." But the tone had been set, and it did not help matters when an account of the confrontation appeared in *The Wall Street Journal* the next day.

At the same time, the SEC, NASD, and state regulators were starting to cooperate more meaningfully on investigating the abuses of the past. But the national regulators came to the conclusion that in most cases they were miles ahead. "The federal regulators had this e-mail and that e-mail and really solid evidence of abuses. The state regulators at that point hadn't made much progress," said the SEC's Lori Richards. "It made me wish that we had pooled our talent and resources from the very beginning." The one exception, she said, was Spitzer's office. "The New York AG's staff was very very good." Some of the bank negotiators had an even more negative view of the states. "The states did no work but they wanted a piece of the action," one of them remembered. But the other states disagreed. In their view, they were doing their best with far more limited resources than those of either New York or the SEC. "All these folks don't work for you. They've approached it how they want to approach it," Bruenn said she reminded the SEC participants.

Despite Richards's vote of confidence, Spitzer's investigators weren't having much luck turning up evidence against Morgan Stanley's star Internet analyst Mary Meeker. The firm told regulators that it had failed to save many of its employees' e-mails. Those e-mails that did make it into regulators' hands were routine correspondence that did not disclose Meeker's private views of the companies she rated. Morgan Stanley was able to show that Meeker had privately lobbied against doing some IPOs when she felt the underlying companies weren't sound business propositions, which they said helped lead the firm to turn down one billion dollars in investment banking fees. Furthermore, according to statistics prepared by the company, Meeker's stock-picking record had outperformed the market in every year except 2000. The firm's general counsel, Donald Kempf, compared Meeker's record to that of baseball great Ty Cobb, who routinely led the league in batting but hit only .240 in 1905. (The comparison, while tempting, wasn't apt. Cobb hit .240 in his first year in the majors, when he played only forty-one games, while Meeker's bad year came at the height of her career.) Though Waldman continued to have questions about Morgan Stanley's ratings process, he reluctantly concluded that "without e-mails showing a disconnect between Meeker's public statements and private beliefs, there was not the kind of demonstrable fraud that there was in certain other cases." Ultimately, neither the SEC nor Spitzer's office ever brought any charges against Meeker.

By contrast, Topman's Citigroup investigation seemed to qualify as one of those "certain other cases." While Jack Grubman's WorldCom reports had gotten him into hot water with Congress, Spitzer's office was more interested in the way Grubman had covered telecommunications giant AT&T, particularly his 1999 decision to upgrade the stock after years of telling investors the company was a behind-the-times behemoth. Spitzer, and other regulators, suspected that Grubman's upgrade might have been related to AT&T's decision around that time to spin off its cellular phone division, an investment banking deal that would be worth millions. Certainly the timing looked suspicious— shortly after Grubman's upgrade, in November 1999, Citigroup had been selected to work on the deal and had received sixty-three million dollars in fees when the deal closed in April 2000. Grubman down- graded the stock a month later. Asked to turn over all of Grubman's e-mails, Citigroup initially came up as empty as Morgan Stanley had on Mary Meeker—only a few dozen e-mails, none of them incriminating.

Then the investigators had a stroke of luck. When NASD investiga- tors had deposed Grubman in April, while preparing for the Winstar case, their boss, Barry Goldsmith, had run into Grubman in the hall- way during a break. The analyst was feverishly sending e-mails on his handheld BlackBerry device. Goldsmith realized that something major had to be missing from Citigroup's e-mail file. So his team put their computer experts on the phone with Citigroup's technicians and de- manded a more exhaustive search.

In mid-October, about the time the regulators were conferring at the Georgetown Club, Citigroup's attorneys placed urgent calls to Spitzer's office and to the national regulators in Washington. Lewis Li- man, one of the bank's outside lawyers from the firm Wilmer, Cutler & Pickering, was already well liked among the attorney general's staff be- cause he had helped defend Spitzer's office against the gun industry's antitrust lawsuit. So when Liman called Beth Golden to say, "We need to come in, today," she knew they were about to get something hot. Li- man arrived with senior partner Bob McCaw. Both of them seemed oddly embarrassed as McCaw read what appeared to be a scripted set of talking points and then handed over a packet of e-mails between Grubman and Carol Cutler, an analyst for the government of Singa- pore. As Spitzer's lawyers read the e-mails, the reason behind the lawyers' odd manner became clear. The e-mails were sexually explicit, offering investigators a real-time peek into a kinky, but entirely virtual, relationship between Carol Cutler (who is not related to Steve Cutler, the SEC Enforcement Division chief) and Grubman, who was married and the father of twins. Amid the flirting and references to private parts was a potentially explosive exchange from January 13, 2001, that offered an entirely unexpected explanation for Grubman's 1999 upgrade of AT&T. Rather than being a ratings-for-banking-business swap, as investigators had suspected, Grubman contended that the upgrade had had to do with internal politics at Citigroup and an internal struggle between the company's chairman, Sanford I. "Sandy" Weill, and John Reed, who had headed the company's Citicorp unit before it merged with Weill's Travelers Group. "You know everyone thinks I upgraded T [AT&T's stock symbol] to get the lead [banking role for the wireless deal]," Grubman wrote to Carol Cutler. "Nope. I used Sandy to get my kids in 92nd St. Y preschool (which is harder than Harvard) and Sandy needed [AT&T chairman Michael] Armstrong's vote on our board to nuke Reed in showdown. Once coast was clear for both of us (ie Sandy clear victor and my kids confirmed) I went back to my normal negative self on T," Grubman wrote. "Armstrong never knew that we both (Sandy and I) played him like a fiddle."

Liman and McCaw spent much of the meeting with Spitzer's lawyers emphasizing the weirdness of the Cutler-Grubman relationship and the other strange missives Cutler had written to the telecommunications analyst. But the investigators recognized a crucial distinction. The allegation that Grubman had slanted his ratings for personal considerations came straight out of his keyboard, not Carol Cutler's. If his story were true, they might have a securities fraud case not only against Grubman but also against Weill, one of the richest and most powerful men on Wall Street. "We had a ticking time bomb there," Golden remembered. Then Bruce Topman uncovered a memo Grubman had written to Weill with the subject line "AT&T and the 92nd Street Y," which was dated just a few weeks before the 1999 upgrade. Though Grubman never explicitly linked the two subjects, he spent the first part of the memo explaining the steps he was taking to review AT&T's rating and then switched gears to remind Weill that he, Grubman, hoped to get the twins into the 92nd Street Y, a fifteen-thousand-dollar-a-year Upper East Side preschool with strong ties to the upper echelon of New York Jewish society. "There are no bounds for what you do for your children," Grubman wrote. "It comes down to 'who you know.' . . . Anyway, anything you could do Sandy would be greatly appreciated. As I mentioned, I will keep you posted on the progress with AT&T which I think is going well." Joan Tisch, one of the Y's directors, confirmed that Weill had talked to her about a month after the AT&T upgrade, saying he would be "very appreciative" if she would help Grubman, a "valued employee" at Citigroup. After Grubman's twins were admitted, the Citigroup Foundation agreed to donate one million dollars to the Y. Spitzer decided the office needed to take the next step and warn Citigroup and Weill that the chairman was fast becoming a potential target and probably needed a personal lawyer.

Jack Grubman arrived for two days of interviews in late October. Unlike Henry Blodget, he was never formally deposed, so no transcript exists. But Assistant Attorney General Maria Filipakis, newly added to Spitzer's research analyst team because she had trial and deposition experience, remembered thinking that the analyst had clearly spent significant time preparing for the confrontation. Shorter than Filipakis had expected, Grubman had left his larger-than-life analyst persona at the office. He also looked nothing like the former boxer he had often claimed to be. Grubman immediately disavowed his e-mails about the 92nd Street Y. In a later written statement he said, "The contents of these particular e-mails, while personally embarrassing, are completely baseless. Regrettably, I invented a story in an effort to inflate my professional importance and make an impression on a colleague and friend. My research on AT&T was always done on the merits."

Sandy Weill's turn came two weeks later, on the day that details of the Grubman-Cutler e-mails first began appearing in *The Wall Street Journal*. The investment banks were absolutely convinced that Spitzer's team had leaked the information to put pressure on Weill, but both the attorney general's staff and the reporter who wrote the story denied that Spitzer's people were the source. Like Grubman, Weill was not placed under oath, and his words were not recorded. Spitzer's staff also agreed to conduct the interview at the Midtown offices of Weill's lawyers, Wachtell, Lipton, Rosen & Katz, rather than forcing the easily recognizable Citigroup chairman to run the gauntlet of reporters camped outside Spitzer's downtown headquarters. Weill survived the interview largely unscathed, even in the view of the team trying to build a case against him. Citigroup had written policies that theoretically guaranteed its analysts' independence, and as CEO, Weill could plausibly claim that he did not know exactly what was happening on the ground in his firm's research department. He did not personally use e-mail (not unusual for a sixty-nine-year-old executive), so there was no paper trail to contradict his claims. Weill and his legal team also handled the 92nd Street Y issue skillfully. In a company memo released to the media, he readily conceded he had asked Grubman "to take a fresh look at AT&T" but insisted, "I never told any analyst what he or she had to write." He said much the same thing to Spitzer's investigators. "His basic worldview was 'I never told any analyst what to do or what to say. I thought Grubman had an outdated picture of what was happening at AT&T. I was on the AT&T board and I knew AT&T had gone through so much change and had such fine new leadership that it really warranted taking another look. That's what I asked him to do and all I asked him to do,'" Weill's attorney John Savarese remembered. Weill also freely admitted that he had intervened on behalf of his fifteen-million-dollar-a-year analyst and gave a donation to the 92nd Street Y preschool, but said he would have done the same for other highly valued employees. Weill's lawyers also put together an impressive list of their client's other charitable giving, including monumental donations to Carnegie Hall and Cornell University, where the recital hall and medical school, respectively, were named after the Citigroup chairman and his wife. The contrast between Grubman and his ultimate boss could not have been clearer. "We had Grubman pretty good," Topman remembered. "With Weill, we just didn't have it. . . . He was very good in the interview. He wasn't evasive. He was very practical about things. He didn't try to duck the hard issues."

Election Day on November 5, 2002, brought with it two key developments—Spitzer handily won reelection, as expected, beating the little-known former state judge Dora Irizarry by more than thirty-five percentage points, and Pitt announced his resignation from the SEC. Between his 2001 speech, which seemed to promise a "kinder and gentler" SEC, and his failure to beat Spitzer to the punch on analysts, Pitt had become a political liability in an era of burgeoning corporate scandals. The last straw proved to be an imbroglio involving William H. Webster, Pitt's choice to head the new board designed to restore confidence in corporate accounting. Though Webster was a respected former FBI director and judge, he had also served on the board of a failed Internet firm whose chairman was under investigation for fraud. "I came to a conclusion that it was not going to stop, that one way or another I was going to be the story," Pitt remembered. The SEC chairman stayed on until February and continued to attend the negotiating dinners with the other regulators, but his announcement temporarily made Steve Cutler, already the commission's point man in the global settlement, the face of the SEC. It was a development that boded well for everyone involved. An academic star both at Yale College and Yale Law School who had spent much of his career in private practice, Cutler was widely seen as one of the brightest securities lawyers of his generation. Intense and thoughtful, he could more than hold his own with Spitzer, and he genuinely cared about forging a settlement that functioned as well in practice as it did on paper. While Spitzer generally worked through his deputies, Cutler took personal charge of drafting the agreement that would govern the behavior of the banks. He kept the master copy on his personal computer and would often devote his lunch hour to getting all the regulators on the same page and drafting new language to address points that had been raised during negotiating sessions. "More than anyone sitting at the table, Steve tried to make sure that the final terms of the settlement not only dealt with the very real enforcement issues, but that at the same time we got something that did not disrupt the capital raising structure," said NASD chief enforcer Barry Goldsmith.

Smack dab in the middle of the negotiations, Spitzer was invited by *Institutional Investor* magazine to be the keynote speaker at its annual awards dinner for top research analysts on November 12. The occasion was a celebratory one; dozens of individual analysts would be honored in front of their families at the Ritz-Carlton in downtown Manhattan. But Spitzer—then fielding angry phone calls from the chieftains of Wall Street almost daily—was in no mood to make nice. Instead, he and Deputy Attorney General Avi Schick came up with a way to underscore the need to overhaul Wall Street research. The office spent weeks gathering every buy or sell recommendation issued by the honored analysts and building a database to determine how an individual investor would have done if he or she had followed the recommendations. Schick then crafted a speech for Spitzer that would excoriate what he called "industry-wide failure" and criticize the fifty-one all-star analysts for turning in "lackluster performances" and "dishonest advice." The draft got angrier from there: "Small investors were advised to buy stocks that the analysts believed they never should have owned, and told to hold stocks that they long ago should have sold."

But an hour into the dinner, as Schick watched the honorees smile and pose with their Lucite statues, the deputy began having second thoughts. "I'm thinking, man, this speech is going to seem gruesome," Schick remembered. So he grabbed a copy and began to pencil in changes that would tone down the language and make the attack less harsh. When the presentations stopped for the main course, Schick sought out his boss and offered him the milder version. Spitzer stopped him cold. "If it was the right speech to give at the office, it's the right speech to give now," the attorney general said and walked onstage knowing he was about to mortally offend a ballroom full of people.

Spitzer started out with a joke: "It is wonderful to be here this evening, because it allows me to put faces to the names in all those e-mails we have been reviewing." Then, amid the nervous laughter, he plunged in the knife, attacking the evening's honorees for the quality of their work. "When measured by the performance of their stock recommendations, only one of this year's fifty-one first-team all-stars included in the study ranked first in their sector. . . . More than 40 percent of this year's first-team all-stars did not perform as well as the average analyst for their sector." As the attorney general spoke, some guests stormed out. "I'm not going to sit here and listen to this shit," one departing guest said as Spitzer plowed on through the speech. The room was silent when he finished. One of the analysts turned to Schick and asked if he had had anything to do with drafting Spitzer's remarks. When Schick acknowledged that he had, the analyst cursed him, too: "You flaming asshole." Unlike Schick, Spitzer was unfazed. "That summarizes why he is so successful," Schick said. "He's not going to worry, am I going to be friends with them, am I going to play tennis with them. He doesn't care if one thousand people get up and say, 'You're a flaming asshole, Mr. Spitzer.' He's able to filter all that stuff out and do what's right."

Spitzer also didn't seem to care that he was being blamed for leaking to the press the most sensitive details of the ongoing negotiations. In late November, the regulators scheduled individual meetings in Washington or New York, one with each bank, to discuss the evidence that had been uncovered, each firm's possible defenses, and the proposed penalties. But lawyers for several banks walked into their meetings already apoplectic because they had learned about their likely fines by reading about them in the newspapers. "How can you negotiate off that? It was horrific," one of them remembered. Morgan Stanley's general counsel, Donald Kempf, took a particularly confrontational approach at his meeting, telling the national regulators that they had been "asleep at the wheel," and comparing Spitzer, who was not present, to Thomas E. Dewey, the New York prosecutor of the mob organization Murder Incorporated, who later served as governor of New York and ran unsuccessfully for president. Those in the room were not sure whether he meant it as a compliment. Later in the same meeting, Kempf got so "belligerent and abusive," in the words of one regulator, that the SEC's Lori Richards walked out and did not return until the Morgan Stanley lawyer had apologized. "I have a way with words and sometimes that can strike people as funny, and other times people see it as out of bounds," Kempf explained later.

Spitzer wasn't the only state official to draw the banks' ire. Bill Galvin, the Massachusetts secretary of the commonwealth, had struck out on his own, filing a two-million-dollar civil suit against Credit Suisse First Boston that alleged that the firm had improperly spun IPO shares to technology firm executives and issued tainted research to win investment banking business. California's corporations commissioner, Demetrios A. Boutris, threatened to hold up the entire global settlement because he thought the penalties were too low—particularly for Deutsche Bank and Thomas Wiesel Partners, which his office had been responsible for investigating. Several of the smaller investment banks joined forces and began making noises about pulling out of the global settlement talks, while Spitzer and national regulators began pressing all the harder to get a deal done before things could unravel further. It was unclear how serious the revolt really was—some regulators thought the midsize banks were simply trying to push their penalty payments down. But Grasso and others reached out to Richard Fuld, the CEO of Lehman Brothers, and persuaded him to sign on for eighty million dollars. Their coalition in tatters, most of the other midrange banks quickly followed suit.

Then another snag developed. Citigroup, already facing the largest payment—four hundred million dollars—made clear it would not participate in any deal unless all the regulators agreed not to go after its chairman, Sandy Weill, personally. After consulting with his staff, and after a couple of anguished jogs around the reservoir in Central Park, Spitzer decided he could live with giving Weill a pass. Though the case would be a media bonanza, winning would be incredibly difficult, because Spitzer would have to prove not only that Weill pushed for an upgrade on AT&T but also that he didn't believe the company deserved it. Though the 92nd Street Y link looked suspicious, there was no e-mail trail to suggest that Weill had ever disparaged AT&T. He had even bought the company's stock on a number of occasions. "We will never be able to disprove that he believed in the stock. He will take the stand and say, 'I bought the stock. I believed in it.' That trumps all the other things that would suggest" fraud, Spitzer remembered thinking.

But Spitzer's fellow regulators balked. The NASD enforcement staff, which had helped uncover the 92nd Street Y evidence, wasn't willing to give up so easily. They wanted more time. Christmas was fast approaching, and Spitzer wanted the deal done before he left for vacation, for fear of losing the momentum. So he called NASD vice chairman Mary Schapiro directly and began to pressure her to make a decision. Talking loudly and quickly, he made clear that he wanted the deal done before the calendar year was up, and that she was standing in the way. "Look, there's no case here," he remembered saying. Schapiro refused to bend, telling Spitzer she would get back to him when she could. In truth, her staff was nearly done with its review of the evidence and they had come to the same conclusion. "We made our own decision in our own time about whether to bring an action against Sandy Weill," Schapiro remembered.

On Wednesday, December 18, Spitzer's aides started telling representatives from most of the biggest banks to be in his office by noon the next day for what became known in retrospect as his "Come to Jesus" meeting. Citigroup's representative, Charles Prince, already had a separate meeting scheduled with Spitzer's staff that morning, so he came in first, without the other banks. Spitzer laid into him, telling him that the giant bank had to sign the global settlement, or else. But that was just a warm-up—Citigroup had been far more cooperative than many of its counterparts. Spitzer then strode down the hall to his own office, where half a dozen general counsels and their outside lawyers were packed in around the conference table. Morgan Stanley had sent its chief executive, Philip Purcell, and he looked like he was going to give his general counsel an earful as soon as the meeting broke up. The Spitzer staffers mostly stood—they knew their boss would be terse. Spitzer sat down and got right to the point. "I'm done with this," he said. The banks had been acting like "children in a sandbox." He wasn't going to wait around any longer. "Give me your agreement, or I'm going to court." Each bank would receive, sign, and fax back a one-page document agreeing in principle to pay its share of the $1.4 billion settlement within hours, or Spitzer's team would start filing Martin Act complaints much as they had done with Merrill Lynch. "Any questions?" Spitzer asked. Everyone stared at their shoes. The bank executives were aghast. Who was this lunatic who was ranting and raving at them as if they were errant schoolchildren? But Spitzer's staff and some of the lawyers who knew him well believed they were witnessing a calculated performance. Spitzer wasn't out of control. He didn't scream. He didn't yell. The whole thing lasted less than fifteen minutes. And he had made his point. Acceptances started rolling in, even from firms such as Deutsche Bank, which had not attended the meeting. "Eliot can be very blunt. He understands the leverage he has and he uses it," said a top lawyer for one of the banks.

Some of the firms continued to dicker over individual provisions and particular words in the tentative agreement, and some warned Spitzer it would be well after the close of business before they got back to him. But he was too pumped up to leave the office. Sounding like a precinct captain on Election Night, he demanded that Dinallo put out calls to all the general counsels at home and track their responses on a spreadsheet. Eventually Spitzer let most of the staff go home, and he and Beth Golden manned the fax machines themselves. One by one, the responses trickled in from most of Wall Street's largest firms.

Morgan Stanley kicked and screamed to the last, and Bear Stearns didn't sign on until the morning of December 20—Spitzer was practically on his way out the door to the press conference at the New York Stock Exchange when the firm's acceptance arrived.

A deal had been rumored for days, so the NYSE's sixth-floor boardroom was packed with reporters when on Friday, December 20, the regulators finally announced they had an agreement in principle. Grasso was an effusive master of ceremonies, and graciousness was in the air. Cutler opened with words of praise for Spitzer and his staff for doing "an incredible job bringing some of this misconduct to light." For his part, Spitzer buttered up Grasso as a "consummate diplomat" and said nice things about the other state regulators as well. Then he got serious. This investigation, he said, "has been only about one thing. It has been about ensuring that retail investors get a fair shake. Retail investors know there is no guaranteed return in the market. They know there is risk. But the one thing they deserve is honest advice and fair dealing. That is what this deal is designed to produce." His critics were quick to note that despite his stated focus on the small investor, New York's share of the settlement would go to the state treasury, while the national regulators vowed to devote every penny of their $432.75 million to investor restitution. Spitzer replied that he did not have a mechanism for funneling state penalties back to investors.

Despite the happy smiles, it would take four more months and endless dickering to forge a final written settlement that both described the banks' past conduct and spelled out the remedies that would protect investors in the future. To Golden, who generally represented the Spitzer team, much of the later wrangling about the descriptive section "was a painstaking negotiation over what, in many instances, was the placement of commas." To the industry, the details were critical. The banks were concerned about their exposure to investor lawsuits and wanted to control exactly how their past behavior would be described. The remedy section was equally contentious. Spitzer had blown up the existing system. The SEC and the industry would have to live with whatever replaced it. "It could have a huge impact on how the capital markets worked. You're balancing investor protection with efficiency of capital formation," Cutler explained.

The banks found the entire process extremely frustrating. They saw the settlement as a kind of back-door rulemaking that deprived them of their right to fight back against new regulations that they believed would be impractical and expensive. Ordinarily, the SEC spent months or years on new rules and engaged in an extensive comment and revision period before imposing its views. With Pitt on his way out the door and the commission staff determined to keep pace with Spitzer, the global settlement negotiations had taken on an entirely different tone. Speed and horse trading seemed to be the order of the day, and some of the proposals—such as the requirement the banks provide chaperones for all conversations between bankers and analysts—seemed ridiculously expensive to some participants. "They flushed down the toilet notice and comment; it also flushed down the toilet regulatory history. You have a twenty-page ill-conceived document" that no one knew how to interpret, one of the bank lawyers complained later. Morgan Stanley's ever-mercurial general counsel, Don Kempf, gave voice to some of the banks' frustrations during a late-winter negotiating session. The banks had already agreed to pay more than four hundred million dollars in restitution to investors, but how to divide and distribute the money became a point of endless contention. As the banks and regulators went around and around, Kempf lost his temper. "For all I care, you can open up a phone book and start picking names," he said.

In addition to detailing how the money would be spent, the final settlement also spelled out the fates of Henry Blodget and Jack Grubman. Blodget agreed to pay four million dollars in fines and restitution. The settlement document included allegations that Blodget's report on GoTo.com was "materially misleading" and his reports on InfoSpace and five other companies "were not based on principles of fair dealing and good faith." Grubman paid fifteen million dollars, and the regulators alleged that his reports on two telecom stocks were "fraudulent," and his reports on six others "were not based on principles of fair dealing and good faith." His 1999 AT&T upgrade was labeled "misleading." Blodget and Grubman neither admitted nor denied wrongdoing and both were barred from the securities industry for life. The regulators took no action against Citigroup CEO Sandy Weill, but the settlement included a special provision that barred him from talking directly to the firm's analysts without a lawyer present.

By the time the final deal got done in April, the federal regulators and the New Yorkers were practically best buddies. During the fights with the banks over particular clauses and requirements, the SEC and New York delegations often saw issues the same way. Both sides also acknowledged that Cutler's eye for detail and Spitzer's willingness to knock heads together had made the whole thing possible. The arrival in February of the new SEC chairman, William H. Donaldson, also helped. A leading banker and former chairman of the New York Stock Exchange, Donaldson made an early effort to reach out to Spitzer, inviting him to Washington for a chat that observers said was markedly less tense than the Pitt-Spitzer meetings. Imbued with the new spirit of cooperation, Spitzer agreed to let Donaldson host the April 2003 press conference announcing the final global settlement at the SEC. The commission staff returned the favor by sponsoring a congratulatory dinner in Washington for all the regulators after the final settlement was announced. The point, remembered Lori Richards, was to mend fences and to show Spitzer's lawyers and the other regulators that the SEC really did understand and appreciate their work. "This was a 'regulators do a great job together' event. Let's join arms; we're all on the same team," she said.

A few weeks later, Spitzer and Cutler were both invited to address the SEC Historical Society. Cutler used the event as an occasion for levity, offering an impromptu roast of his New York counterpart using fictional e-mails he claimed to have recently received. One was supposedly from Spitzer to Michael Powell, the chairman of the Federal Communications Commission. "Dear Chairman Powell: I believe the FCC's sweeping overhaul of bandwidth ownership is not being handled properly. Our interpretation of the Stamp Act of 1785 allows us to tax all products that flow through New York, which obviously includes bandwidth. Please call for my ideas."

Cutler went on. The next one was "from Eliot to the Vatican. 'Dear Pontiff: I have some comments on recent papal edicts. While you are and should be the primary regulator of Catholicism, I believe you may be asleep at the switch on this whole business of transubstantiation. As

I read the Stamp Act of 1785, I have the authority to tax and regulate all items passing through New York, which we believe includes Catholicism.'" The final e-mail was purportedly "from Eliot to Heaven. 'Dear God: It's my understanding that you are everywhere, including, apparently, the State of New York. As I read the Stamp Act of 1785, you are subject to regulation and taxation by the State of New York. While you are and should be the primary regulator of humanity, I have some ideas I'd like to share with you.'"

The audience laughed, but the banks and their Republican supporters in Congress weren't nearly so appreciative—if anything, they felt the newly aggressive SEC and NASD had gone too far in their efforts to make peace with Spitzer. So, in July 2003, they had another go at cutting the legs off state enforcement. This time, Representative Richard Baker was the instigator. Hours before his Capital Markets Subcommittee took up legislation to strengthen the SEC's enforcement powers and increase the size of the fines it could impose, Baker unveiled a "preemption" amendment that would limit what state regulators could demand from brokers and investment banks as part of a fraud settlement. Much like the proposal Morgan Stanley had pushed for unsuccessfully the year before, Baker's amendment sought to prevent state attorneys general and securities regulators from requiring new oversight and disclosure to clients of conflicts of interest—the central issue in the research scandal. Calling his amendment "very straightforward," Baker claimed to be reasserting the existing legal order: "Market structure remains in the providence [sic] of the SEC and they retain their primacy as the national securities regulator," he said. But the Democrats recognized immediately that Spitzer was Baker's ultimate target. Despite their protests, the Republican-dominated subcommittee approved Baker's language twenty-four to eighteen and sent the bill on to the full Financial Services Committee.

When Spitzer's team learned of the proposal, they couldn't believe it. After months of working with the federal regulators to forge the global settlement, they were under attack again. "We are living Groundhog Day," Spitzer told the New York Post. This time, Baker's amendment had been attached to a bill that both consumer advocates and the SEC badly wanted passed, and there was no WorldCom collapse to galvanize public sentiment. Representative Barney Frank of Massachusetts, the ranking Democratic member of the House Financial Services Committee, was not optimistic. The Republicans had a majority in the committee, and two Democrats were thinking of defecting, he told Bill Galvin, the Massachusetts securities regulator. "I think we'll lose," Frank said, but "it'll be a great issue" on the House floor and in future political campaigns. Galvin was appalled. "We can't lose," he replied. He and the other state securities regulators believed they would basically be out of a job.

Spitzer and Galvin huddled. Whom did they know on the House Financial Services Committee? Were any of them close to their state securities regulators? How could they be influenced? Spitzer's chief of staff Rich Baum became the organizer, keeping lists and setting up phone calls. Spitzer's first attempt, a call to Representative Sue Kelly, the lone New Yorker to vote for the proposal in the subcommittee, blew up in his face. "Sue, do you realize what you have done?" Spitzer asked. "Your vote in committee eviscerates state enforcement."

"Well, what are you going to do?" she replied. Kelly was shocked by what happened next. "He just started lighting into her," said a Kelly staff member who listened in on the call. "She's a member of Congress. People at that level communicate in a certain way. He treated her very condescendingly, and he just spoke over her." Both Kelly and the staffer believed that Spitzer was threatening to campaign against her unless she changed her vote. "He was basically screaming and wouldn't let her talk. It was appalling," said the staffer, who now works for another member of Congress. Two Spitzer aides who also listened in reacted differently. They said Spitzer never raised his voice or made direct threats, but they agreed that his insistent questioning and promises to "tell people what you did" made Kelly extremely angry. "He was firm and clearly disagreed with her, but it was not an aggressive call by the measure of Eliot's norm or anyone else's," Baum said. In his view, Kelly was the angry one. "She blew up at him," he said. (Though hard feelings remained, when the preemption issue came up again in the banking context, Kelly was far more supportive of state prerogatives.)

A few days later, Spitzer and Galvin hit on the strategy of using a press conference about Galvin's latest securities fraud case to rally public opposition to the Baker bill. Spitzer—who by then could attract far more national media coverage than Galvin—flew up to Boston and stood by Galvin's side on July 14 as the Massachusetts regulator announced that he had uncovered improper mutual fund sales practices at Morgan Stanley's office in Boston. Brokers were secretly being offered prizes to push the firm's own funds, and the firm had lied about it to state regulators, Galvin alleged. Spitzer told the assembled cameras that the global research settlement had proved that state and federal regulators could cooperate and that the preemption bill was simply removing a level of investor protection. He also issued a veiled threat to the new SEC chairman, William H. Donaldson, asking him "to stand up loudly and clearly reject this amendment. . . . Say it is not good for investors. Say it is not good for the integrity of the marketplace. If you do not do that, I will have to draw the conclusion that you have not learned the lessons of the last five years." Newspapers around the country ran articles about Baker's effort to defang the state securities regulators and began asking whether consumers would be well served by the provision. But Spitzer's efforts to enlist Donaldson's aid backfired, at least on the public side. Although the SEC's new leader had no interest in picking a fight with Spitzer, he also was not about to speak out against a bill that reasserted the SEC's primacy. Pressed by reporters the next day, Donaldson made this clear. "You can't have a system in which there are 50 different structures," he told *The Washington Post*. "It will paralyze business. . . . The SEC must be supreme." Later, Spitzer contended that he never expected Donaldson to come out against the bill. Rather, he said, he was hoping to encourage the SEC staff to work against the bill behind the scenes. "The only way I could put enough heat on them was to go after them publicly. I had to go to war with them so that privately they could go back to their side and say 'let's forge a compromise,'" Spitzer said.

By the time the preemption bill came up for a vote in the full Financial Services Committee, Baker had a full-blown fight on his hands. The SEC was still studiously avoiding taking a formal position on Baker's language, although the staff privately let reporters know that the commission had not put Baker up to this maneuver. Peter King, an independent-minded senior Republican from Long Island, had come out publicly against the preemption language. "As Republicans, we do believe in states' rights, state prerogatives, and state control," King told *The Washington Post*. "It's state officials who have been cracking down on corporate corruption. . . . I would never vote for Eliot Spitzer for any office, but he has made real inroads in uncovering corporate corruption and bringing a sense of justice to the market." Other Republicans were shaky as well. Galvin had convinced Ohio's Republican governor Robert Taft to write a letter formally opposing the proposal, and regulators from other states were also lobbying their congressmen. Angrily, Baker, the Louisiana Republican, pulled his bill. Announcing he was "not pleased," Baker promised he would bring the proposal back in the fall. "I would kindly caution opponents of this bill not to misunderstand this postponement as a victory," he said. But before Baker could reload, Spitzer would explode another bomb.

6

BETTING TODAY ON
YESTERDAY'S HORSE RACES

"YOU'RE FROM WALL STREET. WHAT'S NEXT?" ELIOT SPITZER ASKED HIS newest hire, his Harvard Law School classmate David Brown IV, in the spring of 2003. Brown had spent his career working for the securities industry, helping the big firms cope with regulators and litigation, and he had a ready answer: "Mutual funds."

While working as an in-house lawyer for Goldman Sachs, Brown had read a *Journal of Corporation Law* article that alleged that the seven-trillion-dollar mutual fund industry routinely overcharged millions of middle-class investors by charging fees that were on average twice as high as those levied on pension funds and other large customers for similar services. "It's a funny business . . . where people don't eat their own cooking," Brown explained to Spitzer, using Wall Street slang for products that are ripe for abuse because they are marketed to the public but rarely used by insiders. "The potential overcharges are in the billions because of the amount of money involved. If we could do something here, the savings for consumers are enormous."

Though the mutual fund industry had been largely scandal-free for several decades, Spitzer was instantly enthusiastic. "Go for it," he said. "This is the next logical step from analysts. Analysts are the intermediaries between investment houses and those assembling stock portfolios for themselves . . . but most Americans own stock through a mutual fund, where the investing is done by someone else."

Brown, who had been waiting for years to use his skills for investors rather than against them, didn't need to be told twice. He had recently resigned from Goldman, sold his home in Jersey City to cash in on the appreciation, and begun moving his wife, three kids, and a baby on the way to the Albany area. There, where housing prices were lower, he would be able to afford to work for the government. Inspired by the *Journal of Corporation Law* article, which was written in 2001 by John Freeman and Stewart Brown (no relation), David Brown initially focused on mutual funds' unusual management structure and whether small investors were paying higher fees than they should. As the name suggests, mutual funds are baskets of stocks and bonds owned collectively by thousands of individual investors who are seeking to share both risks and profits. Under the federal Investment Company Act of 1940, funds must be overseen by a board of directors who are supposed to act in the investors' best interests. But the directors don't do the investing themselves. Instead, they hire a management company to run the fund. The problem with that arrangement, according to the law professors, was that at many fund companies, the chairman and several of the members of the supposedly independent board were actually executives of the management company, and the rest of the board generally sat on the boards of all the funds run by the same management company. This meant that they had little motivation to negotiate hard to keep fees down. As a result, Freeman and Brown estimated, fund fees on average were twenty-five basis points—one-quarter of a percentage point—"higher than they need to be in order to furnish fund [managers] with fair and reasonable compensation. . . . This translates into equity mutual fund shareholders being overcharged to the tune of nearly $9 billion-plus annually."

The main mutual fund trade group disputed the methodology, and the financial industry had reacted to the article with a collective yawn. "This Is News?" asked *The Wall Street Journal.* But David Brown thought the idea of compromised boards and excessive fees just might add up to securities fraud. Spitzer read the article and immediately agreed. "We believed there was something very genuinely amiss in the mutual fund world," he said. Even if fees turned out to be only fractions of a penny too high, Spitzer thought, that was unacceptable, because many mutual fund returns lagged behind the market indexes or barely beat them. "My core belief is that very few investment vehicles beat the market long term. The impact of fees on total return is huge, and people don't understand that," Spitzer said, citing his Princeton economics professor, Burton G. Malkiel, who made that argument in his classic 1973 book, *A Random Walk down Wall Street.*

With Spitzer's blessing, in the spring of 2003, Brown started drafting subpoenas to send to mutual fund companies that seemed to have excessively high fees. "The idea was maybe you could do a case based on a failure to disclose to investors that there's this conflict and the management fee isn't set competitively," Brown said. "If there are problems with mutual funds, I was convinced that they would show up graphically in the e-mail traffic, particularly because the mutual fund industry hadn't been investigated recently." But before he could move forward, another lawyer on staff, Lydie Pierre-Louis, came into his office to discuss an anonymous message she had received on her voice mail. "I think you should investigate mutual funds," said a clearly nervous female voice. "People are doing way too many trades and doing late trading after the close of business. There are violations of security laws by the hedge funds and mutual funds." Pierre-Louis had no idea what the caller was getting at; Brown thought the tip sounded harebrained. Everyone knew that mutual fund prices were fixed at 4:00 P.M., when the New York stock markets closed, and orders placed after that time got the next day's price. "Who would trade at an old price and why would they do it?" he asked Pierre-Louis. "Who's going to step up and lose money?" They could see why someone might want to buy or sell at an out-of-date price, but why would anyone take the other side of the transaction? So they waited to see if the tipster would call back.

"**D**oesn't this woman ever answer her phone?" Noreen Harrington thought to herself in early June 2003 as she tried once again to reach a live person at Spitzer's shop. This was positively the last time she was going to call. She had already left one cryptic message about mutual funds, and if this Pierre-Louis woman couldn't follow it, that was Spitzer's problem. Harrington wanted to clear her conscience, but not enough to leave her number. Surely five or six attempts to get through were enough. Surprised when Pierre-Louis actually picked up the line, Harrington blurted out, "I'm that woman who was calling you about mutual funds."

"Oh, I'm so glad you called," Harrington remembered Pierre-Louis saying. "We really want to look into this but we don't understand it. We want you to come in." No way, Harrington thought. "I can explain it on the phone," she said and started talking in rapid-fire Wall Street fashion about "capacity," "market timing," and after-hours trading. Pierre-Louis was encouraging but sounded confused. Here Harrington was, reporting what she thought was a crime—that small investors were being ripped off by hedge funds making improper mutual fund trades—and the lawyer on the other end of the line didn't seem to get it. Eventually, Harrington was persuaded that she was going to have to do more, so she agreed to come into the office where Brown, and others who knew more about the fund industry, could question her.

But when the day came, Harrington almost didn't make it through the lobby of 120 Broadway. So nervous that she hadn't even put the appointment in her date book, she grew agitated when she was forced to stand in line to check in with security and almost walked out. Upstairs, David Brown, Roger Waldman, and Lydie Pierre-Louis were nearly as anxious. Could this woman be for real? They peered down the hall at the elevators, waiting for the first glance of their tipster. When Harrington walked off the elevator, the excitement in the room was palpable. Trim, neatly dressed, with well-groomed graying hair, Harrington looked every inch the former Goldman Sachs trader that she said she had been. "That doesn't look like a nut to me," Waldman said, half to himself, just before Harrington walked into the room.

It took Brown and the others several interviews to understand and piece together Harrington's story. But in essence, here was what she had to say. She had been working for Edward J. Stern, the younger son of one of New York's richest and toughest business magnates, Leonard Stern, who had built a three-billion-dollar fortune out of pet supplies and real estate. Since 1999, Eddie had been managing the family investments. Harrington, a former bond trader and saleswoman for Goldman Sachs and Barclays Bank, had joined the Stern family's Manhattan office in March 2001. The Sterns had just sold their pet supply business, Hartz Mountain, for an estimated $250 million, and Harrington was charged with running a "fund of funds." That is, she helped the family invest its money in a variety of different outside hedge funds, largely unregulated investment pools aimed at wealthy people. Harrington's tip concerned another part of Eddie Stern's business, two internal hedge funds—known collectively as Canary Capital Management—that specialized in trading mutual fund shares. Managed by Noah Lerner, a close adviser of Eddie Stern, and Andrew Goodwin, a young Harvard-educated trader, the funds sought to make money by engaging in a practice known as market timing. In English, that meant they were trying to exploit the fact that stock prices changed all the time, but mutual funds were priced just once a day. They would move millions of dollars into a particular mutual fund whenever they thought its prices were "stale"—lagging behind the actual value of the underlying assets—and then sell their shares as soon as the fund price caught up, usually within a few days. Dozens of hedge funds were trying this strategy, and many mutual fund managers hated them because the sudden inflows and outflows increased costs and cut into profits for long-term investors. But the Canary team stood out from the pack. In fact, they had been so spectacularly successful that Eddie had moved beyond the family money and started taking in millions from outsiders. In January 2002, Stern told his investors that Canary had $400 million in assets—$160 million of it from outsiders—and had made a return of more than 25 percent in 2001, a year in which the standard stock indexes had all lost between 7 and 21 percent.

Harrington initially paid the Canary traders little mind. Their hedge funds were based in the Sterns' Secaucus, New Jersey, offices, while she worked mostly in Manhattan. But one evening in 2002, when she happened to be working late in New Jersey, Harrington watched the Canary team begin to celebrate a big score. "We just picked off this fund," Harrington remembered a trader crowing as the group crowded around a computer terminal they referred to as "the box." The whole scene seemed odd to her. Same-day mutual fund trading was supposed to stop at four o'clock. This was well into the evening. "Who are you trading with? Japan?" she asked. No one answered. Now on the alert for odd behavior, Harrington noticed that the Canary traders routinely wrote order tickets in the hours between 4:00 P.M. and 8:00 P.M. She also began to wonder if the trading was connected to a call Stern had asked her to make to Goldman earlier that year. Eddie wanted to make frequent trades in and out of Goldman's mutual funds, but the honchos there had turned him down. Stern had hoped Harrington could find him another way in. No dice. "Noreen, you can't do that, it's illegal," Harrington's pals at Goldman had said. "We can't have that kind of turnover in our funds." The conversation hadn't rung alarm bells at the time—"I thought it was a Goldman issue," she said, meaning that she had believed that her old firm had stricter rules against short-term trading than the other fund companies Stern did business with. Now she was concerned. She tried to sleuth discreetly, asking fellow employees a few questions here and there, without attracting attention. One of them, James Nesfield, a former trader now based in North Carolina, told her his job was to find "capacity," funds where Stern's team could make their enormous investments and then pull out within days without having to pay a fee, usually known as a redemption charge. Some funds welcomed Stern's money, Nesfield said. Others were in the dark about what was happening. "We go back door through some of them. They don't know it's us," Harrington remembered him explaining.

That kind of cat-and-mouse game sounded wrong, so Harrington went directly to Eddie Stern. "Is this legal?" she asked. A lithe and smooth-talking Haverford graduate who could ooze charm when he wanted to, Eddie sidestepped the question. "If the regulators ever look at it, they'll want the mutual funds, not me," he assured Harrington. By Labor Day 2002, Harrington had left the Stern family business. She said she had become increasingly uncomfortable with the way Eddie Stern was doing business and that he had made clear that her questions were unwelcome. Others familiar with the situation said that Harrington had been forced to compete directly with a coworker for Stern investment funds and was losing when she left. In any case, her separation agreement said that Harrington and the company "amicably terminate their relationship."

Initially, Harrington kept quiet. She believed Stern's trading was an isolated problem, and she wasn't inclined to jeopardize her own future on Wall Street by rocking the boat. But her next job, with a private investment boutique, brought her into contact with lots of hedge fund managers who openly engaged in market timing. When she asked them about after-hours trading, they tended to tiptoe around the subject rather than reject the idea outright. She also began to focus more on the harm that Stern was doing. In April 2003, Harrington's sister, Mary Ellen Corrigan, was so appalled by the shrinking value of her 401(k) retirement account that she sent Noreen a copy of her statement, accompanied by a bitter joke: "I guess I'll have to work forever." On the statement, Harrington recognized the names of several fund companies that she knew had been granting Stern special trading privileges. She realized with a start that she had been working for a reverse Robin Hood. "Money isn't created," she observed. "It's taken from one person to another. [Stern was making money off] people who had no money." That same month, an old friend independently called Harrington and asked her to give him a reference for Stern because the friend's bank was about to lend money to Canary. "Don't do it," Harrington warned. "Something is terribly wrong."

By late May 2003, Harrington was convinced she had to do something. "I'm a senior person in the industry. We're supposed to police ourselves. I don't want people to think we're all crooks," she remembered thinking. But where should she go? For the last few months, the papers had been full of articles about Eliot Spitzer and his ambitious "global settlement" that had reformed Wall Street stock research. "He had a profile in the paper that was clear; he was a man on a mission," she said. Harrington also believed that what she had witnessed was a crime, and she knew that the Martin Act gave Spitzer criminal enforcement powers that the SEC lacked. So when she finally plucked up the nerve, Spitzer's office was the first place she called.

The more David Brown thought about Harrington's story, the odder it seemed. Why would the fund companies allow Stern the special privileges Harrington had described? Academic studies and Wall Street lore made clear that market timing increased expenses and cut into overall returns for long-term investors. So Brown decided to call some of his friends in the mutual fund business. They assured him that most portfolio managers would fight against the practice because it hurt their customers and made their investment results look bad. But Harrington had a ready answer for the fund managers' duplicity: "For the fees, of course," she explained. Fund companies made money by charging customers a management fee based on a percentage of the assets they invested, and as a fund company's funds grew, so did its income. During the rollicking 1990s, fund assets grew exponentially, both through internal growth and because small investors were pouring their retirement and education savings into mutual funds and 401(k) plans, hoping to ride the stock market wave. Then the bear market hit in 2000 and 2001, prompting many small investors to pull out of stock-based mutual funds. Suddenly fund companies were seeing their assets under management—and hence their fees—decline. Market timers offered these companies a way out: in exchange for permission to jump in and out of individual funds, these short-term traders would usually agree to park a certain amount of cash with the fund company overall, generating a steady stream of fees. Suddenly Harrington's tip and Brown's earlier worries that fund companies cared more for their profits than for their investors didn't seem so far apart.

Brown set his law school interns to work, looking for information that would help bolster Harrington's story. One of them, Delfin Rodriguez, had been a systems administrator before heading to NYU, so he started surfing the Internet, looking for information about market timing. He quickly hit pay dirt, a mutual fund chat room where investors trolled for "timing capacity" and promised to "pay top dollar." Among the many messages was a June 20, 2001, e-mail posted by James Nesfield—the Canary employee from North Carolina—that read, "We work for a Market Timing Investment Manager that employs Mutual Fund Shares in their strategy. We are seeking a negotiated timing arrangement." Even better was a November 2002 exchange in which a Seth Fox of fundtiming@hotmail.com announced he was "Looking for timers who need Capacity" and received a November 24 reply from an ejstern@canarycapital.com. "Run a very large timing pool. $2 Bn. Call me if this is for real. Don't waste my time if it isn't. ES." Both the phone number and the e-mail address traced back to the Stern family offices in Secaucus.

On June 30, Brown was ready to send out subpoenas. He called Nesfield's North Carolina home first and asked if he would accept a subpoena. Brown hoped that the consultant, who no longer worked for Stern, would reach out to his former employers and that a later subpoena to Canary would pick up their e-mails and conversations. Indeed, when Nesfield got Brown's request, he did call Stern's office, partly because he felt he owed his former employer a heads-up and partly to find out if Stern would get him a lawyer. "I think you need a lawyer, too," Nesfield added. "I recommend Harvey Pitt." Nesfield said later that he believed the former SEC chairman knew the industry and its rules better than anyone else around. Stern told Nesfield he was on his own. So the North Carolinian called Brown back and asked what the Attorney General's Office wanted. "I didn't do anything wrong," Nesfield reasoned. "So why am I going to act like I did? Spitzer has a reputation for doing the right thing."

At first, Nesfield would acknowledge only that he had "heard" of "late day access" or "backward pricing," but soon he was talking freely about brokers who offered that "capability" when they sold Stern the "capacity" to engage in market timing. Nesfield's jargon was sometimes hard to understand, but the man clearly wanted to cooperate. So he and Brown agreed to meet in person. Nesfield then threw sixteen boxes of documents and his laptop—filled with trading records—into the back of his Ford F-150 pickup and drove the nearly five hundred miles to Manhattan. Nesfield was rambling and emotional when he arrived at Spitzer's office on July 22—at one point he broke down in tears while explaining that he admired the Stern family's philanthropy and that it pained him to cause them trouble. A self-described "gnome" who had dropped out of college and spent years immersed in the inner workings of the securities industry, Nesfield told Brown he had been thinking for years about the best ways to engage in market timing. By the time Stern found him through a résumé posted on the Internet, Nesfield had come up with two ways to circumvent the mutual fund compliance officers who were charged with keeping short-term traders out. The first strategy was to "fly under the radar"—make trades through brokers and other intermediaries. This worked because most funds accepted huge bundles of trades from intermediaries, and—with the brokers' connivance—the timing transactions could be hidden among dozens or hundreds of other trades, making them hard to detect. The second course was to tackle the fund companies head on by finding an executive who would grant a secret exemption from the anti-timing rules. This eliminated the risk that the trades would not go through, but it cost additional money because the timers had to agree to park large amounts of cash in funds that were generally struggling.

Nesfield told Brown about his unusual employment relationship with Eddie Stern. Working out of his house for fifty dollars an hour, amid the chaos caused by four children, chickens, and an old swaybacked horse, Nesfield scored an immediate success. Beginning in May 2000, Security Trust Company (STC), a Phoenix-based company that processed mutual fund trades for retirement plans, allegedly hid Canary's trades among those of their other customers in exchange for a processing fee. Even better, STC said it would accept orders as late as 9:00 P.M. Nesfield said he couldn't say for certain whether the Canary traders exploited this window to capitalize on news that was announced after the stock markets closed at 4:00 P.M. and after the mutual funds had set their prices. But his story certainly helped corroborate Harrington's tip. Spitzer's team learned later that STC had placed hundreds of trades for Stern between 2000 and 2003, 99 percent of them after the market had closed. In exchange, STC received a 1 percent fee on the assets it held for Canary plus 4 percent of the hedge fund's trading profits. Nesfield said Stern was so pleased with the arrangement that he gave his consultant a cut of the STC trading and began referring to the former broker as his "secret weapon."

But that wasn't all Nesfield did for Eddie Stern. Flying under the radar was all well and good, but a lot of other hedge funds were doing the same thing, making it that much harder to stay one step ahead of the "timing police," as the mutual fund compliance officers were known. It would be much simpler if Nesfield could find some fund families that would welcome Canary in. Nesfield went to work, using a simple strategy: he would watch the news about mutual funds and look for troubled companies where investors were leaving faster than new money was coming in. Often these firms reacted by replacing top managers, in hopes of stemming the outflow. That's when Nesfield would strike. "I would call the new guy and say, here's how I can help you save your job," he said. If the fund would allow Stern to make huge rapid trades in and out of the small-company stock funds and international funds, where the timing profits were usually biggest, Stern would promise to leave large amounts of money in the firm's other mutual funds, or, in some cases, high fee–generating hedge funds run by the same management company. The market-timing money plus the "static" or "sticky" assets would allow the fund company to boast that its total assets under management had increased, creating the illusion that its problems with departing investors had been solved. Most of the time, Nesfield said, he made the early approach to the fund companies, but Stern actually closed the deal. "Eddie liked the idea of having the big organizations call him," said Nesfield, who said he was pulling in one hundred thousand dollars a year while Stern was making millions. "They were being wined and dined by" big financial companies anxious to get "a piece of the Stern family's money." Eventually, Stern pushed Nesfield out. "The Street started calling them as an entity. They got a little cocky. They felt like they didn't need me," he said. "I didn't make the yuppie cut."

Andrew Goodwin, a former Canary portfolio manager, came in the next day with his lawyer. His first phone conversation with Brown was less than forthcoming—Brown remembered that when he asked Goodwin if he had worked for Canary, Goodwin replied, "I can't help you with that." For his part, Goodwin initially wondered if a friend was playing a prank and asked if he would really be contacting the Attorney General's Office if he called the number Brown had provided. Then he had his lawyer make the actual call to explain that Goodwin was bound by a confidentiality agreement and could not talk about his Canary days unless the Attorney General's Office issued him a subpoena. Brown obliged with alacrity. Once in the office, Goodwin came across as guarded but extremely bright. A short and solidly built redhead, he had studied social anthropology at Harvard but spent his free time in the business school library, reading books on the markets, and trying out the techniques he had learned by trading from his dorm room. By the time he and Stern connected, in 2000, he was in his early thirties, had written a book called *Trading Secrets of the Inner Circle,* and was running a one-man money management shop in Midtown Manhattan. At Canary, he became the whiz kid, setting up the computer programs that used statistical models to determine when Stern's team should put their money in or pull it out. Even better from the investigators' point of view, Goodwin had been forced out of Canary in December 2001 over a dispute about the way he had handled an e-mail containing salary information. Now the investigators had a former insider who could confirm Harrington's allegations and explain exactly how Stern's business model worked.

Much of what Goodwin said also appeared in the documents that were rolling into the office from Bank of America, Janus Capital Management, and the other fund families that Brown had subpoenaed based on Harrington's tips. But it was the eleven hours of interviews with Goodwin, who had an eye for detail and a capacity for quoting entire conversations and e-mails, that brought these operations to life. "Absent him stepping up and saying, it is real, I think we still would have had some doubts about the case at that time," Brown recalled. "I was absolutely astounded that the mutual funds would allow this. These people had a fiduciary duty to look after investors."

As Brown reconstructed events, Canary traders had made hundreds of after-hours mutual fund trades through Bank of America, at first through manual trades they phoned in to a broker named Theodore C. Sihpol III and then through Canary's own dedicated computer terminal, which allowed the hedge fund staff to enter trades directly into Bank of America's clearing system until 6:30 P.M.—this was the "box" that Harrington had seen. To Spitzer's team, the manual trades sounded blatantly deceptive. Sometime before 4:00 P.M., Canary would call Sihpol with a list of proposed trades and the broker would write them down on order tickets stamped before 4:00 P.M. Then, after the markets closed, a Canary employee would call back and tell Sihpol which trades the fund wanted put through, and the broker would put the other order tickets into the wastebasket.

Goodwin had been anxious about the legality of the late trades long before the Attorney General's Office called. After Nesfield had set up the deal with STC, including a provision allowing for trades until 9:00 P.M., Goodwin remembered sending STC president Grant Seeger an e-mail that essentially questioned the arrangement: "Are you sure we can trade until 9 P.M. I didn't think it could go that late?" he recalled writing. Then, as the Bank of America deal kicked into high gear, Goodwin pressed Stern about that after-hours arrangement as well. Stern brushed off his concerns, saying, "I have an expert SEC lawyer who has confirmed that the mutual funds don't like it but we can do it." Eventually, the young trader demanded and received a written guarantee that Canary would cover his legal costs if he were ever sued for his role in placing the hedge fund's mutual fund trades. When he showed that "indemnification" to Brown and Topman, they laughed out loud. It is legally impossible to indemnify someone for an illegal act.

Even as they interviewed Stern's former employees, Brown was also applying the screws to the fund companies and brokers who had worked with Stern. Fresh from the stock analyst investigation, Spitzer felt strongly that the office needed to keep up the time pressure and not allow the investigation to drag on. So Brown sent out subpoenas requiring the firms to turn over their Stern and market-timing–related documents in fourteen days or less. When the fund companies begged for more time, he would prioritize what he wanted but he granted extensions only with the greatest of reluctance. "I had been on the receiving end of subpoenas like these my whole career; if I had been served with these ones I would have tried to stretch out my response for an entire year," he said. "We realized we were on to something important and nobody else was. We didn't want to attract the attention of the SEC or anyone else."

Unlike the investment banks that had been the Spitzer team's last target, the Stern family took the Attorney General's Office seriously from the outset. Their pet supply company had settled a civil antitrust suit, criminal perjury charges, and antitrust charges in the late 1970s and early 1980s, working out deals that had spared the family and the other top executives criminal charges. (Leonard Stern told *BusinessWeek*, "I wasn't aware of any of this corruption when I was heading the company. The bottom line is that they didn't have the goods against us.") Eddie went out and hired Gary Naftalis, a top Manhattan criminal defense attorney with a résumé that included work for Kidder Peabody, for Salomon Brothers, and for Gary Winnick, the chairman of the telecommunications firm Global Crossing. Leonard advised his son to be cooperative. "I told Eddie to tell the attorney general 100% of the truth—to vomit it out. Don't filter it," Leonard Stern said in the *BusinessWeek* interview.

Naftalis and his team quickly realized the danger their client was in. Though late trading had never been prosecuted before, the Martin Act was so broad that it would probably allow Spitzer, if he so chose, to bring criminal charges against Stern. Within weeks they made clear to Spitzer that Stern was interested in a deal. "This wasn't going away, and we were certainly in the crosshairs. This was not a case where it was in Eddie's interest to fight if we could reach a settlement that protected him and his investors," Naftalis remembered. From Spitzer's point of view, Stern had much to offer. As one of the biggest and best-connected members of the close-knit market-timing world, he could give the office the goods on dozens of mutual fund firms and brokerages. To whet the investigators' appetite, Naftalis and his colleagues turned over a couple of key documents that made clear the gold mine Stern could become. For the first time, Brown had written proof that late trading had occurred: signed agreements with two brokers— Kaplan & Company and JB Oxford Company—that specifically allowed Stern to place mutual fund buy and sell orders as late as 4:45 P.M. The defense lawyers also faxed over a May 1, 2001, letter from Stern to Sihpol, in which Stern laid out his plans to move up to $16.8 million a week out of four of Bank of America's mutual funds. In exchange, Stern promised, he would borrow money from the bank—paying interest of course—and park an equal amount of capital in the mutual funds, where it would generate more fees for Bank of America. The letter also obliquely referred to late trading; Stern's lawyers highlighted a sentence in which Stern said that Canary planned "on transacting our trades . . . at a time of day that is a little bit earlier than Matt specified." "Matt," Brown learned, was Matt Augugliaro, a Bank of America official who had told Stern that they had set him up with an electronic trading platform that would process trades as late as 6:30 P.M.

The Spitzer team also learned from their growing pile of subpoenaed documents that Stern had hedged his bets another way. Market timing works best when the market is rising—then the "stale" prices are often lower than the fund's actual value. But a falling market brought dual risks for timers such as Stern—a short-term investment was more likely to lose value than gain, plus the "sticky assets" that he had to put up in order to get permission to engage in timing were often invested in lousy, money-losing funds. So Stern's team came up with a way to get around SEC rules that barred investors from selling mutual funds short, essentially allowing him to bet that the fund values would fall. Working with Bank of America's derivatives desk, the Canary team created baskets of stock and bond short positions that closely mirrored the holdings of the mutual funds that Stern was timing. Stern would park his sticky assets in the lousy funds and short the exact same investment, making that part of the deal completely market-neutral for him. He also would short the funds he was timing when he thought the value was more likely to fall than to rise. These "synthetic" baskets of stocks were only possible, the investigators learned, because Bank of America and other mutual funds would regularly update Canary on the changing portfolios of their mutual funds—information the general public only got to see twice a year.

When Eddie Stern finally showed up in Spitzer's office on August 5, he was a far cry from the confident son of privilege who had assured Harrington and Goodwin that they had nothing to fear from the regulators. Visibly nervous, Stern lingered in the doorway of the Investment Protection Bureau's twenty-third-floor conference room, as if resisting his lawyer's plan to have him come in and tell all. Much of the meeting was spent on background material. The investigators wanted to size up Stern and learn more about his Canary operation and its connection to the larger Stern financial empire. Eddie seemed reluctant to talk. When asked questions, he mumbled, looked down, and began to sweat. Naftalis had negotiated a "queen for a day" arrangement, which meant that nothing Stern said to Spitzer's team could be used against him in court unless he lied. But that didn't stop Brown and another lawyer from Spitzer's staff, Charles Caliendo, from asking the key question.

"Did you do late trading?" they pressed him.

"Yes," Stern replied, his body hunched over, his arms crossed across his chest with his hands cupping his elbows. The Canary traders had called such trading "nice insurance," he later acknowledged.

Stern did not initially behave like a man seeking to win a deal protecting him from legal action. "We felt as if we were having to dig stuff out of him," Brown remembered. "He was answering, but only if we asked the right questions. We thought, 'If you're trying to convince us you're going to be a great witness, you're going to have to work a lot harder.'"

By now, Spitzer was supervising the investigation personally because Eric Dinallo had taken a job at Morgan Stanley. Spitzer was reading the scholarly articles on market timing and keeping a stack of the hottest e-mails on his desk. One cache of e-mails from Strong Capital Management included correspondence from Stern in which he asked to double the size of his short-term timing bets and in exchange promised to double his investment in a high-fee Strong hedge fund. An e-mail from Richard Garland, the CEO of Janus International, read, "I have no interest in building a business around market timers but at the same time I do not want to turn away $10–$20m! How big is the [Canary] deal?" (Janus ultimately turned down that particular deal but approved others involving market timers.)

Though the evidence continued to mount, Spitzer and Brown sometimes felt dubious about the investigation. "There were moments over the summer where we thought, it's not real. The evidence of late trading or market timing would seem to fall apart," Spitzer remembered. And Brown kept worrying that there was some aspect of the market-timing deals that the Attorney General's Office had misunderstood. "I knew what we had was bad, but on the other hand I just couldn't believe it," he remembered. "I was so afraid we'd missed something." At one point, Spitzer even asked Marlene Turner, his executive assistant (who was herself a lawyer), to cold-call legendary investor Warren Buffett to ask for advice. Buffett not only took the call but referred Spitzer on to Jack Bogle, the semiretired founder of Vanguard Investments, who had built one of the nation's largest mutual fund companies by emphasizing low fees.

By mid-August, Spitzer had decided that the investigators needed to take the next step, and he asked Brown to write up their findings in the form of a civil fraud complaint. The Canary lawyers were still interested in hashing out a deal, but negotiations kept bogging down. Spitzer's already legendary radar for hot issues had spotted this one, and he wanted to move quickly. "This could be bigger than the research analysts," he observed to his deputy, Beth Golden. Charles Caliendo, the staff attorney who had helped interview Eddie Stern, focused on describing Stern's deals with a few particular brokers and fund companies, while Brown concentrated on explaining the concepts at the root of the alleged fraud. Their first efforts at a draft complaint flopped badly. Brown was convinced he had to explain the complicated financial principles behind market timing before he got to the more egregious problem of improper after-hours trading, and Caliendo was worried about their overemphasizing late trading because the language in the SEC rules about when trading of mutual funds had to stop was not completely clear. Spitzer intervened, urging them to "lead with the late trading," Brown remembered. The Investment Protection team also struggled to find a way to explain Stern's advantage in terms that ordinary people could understand. They toyed with comparing the scheme to "loaded dice" and "marked cards" but the one Spitzer liked was "betting on a horse race after the horses have crossed the finish line." Others in the office had doubts about that characterization; buying mutual fund shares after 4:00 P.M. increased Stern's ability to predict where the market was going, but it didn't guarantee a profit. In fact, Stern and Goodwin had told them that Canary had sometimes lost money on its after-hours trades, when even later events shifted the direction of the stock market. Rather than question Spitzer's choice, the staff added some wiggle room to their legal document. They chose not to assert that late trading was anything in particular, instead they wrote that it "can be analogized to betting today on yesterday's horse races."

Spitzer blessed the draft and then headed off to North Carolina for his annual family vacation on the Outer Banks. But a key question remained unanswered: Would the office be able to work out a deal with Stern before Spitzer got back and went public with what they had found? Stern and his lawyers wanted to settle, and Spitzer's team knew that their cases against the mutual fund companies, which they considered the primary target, would be far stronger if they had Stern as a cooperating witness. After a couple of rounds of hard haggling, the two sides agreed that Canary would make a total payment of forty million dollars—thirty million in restitution to investors in the mutual funds in which Canary had made improper trades and a ten-million-dollar penalty—and Spitzer would agree not to go after the investors who had profited from Canary's trades, including Stern's family and friends. "Eddie felt strongly that his investors shouldn't be hurt because they didn't know what he was doing," Naftalis said. But as the Labor Day weekend approached, the deal kept coming apart. Stern's lawyers wanted the settlement document to say that the money payment covered only their client's late trades and not his general market-timing activities, because they hoped to limit Stern's exposure to civil suits filed by mutual fund investors. But Brown wanted the settlement to make clear that both deceptive market timing and late trading were improper. The two sides also went round and round on smaller issues—as part of the deal, Stern was going to be banned from investing in mutual funds on behalf of nonrelatives, but the two sides disagreed on what constituted a family member. Efforts to resolve the issues were further complicated by the fact that both Spitzer and Naftalis were calling in from their respective beach vacations. "That was my one week of vacation, and I spent the entire time on the phone," Naftalis remembered.

At 7:38 P.M. on Friday, August 29, Caliendo e-mailed Eric Tirschwell, the junior defense lawyer who had been left minding the store, with one final demand: "We need your signature and your client's signature within 15 minutes." No reply. David Brown packed up his things and left for the weekend. On the subway, he sent a resigned e-mail to Spitzer and the senior staff: negotiations had broken down. "At that point I thought we were going to have to sue them," Brown remembered. "I thought that it was a good complaint and we could win."

Back at the office, the phone rang. Bruce Topman, who was working late and half-hoping that Stern's team would reconsider, rushed to pick up the phone. It was Tirschwell. "This is crazy. We aren't that far apart. Can't we get this back on track?" the defense lawyer said. Topman promised to do what he could. "I called Eliot and I told him that this was what the guy was willing to do. I conveyed to him that in the overall scheme of things . . . it was more important to get this done than to stick on these less important issues. If we could get the Stern settlement done, then when we went to the mutual funds, it would give us momentum and it would give us credibility to get the structural reforms," Topman remembered saying.

Down in North Carolina, Spitzer was watching the U.S. Open tennis tournament on television, and he sent word to the Canary defense team that if they couldn't work out a deal by the time the match finished, all bets were off. Finally, between ten and eleven o'clock, he and Naftalis were able to cut through the clutter—the settlement language about market timing versus late trading allowed Spitzer to claim that the settlement covered both but did not prevent Stern from arguing in civil cases that he was not liable for timing. Then another snag arose— the fax machine at Spitzer's beach house had broken down. He went down the street to a local deli. "They wondered who I was," Spitzer remembered, but they let him use the fax machine anyway. As a result, the settlement papers that sparked one of the biggest scandals in the history of the mutual fund industry were all stamped "Tommy's Market."

In the end, Spitzer's decision to cut a deal with Stern was heavily influenced by his experience in prior cases. The early apology from Merrill Lynch's CEO had helped push the rest of Wall Street to take Spitzer seriously. The gun industry's absolute refusal to accept responsibility for illegal gun violence had helped doom that initiative. Spitzer believed he would find it far easier to force broad-based change in the mutual fund world if a key participant was on record acknowledging that the status quo was wrong. Getting a settlement and cash penalty from Canary would instantly change the tone of the debate about late trading and market timing. As Spitzer remembered it, he weighed the costs and benefits like this: "Do we want to file the first case against him and Canary and litigate with them where they contest every issue where it might take a year and a half or do we want to settle with them in a way that allows us to blow the whole thing open? I chose the latter. You end up with an accepted base of facts that becomes the base from which you spring to other entities." Spitzer knew that a Stern deal would have a significant downside: by allowing Eddie to escape criminal sanctions and keep a significant portion of his trading profits, Spitzer would make it that much harder to exact tough penalties from other late traders and participants in the Canary scheme. The deal would also renew old criticisms that Spitzer was too quick to seek deals and unwilling to challenge really tough customers. Spitzer decided he didn't care. "When *The Wall Street Journal* complains about [my cases], 'they're all settlements or plea bargains,' well, 99 percent of the cases in the Manhattan D.A.'s office are plea bargains. That's the way the criminal justice system works and nobody complains about it unless [the defendant is] somebody who looks like" the editorial writers, Spitzer expounded.

But the challenges and criticisms would come later. Right now, he had a press conference to hold. "The full extent of this complicated fraud is not yet known," Spitzer told the cameras and reporters on Wednesday, September 3, before focusing anew on his core message that the markets must play fair with all investors, even the small ones. "But one thing is clear: The mutual-fund industry operates on a double standard. Certain companies and individuals have been given the opportunity to manipulate the system. . . . We will do our best to get funds back to those injured." The next question was: How?

7

TWO SETS OF RULES

THE NEWS THAT THE NEW YORK ATTORNEY GENERAL HAD UNCOVERED another financial scandal set off explosions across the country. Bank of America chairman Kenneth Lewis was on vacation in California when he learned that his company was being featured as a bad guy in Spitzer's televised press conference about the Canary settlement. On Wall Street, the stocks of the fund companies specifically mentioned by Spitzer began to fall. The shares of Janus Capital Group dropped more than 10 percent on September 3 and 4. Bank of America, which was more diversified, fell 4 percent. In Washington, Matthew Fink, the president of the Investment Company Institute, the powerful mutual fund lobbying group, immediately scrapped his plan to announce his retirement that week. As he watched Spitzer's masterful performance on television, he thought ruefully of an encounter he had with the New York attorney general just two weeks earlier, on a Washington tennis court. Spitzer had asked how the fund industry was doing, and Fink said that it was under scrutiny but holding up well. "Just wait," Spitzer replied with a smile. Congressman Richard Baker, who had tried just two months earlier to gut Spitzer's authority, now had words of praise for him. "We should all be outraged to learn about fraud like this, and I commend the attorney general for helping to shine a bright light on the murky world of mutual fund fees," said Baker, who was pushing his own mutual fund reforms.

The Canary probe hit with particular force across town at SEC headquarters. Despite the many months the commission staff had put into working side by side with Spitzer on the global research analyst settlement, letting him take much of the credit while they did much of the detail work, Spitzer had not even given them the courtesy of a heads-up call. Instead, Steve Cutler found himself back in the position where he had been in April 2002. He learned from the media that Spitzer was about to drop another bombshell squarely on the SEC's turf. Half an hour before the Canary press conference, Spitzer returned a phone call from Cutler. "Eliot, this is the worst day of my professional life," Cutler said. With a few hours' warning, the commission could have had inspectors on the doorstep of every major mutual fund. Instead they were being caught flatfooted again. "I really would have thought after all we've been through you would have said at some point, 'I've got this whistleblower; let's work the case together.'"

Spitzer professed not to see a problem. "Steve, this isn't a betrayal. This is the way the system works," he said. "Why should we call you before breaking a case you haven't been involved in?" Later he said that the thought of calling the SEC hadn't even crossed his mind. "If it had, I would have dismissed the thought," he said. "The FBI, in all my years as a state prosecutor, has never called us and said, 'Do you want to join us on a case we have investigated?' And we've never called them."

Still, Spitzer allowed, now that his team had broken the issue open, he would be glad to have the SEC's help. Edward Stern had given them the names of more than thirty fund companies that had allowed him or other market timers to cut deals to make short-term trades at the expense of the funds' longer-term investors; Stern had also fingered lots of other players—brokers, other market timers, and banks that financed this kind of predatory trading. Unlike the New York attorney general, the SEC had offices all over the country and the kind of manpower needed to tackle the entire industry. The commission also had the authority to write new rules to protect investors against late trading and market timing. As with the research analysts, Spitzer wanted to find the solution but he was more than happy to share the work of getting there. "We've done what we can do, which is to be a catalyst, to get the national entities to focus on the issue," he said. "Our value has been both recognizing and standing up and saying very loudly, 'Here is a problem.'"

Despite his personal feelings, Cutler was publicly magnanimous. The day after the Canary press conference, Cutler told a gaggle of reporters, "God bless Eliot Spitzer. He got a tip and pursued it. . . . This should not be a zero sum game." Privately, he agreed with Spitzer that they had to work together. "At the end of the day, what it's about is not turf or territory. It's about protecting the markets," Cutler explained. A few months earlier, he had warned the incoming SEC chairman William Donaldson not to get into a pitched battle with Spitzer, saying, "If you make Eliot the enemy, you are making yourself the enemy of the people because that's how Spitzer is portrayed, as the people's protector. You've got to find another way of dealing with him." Now Cutler took his own advice. Still, he couldn't help feeling "perplexed. . . . If the tables were turned I think I would have done it differently."

On September 4, Cutler and Lori Richards of the inspector's division sent a letter to the eighty-eight largest fund companies and thirty-four largest brokers, demanding that they turn over information about late trading, market timing, and any special deals they had cut with short-term traders. "Steve and I decided we wanted to do an industry-wide investigation to see how big and broad the problem really was," Richards remembered. The results proved that Spitzer had been on to something big: one-quarter of the brokers had helped clients improperly trade after hours, and employees at 10 percent of the fund companies knew that the late trades were happening. Half of the fund companies had secret deals allowing market timing, and 30 percent of the brokers had helped clients circumvent rules against the practice. Other whistle-blowers started to step forward. In Massachusetts, Bill Galvin's office got a call saying that the boilermakers union was market timing the Putnam Investments funds in its retirement plan. And Cutler got a personal phone call that blew open one of the most shocking cases of all.

The tipster, who has never been publicly identified, told the SEC enforcement director on September 8 that if the commission was serious about investigating market timing, "here's where you really want to focus." The caller mentioned Boston-based Putnam, the same firm that Galvin was investigating in connection with the boilermakers, but for an entirely different reason. "You really should be looking at Putnam and at the trading of their portfolio managers," the tipster said, alleging that some Putnam executives had engaged in market timing of the funds they managed. In other words, they had profited personally at the expense of the funds they were charged with running. "I called the head of our Boston office and said, 'Get on this immediately,'" Cutler remembered.

The SEC was off and running, and this time the commission and Spitzer planned to pay more than lip service to the idea of a joint investigation. Cutler and Spitzer agreed that they would work together on all of the cases that stemmed from Canary's trading. Initially, the main beneficiary was the SEC, because it could rely on the work Spitzer's lawyers had already done; later, Spitzer's small team would get credit for cases where the SEC had provided most of the manpower. On September 10, representatives of the SEC's New York office arrived at 120 Broadway for a get-acquainted meeting. Both sides were at once suspicious and determined to make nice. They began to divide up the fund companies and brokers that Stern had identified as possible targets, creating joint SEC–New York teams to work on each one. Many of the companies were headquartered far from New York, so the SEC staff planned to parcel out the cases to its regional offices. Mark Schonfeld, the head of enforcement at the New York office, would lead the SEC's side of the effort and be the main point of contact for the Spitzer team. The two sides also agreed to schedule joint debriefing sessions with Eddie Stern so that Spitzer's cooperator could bring the SEC up to speed on everything he knew about their targets.

With things going so swimmingly with the SEC, Spitzer made little effort to work with the other states, at least at first. Christine Bruenn, the Maine securities regulator who had represented the states on the research analyst task force, said that this caused "hard feelings" among some of the other state securities regulators, who had expected Spitzer to adopt the same sort of task force approach he had tried after his Merrill Lynch case. Spitzer was intent on pressing forward and didn't really want to spend the time bringing other regulators up to speed. After particular state officials complained, Spitzer and the SEC invited them to participate in their local cases—Wisconsin worked on Strong Investments, Colorado was involved in Janus—but New York and the SEC shied away from big group efforts wherever possible.

In mid-September, Spitzer decided it was time to add a new ingredient to the mix: criminal charges. For the first time since he had ventured into the world of Wall Street, he decided he would try to put someone in jail. Spitzer's target was Ted Sihpol, the Bank of America broker who had helped Stern put through after-hours trades by preparing and time-stamping order tickets for "proposed" orders before 4:00 P.M. and then waiting for Canary traders to tell him—after the market closed—whether to submit or discard the orders. Spitzer didn't initially alert the SEC to his plans, but when Cutler pressed him a few days after the big summit meeting, Spitzer let him in on the secret. The New York attorney general had a good reason for inviting the SEC to join his case. The SEC rules specifying the cut-off time for same-day mutual fund trades were somewhat fuzzy, and criminal cases have higher standards of proof than civil actions. Spitzer knew his case would look stronger if he had the SEC on record saying that late trading was illegal. If Cutler's team could throw together a complaint over the weekend, Spitzer said, they could do a joint press conference. The SEC lawyers assigned to the fund probe were stunned. It was only a week after the Canary filing and they were just getting started. What was the hurry? But Spitzer wouldn't budge. He wanted to build up the pressure for systemic change, and to do that, the investigation had to stay in the headlines. New charges had to be brought. So Schonfeld got down to work and banged out a civil fraud complaint, and the five SEC commissioners approved the action late Monday night. On Tuesday, September 16, Cutler stood shoulder to shoulder with Spitzer at a New York news conference announcing their first joint action against late trading. Spitzer promised there would be more to come. "This is an investigation with an ever-widening reach," he said. As always, Cutler was more circumspect: "Whether it is the tip of the iceberg or the entire iceberg, the conduct alleged today is serious," he said.

The Sihpol case would take years, but the pattern it established would be repeated over and over in the fund probe. Spitzer would decide that the investigation was flagging, that the public needed to learn more about the abuses or see more tangible results. His office would then rush to complete a new complaint or demand a settlement from one of its targets, forcing the SEC staff to choose between pushing the commissioners (ostensibly their bosses) to move faster than usual, or being left in Spitzer's dust. Even worse, Spitzer wanted to announce each deal as soon as both sides had agreed to a broad outline of an agreement, known as a term sheet—lest news of the settlement leak or the company try to put its own spin on the deal. That practice caused trouble between the SEC staff and some of the commissioners because it meant that deals were being announced before the commissioners had had a chance to vote on them. As the months wore on, the process became ever more galling to the SEC staff because they felt they were doing much of the substantive work on the later cases—sorting through documents, interviewing fund officials and traders, and in some cases writing the settlement documents.

Defense lawyers and Spitzer's team agreed that the two agencies had radically different approaches to the mutual fund investigations. The Spitzer folks routinely required the fund companies to produce annotated binders that listed all of their arrangements with market timers and then highlighted which e-mails were related to which arrangement. The SEC teams wanted the binders too, but they would also ask for a broader swath of documents and do their own sorting and searching. One mutual fund defense lawyer said the contrast between the Spitzer lawyers and the SEC was startling. The Spitzer team "made us do all the work. You find the documents, you explain it to us. Then they would ask, 'What was that thing you told us was important last week?'" the lawyer said. "We would produce boxes and boxes and we would hear from our couriers that they were just stacking them on top of the unopened boxes from three weeks ago. The SEC was actually reviewing the documents and asking the intelligent questions." Yet when time came to settle that particular case, the Spitzer people drove the train, making most of the demands and setting the schedule.

To some defense lawyers, the Spitzer team appeared lazy, and their ultimatums came dangerously close to being unconstitutional demands for self-incrimination. The office, like most regulators, gave extra credit for cooperation, and many of Spitzer's targets felt—correctly or not—that they had to help build a civil case against themselves or face the crippling possibility of a criminal indictment. "Often because the indictment itself would have such a devastating effect, you have to forfeit a worthy defense," said Stanley S. Arkin, a prominent member of the defense bar who tangled with Spitzer during the investigation of the Strong funds.

Spitzer and his deputies viewed the matter quite differently. With fewer than a dozen lawyers assigned to the mutual fund cases, the office freely admitted that it didn't have the manpower to investigate every allegation in every case. But they believed that they did the heavy lifting when the case called for it. "We only have the leverage that we have because of the hard work and accuracy of our cases," said David Brown, who was promoted to head the Investment Protection Bureau in the middle of the mutual fund investigation. "We have been right 100 percent of the time." Since the SEC's regional offices had gotten involved, and many of the fund companies were eager to cooperate and settle as quickly as possible, why not let the defense lawyers and the federal investigators do much of the work? A lifetime of defense work had taught Brown that most of the companies were doing internal investigations and collecting damaging documents for their own purposes, so why shouldn't the regulators and prosecutors benefit from work that was being done? "I've called people [on the defense side] and said, 'I want the written market-timing agreements. I know there are written agreements, and you are probably holding them right now,'" Brown remembered. "Then there's this long dead pause."

Spitzer acknowledged that defense concerns about forced self-incrimination were legitimate, but he argued that prosecutors had been requiring companies accused of wrongdoing to investigate themselves for years. On the federal level, the Justice Department had refined "required cooperation" to an art form, spelling out in a January 2003 memo by Deputy Attorney General Larry Thompson exactly what companies had to do to get in good with federal prosecutors. "This is the reality of the white-collar world for the past decade. I didn't invent it," Spitzer said. "There's a very legitimate long-term corrosive effect we have to worry about . . . but there's balance that has to be struck. Government could never do these investigations in a timely manner."

Eager to keep the momentum going after Sihpol's arrest, Spitzer and his team jumped quickly on reports from Millennium Partners LP that one of its hedge fund executives, Steven B. Markovitz, had placed numerous trades after 4:00 P.M. as part of his efforts to market time international mutual funds. The evidence against Markovitz was in many ways stronger than the case against Sihpol. Months before Spitzer's Canary case, Markovitz had been told by his bosses at Millennium to stop trading after hours and had been advised by the company's general counsel that the practice should be avoided because it could be considered illegal. But when Spitzer sent Millennium a subpoena, Markovitz acknowledged to the firm's general counsel and an outside lawyer for the company that he had "fallen off the wagon" and started trading after hours again. Under pressure to produce results, the lawyers in Spitzer's criminal division gave Markovitz less than twenty-four hours to plead guilty. If he didn't, they said they would arrest him at home in front of his child and pregnant wife. The trader quickly opted for cooperation, pleading guilty on October 2 to violating the Martin Act, a Class E felony. Once Spitzer had another scalp, the office seemed to lose interest. Although the SEC barred him from the securities industry and imposed a two-hundred-thousand-dollar penalty, more than two years later Markovitz still had not been sentenced. (Millennium, its founder, and several top executives would agree in late 2005 to adopt reforms and pay $180 million in restitution.)

Fear was sweeping the securities industry. Spitzer had promised a wide-ranging investigation and now he was coming through. Every day, it seemed, new firms were announcing employee suspensions and revealing that they had uncovered secret market-timing deals or after-hours trades. At Fred Alger & Company, a fund company that had done deals with a market-timing hedge fund called Veras Investment Partners, chief mutual fund officer James P. Connelly, Jr., panicked and directed employees to begin destroying e-mails about late trading even though he knew the firm was under subpoena. He also coached subordinates to lie to internal investigators. As a result, Alger told Spitzer's office—incorrectly—that they had no records relating to late trading. When the investigators learned the truth, they wanted to see Connelly immediately. The Alger executive compounded his problems by being less than forthcoming with investigators. Then, in the cab ride back to the office, he broke down and cried. On October 16, Connelly pleaded guilty to tampering with physical evidence, paid a four-hundred-thousand-dollar penalty, and was barred from the securities industry for life. After a heartbreaking hearing in which Connelly's attorney, Alan Vinegrad, described the fund executive's bond with his severely disabled daughter and his work rebuilding Alger after much of its top staff perished in the September 11 terrorist attacks, Connelly was sentenced to one to three years in prison.

Unlike Spitzer's other targets, Sihpol was still refusing to fold. A mid-level player who had already been forced out of the industry, he had little to lose and much to gain by fighting the criminal charges. Spitzer said he offered the former broker a deal—plead guilty to a Class D felony, which carries up to three years in prison, and leave the actual sentence up to a judge. Sihpol's lawyers turned him down. They wanted a guarantee of no jail time. Spitzer said no thanks. "We had people who had pled guilty who were sentenced to jail time. There is a horizontal equity issue," he remembered. The case would drag on for years. "Maybe I should have taken the deal," Spitzer said.

By late October 2003, the SEC had a host of mutual fund initiatives under way, including plans for industry-wide rules that would make it harder to engage in late trading and market timing. Cutler's Enforcement Division was ready to bring its Putnam case. After some false starts, they managed to coordinate their work with Massachusetts officials and, on October 28, bring a joint federal-state action against the firm's portfolio managers. The charges proved to be the sexiest yet: Putnam knew that two portfolio managers had profited from hundreds of short-term trades in the funds they managed yet had done little to stop them, the regulators alleged. Suddenly everyone was talking about the SEC and Galvin, rather than about Eliot Spitzer.

As was his wont, Spitzer immediately grabbed the spotlight back. Putnam might have troubles with misbehaving portfolio managers, he told the media on October 29, but his investigators had uncovered "one of the most scurrilous tales I've seen yet. . . . If you want proof that there were two sets of rules—one for the powerful and one for the small guy—this is it." Richard Strong, the CEO of Strong Capital Management and the chairman of the Strong funds' boards, had been timing his own funds, Spitzer revealed. Giving an interview about a pending investigation was, to put it mildly, an unorthodox step. Spitzer's Criminal Division had already opened a grand jury probe of Strong, and prosecutors are legally required to keep grand jury proceedings confidential. Spitzer's comments and revelations came very close to breaking that rule. He followed up by lashing out publicly at the SEC with language that his erstwhile allies found uncomfortably personal. "Heads should roll," he told *The New York Times*. "There is a whole division at the SEC that is supposed to be looking at mutual funds. Where have they been?" The news about Strong combined with the sharp criticism of the SEC swung attention back to Spitzer's efforts to expose conflicts of interest in the fund industry. But the contretemps also deepened his reputation for self-aggrandizement and calculated leaking when publicity suited his purpose. "I thought that the use of the public bludgeon was something that a public prosecutor should never do prior to the action of a grand jury, and [was] just generally extremely unfair," remembered Richard Strong's lawyer Stanley Arkin. Spitzer said later that he was simply talking tough to cut through what he saw as deceptive rhetoric. "It's speaking to the public in a manner they understand," he said. "You get the message through. I'm not going to apologize for that."

Amid all the discussion about late trading, market timing, and leaking, Spitzer didn't forget the issue that had originally gotten him and David Brown interested in the mutual fund world: high fees. Market timing and late trading were shocking and did cut into investors' returns, but academic studies suggested that their impact was relatively small, perhaps hundredths of a percentage point a year, while fees could be as high as 2 percent a year. "I'll be damned if I'm going to come this far and not get lower fees," Brown remembered saying to Spitzer during a mid-fall conversation. "The fees are where the real money is and where the real consumer harm is."

"Absolutely," Spitzer replied. So when he was invited to Capitol Hill to testify before both the Senate and the House about the scandal in early November, Spitzer seized the opportunity to rail about high fees. Referring to his market-timing cases as "low-hanging fruit," Spitzer told Richard Baker's subcommittee that investors were suffering "enormous losses" because of high fees, and he urged the subcommittee to tackle that issue as well. "Your efforts here today are critically, critically important," he said. "We are not adequately protecting the tens of millions of Americans, whom we have invited into the marketplace and whose capital we desperately want to see flowing into the marketplace."

When Spitzer tried to make the same point the next day in front of the Senate, he all but lost his audience, according to Bill Galvin, the Massachusetts regulator who sat with him on the panel. "While we were still describing to the Senate the fundamental nature of the problem of market timing, Eliot was already onto the remedy. He was off on basis points and fee reduction," Galvin remembered. "He was working himself up and getting more and more detailed and talking faster and faster. I finally gave him a little elbow in his ribs, [and whispered] 'I don't think they're following you.'" (Spitzer said he didn't recall the exchange.)

Still, Spitzer felt he had thrown down the gauntlet and made clear that he felt lower fees had to be part of any solution to the market-timing problem. He even made public data that he said showed that Putnam charged its large institutional customers significantly less than small investors for similar services. So he was absolutely outraged two weeks later when the SEC worked out a partial settlement with Putnam Investments that made no mention of the fee issue. Cutler and

Peter Bresnan, the newly installed head of the SEC's Boston office, had taken a page out of Spitzer's own book and not consulted him in advance on their negotiations with Putnam. When Spitzer complained, Cutler told him, "Look, I couldn't. It wasn't your case." The SEC had also approached the negotiations differently than Spitzer would have. The New York attorney general usually viewed his first settlement strategically, seeing it as setting down a marker for the rest of a given industry. He preferred to demand big cash settlements up front. Cutler and Bresnan had instead opted for a deal in which Putnam agreed to make quick institutional reforms and leave until later the thorny question of how big a penalty the firm would pay. "This is not intended to be an industry template, and it includes very serious relief for investors for all the problems alleged in the complaint. The relief we are getting, we are getting now, and we haven't given up anything," Cutler said when the deal was announced. As for the money, the settlement "left the money open because the damages weren't clear at that point," he remembered later.

Spitzer wasted no time before going on the attack. "I am disappointed that this happened. This document is not a settlement with me," he told *The Washington Post*. "It does not address the most fundamental issue, which is, how do you control fees?" A day later, he moved on from the agreement to the people who had negotiated it, saying he "wouldn't let them handle a house closing." SEC officials were understandably furious. Putnam was their case, not Spitzer's, and they felt confident they would eventually win ample restitution for investors. (Putnam agreed in April 2004 to pay $110 million in penalties and restitution.) In the meantime, the Boston-based fund company was in serious financial trouble and was promising to install what the SEC considered meaningful institutional safeguards to protect investors from future problems. As for the fee question, to the SEC the two issues seemed like apples and oranges. This was a settlement about improper market timing. If Putnam's fees were too high, that was something that should be addressed separately.

As with many of Spitzer's spats with SEC officials, the fight stemmed largely from their different perspectives. As Spitzer ruefully observed in a speech to the SEC Historical Society, the SEC "has the capacity to issue rules. We don't, even though that may surprise people. We know we don't and, therefore, we are only left with the option of sort of crafting changes in the form of injunctive relief in the form of settlements." To him, the SEC's deal with Putnam seemed to be a wasted opportunity. The SEC officials had more options. If they uncovered broad problems in the fund industry, they could address them by writing new rules. For example, both Spitzer and SEC chairman Bill Donaldson believed that the chairmen of fund boards should be independent of fund management companies. Spitzer made independent chairs part of his settlement demands from the firms that had engaged in market timing. Donaldson and two other commissioners pushed through a rule that affected the entire industry.

What made the Putnam disagreement stand out was the bitterness of Spitzer's criticisms at a time when the state and national regulators had appeared to be working well together. "They believe you put a little Band-Aid on it and they're done," Spitzer complained. He acknowledged later that his choice of words, particularly the "house closing" remark, had been less than politic. "It was gratuitous," he admitted. "It was probably not the smartest thing to say. But it was fun." To Spitzer, the harsh words were simply the way he played the game. After all, he was raised by parents who fought such pitched intellectual battles that their children joked about hiding under the furniture. But Spitzer's penchant for angry rhetoric put a strain on the relationship between the attorney general's staff and the SEC. After the "house closing" remarks, the SEC's Mark Schonfeld told Peter Pope, who by now was handling the criminal side of Spitzer's cases, that the attacks were undermining efforts to get the SEC and the Attorney General's Office to work as a team. Relations never broke down entirely, and David Brown went out of his way to call and tell Schonfeld he had "the highest regard for you." But Spitzer's attacks left a bitter taste in the mouths of many federal regulators.

Spitzer's comments also irked some Democratic Party elders, who worried that his attacks were undermining the authority of the SEC at a time when investors needed reassurance. The last thing the party wanted was to have one of its rising stars tarred as an antigovernment populist. When Spitzer returned to Capitol Hill on November 20 to testify for a third time about the scandal, Senator Paul Sarbanes of Maryland and Senator Christopher Dodd of Connecticut, both Democrats, gently cautioned him to stop picking fights with the SEC. After praising Spitzer's work uncovering the mutual fund scandal as "diligent" and "critical," Dodd went on to say, "I would also be remiss if I didn't express some concern over the seemingly lack of coordination. . . . While I do not doubt that both the SEC and the state enforcement officials have the best interests of investors in mind, I would urge all the parties to work in a more complementary fashion in order to fight securities fraud and abuse in our nation." Spitzer responded politely but was unbowed. "My office and the SEC have worked together cooperatively since the day I announced the settlement with the Canary hedge fund. Each day since then there have been, and will continue to be, dozens of points of contact, coordination and cooperation. On rare occasions, we have disagreed," he said. "I will continue to speak up for investors when necessary."

In truth, the agencies were coordinating well. As if to punctuate that point, Spitzer and the SEC unveiled another joint case that day. This one was the first in the scandal to target a company's top executives: Gary Pilgrim and Harold Baxter, who had founded the high-flying fund company Pilgrim Baxter & Associates. According to the legal documents, Pilgrim, the firm president, had personally profited from a hedge fund that engaged in market timing of the mutual fund he managed, while Baxter, the CEO, had shared secret portfolio information with a friend who was a broker, who in turn passed it on to Eddie Stern. Baxter also allowed the broker's clients—Stern among them—to market time his firm's funds. Spitzer told *The Washington Post* he wanted the firm to return all the management fees it had earned on the funds that were being used for market timing. "You don't cheat people who have trusted you with their money," he said.

In early December, Alliance Capital showed Spitzer and Brown the way to the fee cuts they had been seeking. Known in the industry for having higher-than-average fees, Alliance was particularly vulnerable to Spitzer's pressure for reductions. Its management was in turmoil, and many of its big institutional customers, such as pension funds, were talking about pulling their money out because of the market-timing scandal. The evidence against the firm was also particularly bad—an e-mail sent to the firm's president and the vice chairman of its board made clear that Alliance was allowing a Las Vegas–based investor to market time its mutual funds in exchange for a promise to park fifty-one million dollars in its high-fee hedge funds. "Bruce Calvert is okay with this," the January 2002 e-mail said, referring to Alliance's chairman. A delegation of the firm's outside lawyers came to Brown with a proposal. "It is our intention to settle this . . . and as part of our settlement we would offer a reduction in fees," Brown remembered them saying. "For me, it was really significant that our first settlement was big, that it involved a big company, and that it involved fee reductions. It was great for consumers. It was a great 'do good' moment." While sitting in the meeting, Brown used his BlackBerry to e-mail Spitzer that the company had "something big" to discuss, and then told his boss of the firm's offer. "Fees, fees, fees—that's the big money," Spitzer crowed in response, according to a *Wall Street Journal* reporter who happened to be present. "When we have a company in this position, we shouldn't give up our leverage to negotiate about the issue that's the 800-pound gorilla."

Within weeks, Alliance had agreed to pay $200 million in penalties and restitution for the market timing and to cut fees by 20 percent for each of the next five years—a concession Spitzer valued at $350 million. But when Cutler and Schonfeld took the offer to the five SEC commissioners, they turned it down. The problems with Spitzer's approach were twofold, the commissioners said: mandating fee cuts came far too close to imposing price controls, and the measure would benefit Alliance's present and future investors, not the ones that had been hurt by the past market timing. "We believe that any monetary benefits of a law enforcement settlement should go to the victims of the misconduct," Donaldson said at the time. "The SEC should not serve as a fee setter." Cutler took the bad news back to Alliance. The fee cuts "are valueless to the commission, and in light of this we don't think this is a high enough number" for a possible cash payment, he told the company's lawyers.

Spitzer had no such qualms because he did not believe the fees had been set by a fair market process in the first place. By now, he was firmly committed to a legal philosophy that reconciled his simultaneous support of free markets and strong government regulation. He and Andrew Celli would explain it in *The New Republic* a few months later, by hearkening back to the great reforms of the Progressive Era: "Our commitment to market capitalism cannot obscure one glaring and immutable fact: that, in a number of important ways, an unregulated market does not safeguard certain core American values. That's why our government—with broad bipartisan support—has instituted child-labor laws, minimum wage laws, anti-discrimination laws, and certain safety net protections designed to ensure that people do not fall below a basic level of sustenance." In Spitzer's view, using government pressure to force down mutual fund fees fit right into that grand tradition.

In the end, Alliance gave both the SEC and Spitzer what they wanted. New York got $350 million in fee cuts over five years, and the company sweetened the cash payment by $50 million, to $250 million, all of which would go to the investors who had been harmed by the market timing. Alliance officials said they intended to go public with the settlement news immediately. But Donaldson and the other commissioners hadn't yet approved the deal. Spitzer wondered whether he should try to stop Alliance from talking, but Cutler urged caution, saying, "You don't want to be in the position of telling the shareholders of a public company, 'It was me that prevented you from getting information.'" So Spitzer pushed the SEC instead, telling reporters about his deal with Alliance shortly before the commissioners took their vote. "This deal will show that when a mutual fund has failed to look out for its investors, the payments back to shareholders will be enormous, the structural changes will be significant, and fee reductions can play a part," Spitzer told *The Washington Post*. The SEC commissioners kept the turf battle going by including an unusual one-page explanatory statement with the customary press release that reiterated their unanimous opposition to imposing fee cuts as part of market-timing settlements.

* * *

Other settlements and enforcement actions quickly followed: Massachusetts Financial Services (MFS) paid up in early February, offering fee reductions to Spitzer and cash for investors to please him and the SEC. Bank of America and FleetBoston did the same, just in the nick of time before their slated March 2004 merger. That $675 million deal, the largest settlement in the entire fund investigation, saw Spitzer try another new and controversial tactic. Still convinced that the lack of strong-willed independent directors was at the root of most mutual fund problems, he decided to make an example of eight Bank of America directors. Unlike the boards of most funds involved in the scandal, the Bank of America fund board had actually been briefed on market timing and had not objected to the company's plan to exempt a large investor from a general crackdown on predatory trading. Spitzer decided that the board had to go. "These directors clearly failed to protect the interest of investors," Spitzer said as the deal was announced. "They acknowledged the problem of market timing but then allowed a favored client to engage in that harmful practice. The departure of these board members should sound an alarm for all those who serve in similar capacities."

There was only one problem—Bank of America believed Spitzer had overstated his accomplishments. Mutual fund directors are legally independent of the management company. On paper, there was no way Bank of America could force them out. Though Spitzer and his staff insisted they had a deal, officially the company had promised only to "use its best efforts" to encourage the board to adopt various new governance rules, including a ten-year term limit for board members that would have the effect of forcing the retirement of the directors Spitzer wanted gone. The agreement caught the directors by surprise, and some of them were so angered by Spitzer's triumphant comments that they vowed to fight him. The revolt eventually fizzled, but it left hard feelings in the mutual fund community, particularly among directors who believed it was unfair for Spitzer to criticize them for being insufficiently independent and then demand that fund companies treat them as if they weren't independent at all.

By the spring of 2004, the SEC staff was thoroughly sick of Spitzer's breakneck pace and his practice of announcing deals before they were finalized. Not only did the commissioners disagree with his demands for fee reductions, but they remained uncomfortable with publicizing settlements on the basis of a one-page term sheet. Finally, with Donaldson's blessing, the staff quit trying to keep up. The commissioners figured there was little to be gained from sacrificing the deliberate process that they had historically followed. "We kept trying to cooperate. Eliot had made a large contribution. But after a while we decided, let him go ahead," Commissioner Harvey Goldschmid remembered. In April, Spitzer's office and Colorado state officials hammered out a deal with Denver-based Janus Capital Management over market-timing issues. The Colorado attorney general, who was running for the U.S. Senate, wanted to announce the deal immediately. The SEC staff agreed in private that they would accept the same terms—fifty million dollars in restitution and fifty million in civil penalties—but the commissioners refused to play along. They waited nearly four months—until all the papers were drafted—to announce a formal settlement.

While most of the mutual fund companies were stumbling over one another to reach quick settlements with the New York Attorney General's Office, Spitzer faced a far thornier issue in May 2004. Richard Strong and his Wisconsin-based management company were nearly legendary in the fund world. Strong had spent twenty-nine years building a mutual fund empire by focusing on details and customer service. Obsessive about little things, the self-described "six foot three inch farm boy from the wheat fields of North Dakota" insisted that the screws on the light-switch plates at the firm's lavish Menomonee Falls headquarters be aligned vertically, so they wouldn't catch dust. Employees had to pull their cars into parking spots front end first, lest the fumes from their tailpipes stain the garage walls. Viewing his firm as the Nordstrom's of the fund world, Strong instituted the industry's first toll-free 800 lines for investors and later had the company's customer-service computer system programmed to display news headlines from the caller's hometown so that the Strong staffers could make small talk with callers.

To Spitzer's investigators, the firm had initially seemed little different from the other companies that had done business with Canary. Over the summer of 2003, the fund company acknowledged that it had had dealings with Canary and it sent to New York what it said were the relevant documents. After Spitzer's initial mutual fund press conference on September 3 of that year, Richard Strong had sent a personal letter to investors saying that the investigation had come as a "surprise. . . . We can assure you we are turning over every rock at our firm as part of a comprehensive review." But then things started to get weird. When the SEC arrived on September 5 to do an inspection and demanded a list of everyone who had been timing the fund, Strong's management seemed less than forthcoming. A full month later, during a conference call with David Brown, the firm revealed that it had hired new lawyers from the prestigious New York firm of Sullivan and Cromwell, and they had something important to say. "There's another thing you should be aware of," the new defense attorneys said. "Mr. Strong had engaged in a certain amount of trading of his own money in the Strong Funds."

Brown hit the mute button and marveled to a colleague: "He timed his own fucking fund." Soon Peter Pope's Criminal Division had convened a grand jury to investigate whether criminal charges were warranted against Richard Strong. The evidence, as it trickled in, put Spitzer in a serious dilemma. As a fund board chairman, Strong had a fiduciary duty to look after the interests of investors, yet he had engaged in an extraordinary amount of market timing. He had made 1,400 trades over five years, including more than one million dollars in roundtrip trades in 2000, a year when the Strong funds banned nearly 150 customers for similar activities. The firm had also been less than totally cooperative—it had not only waited all summer and part of the fall before telling Brown about Strong's personal trading but had also failed to turn over a crucial piece of evidence, a document that tended to show that Strong knew that what he was doing was wrong. Pope learned of this document only by chance, when another Strong executive mentioned that the company's general counsel had sent an e-mail to all Strong employees in February 1999 warning them that anyone who engaged in market timing would have his or her trading privileges restricted.

Yet Spitzer had always differentiated publicly between late trading, which he considered clearly illegal, and market timing, which could harm investors but was not obviously against the rules. The office had never brought a criminal case based on market timing and it was not clear that Richard Strong was the right place to start. Fabulously wealthy (he was worth an estimated eight hundred million dollars), Strong had hired a skilled and aggressive defense lawyer, Stanley Arkin, who made clear he would fight every issue tooth and nail. For starters, Arkin told Spitzer's office that he would challenge Spitzer's jurisdiction over trades placed by a Wisconsin resident in mutual funds based in Wisconsin. Arkin warned Spitzer that he would have to test his theories in a Wisconsin court, which likely would be less tolerant of the New Yorker's aggressive definition of fraud. A loss in Wisconsin could hamper all kinds of other cases, Spitzer knew. There was also a question of fair notice. Before Spitzer brought the Canary case, no one had ever alleged that market timing was illegal, let alone criminal. "When you get right down to it, Dick Strong didn't do anything terrible. He didn't steal anybody's money," Arkin said. "A criminal indictment would have been an extremely unjust and bad decision."

As had been his habit since his days in the Manhattan DA's Office, Spitzer began thinking about the best way to turn a potentially difficult individual case into another victory for structural change. Was there a way, short of criminal prosecution, to use the Strong case to make the point that fund directors and officers should not and could not engage in personal trading that hurt their investors? After a series of tough negotiating sessions, Arkin and Pope hit on a compromise proposal: Strong would get out of the business by selling his funds to Wells Fargo, pay a substantial fine, and issue a "statement of contrition" for his behavior, much as Merrill Lynch's David Komansky had apologized for Henry Blodget's e-mails. To Arkin, the proposal made sense. "What [Spitzer] always needed was some validation of what he was doing," the lawyer said. To avoid an indictment, "It's not such a costly price to pay."

For Spitzer, the decision was a tough one. One of the biggest criticisms he had faced was that he settled too easily with powerful targets. Lawyers for investors, such as Jake Zamansky, were bitter that Jack Grubman and Sandy Weill had escaped criminal prosecution for the 92nd Street Y issue. At the other end of the spectrum, supporters of Bank of America broker Ted Sihpol were complaining publicly that Sihpol was being scapegoated while his superiors had escaped scot-free. Even former New York attorney general Dennis Vacco had joined the criticism, writing in *The Wall Street Journal* that his successor's "aggressive application of the Martin Act" was "questionable" because he was focusing on "prosecutions—especially against low-level employees to the exclusion of high-ranking executives—[that] are undertaken on an obscure if not tenuous legal theory." If Spitzer agreed to give Strong a pass in exchange for a monetary settlement, he would only be stoking the fire. But what if he brought a criminal case against Strong and the evidence didn't convince a jury? "These cases are very tough," Spitzer said. "Proof beyond a reasonable doubt is very very difficult. It's supposed to be difficult." In the end, he went for the structural solution, as he almost always did, and endorsed the compromise that Arkin and Pope had worked out. Richard Strong ended up paying $60 million personally, and his fund company kicked in another $115 million in penalties, restitution, and fee reductions. "You try and weigh and balance. My judgment was we could get what we wanted through the civil settlement," Spitzer said. "At the end of the day, when there's a decision people are going to criticize, I'll take the blame."

8

SIMPLY TOO MUCH

ELIOT SPITZER WAS SOMBER AS HE STRODE TO THE MICROPHONE ON MONDAY, May 24, 2004. Normally, when he faced the lights in his office's packed press conference room, he was excited about blowing the lid off a scandal or pleased to be announcing a settlement that would bring relief to people he was charged with protecting. But on this day, he was taking on an old friend and starting what was likely to be a protracted and bitter fight. The issue was "outsized CEO compensation packages," he explained. The target was Spitzer's erstwhile ally Richard A. Grasso, the former chairman of the New York Stock Exchange. Months earlier, a public outcry had arisen when it became known that Grasso had amassed a $139.5-million retirement package while heading the NYSE, a not-for-profit organization that regulated Wall Street and set corporate governance standards for public companies.

Spitzer made clear up front that the attack wasn't personal. "The New York Stock Exchange is the issue we address specifically today," he announced. "There is a much larger problem that should be dealt with. . . . The interrelationship among CEOs and comp [i.e., compensation] committees and comp consultants is one that is unsavory; it is one that is evidenced by misinformation, flawed information and self-dealing." Then he moved on to the specifics. He had not asked for this case. Months earlier, the NYSE board had ousted Grasso on its own in order to tamp down the furor over his compensation package. The directors had then asked Spitzer to help get the retirement money back. Spitzer was not stepping on anyone's toes this time. Under New York law, only the attorney general was empowered to enforce a state law that set limits on compensation at not-for-profits, including the Big Board. It was a case, Spitzer believed, that had to be brought. "Compensation must be commensurate with services rendered," he said. "You can't pay the head of a not-for-profit that much money, close to two hundred million dollars. It's simply too much. It's not reasonable. It's not right."

A day later, Grasso fired back. Grasso had devoted thirty-six years to the NYSE, rising from an eighty-one-dollar-a-week clerical position to chief executive. In 2001, Grasso had been lionized as an international hero for reopening the Exchange just six days after the attack on the World Trade Center. Known for a garrulous, back-slapping style that concealed an iron fist, he was the quintessential outsider—a Queens-born college dropout—who was equally at home at both the top and the bottom of New York's clubby financial world. Grasso not only moved comfortably among the boys-will-be-boys floor traders, but he also was extraordinarily adept at persuading multimillionaires and tech innovators to list their companies on the NYSE and donate to the causes that he supported. Now that he was unemployed and had been publicly vilified for the size of his retirement package, he had nothing to lose. "New York Attorney General Eliot Spitzer's decision to intervene in a commercial dispute between the New York Stock Exchange and me over my compensation and retirement benefits smacks of politics," Grasso wrote in a *Wall Street Journal* op-ed piece. "My vindication will come in a courtroom." Many on Wall Street and in the media licked their chops. Finally, someone was standing up to Spitzer, and that someone had a reputation for street-fighting that surpassed Spitzer's own. This was going to be a long, drawn-out, bloody battle. Spitzer didn't care. "I like it when people push back. It's what I would do," he said a few days after the press conference. "I'm ready for a good fight."

It was a remarkable turn for two men who less than two years earlier had forged a crucial alliance to get the global research analyst settlement done. Grasso's intervention in 2002 had helped convince Harvey Pitt and the SEC that they had to work with Spitzer rather than compete with him. Grasso and the NYSE had also provided the setting for many of the crucial negotiations and for the headline-making press conference when the settlement was announced in December 2002. At that event, Spitzer had made a point of praising the Big Board chairman, effusively referring to him as "a consummate diplomat" and "a great chooser of restaurants. My only regret is . . . I may need to find another excuse for us to have dinner together, Dick."

But the relationship started to sour four months later. On March 21, 2003, the NYSE announced that it was nominating Citigroup chairman Sandy Weill to sit on its board of directors, despite all the evidence that had come out about Citigroup's stock analyst problems. Furthermore, Weill would not take one of the twelve spots on the board reserved for the Stock Exchange's member firms but rather would be considered a representative of "the public." The Exchange argued that Weill's nomination was appropriate because the majority of Citigroup's revenue came from sources other than stock and bond trading, and experts noted that William Harrison, who headed JPMorgan Chase, another big bank caught up in the research scandal, had been a public representative since the summer of 2001. But to Wall Street critics, the choice was patently absurd. Not only had Citigroup agreed to pay the single largest penalty in the global settlement, four hundred million dollars, but Weill had been personally investigated for his possible influence on Jack Grubman's reports on AT&T. Furthermore, one of the NYSE directors being replaced by this round of nominations was a former subordinate of Weill's—Michael Carpenter, the ousted head of Citigroup's Salomon Smith Barney unit—who had served as an industry representative. The nomination was such a stretch that even some board members questioned the choice when Grasso briefed them on it, asking whether it was "the right time" for such a selection.

Spitzer read about Weill's nomination as his family was waiting for the elevator en route to catch a cab to the airport for the annual family ski vacation in Colorado. Instantly "apoplectic," he handed the article to his wife, Silda. "You read this," he said, asking for a second opinion.

She scanned the article and said, "This is nuts." Spitzer pulled out his cell phone and tracked Grasso down. "This is going to be a problem," Spitzer said he told the NYSE chairman, adding, "We're still in negotiations with Citigroup" over the final wording of the global research deal. Grasso declined through his lawyers to be interviewed for this book, but others familiar with what happened during the call said that Spitzer also referred to a lavish seventieth birthday party that Weill had thrown himself just weeks earlier at Carnegie Hall, saying, "First the birthday party and now this. I'm not going to be part of the rehabilitation of Sandy Weill." Every big-name politician in New York, it seemed, had been invited to Weill's party, from Republicans George Pataki and Michael Bloomberg to Democrats Bill Clinton and Charles Schumer, but somehow, there hadn't been room for Spitzer. He said later that his issue with the party wasn't his exclusion from it. "It would have been ridiculous to invite me," he said, because of the ongoing research investigation. He added that he would not have attended anyway, but said he was irked by the public fêting of a man whose firm had just agreed to pay hundreds of millions of dollars to settle claims of issuing fraudulent research.

Spitzer remembered being absolutely clear on the early-morning phone call that Weill was an unacceptable choice for the NYSE board. "Can you undo this?" he said he asked Grasso. According to Spitzer, the NYSE chairman blustered, saying he had not chosen Weill himself. The decision had come from the board of directors, an assertion that Spitzer found patently absurd, given Grasso's reputation as something of a control freak. "That was the moment when I had the first significant moment of real doubt about the leadership [of the NYSE] and the decision process there, and had some significant doubts about the veracity of Dick Grasso," Spitzer remembered. Fully exercised, Spitzer told Grasso he would call back after his plane had landed in Vail. When they talked again around 5:00 P.M., Grasso "said he hadn't been able to unwind it." The next day, March 23, Spitzer went public with his opposition, telling *The New York Times* that the nomination was "an outrage" and "a gross misjudgment and a violation of trust."

Faced with Spitzer's fury, Grasso and the Exchange backed down.

Within hours, Grasso released a statement saying that Weill had removed his name from consideration. "When Sandy Weill was informed of the comments and the intentions of the New York State Attorney General concerning his nomination to the board of the N.Y.S.E., Sandy informed me that he wished to have his name withdrawn," Grasso's statement said. The Citigroup chairman "had only reluctantly agreed to serve and was adamantly opposed to engaging in a public debate over his qualifications to do so." The news coverage uniformly portrayed the battle as another victory for Spitzer on behalf of small investors and a black eye for the NYSE's corporate governance. Then SEC chairman William H. Donaldson waded into the fray. He formally asked the NYSE, the NASDAQ, and seven other marketplaces to review their corporate structures. Donaldson had a special interest in the issue—he had been chairman of the NYSE in the 1990s, and there was no love lost between him and Grasso, who had been his deputy. Donaldson told reporters he was particularly concerned about the Weill flap because stock exchanges established corporate governance rules for the publicly traded companies. "If you're going to set standards for other people, you've got to set a standard for yourself," he said.

Spitzer and Grasso insisted publicly that they were still close—two weeks after the Weill fight, Grasso told a gathering of state securities regulators that Spitzer was "a friend who has been a tireless campaigner for consumers and investors," and at the April 2003 press conference announcing the final global research settlement, Spitzer made a point of referring to the NYSE chair as a "great friend." But troubles continued to mount at the Exchange. In mid-April, *The Wall Street Journal* reported that the NYSE's regulatory arm was investigating whether some of the specialists—the member firms that facilitated trading on the Exchange floor—had improperly profited by buying stocks from would-be sellers and reselling them to would-be buyers at a higher price, rather than matching the offers directly. The newspaper account enraged Grasso because it referred to the practice as front running, which was a closely related but slightly different way of cheating customers. Though an investigation was under way, Grasso ordered the Exchange to put out a press release that attacked the *Journal* by name for "erroneous" reporting.

Less than a month later, the *Journal* had its revenge—its reporters ferreted out an estimate of Grasso's salary, previously a closely guarded secret. The reported totals were shocking. The Stock Exchange chief had taken home more than ten million dollars in the down year of 2002 and had amassed between eighty million and one hundred million in retirement pay. Angry investors called the figure outrageous for a man who was—at least part of the time—supposed to be a regulator. Corporate governance experts called the numbers proof that something was rotten in the way the NYSE was structured. But NYSE board members defended their chairman and chief executive. Merrill Lynch CEO David Komansky, who had sat on the compensation committee, said that Grasso had done a "spectacular" job persuading new companies to list on the NYSE and he deserved to be paid at least as well as the Wall Street CEOs he was overseeing. The Exchange tried to quell the controversy by promising to be more "transparent," but the resulting disclosures only fanned the flames.

In late August, the board, which had previously refused to disclose salary and contract information, announced that it had renewed Grasso's contract, guaranteeing him a minimum of $2.4 million a year, and authorized him to withdraw not the estimated $100 million but $139.5 million from his deferred compensation account. Though some of the directors balked at the size of the payout, and a straw poll on the contract had come out in favor of it by eleven to seven, the board agreed to present a united front and make the official tally unanimous. Board member H. Carl McCall, newly appointed to head the compensation committee, acknowledged to the media that the payout was a large one but said that the board believed Grasso was worth the money. "I think the board is very pleased with the leadership he has provided," said McCall, a former New York state treasurer. "We want to make sure that we retain his leadership at the NYSE."

Bill Donaldson, though, was not about to let the issue slide. The SEC chairman was annoyed that the NYSE had approved the Grasso payout before completing the governance review the SEC had requested after the Weill flap. He was appalled by the size of the payout—in the 1990s he had taken a pay cut to head the Exchange and he now earned $142,500 as head of the SEC, which had a broader regulatory mandate. So on September 2, Donaldson sent a strongly worded letter to McCall, as head of the compensation committee, asking for a detailed accounting of Grasso's salary and retirement pay. Noting that the NYSE had not yet completed the corporate governance review, Donaldson wrote, "In my view, the approval of Mr. Grasso's pay package raises serious questions regarding the effectiveness of the NYSE's current governance structure." The Exchange's response only made matters worse. At a press conference, Grasso and McCall admitted to reporters that the $139.5 million wasn't the whole story. Grasso was in fact owed an additional $48 million but had agreed to forgo the extra money. "This institution should not be preoccupied by talking about the compensation of its leader," Grasso said. "I've put this issue behind me." McCall also continued to defend Grasso, saying he had earned the money by more than doubling the number of companies that were listed on the exchange. "Dick was and is the right leader at the right time," McCall said.

Corporate governance experts and the media went wild. "Greedy Grasso," wrote *The Sunday Times* of London, and *The New York Times* editorialized that "Public cynicism about how much of an insider's game Wall Street plays can only be increased by the disclosure of the compensation riches that the New York Stock Exchange pays to Richard Grasso." Many of the floor traders were angry that Grasso had made so much at a time when brokers' fees were rising and the Exchange's reported profits had fallen by three-quarters—from $101 million in 1998 to $28 million in 2002. Within days, a group of NYSE members had organized a petition to call a members' meeting that would allow them to replace the entire board. The state treasurers of New York, California, and North Carolina, all of whom oversaw large public pension funds, also began calling for Grasso's resignation.

But one voice was conspicuously absent. To the surprise of some observers, Spitzer stayed out of the verbal slugfest, letting Donaldson and the SEC take the leading role. The attorney general believed he had more than enough on his plate at the time—he had just revealed his late-trading settlement with hedge fund executive Eddie Stern, and his staff was hip-deep in the mutual fund investigation. "There was nothing to be gained," Spitzer remembered. "The SEC said it was handling it." He and Donaldson and Steve Cutler "were getting along fine and I [was] trying to respect the theory that I have generally tried to follow that if somebody begins something, we don't tag along and cause trouble for them."

Meanwhile, Grasso's support on the NYSE board was crumbling. A number of the directors had not known about the additional $48 million—the handout they had received at the August 7 board meeting when Grasso's contract was approved did not mention future payments, and the subject was never discussed. When McCall told the board about the extra money, hours before the Exchange went public with the news, several directors expressed dismay. Goldman Sachs chief executive Henry Paulson had already been opposed to the general idea of a chief executive taking his retirement pay while still on the job, and for him, the extra money was the last straw. By September 17, he and three other board members who also headed Wall Street firms were ready to push Grasso out, and they believed they had the votes to do it. Another board member, Kenneth Langone, who ran the boutique investment bank Invemed and who had headed the compensation committee when much of the pay package was approved, was trying to rally support for Grasso, with little success. Even Laurence Fink, chairman of the investment management firm BlackRock, who had previously backed Grasso, was moving toward opposition. Warning Grasso that "the tide has turned," Fink urged the chairman to convene an emergency board meeting by conference call that afternoon.

The phone call was a turbulent one. Grasso, who had consulted with an employment lawyer beforehand about how best to position himself, read a speech that the lawyer had prepared. "While I say this with the deepest reluctance, the best alternative, it seems to me, is that I should submit my resignation at the next board meeting, if you wish me to do so." Then he stepped off the call. JPMorgan Chase chief executive William B. Harrison began to make the case for Grasso's ouster. "This is about the integrity of the Exchange," Harrison said. Langone continued to defend the chairman, saying it was ridiculous to force him out just weeks after approving a new contract. "You guys should be ashamed," Langone barked. In the end, the directors voted thirteen to seven against Grasso. McCall was the one to break the news; he called Grasso as several directors listened in. "The board has voted to accept your resignation," McCall said. Grasso consulted quietly with his advisers and responded, "I didn't offer to resign. What I said is that if the board votes me out, I will go." McCall responded, "Well, the board has voted you out." Grasso's statement to the media that day made clear how loath he was to go. "For the past 36 years, I have had the honor and privilege of working for what I believe is the greatest equities market in the world—the New York Stock Exchange. Today, I shared with the board of directors in a conference call that, with the deepest reluctance and if the board so desired, I would submit my resignation as chairman and chief executive officer."

Within days, the board had selected John Reed—Sandy Weill's old adversary at Citigroup—as the Stock Exchange's new chairman and announced plans to radically restructure the way the Big Board was governed. The Exchange also hired Dan K. Webb, a former U.S. attorney from Chicago, to investigate Grasso's contract, with an eye toward finding a way to pressure the former chairman to return some of the money. Webb's report, which was completed on December 15, 2003, made clear just how dysfunctional the Big Board's leadership had become: the report said that Grasso "had the unfettered authority to select which board members served on the compensation committee," and that he had "hand-selected" members with whom he had personal relationships and who were less likely to object to the size of his retirement package because they made huge salaries themselves. The comp committee also used a comparison group for Grasso's pay that included the CEOs of much larger, more profitable, and more complex companies. Even then, the committee often departed upward from its own "inflated benchmarks." As a result, the Webb report concluded, Grasso's compensation was "unreasonable" and "excessive" for most of his tenure as NYSE chairman and "grossly excessive" for the years 2000 and 2001.

The report also cast a jaundiced eye on the process by which the board had approved the $139.5 million payout. Grasso's contract had not been on the agenda at its August 7 board meeting, and the outside consultant who had analyzed Grasso's retirement package for the board did not attend. Compensation committee chairman McCall told his fellow board members that they had no choice about authorizing the $139.5 million payout because the entire sum was fully vested—"all his money," the report said. In fact, thirteen million dollars of it was not. Webb's investigators had also discovered why some directors were surprised when they were told about the forty-eight million dollars in extra money. McCall had erroneously stated at the August meeting that the $139.5 million payout would end the Stock Exchange's retirement obligations to Grasso. McCall told Webb's investigators that he did not understand the contract, even though payments adding up to forty-eight million dollars were mentioned in a set of talking points that had been prepared for him. None of the other compensation committee members who knew about the additional money corrected McCall at the meeting. (Carl McCall's lawyer, William Wachtell, later criticized the Webb report as "inaccurate" and said, "The truth will set Carl free and will demonstrate that what was done was not only proper but was done on the watch of some of the finest lawyers in America.")

Grasso's camp argued that Webb's investigation provided support for the size of Grasso's retirement package. "The Webb report does not take issue with Dick Grasso's exemplary performance as CEO of the N.Y.S.E., but questions the business judgment of some of the most sophisticated men and women in the financial world," Grasso's personal spokesman, Eric Starkman, said in a statement when a judge agreed to Grasso's request to make the report public. "Every dime of compensation was voted on unanimously by a Compensation Committee that, working with its consultants, decided that Dick Grasso was worth a great deal to the NYSE." Even Spitzer's lawyers and the SEC, while appalled by the horrible oversight process described in the report, agreed privately that it lacked a "smoking gun" that proved that the NYSE board had been misled.

Now the ball was squarely in the court of John Reed, the new NYSE chairman. To the surprise of some of his fellow directors, Reed quickly forwarded Webb's report to the SEC and Spitzer's office, asking if they could do something to help get some of the money back from Grasso. Though Reed would later downplay his role, saying the government officials were "under no compulsion to do anything," he got an immediate reponse. The SEC staff roared into action, demanding documents and interviewing board members. But within a few months the commission demurred, deciding that it had no jurisdiction because no federal securities laws had been broken. Spitzer and his top aides viewed the matter differently. They saw the conflict as a potential intersection of two big issues they had been working on for years: improving corporate disclosure and making sure nonprofits used their resources for the purposes they were intended. Since his election in 1998, Spitzer had brought an action to block the sale of the Manhattan Eye, Ear & Throat Hospital; he had indicted the founder of Hale House, a charity for the children of drug-addicted mothers; and he had finished an investigation that his predecessor, Dennis Vacco, had begun of alleged conflicts of interest at the historic Apollo Theater in Harlem, which ultimately resulted in a settlement. "Generally, when we bring actions involving nonprofits, we are seeking to make them do their jobs," Michele Hirshman explained. The Grasso allegations fit right in. "The process that led to the Grasso compensation award was indefensible," she said.

From past cases, Spitzer knew he had a way into the Grasso issue that the SEC did not. New York had a law requiring not-for-profits and their boards to use their resources wisely and to pay reasonable compensation. Vacco had used the same law in 1997 to go after the president of Adelphi University, Peter Diamandopoulos, and seventeen of the university's trustees, charging that they had wasted more than five million dollars. Spitzer believed that the sheer size of Grasso's pay package, plus the information that Webb's investigation had turned up about improper comparisons and inflated benchmarks, was probably enough to bring a case under that law. But he wanted more. The Webb report suggested that at least some NYSE board members had not understood what they were voting on and that some may have been misled on key issues. So Spitzer turned to Avi Schick and asked him to investigate. Schick, a deputy attorney general with an office just two doors from Spitzer's own, gathered together a small team of experienced lawyers, including Bruce Topman, who had done so much work on the analyst cases. They did what the office always did when faced with a hot allegation—they got copies of every document that might possibly be relevant and began burrowing through them.

One of the first places the trail led was to the Chicago law firm of Vedder Price, which had done some consulting work in late 2002 and early 2003 on the subject of Grasso's salary and benefits. The Webb report suggested that Vedder Price partner Bob Stucker had provided almost the only note of skepticism in the entire dysfunctional process, and when Avi Schick read the documents, he "was able to piece together that they [Vedder Price] were the good guys," Hirshman remembered, "so he took a flight to Chicago to see them." The Vedder attorneys walked Schick through their brief and bizarre stint working for the NYSE. On September 23, 2002, the Stock Exchange board's compensation committee had taken up a proposal to extend Grasso's contract and convert $51.5 million of his enormous retirement package from an unfunded line in the NYSE's budget into an actual payout into his deferred compensation account, where it would earn him interest. Kenneth Langone was squarely behind the plan, but three new members of the comp committee—Laurence Fink, Bear Stearns CEO James Cayne, and DaimlerChrysler chairman Jurgen Schrempp—learned for the first time at that meeting that Grasso had by this time accumulated a total of $110 million in retirement benefits. The meeting, according to the notes of longtime NYSE consultant William Mischell, who had provided the board with an analysis of the package, was a "disaster! The new members were shocked by the size of Dick's SERP [the NYSE term for one type of retirement benefit]. They want an independent consultant to say it is ok . . . someone who has never worked with NYSE before."

Soon thereafter, Vedder Price's Bob Stucker got a call from Langone, who said he wanted to hire the firm to attend the next comp committee meeting and answer questions regarding four points—the plan to extend the contract until 2007, to transfer the $51.5 million to the deferred compensation account, to cap Grasso's total pension benefits, and to move up the date (from 2006 to 2003) when a five-million-dollar retention bonus would become fully vested. In their discussions with Stucker, Langone and NYSE human resources director Frank Ashen referred to the proposal as being something along the lines of a "no brainer" and "essentially a done deal" that most of the committee members and two outside consultants had already signed off on. They asked Stucker to be ready for the meeting in a week's time—an extraordinarily tight deadline in the world of compensation matters. On October 3, Stucker delivered a report that included several skeptical notes. He noted that Grasso's pension was one hundred million dollars greater than the median for the so-called "peer" group, and he pointed out that vesting the five million dollars immediately "eliminates the retention" purpose of the bonus. Furthermore, Stucker called the $51.5 million transfer a "rare" proposal that would "significantly erode the retention value of the pension." The board minutes—written by Ashen—said Vedder Price had recommended that the comp committee approve the proposal with the exception of the vesting of the five-million-dollar bonus, but the Vedder Price lawyers told Avi Schick that they did not make a formal recommendation of any kind. (Ashen later conceded that the board minutes were "inaccurate.") The comp committee rejected the proposal to vest the five-million-dollar bonus and tabled the rest.

Stucker and the rest of Vedder Price didn't hear from the NYSE board again until February, when comp committee member Schrempp faxed them a different proposal from Grasso that was due to be discussed at a meeting three days later. This time Grasso wanted all his money—nearly $130 million—and he wanted it in cash rather than in a deferred compensation account that was still under the control of the NYSE. Bob Stucker reported to Schrempp and the comp committee that such cash-out plans were "rare" and presented "due diligence" issues. To Stucker, it seemed that some committee members were concerned that they didn't fully understand the proposal and its alleged benefits for the Exchange. He offered to provide a more detailed analysis by the next meeting, a conference call scheduled for March 28, but the comp committee wanted a firm with more experience in number crunching and greater familiarity with the Exchange. After the NYSE chief financial officer nixed a plan to use the NYSE's auditors, Ashen opted to bring in William Mischell, the Exchange's old standby, who worked at Mercer Consulting. Vedder Price also submitted a third report in preparation for the March 28 comp committee conference call that indicated that business judgment issues were involved, but re-iterated that such cash-outs were "rare" and cautioned that a separate Mercer analysis of the proposal had identified only "some" of the costs and benefits of the plan. But Stucker never got to brief the comp committee or the board—the March 28 call was cancelled. The next time Vedder Price heard about Grasso's contract, it was August and they were reading about its approval in the newspapers.

After talking to Vedder Price, Avi Schick focused his attention on the other consultant who had played a key role in the saga: Mercer's compensation expert William Mischell. He had worked for the NYSE for years and had provided the numerical analysis of the pay package. Mischell told Schick's team of lawyers that Ashen had told him he was turning back to Mercer for analysis and that he was concerned that Vedder was "hedging" about whether it would recommend the compensation package. The NYSE then exerted a strong influence over the contents of the March 2003 report and—in the eyes of Spitzer's lawyers—made it misleading. Ashen told Mischell that the comp committee had decided which scenarios to consider, and he and other Exchange officials reviewed and edited multiple drafts before Mercer turned in a final version. The interactions did not make the process or the Exchange look good. The early drafts of the retirement payout had used an estimate of Grasso's 2003 salary to calculate his retirement package, but by March, the real number was available, and it was substantially smaller. Mischell asked Ashen if he should "true up" the numbers—which would have reduced the estimate of Grasso's potential take by $8.5 million if the Exchange had followed its usual practice of basing retirement benefits on the past few years of salary. Ashen told him not to. (Ashen believed that the true-up was irrelevant because the proposed new contract would permanently peg Grasso's retirement benefits to his 1999–2001 salary.) Spitzer's lawyers found the decision misleading, because it gave the board an inflated view of what it would save if it paid out Grasso's benefits immediately. In addition, when Mischell proposed pointing out to the board that thirteen million dollars of the package could be revoked if Grasso left the exchange, Ashen insisted that Mercer describe the thirteen million as "vested but forfeitable"—Mischell sarcastically referred to this euphemism as "the

Ashen convention." By the time Spitzer's investigators were done, Mischell and his employers had agreed to return $440,275 in fees to the NYSE and sign a cooperation agreement detailing the ways they had helped provide misinformation to the Stock Exchange board.

This left Frank Ashen, who had resigned from the Stock Exchange two weeks after Grasso's ouster. In early interviews with Spitzer's office, the former human resources chief stuck by his former boss and maintained that the board had been fully and properly briefed about Grasso's contract. But by the early spring of 2004, Schick had amassed what he considered a stack of bad evidence against Ashen: he had written the comp committee minutes that misstated Vedder Price's view of the contract changes and he had tweaked Mischell's reports to the board to overstate what Grasso was owed. Schick also found that Ashen had not shared with the board the calculations that Mischell had done in 2001, which Spitzer's investigators believed could have suggested to the directors that every one million dollars more that Grasso received in regular bonuses would net him up to $6.8 million in retirement pay. Finally, Schick had uncovered a series of suspicious-looking charts that Ashen had used to summarize and track Grasso's compensation in 1999–2001. The charts seemed to come in multiple versions, creating a "now you see it, now you don't" description of Grasso's total take. The first chart, developed by Ashen for his own use, showed five kinds of compensation, including a category entitled CAP, short for capital accumulation plan, under which Grasso would receive up to $8.05 million a year in that category alone. But the version of the spreadsheet Ashen gave to the Stock Exchange's board of directors had only four categories. The CAP column was conveniently missing, and the reported "total" had dropped by eighteen million dollars over the years 1999 to 2001. And there was still a third version: when Ashen sent the chart to the Exchange's chief financial officer to tell him how much to pay Grasso, the CAP column and higher totals had reappeared. Spitzer's office thought that the whole process might add up to a violation of section 715(f) of New York's Not-for-Profit Corporation Law: "the fixing of salaries of officers . . . shall require the affirmative vote of a majority of the entire board." If the board wasn't told about the CAP payments, how could it have approved them?

A month after Ashen finished his first day of formal interviews with Spitzer's office, Schick put a call in to Bruce Yannett, Ashen's lawyer: "This is really not going anywhere good for your client," he said. "Tell me now if you want to cooperate." Several days of negotiations ensued, and Ashen came back in and eventually reached a formal settlement with Spitzer's office over his role in the affair. The Spitzer team pushed him to remember specific details that would strengthen the case Schick was building against Grasso and the NYSE. The former Grasso loyalist not only acknowledged that the Mercer analysis and the "now you see it, now you don't" worksheets for 1999 to 2001 were "inaccurate, incomplete and misleading," but he also said he believed the contract should not have been considered and approved at the August 7 board meeting. As part of the settlement with Spitzer, Ashen signed a sworn statement of facts that said, "There were no consultants present and the non-[compensation] Committee directors were not adequately prepared or briefed. . . . Based on a quarter century of work at the NYSE, I felt this was not the way the NYSE conducts business."

During Ashen's interviews, Spitzer's lawyers pressed him hard for information about the compensation committee's processes and about Ken Langone, the committee's chairman during the period when Grasso accumulated much of his huge package. Ashen described several interactions that Spitzer's lawyers believed showed Langone had taken steps to keep information from the rest of the board that might have slowed down or halted Grasso's payout. Specifically, Ashen said, Langone had told him in the fall of 2002 that he was angry that Vedder Price had written directly to individual board members. "I understood he wanted all communication to flow through him," Ashen said in the statement of facts. By the time Grasso decided to change his proposal and seek a cash payout in January 2003, Ashen had already briefed all but two comp committee members, but he said Langone told him not to "circle back" and inform them of the substantial changes because the whole committee would discuss the proposal at their next meeting. (The remaining two members were told about the proposal.) A few months later, Ashen said, Langone told him he was going to call Martin Lipton, a leading Wall Street attorney, "to inquire whether it would be okay not to tell the full board the amounts to be paid to Grasso" under the payout plan.

The Langone information presented an issue for the Attorney General's Office. Spitzer and his lieutenants were leaning away from filing suit against most of the NYSE directors personally. The office had no problem suing the Exchange for having bad policies and procedures— and in fact they decided to do just that—but they worried that going after the directors would make it hard for charities in the state to fill their boards. "We want people to sit on the boards of not-for-profits," Spitzer explained. "They are not compensated well for it. If they fear they will be sued for bad decisions . . . they will not serve."

Still, Spitzer and his lieutenants believed the evidence showed that Langone had known more about Grasso's package than many other directors and had gone out of his way to keep the board in the dark. While Langone headed the compensation committee, Grasso's compensation had more than quadrupled. Newspapers had also had a field day with the close relationship between the two men. The *New York Post* illustrated a May 2003 article about Grasso's decision to sit on the board of Home Depot—an NYSE-listed company that Langone had helped found—with a photo composite that purported to show Grasso and Langone in bed together. Spitzer decided his case against the Stock Exchange would make a distinction between "which board members deceived and misled and which board members made a bad decision." Langone, in Spitzer's mind, fell firmly into the first camp.

There was a second Stock Exchange director who had to be considered carefully: Carl McCall, the former New York State comptroller and the first black to win the Democratic nomination for governor. When the $139.5 million was approved, McCall was chairman of the compensation committee, and he had actually signed the contract. Other directors had told Dan Webb's investigators that McCall had not told them about the extra forty-eight million dollars and had resisted having Ashen attend the August 7 board meeting where the contract was discussed, preferring to do all the briefing himself. McCall had told Webb's investigators that he did not fully understand the contents of the package and that as late as September he did not know about the extra payout. That assertion conflicted with the set of talking points that McCall brought—but did not read aloud—to the August 7 board meeting, where the deal was approved. It was also clear that after the board meeting but before Grasso's package was made public, McCall received multiple drafts of the contract that spelled out every dollar Grasso would receive. Moreover, McCall and Langone had given the Webb investigators diametrically opposed versions of the June 2003 meeting where Langone (McCall's predecessor as chairman of the comp committee) handed off responsibility for the pension payout. McCall said that he was "shocked" at the size of the $139.5 million payout, but both Ashen and Langone said the money was fully vested and that the committee had already signed off on the deal. For their part, Langone and Ashen said that McCall had not expressed any concerns at that meeting or at a subsequent briefing by Ashen and Mischell. Langone also insisted that he told the new chairman that "you're not bound by what we've done to date . . . you can proceed as you see fit." (Carl McCall's lawyer, William Wachtell, would later insist in court that Webb's report had been a "hatchet job and somebody lied.")

In his interviews with Spitzer's office, Ashen was particularly critical of McCall, but, like almost everyone else involved in the controversy, he knew that Spitzer was interested in running for governor and Ashen believed Spitzer could ill afford to alienate McCall's supporters. So Ashen was openly dismissive, saying, "I could tell you things about Carl McCall, but you don't want to hear that." In response, Schick reached over to a tray stocked with drinking water, picked up a Dixie cup, and put it down on the conference table in front of Ashen. "You want to piss on Carl McCall, show me what you've got," Schick said. The results, in the eyes of the Spitzer team, were not strong enough to push McCall out of the mass of board members who were misled and into the Langone/Grasso group that had allegedly done the misleading. Spitzer's lawyers believed Langone was liable, because he had allegedly failed to share information with the board for several years about the size of the retirement package as it was accumulating, but McCall's role was much smaller: he had headed the comp committee for less than two months before the August 2003 vote, and the information he had allegedly failed to share was about the forty-eight-million-dollar future payment, money that Grasso had never received and had renounced in September 2003 in an effort to save his job.

Schick and his team were also uncovering evidence that suggested to them that Grasso had used his status as a regulator to make sure his salary and retirement benefits went unchallenged. Bear Stearns chairman Jimmy Cayne told investigators that a top executive in his firm's specialist division had urged him to join the NYSE board because he believed the firm would then get better treatment when the NYSE handed out newly listed stocks. One former compensation committee member described an incident in 2000 when he expressed concern privately to Ashen about the size of Grasso's package. "My hesitancy was reported immediately" to Grasso, he said. After approving the package, the director remembered thinking, "Thank God I escaped that one. This man was also our regulator and I'm a member of the New York Stock Exchange. . . . And when he's kind of indirectly your supervisor or your regulator you have to be careful."

Even as Schick was building his case against Grasso and Langone, Spitzer was trying to find another way out. He reached out to Grasso through mutual friends and business partners, seeking a peaceful resolution that would allow both sides to save face. "I tried for months to settle it," Spitzer remembered. "It was better for the Exchange and we could vindicate our theory" that state law put caps on executive compensation at not-for-profit institutions. "I went to Marty Lipton, among others, to try to be an intermediary. I said, 'This is crazy.'" Grasso didn't have to return all of the money, Spitzer said, just enough of it to bring his retirement package closer in line with those of his peers. Spitzer said he proposed that the former Big Board chief forgo his claims on the additional $48 million, return $50 million, and keep the rest of the $139.5 million payout. "Then I could say, fair enough," Spitzer recalled. His office also approached Grasso's official counsel in the matter, bulldog litigator Brendan V. Sullivan, Jr., but with no success. "They rejected it out of hand," Spitzer remembered.

By late May, Spitzer had reached the moment of truth. Negotiating an amicable settlement looked impossible. Going after Grasso would mean taking on a hardheaded, angry man with little to lose. It would open Spitzer up to all kinds of criticism. Why should the taxpayers foot the bill for his interfering in a squabble between an allegedly overpaid CEO and the wealthy NYSE stakeholders who had given him the money? Charging Langone and not McCall would also raise questions of political expediency. But Spitzer and his staff felt strongly that the money was not the NYSE board's to give—the Not-for-Profit Corporation Law said that compensation must be reasonable, and many of the NYSE's floor members had gotten angry when they learned of the size of the payout. They also believed strongly that Langone's behavior had been improper. "The alternative was to do nothing," Hirshman remembered. And Spitzer wouldn't do that. The NYSE had incorporated itself as a not-for-profit entity in New York, and he believed that it could not be allowed to flout the law so publicly. "We would have acted the same if this was the NYSE, the Botanical Gardens, or the Metropolitan Museum," Spitzer said. "We wouldn't allow it to happen anywhere. There are not bright lines that permit you to say ten dollars not eleven dollars. But you can say twenty million dollars not two hundred million dollars."

Spitzer's May 24 complaint named Grasso, Langone, and the Stock Exchange itself as defendants, but not McCall. The fifty-four-page document argued that Grasso's total take was not "reasonable" because it had been based on flawed comparisons with top Wall Street executives and approved in a process that was riddled with conflicts of interest. Many of the directors voting on Grasso's compensation headed companies that he was charged with regulating. But the allegations went well beyond the procedural problems cited in Dan Webb's report and used the information Schick had dug up to allege that the board had been actively "misled" on key pieces of information. "If this case were tried based only on the Webb report, we would win," Spitzer said. "But what we've got is exponentially more powerful."

The response was decidedly mixed. Newspapers across the country played the story across their front pages, and *The New York Times* observed, "Given the amounts involved, and the weight of the evidence, Eliot Spitzer really had no choice but to sue Richard Grasso." But Spitzer drew significant criticism from the business community for stepping into what they viewed as a private contract dispute, and from Republicans who believed he had given McCall a pass for political reasons. *The Wall Street Journal* noted, "Mr. McCall also ran the compensation committee when some of Mr. Grasso's pay was approved, yet he was spared Mr. Spitzer's legal attentions. Far be it from us to suggest that this oversight has anything to do with Mr. McCall's status as a prominent New York Democrat who could help Mr. Spitzer in a future run for Governor." (The allegations of a political quid pro quo would gain traction in 2005, when McCall was quoted in *The New York Times* as saying he had cautioned Nassau County executive Thomas R. Suozzi not to challenge Spitzer in the 2006 gubernatorial primary: "Tom already has his problems in the party, and a primary run would drain resources, create divisions and not be well received," McCall said.)

Many lawyers not connected to the dispute agreed that Spitzer had a good case on the issue of whether Grasso's compensation was reasonable for the head of an entity that had chosen to incorporate under New York's not-for-profit statute. But the evidence that the NYSE board had been misled or was somehow compromised by close association with Grasso was far thinner, these outside legal experts said. Some of the key facts were open to multiple interpretations that made the case hard to predict. Among them:

• Spitzer and his lawyers had made much of Ashen's settlement and statement of facts, arguing that they proved that the NYSE staff had misled the board. But Ashen's lawyer, Bruce Yannett, issued a statement in which he highlighted the part of the statement of facts in which his client denied intentional wrongdoing: "Mr. Ashen recognizes in hindsight that certain mistakes were made, but at no time did he intentionally provide inaccurate or incomplete information to the Board of Directors." When former NYSE board member Gerald Levin was asked later about Ashen's statement of facts, he said he found it "totally offensive . . . I don't know what took place that encouraged Mr. Ashen to sign this piece of paper. So it has no validity from my point of view at all."

• William Mischell had told Spitzer's office that Ashen told him to describe as "vested but forfeitable" the portion of Grasso's bonus money that he would lose if he were fired, because some board briefings used that phrase. In Spitzer's complaint, the phrase had been shortened to just "vested," the same phrase that Mischell used in his written reports to the board.

• The board had received "now you see it, now you don't" charts that omitted Grasso's CAP benefits from the overall total, but the total benefits had been included in the chart shown to the board in February 2003. And even in the years where the CAP numbers were omitted, the program itself was mentioned in a footnote. Spitzer's side argued that the 2003 chart was irrelevant—since Grasso was seeking a payout at that time, he no longer had a reason to hide the totals.

• There was disagreement about the amount of information Langone had shared with the board during his tenure as comp committee chairman. Webb's investigators noted that Langone's speaking points for the February 2002 compensation meeting failed to mention eight million dollars in CAP benefits that Grasso would receive, and Spitzer alleged that the directors were also not told about the money Grasso was getting from another program—the Supplemental Executive Retirement Plan or SERP. But Langone's supporters argued he had made sure the comp committee was fully briefed and noted that the CAP was mentioned in Langone's speaking points for prior years. "Grasso's comp, including the CAP and SERP, were reviewed and approved by the comp committee each and every year," said Langone's spokesman, Jim McCarthy. "The public has the impression that the total amounts were somehow sprung on the directors, as if out of a hat. That's not how it worked. . . . If some of the directors were surprised, that's a reflection on their own lack of diligence." Levin, one of the NYSE board members at the time, would later say that, despite what the speaking points suggested, Langone either specifically mentioned the size of the 2002 CAP award "or it wasn't necessary because he was identifying the variable compensation" that would be used to calculate the size of the benefit. "It was very clear that it was $8,050,000," Levin said.

• If withholding information was going to be the standard for charging directors, Langone's and Grasso's supporters asked, why not charge Carl McCall? There was evidence that Carl McCall had received documents that mentioned that Grasso would be owed millions of dollars more after the $139.5 million payout, yet McCall had failed to tell the board about this at the crucial meeting where the payout was approved. Spitzer's office argued that McCall's alleged omissions concerned the forty-eight million dollars in future payments, which were damaging to the NYSE's image, but not its pocketbook, because Grasso never got the cash.

• The complaint alleged that Langone wanted to ask lawyer Marty Lipton if it was okay not to tell the board about the full extent of Grasso's compensation. Frank Ashen's contemporaneous notes said that Langone had called Lipton "based on a suggestion from Paulson"—Hank Paulson, the CEO of Goldman Sachs—another board member who was not charged with any wrongdoing. Paulson's spokesman said that the only person Paulson advised to consult Lipton was Grasso himself, and Paulson wanted Lipton's advice on whether the $139.5 million payout was legal, not whether to tell the board about it.

• Spitzer also drew the wrath of his old adversary Harvey Pitt for asserting that Grasso had failed to crack down on biased research analysts in 2001 and early 2002, a time when the heads of Wall Street's top investment banks were voting on his pay. "That is false," Pitt said, noting that he had convened a private meeting on the analyst issue in November 2001 with Grasso, other regulators, and the heads of the banks. "Grasso was terrific," Pitt said, and was working on proposals to solve the problem when Spitzer brought his Merrill Lynch case in April 2002.

No one reacted to the complaint with more fury than Ken Langone. Colorful and outspoken, the sixty-eight-year-old Langone had not initially taken Spitzer's investigation seriously. He believed that Grasso was "worth every penny" the Stock Exchange had paid him and that the pay process had been handled properly. If anyone should be ashamed, he said, it was the other board members who had approved the pay package and then ousted Grasso when the public reaction turned negative. "September 9, we gave this man a rousing round of applause, and eight days later we fired him. Nothing had changed," Langone said. Langone's interview with state and federal regulators after the Webb report did nothing to change his mind about Spitzer's probe. The SEC lawyers seemed to be asking most of the questions, while Spitzer's representatives sat silent. Langone fully expected the investigation to come to naught. "I have nothing to hide," he said. So when Spitzer filed his complaint, Langone was outraged. "This is not the public's money; this is our money," he said. "If Eliot Spitzer called right now and said I'll settle for a penny, I'd say Mr. Attorney General, we're going to war. Not one penny. I'm going to get him to apologize for accusing me of misleading people." Langone contended that he had fully briefed the board of directors about the details of Grasso's compensation each year he chaired the compensation committee.

Just as the criticism was reaching fever pitch, Spitzer tried to change the subject by dropping another bomb, this one on federal turf. On June 2, 2004, he brought another high-profile case that touched on the subject of drug safety, ordinarily the territory of the Food and Drug Administration. The case had gotten started nearly two years before, when Spitzer and the head of his Health Care Bureau, Joe Baker, were brainstorming about the kinds of new pharmaceutical cases they could bring. The bureau had in its sights the drug manufacturers who inflated the prices they charged New York's Medicaid program. But Spitzer, who was then in the middle of the research analyst investigation, didn't want to stop there. He was intrigued by the drug research process and whether manufacturers had too much influence on the clinicians who tested their products. "There was this tension," Spitzer remembered. "The doctors were being paid by the pharmaceutical companies to do the testing. I had no evidence that anything of any kind was wrong, but it was roughly analogous to the analysts and underwriters, and there's at least a theoretical issue. I told Joe, 'Poke around that and see what emerges.'"

At the same time, in another corner of Spitzer's office, a new lawyer in the Consumer Frauds Bureau had also begun to look at drug manufacturers, but from a different angle. Rose E. Firestein had come to the office after years of litigating on behalf of children in foster care. In her previous job, she had been shocked by how many children in the foster care system were being put on drugs—especially antipsychotics and antidepressants—that had never been officially tested or approved for use in young patients. Officially, the manufacturers were barred from advertising "off label," or unapproved, uses for the drugs, but somehow pediatric specialists all seemed to know about them anyway. How was that happening? Firestein started scanning medical journals, looking at the advertising and at the studies that referenced the drugs that she was interested in. She found one published article that seemed to support the use in children of Paxil, GlaxoSmithKline's hot-selling antidepressant, but the literature also made references to other studies that seemed less positive. When Firestein went looking for the actual negative studies, she couldn't find them. This piqued her interest. So did a warning in June 2003, from British and FDA authorities, that unpublished studies of Paxil showed that the drug increased the risk of suicides in teenagers. Firestein began to wonder if GlaxoSmithKline had an obligation under New York's consumer-protection laws to share those unpublished negative studies with doctors and patients. She later recalled that when she asked scientists and drug policy experts about her concerns, "People looked at me as if I were crazy. Everyone kept saying, the company owns that data. They can do what they want with it." The lawyers in Spitzer's office reacted differently. "They said, 'This is a little weird, but convince me,'" she said. To some of Spitzer's aides, the issue with the antidepressant studies seemed very similar to the securities fraud rules that banned public companies from selectively sharing information. If a public company releases some information about a topic, it must release all of it, both good and bad. So Firestein asked GlaxoSmithKline for all the Paxil studies and other relevant documents to see what she could find.

In the spring of 2004, the Attorney General's Office caught a tremendous break. Firestein spotted a short article in a Canadian medical journal that quoted a 1998 internal GlaxoSmithKline document that said that clinical studies were "insufficiently robust" to support FDA approval for using Paxil in children and that advised Glaxo-SmithKline staff to "effectively manage the dissemination of these data in order to minimize any potential negative commercial impact." An editor at the journal agreed to send Firestein the 1998 document. Now she had hard evidence that the drug company was deliberately burying negative studies. Her bosses were thrilled. "We knew we were onto something along the Wall Street lines, that had the potential to change the industry," Joe Baker remembered. Medical journal editors had been pushing for years to force pharmaceutical firms to register their trials and to make even negative results public, but the FDA had done little to advance this cause. Part of the problem was legal—most of the buried studies concerned off-label, unapproved uses, an area where the FDA had relatively weak authority. Drug manufacturers were required to report their results to the FDA, but under the Bush administration, the agency had shown little interest in forcing the companies to make the data public.

Spitzer jumped on the idea immediately, giving his lawyers the go-ahead to file a case against GlaxoSmithKline in early June 2004. "The point of the lawsuit is to ensure that there is complete information to doctors for making decisions in prescribing," Spitzer told *The New York Times*. "The record with Paxil, we believe, is a powerful one that shows that GSK was making selective disclosures and was not giving doctors the entirety of the evidence." GlaxoSmithKline denied wrongdoing, saying in a statement that the firm "has acted responsibly in conducting clinical studies in pediatric patients and disseminating data from those studies." As for the 1998 memo Firestein had uncovered, the company said it was "inconsistent with the facts and does not reflect the company position."

Within two weeks, the company had announced plans to post all of the pediatric Paxil studies on its Web site—the stated goal of Spitzer's lawsuit—and to create an online registry to make all of its clinical studies of FDA-approved drugs publicly available. By the end of the summer, the company had agreed to settle the lawsuit by paying Spitzer's office $2.5 million—roughly the profits the company had made from selling Paxil to depressed children in New York. The deal also gave Spitzer's office the power to help design and monitor Glaxo's database of studies. "They were well aware that we had good law on our side," Baker remembered. "We were looking for systemic reform." Yet in some ways, the Paxil case was extremely frustrating for Spitzer and his staff. Other drug companies proved reluctant to follow GlaxoSmith-Kline's example, preferring to keep most information about their clinical studies out of public view. The FDA did little to force further change. "One of the things that is mystifying to me [is] the FDA still has not done anything meaningful. The remedy is so easy: honest disclosure of all testing," Spitzer said.

In the end, the FDA's lack of action fit right into a broad theory of federal regulatory breakdown that Spitzer was beginning to espouse. His office had now brought cases squarely on the turf of the EPA, the SEC, and the FDA. It was investigating allegations of predatory lending by nationally chartered banks (ordinarily handled by the Office of the Comptroller of the Currency) and improper payments from music recording companies to radio stations (a violation of Federal Communications Commission rules). "It is odd how many of these agencies we have had to do battle with," he observed, adding that he blamed thirty years of Republican antigovernment rhetoric. "For thirty years, beginning with Ronald Reagan in 1976, Republicans have argued the ideological viewpoint that government is to be disdained and dismissed, that it interferes with the marketplace," Spitzer said. "The spirit of these agencies has been eaten away. Who is surprised that they end up with a much more limited sense of what they can do. . . . If the CEO of a company for thirty years were denigrating the product, wouldn't you expect the product to begin to suffer?"

Though Spitzer was moving on from the Grasso compensation case, his opponents were not. On July 20, Grasso filed a fifty-million-dollar countersuit against the NYSE and its chairman, John Reed, alleging defamation and breach of contract. Grasso also asked a judge to dismiss part of Spitzer's complaint against him. The countersuit claimed that Reed had engaged in a "campaign of disparagement and defamation," and it sought to force the Exchange to give Grasso the additional forty-eight million dollars he had turned down in his vain effort to save his job. Grasso announced plans to donate any winnings to charity. "I'm not going to stop until I win," he told the journalist Charles Gasparino, who was writing a book on the research analyst scandal. "As far as I am concerned, this is about something bigger than money, it's about my integrity." Langone followed up with his own legal papers two days later, asking the court to dismiss Spitzer's complaint. The angry investment banker then repeatedly protested his innocence, telling *The Wall Street Journal* in August, "I made honest decisions that were thoroughly researched and reaffirmed by 100 percent of both the board and compensation committees. No amount of bluster by Mr. Spitzer can change those essential facts."

9

THE CONCRETE CLUB

THE ANONYMOUS LETTER ARRIVED AT THE ATTORNEY GENERAL'S OFFICE IN Manhattan in an envelope with a Westchester County postmark. The handwriting on the exterior was obviously disguised. Inside, the two-page typed letter had no greeting and seemed to start in the middle of things: "Please know that as a reaction to inquiries from your office, there have been several changes made at Marsh in an attempt to obfuscate reality in the area of directed revenue sharing and allocations."

"Huh?" thought David Brown, the head of Spitzer's Investment Protection Bureau, when the letter was forwarded to him in Albany in April 2004. His staff hadn't made any inquiries at Marsh, the world's largest insurance broker. His domain was Wall Street, not insurance. In the mutual fund world, where Brown had been immersed for nearly a year, the term "revenue sharing" was sometimes used as slang for the increasingly problematic practice of paying brokers to recommend particular products. But Spitzer's chief securities enforcer knew next to nothing about the term's application to the world of insurance. Still, as he scanned the tipster's letter, Brown knew he was holding something hot. Densely written and full of jargon, it was also jam-packed with names and contained a potentially explosive allegation: instead of providing independent advice, Marsh was steering its clients to whichever insurance company paid it the most money, and it was collecting these payments under the cover of bogus "placement service agreements" (PSAs). "Clearly it was a very detailed tip by an informant who has inside information," Brown remembered thinking. So he got on the horn to the boss in Manhattan. "Have you seen this?" Brown asked Spitzer. "You've got to look at this. Let me fax it to you right now." When Spitzer saw the letter, which ended simply with "Thank you . . . Talk to clients too!" he had the same reaction: "This looks real."

Brown had one of his subordinates draft a subpoena, and he tracked down William Rosoff, the general counsel of Marsh's parent company, Marsh & McLennan. Years earlier, Rosoff had been one of Brown's supervisors in private practice, so Brown reached out to him personally. "I've sent you a subpoena. It's not a routine subpoena," Brown explained. "I want to make sure it doesn't get lost." Rosoff, then traveling in Japan, was reassuring, saying that he knew all about the PSA issue. "I'm all over that. It's not a problem. Let me come in, and I'll explain it to you," Rosoff said. Brown agreed to wait for the lawyer's return from Asia, but he wasn't about to let the grass grow under his feet. The Investment Protection Bureau was in the middle of a major expansion. Over the course of 2004, it would ramp up from fewer than two dozen lawyers to about forty. One of the new hires—Matthew Gaul, formerly of Spitzer's first law firm, Paul, Weiss, Rifkind, Wharton & Garrison—had arrived just three days earlier and was looking for something to do. Brown handed him the Marsh letter and subpoena along with another tip, something about fraudulent currency trading that never amounted to much of anything.

Gaul quickly figured out that the practice of insurance companies paying brokers "contingent commissions" was controversial in some quarters—the *Financial Times* had written an article excoriating the practice. The paper argued that brokers were trying to serve two masters, the clients who paid them for independent advice and the insurance companies who paid contingent commissions based on the volume or quality of business referred by the brokers. The insurance giant American International Group (AIG) had even asked the New York State Insurance Department about the issue twice, prompting a brief flurry of questions from the state to brokers and insurance companies in late

2003. That inquiry had gone nowhere, but it appeared to have prompted the tipster to send the letter that arrived in April. Spitzer's office had itself been alerted to the issue before—just two months earlier, the conservative Washington Legal Foundation had written to Spitzer asking him to investigate, but the group's letter had drawn little interest at the time. Now that the office had the Marsh tip, however, it looked like a hot topic. About this time, Spitzer recognized that Brown and Gaul were going to need help understanding the arcane world of insurance. So he had his staff track down Mel Goldberg, a lawyer in the office's Consumer Frauds Bureau. Goldberg, who was en route to Niagara Falls for a family vacation, promised to get on the issue as soon as he got back. And when he returned, he went to the Brooklyn Public Library and checked out a twenty-year-old book on the insurance industry—*The Invisible Bankers* by Andrew Tobias—which began to be passed around the office as more and more lawyers joined the investigative team.

When Bill Rosoff arrived in the office to brief Brown, Gaul, and several other lawyers, he seemed to view the PSAs as completely benign. He acknowledged that the PSAs guaranteed Marsh certain contingent commissions if its clients used particular insurance companies, but he argued that there was nothing wrong or shady about the practice. "The whole industry does this. . . . It's all fully disclosed to the clients," Rosoff explained. Besides, he said, there was a "Chinese wall" between the brokers and the department that handled the agreements with the insurance companies that kept the brokers' recommendations from being improperly influenced by the PSAs. Brown was far from reassured, especially after Rosoff revealed the size of the payments— Marsh had received about $800 million from contingent commissions in 2003, a year when Marsh & McLennan's total profits were $1.5 billion. Brown was equally struck by Rosoff's reaction when he was asked what would happen if an insurance company refused to pay the commissions. The general counsel "shrugged and grinned," and said something about companies receiving less business, Brown and Gaul remembered. (Rosoff said through his attorney that he was prevented by the rules governing attorney-client privilege from discussing his actions in the Spitzer investigation because he was serving as Marsh's lawyer at the time.) After the meeting, Brown recalled, "I went right in to Eliot and I gave him a broad overview: it's eight hundred million dollars, and they say if you don't pay they won't send you any business. I said, 'I think it's a pay-to-play arrangement.'"

Spitzer and Brown decided to broaden their inquiry to include two other major brokerage firms, Aon and Willis Group Holdings. The state insurance department shared the results of its limited 2003 inquiry, including a list of the insurance companies that paid contingent commissions. Brown's insurance team expanded and sent out a flock of subpoenas. Maria Filipakis, by now an Investment Protection Bureau veteran, began to squeeze insurance research in among her remaining assignments from the mutual fund probe. Then Mike Berlin, a new hire, moved over from the Telecommunications and Energy Bureau. When Filipakis heard from her colleagues about the Rosoff interview, she perked up immediately. She had worked on the analyst probe, and the investment banks had also argued that a "Chinese wall" protected their stock analysts from improper influence. "Whenever I hear 'Chinese wall,' bells and whistles go off, and I think: we have to look into this," she remembered. "When you start hearing, 'Everybody knows about this; this is the way the industry works,' that sets off alarms for me. Suddenly I'm very interested. It has the opposite effect of what they hope."

The first one hundred document boxes began to arrive from Marsh just about the time the office's summer interns showed up. The insurance team of Gaul, Goldberg, Filipakis, and Berlin was now known as "the Four Ms" because all of their first names started with that letter. They put the interns to work looking for evidence that the brokers were steering business to the companies that paid contingent commissions. The team hit pay dirt almost immediately. "We found all kinds of e-mails," Gaul remembered. "Sales e-mails: 'These are our contingent commissions, you've got to go out and get the business. We've got to meet our goals.'" Brown started outlining a possible legal complaint on the whiteboard in his office. The team had found evidence of steering, he argued, but, to really make their case, they had to find "steering to detriment"—examples where the arrangements had hurt clients. "Find me the disgruntled broker who says I don't like X company and I'm being forced to choose X company," Brown told his staff.

By early July, it was clear inside Spitzer's office that they were going to bring some kind of insurance case. The question was whether to focus on one broker—Marsh & McLennan was the largest and the source of the original tip—or to take on all three. Dealing with the lawyers for Aon was like pulling teeth. The company's outside counsel, from Kirkland & Ellis, were unusually slow about turning over documents, and Filipakis and Berlin made nearly thirty calls over the course of the summer, trying to hold the lawyers' feet to the fire. When Aon's general counsel, Cameron Findlay, came in for a meeting in late July, he professed not to see a problem with contingent commission arrangements, but he said the firm would be willing to make changes in the way it told its clients about the practice. "We want to settle. We can take care of this right away," Filipakis remembered them saying. But she and the other lawyers were not inclined to be rushed. "I remember thinking, oh no, no, no, this is not just about disclosure," Filipakis said. The team had already uncovered what they considered strong evidence of steering, including a 2003 e-mail from an Aon executive, Carol Spurlock, who dealt with insurance companies that served middle-size businesses. In it, she told a colleague that she had just signed a new contingency deal with Zurich American Insurance. "Going forward we are going to push Zurich. I just today negotiated our incentive so we will get paid next year," Spurlock wrote.

Willis, the smallest of the three firms, tried a different approach entirely. In Joseph J. Plumeri, Willis had the good fortune of having a CEO who had spent the bulk of his career in the securities industry, rather than in insurance. When Spitzer's subpoenas arrived, Plumeri and his general counsel, William Bowden, were in the midst of trying to centralize and improve the firm's compliance and legal department to "make the place more bullet-proof," in the words of one company executive. They took the investigation seriously early on and asked for a personal meeting with Spitzer. At the meeting, Plumeri made clear that Willis was no Marsh. Rather than dismissing Spitzer's concerns about contingent commissions, Plumeri said he shared those concerns.

Expansive and dynamic, Plumeri wore gold cuff links that caught the light as he gestured. As a newcomer to the insurance industry, he told Spitzer, he "didn't like" the arrangements and "didn't think they made any sense. . . . But we couldn't very well change the world as a number three. There are some things you have to do across the board." Plumeri and Bowden told Spitzer that they knew his investigators were likely to find some bad behavior among their brokers—the firm was big and decentralized enough that they couldn't know everything. But they swore Spitzer would not find systematic wrongdoing and that they would crack down on anything he did discover. As for the structural problem, Plumeri volunteered that his firm would unilaterally forswear the payments in the small part of their business where the clients were either individuals or less sophisticated small business owners. Willis would also go along if Spitzer pressed for an industry-wide ban on contingent commissions, he said. (Willis would eventually pay fifty million dollars, far less than the other two big brokers and would settle with Spitzer without ever facing a formal complaint.)

Marsh & McLennan, meanwhile, was being anything but conciliatory. Busy with other assignments, Rosoff had hired not one but two outside law firms—Davis Polk & Wardwell and Wilkie Farr & Gallagher—to help handle the details of responding to the probe. Davis Polk partner Carey Dunne, a law school classmate of both Spitzer and David Brown who was close to both men, became the de facto point man. It fell to him to let Spitzer's office know that his clients had anything but friendship in mind. "I have a message," Dunne told Brown in one phone call that summer. No one involved remembered exactly what Dunne said, but the gist was clear: Marsh & McLennan's leadership was getting tired of Spitzer's requests for information. They believed he was wasting his time and their money. This is not the kind of company that will be cowed or that will pay money for the sake of convenience, Dunne warned. This could be a long, drawn-out process. Brown was shocked. Companies under investigation didn't normally talk that way when the government regulators had already uncovered serious issues. "There was a real arrogance there," he remembered. He picked up the phone and called Spitzer. They called Dunne back together. "We are going to look at this," Spitzer told Dunne. "There is going to be accountability."

Rosoff came in again on August 4, and this time he and Dunne met directly with Spitzer on the twenty-fifth floor. Only three years into his tenure at Marsh & McLennan, Rosoff had little hands-on experience with the insurance side of the business. But based on the interviews his lawyers had done with Marsh employees, the general counsel insisted that his firm had done nothing wrong. He conceded that the Chinese wall did not completely protect the brokers, but he argued that the company was not bound by fiduciary duty to act in the best interest of its corporate clients. Besides, the steering took place only when brokers were choosing between two essentially similar bids, when "it's apples to apples and doesn't harm any clients," Rosoff contended. Spitzer was skeptical. Dozens of e-mails seemed to contradict the company's breezy assurances that steering happened only in rare cases and never cost the clients money. Where did the insurance companies get the money to pay the contingent commissions? Spitzer wanted to know. "Doesn't this increase the cost of insurance?" he kept asking. The Four Ms followed up on the meeting with another set of subpoenas, asking this time about whether the brokers were engaging in "tying" their recommendations to other business. That is to say, did the brokers show favoritism to insurance companies that were simultaneously using the same broker to buy their own insurance (known in the business as reinsurance or finite insurance)? Spitzer's team also went back to Marsh and asked for additional e-mails relating to six specific employees and for more information about eight insurance transactions that had come up in particular e-mails.

On Thursday, September 9, Gaul, Berlin, and Filipakis were getting ready for a deposition by combing through the files of an executive at the insurance firm of Munich-American Risk Partners. They found an extraordinary memo written by a vice president who was compiling the concerns of his subordinates in preparation for a meeting with Marsh's Global Broking arm. In the memo, a Munich regional manager complained, "This idea of 'throwing the quote' by quoting artificially high numbers in some predetermined arrangement for us to lose is repugnant to me, not so much because I hate to lose, but because it is

basically dishonest. . . . It comes awfully close to collusion or price fixing." The three lawyers stared at the document. Could it possibly mean
what it appeared to say? Could Marsh brokers really be rigging the bidding process? Gaul fired off a BlackBerry message to Brown, who was
riding the train home to Albany. "Just when you thought you'd seen it
all," the subject line read. In the body of the message, Gaul typed in
key quotes from the Munich memo. "Jeez," the reply came back, along
with the news that Brown had forwarded the message on to Spitzer and
Peter Pope, who still supervised the office's criminal prosecutors.
"These guys are really in trouble," Spitzer replied.

Pope's criminal investigators charged into the bid-rigging issue,
with Brown's team right beside them. So it fell to the summer interns
to comb through files the Four Ms had requested from Marsh about
specific insurance cases. Craig Winters, a second-year law student at
New York University, was assigned the file on the Greenville County
school system in South Carolina. The full-time investigators had asked
for the information because of an e-mail in which a Marsh executive
appeared to be using the Greenville contract as a carrot to induce an
insurance company to sign a contingent commission agreement.
("Hint, hint," the executive wrote.) On Tuesday, September 14, Winters made a discovery that proved his bosses had been right to be suspicious. He appeared in Gaul's office practically quivering with
excitement. "Oh my God," he said, and held out an e-mail from a
Marsh broker named Glenn Bosshardt to an assistant vice president at
the insurance firm CNA. It said, "I want to present a CNA program
that is reasonably competitive but will not be a winner." The Munich-
American memo had talked about Marsh suggesting collusion and
price-fixing, but the evidence was secondhand. This e-mail appeared to
show Marsh actually soliciting a fake bid. Gaul took Winters to Brown,
and together they ran downstairs to the Criminal Prosecutions division
and pulled Pope out of a meeting. Spitzer was in Washington accepting
an award for "ethics in government," so Brown sent him a copy by
BlackBerry. "Unbelievable Marsh document," Brown wrote.

But the office still didn't know if the bid-rigging problem was systemic or a scheme involving only a handful of out-of-control brokers.
So Pope and Brown decided they needed to track down the key wit-

nesses. They told Maria Filipakis and criminal lawyer Whitman Knapp to hop a plane to Florida. "Do I have time to go home first?" Filipakis asked Brown when he gave her the marching orders. "No. On the way to the airport, stop at the drugstore and buy yourself a toothbrush," he said. They were trying to track down the former Munich-American regional manager who had written the "throwing the quote" comments. They needed to know if the practice was widespread. Arriving in Tampa late on a Friday night, the New York lawyers spent the night in a motel that offered a free "continental breakfast" of orange soda and Froot Loops. The Spitzer team had several different addresses, on opposite sides of the Tampa area, and the first one turned out to be wrong. By day two, Filipakis's black suit was looking decidedly bedraggled in the sweltering heat, but they'd finally found the right place. She and Knapp made the first approach, hoping to sweet-talk their way into the air-conditioning and into the trust of their quarry. The former insurance executive was cordial but wouldn't let them in the house. So they stood on the porch for hours in the sweltering heat with little flies known as "love bugs" swarming around their heads. Awkwardly balancing file folders and legal pads, Knapp and Filipakis showed the witness documents, and scrawled the explanations they received. By the time the two left, "We knew there was something there and we had to dig deeper," Filipakis remembered.

Within days, the criminal side had banged out another subpoena and sent it out to all of the brokers and insurance companies. Spitzer wanted everything and anything related to "fictitious bids" or any "bid that was based on anything other than honest underwriting," and he wanted it by October 1, just two weeks away. "Basically we asked them to investigate their entire company top to bottom and get back to us in two weeks. We made it clear that the deadline was not negotiable," Gaul said. Pope, a veteran of Mafia bid-rigging cases from his days in the Manhattan DA's Office, predicted what would happen. "Watch, there's going to be a race to come in," he told Brown. On September 30, lawyers from the insurance firms of AIG and ACE made urgent calls to Brown. They had information they wanted to share as soon as possible, preferably before the October 1 deadline expired.

Both companies were run by close relatives of Marsh CEO Jeffrey

Greenberg—his father, Maurice, known as Hank, ruled AIG, and Jeffrey's brother Evan headed ACE. But that didn't stop the firms from telling Spitzer's lawyers all they knew about Marsh's bid-rigging scheme. They also encouraged some of the executives involved to cooperate with Spitzer. AIG, it turned out, had benefited from much of Marsh's bid-rigging from 2001 to 2004—whenever an AIG customer's policy was up for renewal, the Marsh brokers would call the carrier and suggest a target premium, called an "A quote." If AIG met the terms, it kept the customer, and other insurance firms were asked to provide higher bids to create the illusion of competition. AIG played along when Marsh provided similar protection for the other carriers in their turn, providing higher backup "B quotes" that would create the impression that the other carrier had won the bidding fair and square. One AIG underwriter described a 2003 bidding process like this: "This was not a real opportunity. Incumbent Zurich [a rival insurer] did what they needed to do at renewal. We were just there in case they defaulted. Broker . . . said Zurich came in at around $750K and wanted us to quote $900K." When responding to B-quote requests, AIG's underwriters rarely did a full work-up because they knew they wouldn't get the business. On the rare occasions when the A quote fell through, they would "back fill" the analysis after the fact.

ACE's lawyers told the investigators that its underwriters also provided false bids. They turned over documents that showed how the firm would sometimes adjust its bids, at Marsh's request, to make sure Marsh's preferred firm won particular competitions. In the case of an Illinois consumer products company named Fortune Brands, ACE executives upped their requested premium from $990,000 to $1.1 million because AIG, the incumbent that was supposed to keep the business, had come in higher than expected. The deal benefited both sides. Marsh vice president Greg Doherty noted in June 2003 that the firm's Global Broking division (which served the biggest accounts) had steered six million dollars in new business to ACE, "which is the best in Marsh Global Broking so I do not want to hear you are not doing 'B' quotes or we will not bind anything." The blatant malfeasance revealed in the documents surprised even Spitzer and his top aides. "It's the same kind of cartel-like behavior carried out by organized crime," the attorney general observed. Peter Pope compared it to "the Mafia's 'Concrete Club' "—slang for construction projects in which a corrupt contractor hired concrete companies based on kickbacks.

It was all Marsh all the time now, but the company seemed oblivious. Spitzer's lawyers had met with Dunne and another outside lawyer in late September and asked for more information about the Greenville and Munich documents. The request caught the company flat-footed. Though Marsh itself had turned over the file that contained the infamous e-mail asking CNA for a "reasonably competitive" bid that "will not be a winner," Rosoff didn't even know about the transaction until Spitzer's lawyers called up demanding an explanation. Even then, the request failed to raise the right red flags—when Marsh's internal investigators interviewed the people involved in the Greenville deal, they wrongly concluded it was a one-time problem. CNA had refused to provide a false bid, and the broker just made one up. In early October, Spitzer's top aides Pope and Hirshman warned Marsh's lawyers that Spitzer was specifically concerned about "cartel-like" behavior and mob-style bid-rigging, senior officials remembered. The company asked for more time, and Rosoff began to get personally involved in the investigation. But Marsh & McLennan's leadership was still flying blind. The company's internal controls were so poor that its lawyers had no way of detecting problems without the cooperation of the executives involved. Marsh didn't have good systems for searching e-mails and no way of making sure that key evidence hadn't been deleted. Marsh & McLennan didn't even have a global compliance officer who would have been responsible for making sure document retention policies were written and followed; Rosoff was still in the process of interviewing people for that position. And when Marsh & McLennan's leadership tried to figure out what Spitzer's team was getting at, they didn't get the help they needed from their own brokers and executives. When contacted by the firm's lawyers, Marsh executives uniformly provided complicated but apparently genuine explanations for the way they ran their business. Yes, they did sometimes solicit extra bids that came in at a higher price. But they were just trying to give their customers more options. No one interviewed expressed misgivings or suggested that there was something illegal going on, even though the interviewees included several people who would later plead guilty to criminal charges. While Spitzer and his team, who had documents from ACE and AIG, were staring at clear evidence of price-fixing, the Marsh defense team hadn't even discovered the B-quote system. "There was a major criminal conspiracy being run out of their business, and their lawyers didn't know it," Brown said he later realized. "I think the senior management didn't know it, either. They would have been insane to do this."

Back at 120 Broadway, Brown and the Four Ms started drafting their complaint. By now they were well aware of Spitzer's emphasis on striking quickly, and they wanted to be ready when he decided he wanted to file his case. They tried first to write a document that would charge both Aon and Marsh with steering. (Willis's cooperation had convinced Spitzer that the firm's problems with contingent commissions were somewhat less systemic.) In the Investment Protection Bureau's view, steering was the more pervasive issue, and much of the best evidence came from Aon's files. But bundling steering, bid-rigging, Marsh, and Aon all together quickly became cumbersome. The B quotes proved too compelling to ignore. These allegations were even hotter than the late-trading claims that had led the complaint against the Canary hedge fund. That case had stretched the Martin Act to cover a new problem—after-hours mutual fund trading. This investigation appeared to be a legal slam dunk. Bid-rigging had been against the law in New York since 1893, and the state's antitrust law had been in almost constant use since then. "Just focus on Marsh. Lead with the bid-rigging," Spitzer advised. Aon would have to wait until later.

By this time, the staff had bought into Spitzer's get-it-done-now mentality. Everyone from top aide Michele Hirshman on down pitched in to get the complaint done. The Four Ms pulled all-nighters in shifts, with Brown providing oversight. Pope contributed a timely rewrite that was so clean and compelling that Brown lobbied his superiors to accept the changes wholesale rather than incorporate them into the earlier draft. For Berlin, who was a veteran civil litigator but new to the way the office handled its high-profile cases, the "incredibly harsh vetting process" was extraordinary. For "every single fact that was in that Marsh complaint, we were asked, 'How can you prove this point?'

ABOVE LEFT: Eliot Laurence Spitzer, shown here at about seven months of age, was born in the Bronx on June 10, 1959. He was the youngest of three children. (Spitzer Family photos) ABOVE RIGHT: Spitzer met his wife, Silda Wall, at Harvard Law School, where he was an editor of the law review. They graduated in June 1984. (Spitzer Family photos)

Spitzer's father, Bernard, built a real estate empire and his mother, Anne, taught college and high school English. Shown here on the campaign trail with their son, they provided crucial financial support for his first two campaigns for attorney general. (Spitzer Family photos)

Spitzer and his wife have three daughters (*left to right*), Elyssa, Jenna, and Sarabeth. (Photo by Pamela Fox)

SEC chairman Harvey Pitt was caught by surprise in the spring of 2002 when Spitzer went public with allegations that Merrill Lynch had published fraudulent research. They eventually combined forces to tackle the problem of biased research. (Carl Cox Photography)

As director of the SEC's enforcement division, Stephen M. Cutler worked hand in hand with Spitzer on the stock analyst and mutual fund probes. Cutler was instrumental in making sure Spitzer's revelations of bad behavior led to industry-wide changes. (© 2003, *The Washington Post*. Photo by Ray Lustig. Reprinted with permission)

On April 28, 2003, Spitzer, the SEC, and other regulators announced the final terms of their $1.4 billion settlement with ten major investment banks that revamped the way the banks provided stock research. Shown from left to right are NASAA president Christine Bruenn, Stephen Cutler, Spitzer, SEC chairman William H. Donaldson, NASD chairman Robert Glauber, and New York Stock Exchange chairman Richard Grasso. (Stefan Zaklin/Getty Images News/Getty Images)

David D. Brown IV left a cushy job on Wall Street to join Spitzer's office because he wanted to do public service. Before long he was spearheading a high-stakes investigation of improper mutual fund trading and later oversaw inquiries into insurance kickbacks. (Suzanne DeChillo/*The New York Times*)

Noreen Harrington is the whistle-blower who kicked off Spitzer's mutual fund inquiry. She told his office that the Canary Capital Management hedge fund was trading mutual fund shares after hours and profiting at the expense of ordinary investors. (© 2004, Gabrielle Revere)

Edward Stern, the head of Canary Capital Management. He and Canary agreed to pay $40 million to settle allegations of improper after-hours mutual fund trading and to tell Spitzer's investigators everything he knew about the practice. (Seth Wenig/ *The New York Times*)

New York Stock Exchange chairman Richard A. Grasso and Spitzer were close during the stock analyst investigation, when this photo was shot, but their friendship frayed when the NYSE revealed that Grasso had amassed a $140 million retirement package. (Stefan Zaklin/Getty Images News/Getty Images)

Investment banker Kenneth Langone, a former member of the New York Stock Exchange board, became one of Spitzer's most vocal critics after Spitzer accused him of misleading his fellow board members about the size of Grasso's compensation package. (Courtesy of Ken Langone)

American International Group chairman Maurice R. "Hank" Greenberg was a legendary figure in the insurance world. But Spitzer's investigation of a reinsurance deal between AIG and General Re put Greenberg's thirty-nine-year career in jeopardy. (Courtesy of Maurice Greenberg)

Marsh & McLennan chief executive Jeffrey Greenberg, Hank's son, incurred Spitzer's wrath in 2004 when Spitzer's investigators uncovered evidence that suggested Marsh brokers were taking kickbacks and soliciting fake bids. (© Jim Bourg/Reuters/Corbis)

Former state prosecutor Michael Cherkasky was one Spitzer's early mentors at the Manhattan District Attorney's Office, but he took over a company on the receiving end of a Spitzer investigation when he became chief executive of Marsh & McLennan during the insurance probe. (Dan Nelkin)

Spitzer shocked the business world in October 2004 when he announced that he had uncovered bid-rigging at Marsh & McLennan's brokerage arm and said he would not negotiate with the firm's current management. (Keith Bradford/*The New York Times*)

Former Goldman Sachs co-chairman John Whitehead publicly raised the issue of Spitzer's temper in December 2005 when he accused the New York attorney general of threatening and verbally abusing him for writing an op-ed piece in support of one of Spitzer's targets. (Andrea Mohin/*The New York Times*)

Bank of America broker Theodore Sihpol III was one of the few people to stand up to Spitzer in court. Accused of fraud for his role in processing after-hours mutual fund trades, Sihpol refused to accept a plea offer. He and his wife are shown here outside Manhattan Supreme Court in 2005 as a jury was deliberating his fate. (Associated Press)

In early 2006, Spitzer was running in earnest for governor and surprised much of the Democratic Party establishment by tapping State Senator David Paterson to be his choice for lieutenant governor. Though many party elders were supporting other candidates, eventually most came around and endorsed the ticket. (Keith Myers/ *The New York Times*)

We took out things that by the standards of a civil complaint clearly could have been in. 'If you are 95 percent certain of this, we're not putting it in,'" he remembered being told. "It always makes me laugh when you hear people saying this office is reckless. When you talk about factual allegations, this office is super cautious, which is how it should be."

By Friday, October 8, Bill Rosoff at Marsh & McLennan could see the writing on the wall, though he still wasn't exactly sure what Spitzer was so angry about. "We've got a real crisis," Rosoff told Michael Cherkasky, Spitzer's former supervisor and friend, who had joined Marsh & McLennan four months earlier, when the firm bought the corporate security firm Kroll. Cherkasky had deliberately steered clear of the investigation thus far. ("I don't do Spitzer," he had told CEO Jeff Greenberg at the time of the acquisition.) But now Rosoff needed help. "This is a real crisis," the general counsel said again, and on Sunday, October 10, a team of Marsh executives drove out to Cherkasky's suburban home to brief him about the situation. Though Marsh's lawyers had still not uncovered the worst of the bid-rigging, Cherkasky immediately understood how bad the firm's business methods would look to a prosecutor. "I told them how serious it was," he remembered. But his warning didn't get through. "It's everything about perspective. Some of the stuff, if you looked at it from an industry perspective, it looked different," Cherkasky remembered. "This was a group of people sitting in a position where [Spitzer was questioning something that] had been a practice for seventy years." The disconnect paved the way for a bizarre week. Cherkasky, who was talking to Spitzer behind the scenes, knew that Marsh was about to get hit with a devastating legal blow; the rest of Marsh's leadership remained largely in denial.

On Tuesday, October 12, Spitzer and his team were ready to go. Even Rosoff and Dunne sensed that a case was imminent when they arrived at 120 Broadway for the first of two meetings that day. But Spitzer hadn't pulled the trigger. The mutual fund case had started with a settlement, and he held out the remote possibility that Marsh & McLennan's management would change its tune after being told specifically where to look for evidence of bid-rigging. The first meeting was with Spitzer's staff. More than a dozen lawyers who had worked on the case gathered in the twenty-third-floor conference room to wait for Bill Rosoff's arrival. Michele Hirshman cautioned them to hold their tongues. This was Marsh's opportunity to talk its way out of trouble. No one should interrupt.

When he arrived, Rosoff did most of the talking. He was aware, he told the room, that Spitzer's investigators had discovered e-mails they found troubling. He then acknowledged that one of his outside lawyers, from Davis Polk, had found them troubling as well. But that, he said, just showed their lack of experience with insurance. Then he passed on the explanation that Marsh executives had given to him and to the Davis Polk lawyers. Corporate insurance was a highly specialized market with relatively few competitors for each specific contract. When clients wanted more bids, Marsh brokers obliged by going out and getting them. Often those extra bids were higher than the original bid, but they were genuine offers to do business, not any kind of fake arrangement. No one was being hurt by the practice, he said. "He was really clear that we didn't understand the insurance industry and neither did his lawyers," Hirshman remembered. "It was polite, but it was clear there was not a meeting of the minds."

The gathering lasted less than half an hour, and as soon as Hirshman ushered the Marsh lawyers out, the room exploded. "Can you believe they're still sticking to that story?" the Spitzer staff members asked each other. "It's the same old song and dance." Indeed, the two sides were now talking past each other. Rosoff and Marsh thought that Spitzer was still talking about the general issue of whether contingent commissions influenced recommendations to clients, a potentially questionable practice but not one that was clearly illegal. They didn't know the attorney general was sitting on solid evidence of bid-rigging.

That afternoon, at Spitzer's twenty-fifth-floor conference table, Rosoff repeated his mistake, albeit in a less confrontational tone. "I'm here to resolve this if I can," he said. He knew Spitzer wanted the company to confess to something, he said, but he didn't really understand what. Insurance was a complicated business, and the internal e-mails about bids were easy to misunderstand. "We'd be happy to explain if we knew what you were focused on. . . . Why won't you tell us what we did?" Rosoff said. Spitzer's aides were amazed. They felt they had given the company ample direction—how hard was it to figure out what terms like *cartel, concrete club*, and *fictitious bid* were getting at? Spitzer was stern. He was not interested in negotiating with Rosoff on these terms. Marsh's leadership should know by now what was wrong with their business practices and have meaningful plans to change it. "Neither Jeff [Greenberg] nor Bill Rosoff ever demonstrated an understanding that there were problems with the underlying facts," Spitzer remembered. "They did the opposite of what you would expect good corporate leadership to do. . . . At that meeting, we laid things out, and Rosoff said, 'You don't understand the insurance business.' "

Spitzer told his staff to be ready to file the complaint on Thursday. As usual, they worked through the night. Brown's Investment Protection team fine-tuned the legal language and selected e-mails that could be blown up and put on posters for the press conference. Pope's criminal lawyers negotiated with the defense attorneys for several cooperating AIG and ACE executives, arranging for them to be ready to come to court and plead guilty to charges related to the bid-rigging scheme. Cherkasky made one last telephone call to Spitzer on Marsh & McLennan's behalf. The company wanted to settle. Couldn't the lawyers negotiate an agreement before Spitzer went public? "Too late, Mike," Spitzer replied. "It just can't be done."

Spitzer mulled over his concerns about executive accountability. He had not spoken directly to Jeffrey Greenberg, but he believed that Carey Dunne's "message" over the summer and Bill Rosoff's lack of contrition had come directly from the top. "The stuff as we were laying it out to Rosoff, if he [Greenberg] didn't get it, then he shouldn't be running the company. It's not that we're so smart. This stuff isn't that complicated," Spitzer remembered. "There simply is no reasonable justification for a system that rigs bids, stifles competition, and cheats customers." Spitzer knew he couldn't call for Greenberg's resignation in so many words. That really would be interfering with Marsh & McLennan's corporate governance. But the federal government had long insisted on complete cooperation from companies that hoped to avoid a corporate indictment. Spitzer believed he could use his press conference to do the same thing, and make clear that for Marsh, complete cooperation included a change of leadership. "The company is not entitled to a settlement. If it wants to settle with me, it needs a different CEO," he later explained. "I will not settle unless there is a CEO on the other side who shares an understanding that this is wrong. . . . [Greenberg] clearly has demonstrated that he won't accept that this is wrong." Though Michele Hirshman initially raised questions about Spitzer's plan to announce publicly that he would not negotiate with Greenberg, in the end she didn't object. "To do it at a press conference was unusual," she conceded, but she noted that plenty of white-collar-crime cases from the 1980s resulted in "a swift and certain removal of upper management." David Brown found he rather liked the idea. "I remember thinking, 'That is aggressive but it hits the nail on the head,'" he said. "I wouldn't have thought of doing it that way, but if it's ever appropriate, it's appropriate here."

The reaction to Spitzer's press conference on Thursday, October 14, was explosive. His statement that the leadership of Marsh & McLennan "is not a leadership I will talk with. It is not a leadership I will negotiate with" resounded on Wall Street. Marsh & McLennan's stock dropped nearly 25 percent, and the share prices of three of the insurance companies mentioned but not charged in the complaint—AIG, ACE, and Hartford Financial Services Group—each dropped between 6 and 11 percent that day. On Friday, other insurance stocks fell, and analysts from Moody's warned that the credit ratings of the firms involved in the scandal could be affected. By Monday, all three of the companies headed by members of the Greenberg family, Marsh & McLennan, AIG, and ACE, had forsworn the use of contingent commissions. "It was a type of validation for us," Brown remembered. "We felt like the market had spoken."

In the meantime, Marsh & McLennan's headquarters were in chaos. Company executives who had watched Spitzer's press conference on television weren't sure how to respond to his demand for new leadership. True to his tough-as-nails reputation and the warning Carey Dunne had passed on over the summer, Jeffrey Greenberg initially tried to fight back. The night after Spitzer's press conference, he ousted the head of the Marsh brokerage business and replaced him with Michael Cherkasky. Together they decided that Marsh would take the lead in renouncing contingent commissions, and Greenberg scheduled a telephone press conference to rebut the worst of the allegations.

On Friday, Cherkasky went to see his old protégé. In an effort to keep things cordial, Spitzer had his staff order sandwiches, but the meeting was far from an ordinary encounter between two old friends. Spitzer was "snippy," Cherkasky recalled, and made it crystal clear that he was dead serious about his demand for new leadership at the top of Marsh & McLennan. "Friday, October 15, is the first time I understand the intensity of his feelings about Mr. Greenberg," Cherkasky remembered. "Spitzer is not persuadable. . . . It's very, very tough, what Spitzer's willing to do and not do, and whether he will charge the corporation criminally is very much in the air." By the meeting's end, Cherkasky hadn't eaten a bite of lunch, so Spitzer urged him to take along a sandwich.

Marsh & McLennan canceled Greenberg's planned press call, and the CEO hired a personal attorney—Richard Beattie, the chairman of the prominent firm Simpson, Thacher & Bartlett, a former Carter administration official and a respected legal eminence. Greenberg told Beattie that he had never even talked with Spitzer about the bid-rigging allegations and that he had not realized that the New York attorney general was so angry. They discussed whether it was worth making a personal appeal to Spitzer but decided against it. Beattie told Greenberg that the board should be the ones approaching Spitzer, but added that it was probably too late because "Eliot was so far out on a limb that he couldn't get back," Beattie remembered. Instead, he and Greenberg drafted a letter to Marsh & McLennan's board in which Greenberg offered to resign.

But when the board members received the letter on Monday, October 18, they weren't sure what to do. The bid-rigging scheme had started well before Jeff Greenberg's tenure at the company, and some firm directors resented Spitzer's high-handed demand for a leadership change. Zachary Carter, a former U.S. attorney who had joined the board after the previous year's market-timing scandal at Marsh & McLennan's Putnam Investments subsidiary, decided to reach out directly to Spitzer, and he led a small group of independent directors who met with Spitzer on Wednesday, October 20. "Is this personal?" they asked. "Do we really have to get rid of him?"

"I was rigid on that point," Spitzer remembered. "It doesn't seem right to leave a CEO in place who, after having the evidence laid out for him, has refused to acknowledge the impropriety. I said, 'Get me a CEO who understands what needs to be done.'" By the next weekend, Greenberg was out, and the board had tentatively offered the job to Charles Davis, then head of Marsh & McLennan's private equity firm, MMC Capital. But when Cherkasky heard the news, he balked. He knew that both Spitzer and *The New York Times* were looking into allegations that MMC Capital had conflict-of-interest problems and that Davis's appointment would jump-start those inquiries. "It wasn't that I thought it really was a conflict of interest," Cherkasky remembered. "It was that there was going to be an investigation. It was not the reality. It was the appearance. We could not afford it."

On Monday, October 25, Cherkasky told the Marsh & McLennan board that if Davis became the CEO, he would quit. Convinced that they needed Cherkasky and his reputation as a straight-shooting former prosecutor to allay Spitzer's and the public's concerns, the members of the board capitulated and gave Cherkasky the top spot instead. The change could not have been starker—Jeffrey Greenberg had been imperious and demanding but had been steeped in the insurance business almost from birth. Cherkasky was rumpled, unpretentious, and an old friend of Spitzer's. But his expertise was corporate security and investigations. He had a lot to learn about Marsh & McLennan's core insurance and mutual fund businesses.

Still, the board's gamble paid off, at least initially. Moments after Cherkasky learned of his appointment, he, Carey Dunne, and Robert Fiske—another Davis Polk partner and a former U.S. attorney— hopped in a car to Spitzer's office to make the case that Marsh & McLennan should not face a corporate indictment. Fiske presented a package of proposed reforms, including the end of contingent commissions, a slew of personnel changes, and more disclosure to clients, but the meeting quickly devolved into the "Eliot and Mike show." Cherkasky explained to Spitzer that Marsh was in an "Arthur Andersen situation" and would either collapse entirely or hemorrhage people and clients indefinitely until Spitzer stated publicly that he was not going to indict the firm. "He got it right away," Cherkasky remembered. Pulling Cherkasky aside, Spitzer showed him a brief statement that he had scribbled out on a piece of paper. "Will this work?" Spitzer asked. Later that day, the Attorney General's Office used the same phrases in a press release, and Spitzer made a series of phone calls to key reporters to make clear that he would work with the new management. "This is a fundamental shift," Spitzer told *The Washington Post.* "Mike and the new leadership of Marsh are completely dedicated not only to rooting out the wrongdoing but to ensuring that the dynamics that caused it are changed."

Spitzer's critics viewed Cherkasky's installation as head of Marsh as evidence that Spitzer had stooped to corporate blackmail. "When an ambitious political figure, eager to become governor, essentially assassinates CEOs in public, isn't that an abuse of power?" *Chief Executive* magazine complained in an editorial. "The proper role of government would be to pursue remedies, perhaps legislatively or in quiet backroom discussions. But to hit with a full barrage of criminal and civil charges was wrong. Spitzer is building his political career by collecting trophies." And former federal prosecutor Leslie Caldwell, who had headed the federal task force investigating Enron, told *The Wall Street Journal,* "Normally, the prosecutor's role is not to decide what specific management changes should be made—it is to determine whether the company is cooperating in good faith and whether the company is taking appropriate steps to address whatever the problem might be."

But Spitzer believed that the two weeks of whirlwind change proved he had been right: going public had compelled Marsh to address immediately the industry-wide and company-wide problems his staff had discovered, rather than spending years investigating and negotiating settlements. "Filing the complaint forced [Marsh & McLennan] to change their behavior. They had a major crisis with clients and the market," he explained. "That is the virtue to filing a document that lays out the facts. It permits other participants to apply the necessary pressure. This is where transparency plays its part."

10

FOOT FAULTS

========

TWO MONTHS AFTER THE MARSH PRESS CONFERENCE, WITH THE INSURANCE investigation still being featured prominently in the news, Eliot Spitzer made official what many in New York and national politics had long assumed. On Tuesday, December 7, 2004, he made a series of low-key phone calls to political reporters around the state to announce that he would be a candidate for governor in 2006. Political analysts viewed the extraordinarily early declaration—it was twenty-three months before the election—as an effort to scare off challengers. One early possibility, U.S. senator Charles Schumer, had taken his name out of the running a few weeks earlier, and Spitzer's announcement coincided with polls that showed that the incumbent governor, George Pataki, would lose to Spitzer in a head-to-head race. (Pataki would wait another seven months to announce that he would not seek reelection to a fourth term.) Spitzer followed up his announcement with a celebratory speech to supporters two days later at a New York City fund-raiser in which he touted the state's progressive past and promised "to re-energize state government: make it smarter, more efficient, responsive, accountable and ethical." Though anticlimactic, the announcement caused problems for Spitzer a few weeks later when *The New York Times* misinterpreted comments he had made about reinvigorated federal regulators and wrote in a Christmas Day article that Spitzer was "ready to cede" his investigations to the national regulators. Calling the move a "remarkable turnabout," the front-page article speculated that Spitzer was changing his tune because he needed to raise campaign funds. Spitzer, who was spending the holiday with his in-laws in North Carolina, went ballistic. As he viewed it, his entire career had been based on reform, and he was not about to sit still for an accusation that he was trimming his sails for political reasons. "If there's one thing I guard jealously, it's the integrity of what we are doing here," he said. Spitzer and his spokesman, Darren Dopp, spent most of the holiday on the phone. Neither of them got to sit down for their festive meals, and they kept up their assault until the *Times* agreed to run both a correction and a corrective article.

Spitzer also made clear in practical ways that he was still patrolling the financial beat, bearing down on his staff to forge settlements with the insurance brokers. Marsh came first. Though Cherkasky had promised that he would do what was needed to settle the case, the actual terms took several months to hammer out. The new CEO and his lawyers made extensive presentations to Spitzer and his aides about the firm's reform efforts and its desperate financial straits. In the wake of the bid-rigging allegations, Marsh & McLennan had let go more than three thousand employees, and its stock was down nearly 40 percent since the October 14 complaint. Cherkasky had eliminated perks for himself and other top executives and had arranged emergency financing to keep the doors open, but the end of contingent commissions had blown an eight-hundred-million-dollar hole in the company's ten-billion-dollar annual revenue stream. There was only so much more punishment the firm could take. It couldn't pay the one-billion-dollar penalty that the newspapers were speculating about. It needed a "survival discount," Cherkasky argued, and suggested half that much. In late January, the two sides settled on $850 million, but all of it had to go to customers, Spitzer insisted, not to Marsh shareholders angry about the falling stock price. "This wasn't an effort to squeeze the last penny out of the rock," Spitzer remembered. "All the way back to Merrill, the notion was don't fundamentally destroy or injure the company but get rid of its bad behavior."

At Spitzer's insistence, Marsh & McLennan agreed to make a public apology for "unlawful behavior" by the employees who rigged bids and to make its fee arrangements clearer to its customers. But the deal kept bogging down over smaller issues: how to distribute the settlement money, how Marsh would disclose its revenue to customers, and whether the reforms Spitzer was insisting on would apply to Marsh's foreign subsidiaries as well. Spitzer's lawyers spent the entire weekend of January 29–30, 2005, at the office, where they debated individual points by phone with Marsh's legal team. Spitzer himself was pacing around at home on Fifth Avenue, watching television with the sound off, helping one of his daughters with her homework, and generally trying to stay out of his aides' way. But each time the lawyers' spats got really bad, he and Cherkasky went straight to each other. "I never scream and I hardly ever curse," Cherkasky remembered, "but this weekend, I'm exasperated at my legal team and at Michele [Hirshman] and Dieter [Snell]. I want to kill every one of them. Eliot is the only person I can talk civilly to." Spitzer agreed. "Whenever we reached a point where the sides were dug in, somebody needed to rise above it. So I tried to rise above it," he remembered.

Then, in the middle of the afternoon on Sunday, Marsh & McLennan's leadership seemed to disappear. The company simply stopped returning calls from Spitzer's deputies. "Everybody was frustrated it was a Sunday," remembered Dieter Snell. "We didn't want to be there and we didn't understand why it was taking so long." In fact, Cherkasky's management team was in full-blown revolt. Convinced that the CEO was giving away too much, Marsh's top executives basically held their leader captive, away from his office phone, so that he couldn't talk to Spitzer. Finally, after what seemed like hours, Spitzer, who had come into the office to nail down the deal, told Pope to place a call to Cherkasky's wife, Betsy, at home and ask for help in tracking down her husband. Once connected, the two men started horse-trading, each giving way on a few points. "It turned out there wasn't that big a gap," Cherkasky remembered. "We worked out those last items, and I went back to my staff and said, 'This is it. No discussion.'" When the CEO got home late that night and revealed to his wife that Marsh had agreed to pay $850 million, she practically laughed at him. "Only cigarette companies pay $850 million," Betsy said, adding sarcastically, "Thank God he's a friend of yours."

Spitzer, on the other hand, was still raring to go. Marsh was just one company, and he had an industry to revamp. Though it was 10:30 P.M., he looked around at his troops and said, "So everyone is going to be back here at 8 a.m., right? We have got a ton more work to do." Indeed, the staff attorneys in the Investment Protection Bureau had just about reached crunch time in their investigation of Marsh's biggest competitor, Aon, and its longtime CEO, Patrick Ryan. Revered in Chicago, where Aon was headquartered, as a co-owner of the Chicago Bears and a major philanthropist, Ryan had spent twenty-one years building Aon into the world's second largest insurance broker, with nearly fifty thousand employees and ten billion dollars in sales. Charismatic and hands-off, he often talked about Aon's strong ethics—every new employee was given a "Values Card" touting the company's "unyielding focus on what is best for our clients." However, several insurance company executives told Spitzer's team that Aon had a reputation for bullying and throwing its weight around. To make matters more complicated, Aon had retained Spitzer's old friend and former law partner Lloyd Constantine, who had run the 1998 transition team at the Attorney General's Office and had helped hire many of Spitzer's top deputies. He and Spitzer had even given up their regular early-morning tennis game, lest it appear to create a conflict of interest.

Since the Marsh filing in October, several Investment Protection Bureau attorneys had been focused nearly full time on Aon, and the evidence they had turned up wasn't pretty. Though there wasn't anything like Marsh's organized system of bid-rigging, the attorney general's team had uncovered multiple e-mails that they believed showed that Aon brokers had steered clients to insurance companies that paid higher contingent commissions. The probe had also uncovered documents suggesting to Spitzer's lawyers that Aon had encouraged insurers to inflate their bids. In September 2003, Aon told Zurich American that its $247,000 bid for workers-compensation insurance for Fieldstone Investment Corporation was too low and could be raised to $290,000 without jeopardizing the contract. Aon officials explained the move as a way to "make it up to" Zurich for $18,000 in unexpected expenses on a completely unrelated account. But the most explosive allegations of all involved a claim that Ryan himself had promised to favor a particular insurance company by steering clients' business to the insurer if it agreed to use Aon as its broker for buying reinsurance.

Nailing down the Ryan allegation fell to antitrust specialist Peter Bernstein and a new member of the insurance team, David Axinn, who had transferred into Investment Protection from the Appeals Bureau just weeks before the Marsh complaint. For Axinn it had been a heady experience. In his four years of working on appeals he had had direct contact with Spitzer only a handful of times. Now he was attending regular meetings in Spitzer's twenty-fifth-floor office.

The trail started with some handwritten notes taken by an employee of Carvill, a rival reinsurance brokerage firm, during a conference call with some executives at Chubb in the fall of 2000. According to the notes, Chubb officials told Carvill that they were moving their reinsurance from Carvill to Aon because Ryan had personally leaned on Chubb's CEO Dean O'Hare, who had since retired. According to the notes, Ryan had met with O'Hare in Chicago and then tracked him down in South America to make sure Chubb made the switch. In return, the notes said, "Ryan [was] willing to put his personal credibility and friendship on the line to make sure Chubb receives preferential treatment from Aon" when the broker made personal insurance recommendations to its clients. Axinn and Bernstein worked their way through the ranks of the top Chubb executives and amassed evidence that O'Hare had indeed met with Ryan in September 2000, been in Brazil that October, and had made a unilateral decision to move the reinsurance to Aon at that time. Told by O'Hare's lawyer that the retired CEO was too ill to travel, Axinn and Bernstein flew to Florida to interview him. The trip proved disappointing. In between frequent smoking breaks, O'Hare told the Spitzer lawyers "he couldn't remember a goddamn thing. Maybe he met with Pat Ryan. Maybe he didn't. Okay, he did, if we said so, but he didn't remember any promises," Axinn recalled.

A few days later, on November 4, Ryan himself came to New York for an interview with the investigators. Tall and silver haired with a

deep voice, he seemed larger than life. Ryan was also cordial, cooperative, and intent on moving the case toward an amicable settlement. He
and Lloyd Constantine had come in prepared to talk about the larger
issues at the company, including allegations of steering and improper
links between different lines of insurance. They were caught by surprise when Bernstein threw in a few questions about the O'Hare meeting. After a somewhat boisterous legal argument, the Aon chief waved
off his lawyers and answered the questions. But the results were
unsatisfying—he professed to remember little or nothing about any
conversations with O'Hare. In a meeting six days later, Spitzer told
Ryan and Aon's general counsel, Cameron Findlay, that the firm would
not be facing bid-rigging allegations as Marsh had, but that steering
charges were definitely on the table. The attorney general dismissed
Aon's internal studies that the company said showed that its brokers
had largely declined to send clients to particular insurance firms.
Spitzer's top aides also decided to include the allegation about Ryan
pressuring O'Hare in their draft complaint, albeit as the fourth of four
topics. Now they had to see what Aon would do.

In early February, Constantine was on a long-planned vacation in
New Zealand when his Aon clients called in a panic. Though he had been
assured that the Aon matter was not on a particularly fast track, the investigation had suddenly taken a different turn. Get back here, the Aon executives said; Spitzer wants to settle this case right now, but we don't want
to buy a pig in a poke. On February 15, a jet-lagged Constantine joined
Findlay at a meeting with Michele Hirshman and other staff members
working on the case. Aon would not settle, Findlay said, until they knew
what Spitzer planned to allege in his public complaint against the company. Finally, Hirshman agreed to paraphrase Spitzer's draft aloud. When
she reached the personal allegations about Ryan, Constantine exploded.
"It's not true," he said, pounding the table. "You're a public official. You
have an obligation to get it right. Have you even spoken to him?"

The outburst sent the Spitzer team scrambling to reexamine the evidence. Then Ryan sent word that he wanted to fly in from Chicago to
meet personally with the attorney general. Spitzer called Axinn into his
office. He was seated behind his desk, with Hirshman and Snell nearby.
This would not be a jocular team meeting at the conference table.

"Other than the Carvill notes, what do you have?" Spitzer asked.

"Well," Axinn replied, "the best evidence I have is that the Carvill notes reference a trip to South America, and we have Dean O'Hare's itinerary, and he's in Brazil on that very day."

Spitzer wasn't satisfied. "That's still Carvill notes. . . . We can't do it," he said sternly.

Axinn started shuffling through the documents he had brought with him. "We do have a few things," he said anxiously and pulled out an October 30, 2000, letter in which a top Aon executive, Michael O'Halleran, thanked a Chubb executive for moving the reinsurance to Aon and promised to follow up with Aon's personal insurance and executive risk brokers. It appeared to be exactly the type of trade-off the Carvill notes had alluded to. Axinn handed his find to Hirshman, who scanned it and smiled.

"That's pretty good," she said.

By the time Ryan arrived and made a personal pitch to Spitzer, the office stood squarely behind the additional evidence Axinn and Bernstein had uncovered. "I had no doubt," Snell remembered. Ryan "was in the middle of it. The documents are very clear that he was a part of it, and the more we looked into it the clearer it got." Aon completely disagreed—they believed the Carvill notes were simply the excuses of a disgruntled competitor and that the O'Halleran letter showed that Pat Ryan and Dean O'Hare had arranged a meeting between their people, nothing more. Constantine made a formal presentation to Snell and the team that had investigated Aon, running through the documents, offering explanations, and arguing that no quid pro quo had taken place. But he got nowhere. "I was and I am absolutely convinced that allegation was not well founded," Constantine said. "They were not convinced by my advocacy. I feel like I failed."

Aon ultimately capitulated, agreeing to a $190 million settlement even though the complaint would include the personal allegations against Ryan. "They were not happy. They thought that the actual amount of money was too harsh," Constantine remembered. "The company decided to settle because of the brooding omnipresence of that investigation. . . . It would have been a problem for them for as long as it went on." Spitzer, meanwhile, found the deal easier to agree to because Ryan was already on his way out as CEO—in a move unrelated to the Spitzer inquiry, he had announced the prior September that he planned to move from CEO to chairman. "We did not pull any punches. He was leaving the company anyway. That had begun independent of us, but it made it easier. We did not have to say anything about going forward," Spitzer remembered.

The Aon settlement was announced on Friday, March 4, and once again there would be no rest for the weary Investment Protection team. Gaul, Filipakis, and Brown were already enmeshed in a high-stakes investigation of an entirely different problem with insurance companies: allegations that AIG—run by Jeffrey Greenberg's father, the legendary insurance executive Maurice "Hank" Greenberg—had used complicated reinsurance deals to make its books look better to investors. Spitzer's team was ostensibly working in tandem with the SEC and federal prosecutors in Virginia, but cooperation was rapidly giving way to a horse race, as each office sought to put its own stamp on the investigation.

At Spitzer's office, David Brown had gotten two separate calls from friends on Wall Street right after the filing of the Marsh complaint. Both callers said, if you're looking at insurance, you should really look at the whole issue of finite insurance and its impact on publicly reported companies' books. Brown and his team did some quick research and learned that in 2003 the SEC had brought an action against AIG for selling a telecommunications firm called Brightpoint a "purported 'insurance' product" that was really a loan that Brightpoint had used to hide losses and overstate its earnings. The settlement also noted that AIG had been uncooperative and "withheld documents" from the SEC. Convinced that the Brightpoint case might be the tip of an iceberg, the Investment Protection Bureau dashed off a subpoena to AIG in November 2004. Almost immediately, they got a call from the SEC's Steve Cutler. The SEC Enforcement chief told Brown, we've been investigating this issue for two years now and we're on the verge of announcing a $126 million settlement with AIG for selling PNC Bank an "earnings management" product. Our deal will also require AIG to come clean about its other finite-insurance sales. Cutler's message was cordial but clear: we're on the ball here; don't mess things up. Brown checked with his bosses and immediately called Cutler back. "We're going to back off this one out of comity," he said, "but I think this is a very serious topic." The two men then agreed that their staffs would work on the issue together.

For the next two months, the SEC's New York office and the Four Ms from Spitzer's office sent closely coordinated subpoenas to a batch of insurance companies asking for information on finite insurance, a hybrid product that was part transfer of risk and part financing arrangement. Unlike traditional insurance, which covered unexpected losses of uncertain size, these contracts covered a specified—or finite—amount of losses. Insurance companies routinely bought such coverage from their peers or from reinsurance firms to minimize their exposure to potentially catastrophic losses. But the investigators learned that the deals were often driven by the need for financing and were sometimes structured so that the size of the loss was nearly certain and the total premiums paid were almost equal to the total insurance payout. The contracts, then, included the barest minimum of risk required to qualify for accounting treatment as an insurance contract rather than a loan. "Finite insurance was the drug of choice among insurance companies, and selling it to other non-insurers was a relatively small part of the business," Brown said. His bosses upstairs on the executive floor were skeptical. The issues with finite insurance seemed "inchoate," and Brown's staff was already up to their ears in the contingent-commission investigation, Snell remembered. Spitzer was even more skeptical. "Is this ever going to be a case? This is so complicated that even if there's something there, is it ever going to be a case you can bring to a jury?" Spitzer asked Brown. Even worse from Brown's point of view, "It was in the papers every time we sent a subpoena, and I didn't like that. I didn't want to raise expectations."

Unbeknownst to the Spitzer team, the federal Department of Justice was also on the case, because its investigation of a troubled Virginia malpractice insurance company had turned up examples of the same issue. Then, on December 30, 2004, Filipakis received a call from two SEC lawyers who said they wanted to inform her that they had sent a letter requesting information on finite insurance to General Re (Gen Re), a Connecticut-based subsidiary of Berkshire Hathaway, the firm headed by famed investor Warren Buffett. Filipakis was non-plussed. The two agencies had been sending out joint subpoenas to a variety of companies, so why had the SEC done something on its own? "Why would you send an information request rather than a subpoena unless you didn't want us to know about it?" she asked. The SEC attorneys got very quiet, and one of them said something halting about having asked for permission to tell Spitzer's office but not having gotten the go-ahead. While he was speaking, Filipakis did a Google search on the company name and up popped Gen Re's own public announcement that day that it had received the SEC request. "Wait a minute. I have the news release here," she said. "You didn't want us to know about it." Then her search also pulled up an earlier e-mail from another SEC lawyer asking her to remove Gen Re from one of the earlier joint subpoena lists. Though no one mentioned the Justice Department by name, Spitzer's lawyers quickly figured out what had happened. The federal prosecutors, who were in the middle of negotiating a cooperation agreement with Gen Re, had gotten the SEC to take Gen Re off the joint list in November because they wanted to keep their grand jury probe secret and were afraid an additional request from Spitzer would spook Gen Re's officials. But the Justice Department had not counted on Buffett's reputation for transparency. Concerned that they were behind the eight ball, the Spitzer lawyers banged out a subpoena and got it to Gen Re.

Rather than get caught up in the rivalry, Gen Re and its lawyers agreed to share the results of their internal investigation with everybody at the same time. Their February 8 presentation at the New York offices of the SEC was unusual for its candor. Gen Re's lawyers said flat out that they believed they had uncovered a transaction with AIG from the third quarter of 2000 that appeared to be bogus, and they proceeded to demonstrate why they thought certain documents had been faked. Essentially, the allegations boiled down to this: In late October 2000, AIG's share price began to drop amid reports from analysts that the company's long-term reserves were shrinking and might not be big enough to cover unexpected losses by its customers. The day AIG chairman and CEO Hank Greenberg was told of the market's concerns, he had called Ronald Ferguson, the president of Gen Re, to propose a transaction. Greenberg wanted Gen Re to buy five hundred million dollars worth of reinsurance from AIG, which would allow AIG to increase its publicly reported long-term reserves, but he also allegedly wanted Gen Re to guarantee that it would not make a claim against the policy, making the deal "risk free." The combination made no sense and violated accounting rules, not to mention the fact that it made the insurance completely worthless to Gen Re. But, Gen Re's lawyers continued, Greenberg told Ferguson he would make the deal worth Gen Re's while, and their subordinates worked out a series of wire transactions to make that happen. Although a Gen Re subsidiary officially paid ten million dollars for the worthless reinsurance, AIG returned the money along with an additional five million. Gen Re and AIG officials also cooked up a series of after-the-fact documents that made it look as if Gen Re had approached AIG and not the other way around. AIG officially booked the deal in two parts, adding two-hundred-fifty-million dollars to its reserves in the fourth quarter of 2000 and again in the first quarter of 2001. (Greenberg's spokesman, Howard Opinsky, said, "Mr. Greenberg never requested nor intended to participate in any sham transactions." Greenberg's lawyers also pointed out that AIG's publicly reported loss reserves at that time were more than twenty-five billion dollars, more than a hundred times the size of each Gen Re transaction.)

Gaul, Berlin, and Filipakis attended the Gen Re presentation for Spitzer's office, and it was not until the next day that they caught up with Brown and briefed him. He was stunned by what they had to say. Gen Re had done "as good a job of serving facts up to enforcement as I have ever seen," Brown said. "It's really extraordinary. They did it the right way." He rushed right up to see Spitzer. "Eliot, you should hear this," he said. "I think it's real, and if it's real, it's really explosive." The AIG transaction not only looked bogus but it had also allegedly been proposed and negotiated by Hank Greenberg himself. They needed to hear AIG's side of the story. "Get the subpoenas out," Spitzer said after he had heard the details. "Get them out now." Several hours later, Brown returned to his boss's office. Spitzer was scheduled to speak that night at a private gathering at Goldman Sachs, Brown's old employer, and Brown was planning to go along. When Brown arrived, Spitzer was glaring at his computer screen. "I can't believe this. Look at this,"

Spitzer said. He pointed to a news report on remarks that Hank Green-berg had made on a company conference call for investors earlier in the day. The AIG chairman had been flush with pride to be announcing record profits of eleven billion dollars and pleased that he had finally sorted out AIG's problems with the SEC and federal prosecutors over the PNC deal. Asked by an analyst about a "hostile regulatory environment," the seventy-nine-year-old corporate titan lashed out at regulators who "look at foot faults and make them into a murder charge."

Spitzer was outraged. How could Greenberg be talking that way? He might not know about the finite-insurance probe yet, but he was aware that AIG had not yet settled with Spitzer over its participation in the bid-rigging scandal. Never one to accept criticism with equanimity, Spitzer already had reason to be irked at Greenberg's attitude toward his regulators—the prior October, a public relations company hired by AIG had offered up to twenty-five thousand dollars to financial industry experts if they would criticize Spitzer's insurance industry probe. AIG officials said they had not authorized the effort, but bad blood remained. At the Goldman dinner that night, Brown quietly informed his boss that the subpoena asking for all of AIG's documents on the Gen Re deal had gone out. Spitzer then departed from his speech on compliance to take on Greenberg. "Hank Greenberg should be very, very careful talking about foot faults," he warned. "Too many foot faults and you can lose the match. But more importantly, these aren't just foot faults."

Spitzer and Brown's decision to send out a late-night subpoena to AIG without alerting the SEC caused new friction with their long-suffering partners. Andrew Calamari, who was heading the SEC team investigating AIG, called Brown to complain, saying, "Are we working together or not?" Brown retorted that the SEC had done the same thing over Gen Re, and the two men had words. But the exchange cleared the air, and they agreed to continue doing the investigation together.

Later that same week, Spitzer had another idea. Rather than just asking AIG for information, he wanted to talk to Greenberg directly, to make him testify under oath about the Gen Re transaction. It was an unusual move. When investigating allegations of fraud, most prosecutors and regulators started at the bottom of a company and worked their way up the ranks, building evidence as they went. Spitzer and

Brown wanted to go right to the top. They said there was no connection between their decision to subpoena the AIG chairman and the conference call remarks. Rather, they were investigating a highly unusual transaction and believed Greenberg had the information they needed. "These are fact patterns that revolve around him," Spitzer said. "This is not 'let's see what the CEO knows about some transaction eighteen levels down.' He was intimately involved. . . . Subpoenas should go to the people who have material information." Meanwhile, the SEC had sent its own subpoena to AIG. In short order, Steve Cutler got a call. It was Hank Greenberg. "Why do you have to revisit this stuff? I thought we settled this" as part of the PNC settlement, the AIG chief executive barked. After double-checking with his staff, Cutler explained that the previous settlements had involved AIG's sale of finite insurance to other companies. The new probe was looking at allegations that AIG had used the product to cook its own books. The SEC declined to join Spitzer in subpoenaing Greenberg—they saw no great need to turn up the heat on the AIG chief yet—but Calamari's boss, Mark Schonfeld, by now the director of the New York office, made sure that his lawyers would be allowed to attend and ask questions when Greenberg talked to Spitzer.

When AIG announced on Monday, February 14, that it, like Gen Re, had received subpoenas about finite insurance, the company's stock began to sink. By Friday morning, the share price had fallen more than four dollars, to about sixty-nine dollars. That's when Greenberg, who with his wife owned more than two billion dollars' worth of AIG stock, called in to the AIG trading desk from his private jet. He ordered the traders to use AIG's stock buy-back program to purchase 250,000 shares on behalf of the company, in an apparent effort to prop up the stock price. When Greenberg called back, the trader had only bought twenty-five thousand shares. "I want you be a little bit more aggressive. If you have to go up to half a million shares, go up to half a million shares." (Such a purchase would have cost AIG nearly thirty-five million dollars.) Greenberg called back again as the market was closing. Though companies generally refrained from buying back their stock after 3:50 P.M., to avoid allegations that they were trying to pump up the closing share price, Greenberg ordered the AIG traders to buy more stock. "You can keep buying a little more stock, it's alright. I wanna push it up a little bit if we can," he said. (Greenberg's spokesman, Howard Opinsky, said, "Stock repurchase programs are commonly employed by a wide variety of corporations to boost their stock price when management believes their stock is undervalued. Nothing more than that happened here.")

Meanwhile, a revolt was brewing within the AIG board. In the wake of AIG's earlier SEC troubles, the independent directors had hired their own lawyer, Richard Beattie from Simpson Thacher (who had represented Jeffrey Greenberg at the end of the Marsh & McLennan investigation). The directors now sent word to the SEC that they—not Hank Greenberg—were in charge of the internal investigation of the Gen Re transaction. On February 25, AIG's outside lawyers, a team from Paul Weiss led by Mark Pomerantz, came to the New York office of the SEC to do a presentation about their internal investigation of the Gen Re deal. The AIG independent directors sent their own lawyers, and once again Spitzer's lawyers and federal prosecutors from Washington were part of the audience. The Paul Weiss lawyers laid out facts that were strikingly similar to what Gen Re's lawyers had disclosed, down to the allegedly fake documents. Their conclusions were more measured, however. They called the October 2000 transaction "problematic," but argued that it was still possible that the reinsurance deal had involved a transfer of risk and therefore might be legitimate. In any case, they said the Gen Re transaction had not had a "material" impact on AIG's bottom line. "We think our books are clean," Gaul remembered them saying. When Filipakis asked if the Paul Weiss team had interviewed Greenberg about the transaction, the AIG lawyers squirmed. They had talked to the AIG chairman, they said, but "you don't really interview Mr. Greenberg." Pomerantz and the other AIG lawyers were also trying hard to push off Greenberg's deposition, then scheduled for March 11.

Brown and Spitzer agreed to delay the Greenberg deposition for six days but warned the AIG lawyers that Spitzer wanted answers, and he wanted them soon. On March 9, a big delegation trooped into Spitzer's office. Feisty defense lawyer Robert Morvillo was there on behalf of Hank Greenberg and found he was sitting on the same uncomfortable couch where he had sat during the discussion of Merrill's stock analyst woes. Mark Pomerantz represented AIG. Jamie Gamble of Simpson Thacher was representing the board of directors. Pomerantz asked for more time. "We have clear marching orders that we are to get to the bottom of this," Pomerantz said, "but you have to let us finish this. If you insist on these depositions it will screw that up." Spitzer didn't budge. "We can do our own investigation," he said firmly. "We're not putting off our deposition."

In fact, Gen Re's lawyers had already told Spitzer's office to expect a potential jackpot. The company's Irish subsidiary, for reasons that were never quite clear, had routinely tape-recorded its employees' phone calls, and the tapes from 2000 had captured several Gen Re executives discussing the AIG deal in terms that made clear that they had doubts about its legitimacy. The transcripts would take several more days to show up in Spitzer's office, but news that they were coming gave the investigation even more urgency.

Greenberg's newly hired civil attorneys—noted litigator David Boies and his partner Lee Wolosky—could feel the growing frenzy when they arrived at AIG's headquarters on 70 Pine Street in Lower Manhattan on Friday, March 11, about 9:30 A.M. After consulting personally with Greenberg, Boies had to leave, but Wolosky settled in for what he expected would be a long day of discussions with AIG executives about the particulars of the Gen Re transaction and how the company intended to deal with the regulatory inquiry. Instead, AIG's attorneys stowed Wolosky in an empty corner office, and he watched with growing frustration as they held a series of meetings and discussions without him. Finally, in the middle of the afternoon, Gamble came in and told him that the AIG lawyers were busy preparing for a 4:00 P.M. meeting with at least some of AIG's board and that Wolosky was going to be shut out of that as well. "It certainly was not a consultative process. By 3 p.m., it was clear that, despite the various discussions that were occurring within 70 Pine Street and with regulators, no one wished to speak with Greenberg or his lawyers about this transaction or about the future of the company," Wolosky remembered, adding that he found the development "remarkable."

* * *

March 12, 2005, was a Saturday, and Spitzer was supposed to be taking some time for himself. He was dressed to go running, but his jogging partner—an old friend from college—had cancelled because of illness. Then the phone rang. It was Richard Beattie, calling on behalf of AIG's board. AIG's independent directors were in a quandary, Beattie said, and they wanted to know from Spitzer just how bad things really were. The company was supposed to file its annual report (known as a 10-K) with the SEC in four days' time, yet the company's auditors had warned they might refuse to certify that AIG's books were accurate unless the management changed. The 10-K filing could be put off, but AIG had another problem. Spitzer was scheduled to depose Greenberg later that week, and the AIG chairman was telling fellow board members that his lawyers wanted him to assert his Fifth Amendment protection against self-incrimination. If Greenberg did that, he would run afoul of the company's strict policy—adopted after the SEC's first finite-insurance investigation—requiring employees to cooperate fully with regulators. Yet it would be hard—and controversial—for the board to force out Greenberg, who was legendary for his business acumen and for building AIG into one of the world's largest companies over the past four decades.

Beattie and Spitzer agreed to meet for a walk in Central Park. What, Beattie asked, had Spitzer's investigators found, and was there any chance they would be willing to delay the showdown over Greenberg's testimony? "I was trying to get a sense from Eliot how serious it was for the company," Beattie remembered. "We knew they knew more than we did, but we didn't know how much." Beattie's team had been combing through AIG's files on the transaction with Gen Re and had found some disturbing memos, but they knew that Spitzer had access to Gen Re's files on the deal as well. Spitzer told Beattie that the situation looked grave. There were "transactions, plural" under scrutiny, not just the Gen Re arrangement. Spitzer's investigators had evidence that they thought showed that Greenberg had personally initiated that five-hundred-million-dollar deal and appeared to know that his company was breaking accounting rules. "There are tapes," Spitzer said he told Beattie. "Not with Greenberg on them, but of people discussing what Greenberg knew and wanted. There was no ambiguity that this was risk free." In fact, one particularly intriguing tape had captured a Gen Re executive giving a thirdhand version of what Greenberg had reportedly said to Ronald Ferguson, the Gen Re president: "Ron, I need your help. . . . We've reduced our reserves by five hundred million to boost our third-quarter results, but we've now realized that, come the end of the year . . . the fact that we've taken down these old-year reserves is going to be fairly apparent to anyone studying out [sic] group, and we don't like what's going to happen in terms of stock market reaction. . . . We want to borrow five hundred million of reserves of you for a couple of years." The evidence was hearsay and therefore might not be admissible in court against Greenberg, but Spitzer and his investigators found it compelling nonetheless. (Ferguson was later charged with criminal fraud for his role in the transaction but has pleaded not guilty.)

While Spitzer had previously shied away from filing criminal charges against public companies for fear of driving them out of business, both men knew that AIG might find itself in the crosshairs if the board didn't take corrective action. Still, Spitzer didn't specifically tell Beattie what the AIG board should do with the information about Hank Greenberg. He couldn't. The walk in the park came only a few months after Beattie had personally chastised Spitzer for calling for Jeffrey Greenberg's head. "I had told him he made a mistake with Jeffrey. That was not his role. He gave that board no choice," Beattie said. Beattie told Spitzer he would inform his clients, AIG's independent directors, of what he now knew. "I told him we were having a board meeting on Sunday and I didn't know what the outcome would be," Beattie remembered.

When the board met on Sunday, it was a long and emotional day. Beattie, the lead outside director Frank Zarb, and a handful of others met at 10:00 A.M. The full board joined them at noon. Beattie told the directors about the tapes and reported that Spitzer believed he "had damaging evidence" against Greenberg. Pomerantz gave a presentation about the Gen Re deal and a broader talk about how the regulatory environment had changed after Enron's collapse and how the company might best survive. That information, plus the threat from the auditors, helped embolden a group of directors who had been growing uneasy about the AIG chief's autocratic and irascible ways. In one oft-described incident, Greenberg publicly dismissed as "stupid" a director's concerns about AIG's tangled relationship with several closely related companies that Greenberg also headed. Many of the board members were also well aware that the former independent directors of WorldCom and Enron had recently agreed to pay substantial sums out of their own pockets to settle allegations that they had failed to step in and stop corrupt management practices.

Zarb, the former head of NASD, had joined the AIG board at the behest of Greenberg in late 2001 because the aging AIG chairman wanted a close friend to oversee the transition to new management. But Zarb and other directors had become concerned during the SEC's Brightpoint investigation in 2003, when AIG had to pay a ten-million-dollar penalty. In the course of the settlement, the SEC had made clear that it had doubled the fine because of AIG's failure to cooperate. The same issue reappeared in the PNC investigation a year later—the SEC again found AIG to be uncooperative but was willing to make a deal. At the last minute, Greenberg pulled out, and AIG issued a press release saying that the investigation was "unwarranted." After the SEC formally warned it might investigate the company for "misleading" the public, Greenberg capitulated, but AIG's new $126 million settlement price was $20 million higher than the deal Greenberg had rejected earlier. "We never saw a hint of trouble until Brightpoint came along, and that was argumentative," one director remembered. "Then PNC came along and there was a settlement and we pulled out and then we settled on worse terms than before." By late 2004, some of the directors were pressuring their CEO to consider retiring on his eightieth birthday, which was coming up in May.

Spitzer's subpoena changed the equation. At the directors' meeting with Beattie and their other lawyers, it became clear that much of the AIG board didn't want to wait for Hank Greenberg to make a graceful exit. No formal analysis had been done to determine whether the Gen Re transaction actually transferred enough risk to make it legitimate, and there was no evidence clearly tying Greenberg to the doctored documents that made the transaction look shady. But the momentum had turned against the CEO. "We are here to represent the shareholders, not Hank," Zarb told his fellow directors, making clear that shareholder and employee interests trumped friendship in this battle. Greenberg himself was not present, but he called in several times from Florida, where he was aboard the *Serendipity II*, a yacht owned by one of the AIG-related companies that he also headed, and then later from AIG's private jet. Furious that his entire career at AIG was being tossed aside over a single deal from four years earlier, Greenberg warned that his ouster would destroy AIG. "This company's being run by a bunch of lawyers who couldn't even spell the word *insurance*," Greenberg snapped.

"I felt for him," Zarb remembered. "He was upset." By day's end, the directors had told Greenberg to resign as chief executive or face being fired, although they compromised by allowing him to stay on as non-executive chairman of the board. Unlike some of the Marsh & McLennan directors, who felt they had been railroaded into removing Jeff Greenberg, most of the AIG directors had no bone to pick with Spitzer. "Nobody in that room had a complaint about Spitzer," Zarb remembered. Beattie put in a call to Spitzer to let him know what had occurred. "The board did the right thing," Spitzer said, and then agreed to put off Greenberg's deposition until April.

AIG announced on Monday, March 14, that Greenberg would be replaced by Martin Sullivan, a fifty-year-old executive with the company. During the last-minute vetting process before Sullivan's appointment was announced, Beattie noticed that Sullivan uniformly referred to the former CEO as "Mr. Greenberg" rather than "Hank." When the lawyer asked Sullivan why, he replied, "I started at AIG when I was seventeen, and I've always called him Mr. Greenberg, and he never told me not to." Greenberg, meanwhile, went ahead with a planned trip to visit several far-flung Asian outposts of his empire. Over the next two weeks, Lee Wolosky of Boies's law firm began what appeared to be the reasonably friendly process of negotiating the details of Greenberg's new role and privileges as non-executive chairman of the board. But tensions remained. Media reports were making much of the fact that Greenberg had remained the head of two private companies, Starr International Company (SICO) and C. V. Starr & Company (CVSCO), both of which owned significant amounts of AIG stock and used it in part to compensate top AIG executives.

Over Easter weekend in late March, the volatile situation blew up. Early in the morning on Saturday, March 26, Maria Filipakis got a call from a panicked Paul Weiss lawyer. "She was frantic; she went into this whole big thing about Bermuda and boxes being taken out and she didn't know why or where they were going," Filipakis remembered. Fresh from the mutual fund investigation where at least two people tried to destroy evidence, Filipakis jumped into action. "I sent out an emergency BlackBerry: call me now," she remembered. The clash had started earlier in the week when lawyers from Paul Weiss began securing AIG documents around the world in preparation for turning them over to Spitzer and the SEC. On Thursday, March 24, AIG employees in Dublin seized a computer belonging to a SICO employee who shared their office space but still reported to Hank Greenberg. Later the same day, lawyers from the Boies firm, who were also representing SICO, observed Paul Weiss lawyers representing AIG removing documents that were specifically labeled NON-AIG from an office shared by AIG and SICO. On Friday, the Boies firm responded in kind. Good Friday was a legal holiday in Bermuda, and AIG's lawyers from Paul Weiss had gone home for the long weekend, but the Boies team entered the building, hauled out eighty-two boxes of documents, and was preparing to take out more. Boies insisted that the records all belonged to SICO and other "non-AIG" entities, but AIG employees weren't so sure. Their reports angered and worried the regulators. Concerned that a worldwide effort at document destruction might be under way, Filipakis and Gaul raced to the office to pound out a subpoena demanding the documents' return. They also alerted the SEC, which began drafting its own court order.

Spitzer, who was in Vail, blew his top. He left messages for both Beattie and the Paul Weiss lawyers about what he was calling the "document caper." "Fellas, we're moving along in a way that is all very reasoned and proper, but if we start seeing documents disappear when they are under subpoena . . . the consequences for the company do get much more severe," Spitzer said menacingly. If Greenberg's lawyers were destroying evidence while he was still chairman of the company, Spitzer said, then AIG "could have serious criminal exposure." (Greenberg's spokesman, Howard Opinsky, said, "In retrospect it's clear that the attorney general had jumped the gun because there were no sub-poenas on those documents at that time.")

By the time Spitzer and Beattie connected, it was 10:00 P.M. Saturday on the East Coast, and Spitzer was so agitated that the board's lawyer could barely get a word in edgewise. "I'm going to indict the company. Nothing happens in that company without Hank's approval," Spitzer said. Beattie tried to defuse the situation. "Let me talk to David Boies," he said soothingly. "We'll work things out." Beattie immediately called Boies, who made clear that his firm had already secured the documents and had informed AIG's lawyers they had done so. "Any suggestion that there was any impropriety in our actions with respect to the Bermuda documents of the Starr companies is without basis," Boies said later. "The documents belonged to Greenberg and the Starr entities; AIG was using the fact that these documents were in an AIG-owned building to access and remove some of these documents without our permission; we moved the documents to a secure location where they were held under guard; before moving the documents they were boxed and sealed, and the seals were broken only after a court order expressly permitted it." Beattie and Boies called Spitzer together to explain the situation. The attorney general calmed down immediately. There had to be a formal agreement securing the documents and a process for determining who got access to them, he insisted. But that could wait until morning.

The next day was Easter Sunday. Just before leaving for church, Beattie telephoned Martin Sullivan and Frank Zarb. "Good morning, Happy Easter," the lawyer said. "We have a problem. You're not going to like it." Sullivan sprang into action, sending a planeload of AIG officials to Bermuda to lock down the facility there and fire the employee who had helped SICO's lawyers gain access to the building. Company officials also secured Hank Greenberg's personal office at AIG's downtown Manhattan headquarters, locking out his secretary and other assistants. The AIG board made plans to meet on Monday to cope with the Greenberg problem. Even before the Bermuda mess, Boies and Beattie had been talking about Greenberg's increasingly untenable position. At 5:28 P.M. Monday, just before the board was to sit down, Greenberg sent word from Asia, via Boies, of "his intention to retire" as chairman and to leave the board entirely when his term expired.

Spitzer changed his tune at once, issuing a statement that praised the company's board for moving swiftly. "While there is a long way to go before this investigation is complete, the wise actions of the AIG board will help get this investigation on a path toward resolution," he said. By early April the storm had blown over—it became clear that no important paperwork had been destroyed and all sides agreed to an SEC-drafted court order guaranteeing everyone access to the proper documents. But AIG continued to take a tough line with its former CEO, refusing to allow a moving company to remove Greenberg's personal art and files, including the medical records for Snowball, his dog, and files about his fiftieth birthday celebration three decades earlier. "He is the man who built the greatest insurance company in the history of the business and they, the directors, are treating him as if he is a common criminal. . . . This is a terrible tragedy," said Edward E. Matthews, a retired AIG vice chairman who described himself as "proud to be described as a Greenberg loyalist."

Spitzer's office continued probing, slowly building a case against Greenberg and other top insurance executives. Then, with Greenberg slated to come in for the long-delayed deposition on April 12, Spitzer applied the screws publicly, taking to the airwaves to condemn what the company had done. In an interview with ABC's George Stephanopoulos on April 10, Spitzer asserted that AIG's reinsurance "deals were fundamentally flawed. . . . The evidence is overwhelming that these were transactions created for the purpose of deceiving the market. We call that fraud. It is deceptive, it is wrong. It is illegal. . . . That company was a black box, run with an iron fist by a CEO who did not tell the public the truth." Spitzer's television appearance outraged not only businesspeople but also many current and former prosecutors, who believed that he had crossed an ethical line that prevented prosecutors from making public accusations until they were ready to indict. "Something has gone seriously awry when a state attorney general can go on television and charge one of America's best CEOs and most generous philanthropists with fraud before any charges have been brought, before the possible defendant has even had a chance to know what he personally is alleged to have done, and while the investigation is still under way," wrote former Goldman Sachs chairman John Whitehead in a letter to *The Wall Street Journal*. "Mr. Spitzer has gone too far." Spitzer personally called Whitehead to complain. What happened next is in dispute. Whitehead would later write in the *Journal* that Spitzer called to chew him out, saying, "Mr. Whitehead, it's now a war between us and you've fired the first shot. I will be coming after you. You will pay the price." For his part, Spitzer said that he had called Whitehead to ask where he had gotten his facts but denied having threatened him. (When Whitehead's version became public, in December 2005, Spitzer's spokesman, Darren Dopp, called the account "not accurate. It is embellished and false.")

Spitzer's aides defended his remarks about Greenberg, saying he was simply stating in stronger language what the company had already acknowledged. AIG had said in a March 30 press release that documentation for the Gen Re transaction was "improper" and that a series of other deals "appear to have been structured for the sole or primary purpose of accomplishing a desired accounting result" and would have to be restated. "What I said there was right. The facts speak for themselves," Spitzer said, noting that he never said whether the fraud was a civil or criminal offense. But sympathy began to swing back toward Greenberg. The former CEO's high-priced team of lawyers said that their client was being made the scapegoat for the actions of a large group and that Greenberg should have been allowed to help AIG attempt to clean up its books. *CEO* magazine called for Spitzer's resignation, and *The Wall Street Journal* editorial board wrote, "Why not get on with it and indict the man? If Mr. Greenberg's behavior is so heinous that it warrants a denunciation as 'fraud' on national TV, what is Mr. Spitzer waiting for?"

Greenberg was far meeker when he arrived for his deposition on Tuesday, April 12. Though Spitzer had refused to move or postpone the deposition, his security office had arranged for the former AIG chief to use an often overlooked underground entrance in hopes of giving the media the slip. As was his wont for important interviews, Spitzer greeted Greenberg and exchanged pleasantries with him. But the attorney general didn't stay long. He left before David Brown started reading from his list of prepared questions. "If he had answered questions I would have sat in," Spitzer said. "But I didn't want him to think I was gloating that he was taking the Fifth. He's a wiry guy, hyperactive. Today he seemed remarkably subdued." While Greenberg did answer questions about his identity, age, and educational background, when the subject matter began to touch on AIG, he refused to answer. Instead, with Morvillo, who was still representing him on criminal matters, hovering protectively at his side, Greenberg read a long statement about how he was invoking his Fifth Amendment rights because he had not been given adequate time to prepare or access to the relevant documents. Then he repeated the words "same answer" to everything else Brown and the SEC asked him. It was quite a contrast with the deposition of Warren Buffett, which had taken place the previous day. Spitzer's aides had taken pains to tell the media that Buffett was not a target, and the SEC had provided similar guidance. Grandfatherly and unassuming, Buffett answered all the questions and was so helpful that before the interview was even over a source told *The Wall Street Journal's* online unit that Buffett had been "charming." Some federal regulators and prosecutors blamed Spitzer's staff for the leak, but Michele Hirshman defended Spitzer's team to the hilt, saying to *The Washington Post* that the accusation was "inaccurate and ridiculous." Also, there was ample evidence that others were using Spitzer's reputation for leaking as cover while they filled the ears of the media. (Many of the intimate details about Greenberg's resignation that appeared in *The Wall Street Journal*, for example, were known only to AIG board members and insiders, not to Spitzer's office.)

Still, the spat over the Buffett leak was just one sign that relations among the investigators were breaking down. Though Spitzer's Investment Protection unit and the SEC were accustomed to working together after the analyst and mutual fund investigations, the AIG–Gen Re case also involved Spitzer's criminal prosecutors and the federal prosecutors from the Justice Department in Washington. That was problematic because prosecutors, unlike civil regulators, usually could not bring joint actions because they had to worry about constitutional protections against double jeopardy, which prevented people from being tried twice for the same crime. The two sets of prosecutors quickly started jousting to see who could bring their cases first. The sparring engulfed the SEC and Spitzer's Investment Protection Bureau as well, when Spitzer's criminal investigators moved up a planned joint interview with a key AIG witness and failed to tell the SEC or the Justice Department about the new date. To the SEC and federal prosecutors, it seemed to be a repeat of the "spinning" issue from the research cases, with Spitzer again jumping in front of—and possibly hindering—a federal criminal investigation in his haste to build a civil case. Now the pressure was on for Spitzer's team to get its case before the public before AIG issued the full results of its own investigation. "We thought we had an important story to tell. We wanted to get our facts out first," Brown said.

One way Spitzer's criminal lawyers helped speed the process was by cutting a deal with a senior AIG executive named Joseph Umansky. They put him in front of a grand jury, which under New York State rules meant he had full immunity from prosecution for everything he talked about. Then they quoted from his testimony in the civil complaint they filed against AIG and Hank Greenberg, which had the effect of making it much harder for federal prosecutors to bring their own criminal case against Umansky. The arrangement stuck in the craw of SEC and Justice Department lawyers, who had a far more detailed process for deciding how and when to grant immunity to witnesses. The federal enforcers believed that Spitzer had deliberately thrown a monkey wrench into their criminal probe solely for the purpose of beating them to the punch with a civil complaint. In their eyes, Umansky's value as a prosecution witness had been diminished, because he would have to tell a jury he had not been punished for his work at AIG. In addition, everyone they interviewed now wanted the kind of testimonial immunity that Umansky had gotten. Spitzer gave no truck to their concerns. "We needed to get facts, and we needed to get them quickly against people who were mounting a very aggressive defense. We were willing to make a deal," he said. As for the Feds, "I didn't notice them banging down the door to bring a case."

Umansky had what the Spitzer team considered to be great information. He described how, in the 1990s, AIG had sought to hide underwriting losses from a disastrous experiment with providing auto warranties by disguising them as investment losses, which AIG's investors considered less problematic. The transaction involved investing in a shell company called CAPCO Reinsurance Company and moving the losses there. But for the plan to work AIG had to make it appear that CAPCO was an independent company and not controlled by AIG—otherwise its underwriting losses would have to be included with AIG's. So Umansky had scared up some foreign passive investors who would nominally control CAPCO but let AIG do what it wanted. By the time of Spitzer's investigation, AIG had already told the public that CAPCO had been "improper." What Umansky added was his personal testimony alleging that Greenberg and AIG's chief financial officer, Howard I. Smith, knew about and approved of the strategy.

But Umansky was far from the only source. One of AIG's former general counsels, Michael Joye, contacted Spitzer's office to offer up information about his unsuccessful effort in the early 1990s to stop the company from improperly booking workers-compensation premiums, thereby cheating state governments of millions of dollars. According to Joye's contemporaneous notes, he investigated the allegations and was told repeatedly that Greenberg knew all about the scheme. One AIG employee he interviewed described a meeting about the matter at which Greenberg reportedly asked, "Are we legal?" and was told, "If we were legal, we wouldn't be in business." Greenberg "began laughing, and that was the end of it," the notes said. Joye then reported his findings to Greenberg personally in a January 1992 memo; "AIG makes millions of dollars illegally each year," Joye wrote. These "intentional violations" could "expose AIG to fines and penalties in the hundreds of millions of dollars." Joye recommended an immediate policy change and the firing of everyone involved. Instead, Greenberg hired two outside law firms to look at the issue. Joye, who had been on the job just eight months, quit in protest, and the switch to legal accounting took several years, Spitzer's investigators found. (Greenberg's supporters argued that Greenberg did take corrective action, and pointed to a memo that AIG's president, Tom Tizzio, sent Greenberg just two months after Joye's report. The memo instructed company employees to change their procedures.)

Even employees still working at AIG were turning on their former emperor. When word went out that the new CEO, Martin Sullivan, and the board wanted to know about anything and everything that might be questionable, executives started coming out of the woodwork with stories. Among them were AIG's stock traders, who remembered and resented Greenberg's phone calls in February insisting that they buy AIG shares at the end of the day, when their actions might be questioned by securities regulators. Thanks to them, Spitzer—and federal prosecutors—got their hands on the audiotapes that had captured those demands.

By late May, Gaul and Filipakis were writing and editing feverishly to get the complaint ready for filing, and Berlin was helping fold in sections written by the criminal division. They were disheveled, exhausted, and in the process of pulling their third all-nighter in a row when round about midnight on Wednesday, May 25, they heard someone enter the twenty-third floor. It was their boss, coming to rally the troops. Dressed in jeans and carrying two plastic grocery bags, Spitzer had arrived bearing half an ice cream cake left over from a birthday party for one of his daughters and a batch of Dove bars he had bought on the way downtown. Regular infusions of sugar were part of his management philosophy. Some staff members angled to schedule their twenty-fifth-floor meetings on Fridays because they knew, without fail, there would be donuts available in Spitzer's executive office. Sharing in the long hours was another Spitzer hallmark, particularly when he knew his staff was going through a last-minute crunch before a big case. Often, the investigative team would be working hard in the conference room and the only other light on in the floor would be in Spitzer's personal office. "Being here at night is part of the job even if I am just working on other stuff," he explained. He drove his staff hard, but they drove themselves even harder because they knew he asked nothing of them that he wouldn't ask of himself. "One of the cool things about working for Eliot is that people want to work hard. They want to stay all night," Brown said.

The thirty-seven-page civil complaint Spitzer filed on May 26, 2005, against AIG, Greenberg, and Smith, the former CFO, was rife with telling details that helped back up Spitzer's prior, televised allegations. But unlike many of the celebrated corporate fraud cases that had preceded it, Spitzer's complaint did not and could not claim that the company was a total fraud. Rather than hiding a losing or failing concern, the complaint alleged that AIG executives committed fraud on the margins of an already successful firm to make sure it provided smooth earnings, earned profits from insurance rather than investments, and hit other benchmarks that were important to stock analysts. In fact, when AIG finally filed its revised annual report a week later, the restatement reduced shareholders' equity by $2.26 billion, an enormous number, but it amounted to just 2.7 percent of the company's net worth.

Greenberg and his lawyers quickly exploited that fact by writing to the SEC that AIG's entire management team and its auditors, PricewaterhouseCoopers, had approved the original accounting. In a forty-eight-page legal response, known as a "white paper" (also released to the press), Greenberg's lawyers and supporters painted the entire investigation as an unfair attack on a man who had spent his life building AIG into one of the nation's blue-chip companies. The lawyers argued that "many of the restatement items appear exaggerated or unnecessary" and were "explained in part by the current regulatory environment" and as an effort to justify Greenberg's removal as CEO. The white paper also excused Greenberg's obsession with AIG's share price, saying, "To the extent Mr. Greenberg was from time-to-time concerned with short-term results, it was in furtherance of long-term objectives—for example to prevent other stockholders from being disadvantaged by short-term stock prices that did not fairly reflect the long-term underlying value of AIG." Greenberg's defenders made the further point that Greenberg was well known at AIG for coming up with complex and even visionary business transactions but leaving their execution to others, and that the problems with the Gen Re deal—including the apparently forged documents—had to be viewed through that lens. Greenberg "was never a man who worked on details," remembered Edward Matthews, the former AIG senior vice chairman who joined Greenberg at C. V. Starr after the showdown with the board. "He didn't look at purchase agreements. He'd say yes; he'd say no, but the agreement that was negotiated was all me."

While Greenberg's lawyers were busy constructing a defense for their client against the accounting charges, Spitzer's staff had moved on to a new set of allegations—though the root cause was something very old. They had finally gotten their hands on the dozens of boxes that David Boies's legal team had removed from AIG's Bermuda offices over Easter weekend, and felt duty bound to search through them. In June, a law student summer intern found a decades-old document that would send the office down a new path. It was the minutes of a November 5, 1969, board meeting of C. V. Starr & Company (known as CVSCO), a private company that had been founded by Cornelius Vander Starr, Greenberg's former mentor and boss, who had died the previous year. At the time the minutes were taken, Greenberg was the president of CVSCO. The board minutes reflected plans to sell many of the small insurance companies that CVSCO owned to AIG, in exchange for AIG stock. The minutes said that two weeks earlier, on October 24, Morgan Stanley had issued a preliminary report estimating that the CVSCO-owned companies were worth roughly twenty to twenty-two times earnings, far above their book value. The result, Greenberg said in the minutes, would be a "notable increase in [the] net worth" of CVSCO, a potential "windfall."

The document struck a chord with Bruce Brown, a new member of the Investment Protection Bureau who had transferred in from the litigation defense side of the office. Wasn't there another document from about the same period that said that the "fair value" of CVSCO stock was also its book value? Indeed there was. Greenberg and most of the CVSCO board members also served as the executors of Cornelius Vander Starr's estate, and they were charged with disposing of its assets, including its significant holdings of CVSCO stock. On October 31, 1969, the executors discussed an agreement to sell the estate's CVSCO stock back to the company at book value, even though they had allegedly been told just a week earlier that Morgan Stanley thought the underlying assets were worth far more. To the Spitzer lawyers, the inconsistent prices suggested that the Starr estate had received far less money for its CVSCO stock than the company would soon receive from AIG for much the same assets. What made this potentially even more troubling was that CVSCO was controlled and owned by Greenberg and his associates, who in theory stood to benefit if CVSCO received a "windfall" profit by purchasing the Starr estate's shares at book value and then selling the firm's assets for twenty to twenty-two times book value. Unless there was a good explanation for the apparent price discrepancy, it suggested a serious violation of the executors' fiduciary duty to the Starr estate. (Greenberg's lawyers would later argue that Spitzer's investigators had misunderstood the documents and were comparing apples to oranges. From Greenberg's point of view, the Morgan Stanley valuation was irrelevant to the estate's stock sale because the investment bank was pricing the assets for an entirely different purpose and the CVSCO board had already adopted rules saying that its shareholders, which included both Greenberg and the estate, could only cash out at book value. Greenberg attorney David Boies would also vociferously defend his client's stewardship of both the estate and its main beneficiary, the Starr Foundation, saying, "Under Mr. Greenberg's stewardship the Starr Foundation has grown from $15 million to $3.4 billion and has contributed over $2 billion to charitable causes along the way. . . . Any suggestion that Mr. Greenberg somehow cheated the Starr Foundation is without any basis.")

But the contentiousness would come later. For now, Spitzer's lawyers only knew they had more work to do. It was all so long ago. The transactions had closed more than thirty-five years earlier. "This is very interesting," David Brown told his team. "But are you sure? Is there more?"

11

THE LIMITS OF SPITZERISM

ON JUNE 16, 2005, YET ANOTHER LAWSUIT INVOLVING ELIOT SPITZER HIT THE courts. But this time, the New York attorney general was the defendant. A coalition of eight national banks known as the Clearing House Association was asking a federal judge to stop Spitzer from investigating their lending practices for possible civil rights violations. Hours later, the federal banking regulator, the Office of the Comptroller of the Currency (OCC), followed up with a lawsuit of its own. Under the 1864 federal law that created a dual banking system, both complaints argued, Spitzer had no business asking for lending data from banks that were chartered by the federal government rather than by New York State. Though the banks acknowledged that New York's civil rights laws applied to them, they argued that Spitzer couldn't try to enforce those laws because the OCC had exclusive "visitorial powers" over nationally chartered financial giants such as Citigroup and Wells Fargo. In English, that meant that only the OCC could inspect their books and records, not New York State. "Defendant's actions constitute a violation of federal law and interference with the OCC's authority over the national banking system," the OCC wrote in its complaint. "The OCC is threatened with irreparable harm."

The suits were a startling development for Spitzer. Though the investment banks and the mutual funds had complained in 2002 and 2003 that his office was overstepping its role as a state enforcer, no financial firm had ever challenged his jurisdiction in court before. Spitzer and his Consumer Frauds Bureau said they weren't trying to pick a fight with the federal banking regulator. They were simply following up on government-collected statistics that showed that some banks that operated in New York appeared to be charging much higher rates to minority borrowers. They hadn't singled out the national banks or sought to confront the OCC, said Spitzer's bureau chief, Thomas Conway. In fact they had sent letters—rather than subpoenas—to a variety of state and national banks asking for information because they were trying to be low key and cooperative. Conway found the OCC's hostility bewildering. "It's not like we're trying to take over their job," he said. "If they want to enforce state consumer protection or civil rights laws, that's great. We welcome more cops on the beat. But they're trying to prevent us from doing our job." Then, in October, Spitzer suffered a worse blow, a total defeat in court. "The Attorney General cannot enforce fair lending laws against national banks," wrote U.S. district judge Sidney H. Stein in a forty-page opinion. Stein specifically declined to comment "whether it is better public policy" to cut out the state attorneys general, but he said the law was clear: "The Attorney General cannot compel compliance with a state investigation into potential violations."

Nor was the OCC defeat an isolated incident. In September 2005, the New York–based mutual fund firm of J. & W. Seligman tried a similar tactic after its owners and lawyers balked at Spitzer's terms for settling an investigation into Seligman's arrangements with market timers. Seligman had reluctantly agreed over the summer to demands from Spitzer's Investment Protection Bureau for a monetary penalty and a cut in the fees the firm charged for managing its mutual funds. But Seligman's management balked when Spitzer aides R. Verle Johnson and David Brown insisted on the office's usual package of reforms, including the hiring of a "fund officer" who would report to the funds' board of directors—rather than to the management company—and oversee the annual fee-setting process. Seligman's lead attorney, Daniel A. Pollack, said he told Brown, "Congress said who they wanted to deal with fees. They wanted independent directors, they wanted investors and, as a backup, the SEC. You have no business in this area." Brown, who had already received some fee information from Seligman that concerned him, figured it was time to stop threatening that Spitzer would litigate the fee issue and bring a case. So Brown sent Seligman and its directors additional subpoenas seeking information about fees. "We don't know why year after year this board approves above-market fees but we are at least entitled to look," he explained. "This is as good a case as there is to tee the issue up."

Rather than fight the fee subpoenas in state court, Pollack advised Seligman to file a complaint in federal court alleging that the New York attorney general had overstepped his jurisdiction. "We're going to have to confront this man at some point. Better now than in front of some state court judge who wants a promotion," Pollack told his clients. "What we risked was a money judgment that could shutter us. Better to run that risk than be shackled to this man in perpetuity." The case drew quiet cheers from the fund industry—Seligman's general counsel got a standing ovation at a meeting of industry lawyers—and loud praise from conservative newspapers. "It looks like an investment advisory firm is going to try to do what others have so far failed to accomplish in respect of Eliot Spitzer: stopping the attorney general of the state from trying to patrol areas already regulated by the federal government," cheered *The New York Sun*, which also predicted that the "lawsuit could become Spitzer's Waterloo."

Other financial cases weren't going well either, in the summer of 2005. In June, a Manhattan jury had roundly rejected Spitzer's criminal case against Bank of America broker Ted Sihpol, finding him not guilty of twenty-nine counts and deadlocking on four others stemming from the late trades he had placed for Eddie Stern and the Canary hedge fund. Sihpol had been the first person to face criminal charges in connection with the mutual fund scandal, and his was also the first high-profile white-collar case the Attorney General's Office had brought to trial since Spitzer's election seven years before. Spitzer's opponents jumped on the defeat immediately. "Eliot Spitzer finally found a headline he's not going to like," chortled New York State Republican Party chairman Stephen Minarik in a statement released shortly after the verdicts were announced. "This jury of New Yorkers exposes Spitzer as a politician whose ambition has steamrolled too many hard-working men and women of our state. . . . Looks like the so-called Sheriff of Wall Street had a gun full of blanks."

At the same time, Spitzer's excessive-compensation case against former New York Stock Exchange chairman Richard Grasso was continuing to drag on without resolution, consuming the time and energy of several of the office's top lawyers. As the two sides began deposing former NYSE board members—many of them CEOs of their own Fortune 500 firms—the whole squabble began to seem to some critics like a waste of time. "There are so many unsolved crimes in the state of New York, and Spitzer is attacking the fact that some of the wealthiest people in America had decided to compensate their CEO too much. It's bizarre," said Spitzer's old sparing partner Harvey Pitt, who had become a Washington consultant. Even *New York Times* financial columnist Joseph Nocera publicly implored the attorney general to "let the Grasso case go. You have bigger fish to fry." It didn't help Spitzer's image as a hothead either, when *Newsweek* reported that he had approached former General Electric CEO Jack Welch, a friend of former NYSE board member Kenneth Langone, at the Democratic National Convention and threatened to "put a spike through Langone's heart." (Spitzer said he did not remember making the remark.) Some staff members in Spitzer's office began to joke that they would all be in new jobs by the time the case came to trial.

Though Grasso largely stayed out of the spotlight once the two sides began their depositions, Langone seemed determined to keep the heat on. The self-made billionaire talked openly about bankrolling anyone who would oppose Spitzer in the 2006 governor's race, and he and his wife made contributions to Nassau County Executive Thomas Suozzi, who was considering entering the Democratic primary. "I have no trouble spending tens of millions of dollars on this one," Langone said. "This will be the equivalent of Hiroshima and Nagasaki. He had his Pearl Harbor. Now it's my turn. I made my money fair and square, and it's all mine, and, baby, it buys a lot of bombers."

Langone also asserted in a September 30 *Wall Street Journal* op-ed piece that the depositions in the Grasso case were going strongly his way: "Of the six directors deposed thus far who served on both the compensation committee and the full board, each has said they were not deceived in any way. They all confirm that, as head of the NYSE compensation committee, I provided them and the board with complete and accurate information about Mr. Grasso's proposed compensation—and that they approved it." Langone also insisted he would make Spitzer pay for challenging his integrity. "I have nothing but disdain for this man. He's done incredible harm to New York State. Not a nickel has gone back to investors, and we've lost thousands of jobs that didn't need to be lost," he said. Spitzer countered, "We think the case has gotten stronger as the depositions have been taken."

The malaise surrounding the Attorney General's Office extended beyond the financial world. A year-long investigation of "payola" in the radio industry yielded allegations that Sony BMG and Warner Music had bribed radio stations and their employees to play the firms' recordings and yielded settlements with the two companies. But the mass media greeted Spitzer's first press conference on the subject, about a ten-million-dollar deal with Sony BMG, more as a one-day event than an industry-shaking revelation. The major newspapers ran prominent stories but little follow-up. Even news that the Federal Communications Commission was opening its own investigation into the issue and the announcement of a five-million-dollar deal with Warner in November did not spark tremendous interest outside the music industry.

At the same time, two other longtime Spitzer efforts were facing additional hurdles. Spitzer's early goal of holding gun manufacturers accountable for the spread of illegal guns was rendered nearly unattainable when Congress passed a law that granted the industry sweeping protection from civil suits. In this same period, the federal courts were proving to be less than welcoming of some of Spitzer's environmental efforts. In June, the U.S. Court of Appeals for the District of Columbia Circuit upheld part of the Bush administration's effort to rewrite the rules for power plant modernization, rejecting one of two Spitzer lawsuits contending that the EPA was illegally gutting the Clean Air Act. The ruling was mixed—the judges turned down part of Spitzer's argument while rejecting the power industry's view of some Clean Air Act provisions. But, on the whole, it hurt more than helped

Spitzer's long-running battle to clean up midwestern power plants that dumped pollution on New York State. Then, in September, U.S. district judge Loretta Preska tossed out a suit brought by Spitzer, Connecticut attorney general Richard Blumenthal, and seven other states and cities that had sought to force large power plants to cut emissions of carbon dioxide, which the states considered a culprit in global warming. Lawyers for the power industry had long contended that Spitzer and the states had no business trying to set new air-quality standards for carbon dioxide when the EPA and Congress had declined to do so. Judge Preska wholeheartedly agreed, and her ruling seemed to spell trouble for Spitzer's other environmental cases. "Cases presenting political questions are consigned to the political branches that are accountable to the people, not to the judiciary," Preska wrote.

To Spitzer, in the fall of 2005, the root of the problem seemed clear—Republicans were trying to strip away the consumer and environmental protections that had taken progressives nearly a century to build by appointing "originalist" judges who believed that constitutional rights are static and should not evolve to cover changing circumstances. "What we are dealing with today . . . is a Republican, cold, antiseptic vision of rights," Spitzer told a crowd of New York Democratic activists on October 17. "They want to throw us back to the way it was two hundred years ago." The trend was particularly disturbing, Spitzer argued, because the judges were promulgating ideas that had failed to win majority support in Congress and many state legislatures. "If the originalists had controlled the Supreme Court throughout our history," Spitzer said, "the whole evolution of rights that has been so central to the history of our country wouldn't have occurred."

But Spitzer's critics and even some of his supporters saw his troubles as part of a growing backlash against the New York attorney general and his methods. In the years right after the collapse of the 1990s technology bubble and the implosion of Enron and WorldCom, American investors had been so angry and business leaders so intimidated that Spitzer's penchant for revealing bad behavior and then demanding industry-wide change had won almost universal applause. But as the stock market began to recover and Spitzer's probes hit a wider range of targets, concern was growing. Spitzer could be high-handed and self-righteous, and his proposed reforms were sometimes ineffectual, expensive, and—in the eyes of his critics—misguided. Spitzer's campaign for governor had also focused Republican opposition against him and added weight to their allegations of political grandstanding. Even more telling, after seven years in office, Spitzer now had a long record and a host of imitators in other states. As "Spitzerism" caught on around the country, mutual funds, brokers, and insurance companies were having to cope with competing investigators and contradictory settlement demands. The potential drag on the economy of Spitzer's own investigations and those of his imitators was becoming real. "If you look at the breadth and depth of what Spitzer is doing, there is no precedent. He has too much power and no accountability," said Lisa Rickard, president of the U.S. Chamber of Commerce's Institute for Legal Reform, which led the corporate charge against Spitzer and other activist state attorneys general. The conservative Federalist Society even sponsored a debate in Manhattan, in September 2005, entitled, "Is Eliot Spitzer Good for America?"

Spitzer was far from the first aggressive prosecutor to face claims of overreaching. In the late 1980s, many on Wall Street had complained that U.S. attorney Rudolph Giuliani was using criminal prosecutions to bolster his image and garner publicity for a run for elective office. Giuliani's investigators had pulled Kidder Peabody executive Richard Wigton out of his office in handcuffs, only to drop the charges three months later. Giuliani had also used the threat of corporate racketeering charges to force investment bank Drexel Burnham Lambert into a settlement that helped bankrupt the firm. His office's stock manipulation case against industrial firm GAF resulted in two mistrials, a reversal on appeal, and allegations that the government had withheld crucial evidence from the defense. "There is in your office—I notice it not only in this case but in other cases—a kind of overkill, a kind of overzealousness which is not even . . . rationally related to any legitimate prosecutive objective," said U.S. district judge John E. Sprizzo as he dismissed charges against several defendants in a major Giuliani drug case. The concerns about Giuliani gained even more resonance when he ran for mayor of New York City in 1989 and several of his biggest cases were overturned on appeal. "Why are people afraid of

Rudy Giuliani?" asked one campaign commercial aired by Giuliani's primary opponent. "Because they should be." (Giuliani lost that year, but his confrontational approach won him the mayor's office four years later, when crime was near record levels and the city's economy was ailing.)

By 2005, defense lawyers and corporate general counsels were collecting a stock of Giuliani-like stories about Eliot Spitzer and his legal army. Spitzer's sins, in their eyes, included using the threat of a corporate indictment to improperly pressure Merrill Lynch to settle the stock analyst case; using the threat of imminent public arrest to extract guilty pleas from Steven Markovitz, the Millennium hedge fund trader who had placed late trades, as well as from several insurance executives caught up in the bid-rigging scandal; demanding new leadership at Marsh & McLennan; and helping to force out the chairman of AIG by refusing to put off his deposition. Spitzer even had his own version of a suspect hauled off in handcuffs on a charge that was later dropped. Paul Flynn, a former investment banker with Canadian Imperial Bank of Commerce who had arranged financing for several market timers, had been arrested and handcuffed in February 2004 as he commuted from his suburban New York home to the local train station. When Spitzer dropped the charges nearly two years later, he argued that a criminal prosecution was no longer warranted because Flynn, as the lender, had served as an accomplice, while two codefendants, who had larger roles in actual after-hours trading, had recently pleaded guilty and received probation. Other lawyers were skeptical of the explanation. "This decision begs the question of whether the attorney general's office conducted a sufficiently fair and thorough investigation of Flynn's potential defense prior to arresting and indicting him," former federal prosecutor Evan Barr told *The New York Times*.

Even worse from the perspective of many lawyers and other regulators, Spitzer's investigations were conducted under a white-hot light of publicity. At least twice—once during the 2002 negotiations of the global research analyst settlement and again during the 2005 investigation of AIG—defense lawyers complained directly to Spitzer about specific leaks. In both cases, the attorney general took umbrage and hotly denied that his office had been the source. In both cases, even more details about the investigations appeared in the media the next day. "When it comes to dealing with the press he is absolutely without scruples," said one defense attorney. This attorney reported that a lawyer in the Attorney General's Office—not Spitzer himself—once explicitly threatened to "drag your client through the mud" if the lawyer rejected a settlement offer. "His use of the press is the single most repulsive aspect of the way he's done his job. As a defense attorney I don't like to talk to the press. As a prosecutor you just don't do it," the defense attorney said of Spitzer. Told of the "mud" comment, Spitzer agreed that "that sort of language shouldn't be used," but argued that his staff was making a larger legitimate point: "The facts are going to come out anyway. If we charge you they are going to come out in an adversarial way. If you settle, you'll get more input. Pick your medicine." The criticism also put the office in an odd position: There was no question that Spitzer talked to and used the media in ways that were foreign to the lawyers at the SEC or the Justice Department. Yet he and his staff staunchly denied leaking some of the most sensitive information, such as stock analyst Jack Grubman's e-mails about the 92nd Street Y incident and the details of Warren Buffett's deposition about finite insurance. The staff argued that they were sometimes being blamed for leaks from other sources, who used Spitzer's reputation as cover for their own interest in getting particular information out.

And then there was the *New York* magazine article published in January 2005, in which David Brown seemed to boast about the office's aggressiveness, saying, "Eliot lends a speed and violence to this process that you wouldn't believe. . . . We will come to your house at night." Other regulators and prosecutors cringed. "What Eliot is trying to do is enhance respect for the law, but when you look at his methods, does that end up diminishing respect for the law?" one of them asked. "This is not the way a government official should be acting. Ultimately it's about making sure justice is done and not about using every bit of leverage you have."

For Spitzer's critics, the single most important example of the attorney general acting as an overzealous prosecutor came in the criminal case against Ted Sihpol, the Bank of America broker who had placed after-hours trades for Eddie Stern. Sihpol had been the first white-collar defendant to challenge Spitzer's office directly. First arrested in 2003, he and his lawyers turned down a plea deal because Spitzer's team refused to guarantee that Sihpol would not serve jail time. When the case went to trial in the spring of 2005, Spitzer's prosecutors felt confident because they had tapes of Sihpol agreeing to place trades after the 4:00 P.M. close of the New York Stock Exchange and joking about tampering with time-stamps. But Sihpol's lawyers, Evan Stewart and Paul Shechtman, turned the tables on them, arguing that the deadline for mutual fund trading wasn't as clear as Spitzer claimed and that Sihpol was a mid-level fall guy who had been scapegoated. The jury agreed with the defense arguments, and interviews with the jurors afterward suggested that they were offended that Sihpol was on trial while his Bank of America bosses and Stern had walked away with their freedom and most of the profits. For Spitzer, the loss rankled. "That one bothers me more than everything else," he said. "When they can say, you lost, that kills me. I don't like losing and I blame nobody but myself. . . . The problem [with the Sihpol case] was created in the last week of August '03 when I decided to do a deal with Eddie Stern."

Spitzer then compounded his image as a bully by threatening to retry Sihpol on the four counts for which the jury could not reach unanimity, even as his staff negotiated "no jail time" plea deals with two other defendants in the mutual fund scandal. "Eliot Spitzer just can't take a hint," wrote the *New York Post* in an editorial headlined "Spiteful Spitzer," and Spitzer's predecessor, Dennis Vacco, resurfaced to argue that a retrial would "undermine [Spitzer's] ongoing efforts to raise the business ethics of Wall Street. . . . Sound prosecutorial judgment is best displayed when a prosecutor knows when not to go forward against a target." Spitzer eventually agreed to drop the charges as part of a package settlement with the SEC. Sihpol paid a two-hundred-thousand-dollar fine, was banned from the industry for five years, and issued an in-court apology.

Spitzer's reaction to the J. & W. Seligman mutual fund lawsuit reinforced his critics' view that he was vindictive and that he reacted harshly when people and companies fought back. Three weeks after the privately held mutual fund firm had gone to federal court to challenge the New York attorney general's jurisdiction over mutual fund fees, Spitzer and David Brown fired back. Rather than simply responding in federal court, they used section 354 of the Martin Act to ask a state judge to oversee a public investigation. This was the same legal provision that Spitzer had employed with such success against Merrill Lynch in the stock analyst case, and the filing made public all of the damaging information that Brown's Investment Protection team had gathered. More ominously in the eyes of the defense bar, it allowed the New York attorney general to schedule public depositions of Seligman's top executives as well as its reclusive biggest shareholder, William Morris. The Martin Act filing accused Seligman of fraud on two counts: lying to the public and its mutual fund customers about its involvement with market timers, and secretly charging small retail investors up to twice as much as pension funds for the same services. The market-timing charge stemmed from what Spitzer's office saw as an inconsistency between Seligman's public disclosures and the documents that Verle Johnson had uncovered during the investigation of the firm. In January 2004, Seligman had done an internal investigation and reported publicly that it had made arrangements with four market timers. The funds' board then agreed to accept six million dollars in restitution on behalf of the mutual fund customers. But Johnson's affidavit alleged that the internal investigation had been a whitewash and had attached to it a Seligman internal spreadsheet that listed twelve clients that had allegedly been granted exceptions to the firm's rules against rapid trading. Spitzer also alleged that the market timing had cost shareholders more than eighty million dollars, a charge the firm denied. The second accusation in the Martin Act filing was based partly on information that Daniel Pollack, Seligman's lead lawyer, had provided during the failed settlement negotiations. Rather than turn over detailed information on how Seligman set its fees, Pollack had offered to stipulate that the management company routinely charged its mutual funds—and the small investors who used them—30 to 40 percent more for the same services than it charged institutional clients such as pension funds. Pollack asserted that that spread was common in the industry, but Brown disagreed.

Defense lawyers not connected to either side saw Brown's use of the Martin Act and the associated threat of public depositions as evidence that Spitzer would use every means necessary to force his targets to the settlement table. One white-collar attorney who has handled half a dozen high-profile disputes with Spitzer's office said he has used the Seligman suit as a cautionary tale for clients who wanted to go toe to toe with Spitzer. "This guy, his tactic is, if you kick him in the shins, he'll kick you in the teeth, and he's better at it than you are," the lawyer said he told his clients. Spitzer himself downplayed the conflict, saying the Martin Act filing was "just to ensure we get our discovery"—the legal word for the interviews and documents to which the office was entitled under state law—because negotiations with Seligman had been so contentious.

Pollack vowed to fight on. He expressed confidence that his client would be proven not to have committed fraud. "Seligman stumbled but picked itself up and made good to the funds," with the six-million-dollar restitution, Pollack said. "There's no fraud here. The SEC tells mutual fund companies exactly what they must disclose about fees, and it isn't this. They had no obligation whatsoever to discuss the difference between mutual fund fees [for small investors] and institutional fees." But Brown contended that both the state and federal courts would uphold the office's right to look at mutual fund fraud, whether in fees or elsewhere. The 1940 Investment Company Act gave the SEC jurisdiction over mutual fund fees, but Brown argued that it was not exclusive—federal law also gave state securities officials, including Spitzer's office, the right and duty to investigate and punish fraud. "We simply want to investigate potential fraud, which is our job. The 1940 act doesn't prevent states from investigating fraud," Brown said. "It would be a major setback for consumers if states cannot investigate mutual fund fraud that involves fees."

The critique of Spitzer as overreaching or overly aggressive also included complaints about the way the lawyers in his office conducted their investigations. Rather than start at the bottom, as lawyers for the SEC and the Department of Justice traditionally have done, Spitzer's team headed straight for the heart of the problem—they subpoenaed an entire company's records and demanded interviews with mid-level and even upper-level management almost immediately. The upside was that they often got information much more quickly than their federal counterparts, enabling them to work at warp speed and file lawsuits faster. "It is in and of itself a good thing to have speedy enforcement," Brown said. "Enforcement can have more deterrent value if people know that Eliot Spitzer is capable of rolling up a fraudulent scheme within a few months. When there is an ongoing practice that hurts the public, like mutual-fund timing, bid-rigging, or fraudulent equity research, it is important that regulators act quickly to stop it. Does it really serve the public interest to have securities fraud cases that take two or three years?"

Critics argued that this approach put too much emphasis on cooperation and self-incrimination. Spitzer's focus on public shaming and his wont for making threats, in this view, enhanced his image as the "Sheriff of Wall Street" and got results, but it also opened him up to charges that he was operating like a lynch mob. "Frontier justice wasn't all bad. There were a lot of bad people that were hung," said veteran white-collar attorney Stanley Arkin. "But it has the capacity to be unfair. . . . You need modesty, hesitation, and moderation to have a really good system." In this view, firms that tried to assert their right to defend themselves, such as Marsh and Seligman, got squashed, while the others were frightened into spending millions to cater to the Spitzer team's every demand. "What Eliot has done very successfully is outsource his work by threatening people and subpoenaing them," said Richard Beattie, who represented the former Marsh & McLennan CEO Jeffrey Greenberg and the AIG board of directors. "I think it is a very effective method. He's got many law firms in the city working for him."

Other critics complained that Spitzer's emphasis on fast results and beating rival regulators to the punch made him too quick to favor the first people in the door offering cooperation, especially when they were rich, powerful, and able to fight back. The civil settlement with Eddie Stern, the decision not to go after Citigroup chairman Sandy Weill for his alleged influence over Jack Grubman's research, and the immunity grant to AIG executive Joseph Umansky all opened the Attorney General's Office up to allegations of favoritism. The contrast was particularly stark in the mutual fund case. Critics routinely pointed out that Stern, who was the son of a prominent New York family and had even attended the same pricey private school as Spitzer, came out of the scandal relatively unscathed. He gave up the management fees he received for running Canary, but his investors—including his family and friends—got to keep their trading profits. Meanwhile, Sihpol, a mid-level banker who had simply helped Stern place the orders, faced criminal charges. In this view, the investment banks got off too easy in the research settlement because they didn't have to admit wrongdoing in their settlements, and mutual fund czar Richard Strong should have faced criminal charges. "The record doesn't match the headlines," complained Jacob Zamansky, the arbitration lawyer who brought the first big case against analyst Henry Blodget. "The big guys can buy their way out with him."

Small fry, by contrast, often found themselves left hanging. After being pressured to plead guilty or face immediate arrest, some defendants in the mutual fund and insurance scandals waited months or even years for sentencing. Many of them found it all but impossible to find new jobs with their sentencings still hanging over their heads. When a lawyer for one such defendant, Zurich American underwriter Edward Coughlin (who had pleaded guilty to a misdemeanor antitrust violation), asked the judge to step in after ten months of waiting, Spitzer's office threw a fit. The prosecutor on the case publicly accused Coughlin of violating his plea agreement, which outraged the judge, James A. Yates, who called the claim "unprofessional" and "dishonest." Judge Yates then brought the case to closure, sentencing Coughlin to probation and one hundred hours of community service.

Spitzer's response to some of the criticism was measured. The lower-level defendants who felt they had been left in limbo had a "fair complaint," he said. "It's not in our interest either to have these cooperators waiting around." The problem stemmed from "inadequate resources. When we are doing triage, it just happens." His lawyers often had so many irons in the fire that they had time only for the big-ticket items—extracting guilty pleas or settlements in principle—before moving on to other issues. As for the complaint that he let the big fish go, he said, "We start in the middle because that's where the evidence takes us, and the paper trail doesn't always give you the people at the top. . . . In a twisted way, [the Sihpol acquittal] validates what we've done. If we're not going to bring the criminal case against the guy at the top, go for the structural reform." He called this "more important" than prosecuting lower-level malefactors.

Spitzer's aides noted that despite their hard-nosed image and the Flynn case, they did not make a regular practice of arresting their targets in public. Their record stood in stark contrast to federal authorities, who had recently drawn widespread criticism for forcing several defendants, including John Rigas, the seventy-eight-year-old chairman of Adelphia Communications, to run media gauntlets while wearing handcuffs. Most people charged by the New York Attorney General's Office with crimes were allowed to self-surrender. Indeed, many— although not all—of the defense attorneys who dealt directly with Spitzer and his top deputies on high-profile cases had good things to say about their interactions. While they often disagreed with Spitzer's aggressive demands, in most cases, they said, the negotiating process was spirited but courteous. "We fought very hard for our client and they fought very hard, but it was all very professional," remembered Gary Naftalis, who represented Eddie Stern.

On the larger criticism that he was too aggressive or unfairly enforcing the law in new situations, Spitzer gave no ground. "Where have we been wrong on the facts?" he asked. "Fraud is fraud, and lying to investors is the same species of crime whether you are an analyst, a stock broker, or a Ponzi scheme promoter."

Even many of Spitzer's opponents acknowledged that his investigators were masters at uncovering problems and behavior that needed addressing. Wall Street research was indeed hyped; after-hours trading of mutual funds did harm investors; and bid-rigging had been illegal since the late nineteenth century. Spitzer's tactics were "new, troubling, and have the potential for abuse," said James Tierney, the former Maine attorney general who became head of Columbia University Law School's Attorneys General Program. "But he hasn't drilled a dry hole yet. When has he ever done it and a company turned out to be innocent?" What made Spitzer's record all the more impressive, lawyers and regulators across the political spectrum agreed, was that he did it from a political perch that had been all but inactive in the corporate crime world for years. "That office wasn't even a stop on the railroad for the white-collar bar," said top defense attorney Mark Pomerantz, who negotiated with Spitzer's office on behalf of numerous clients, including AIG. "Now, if it's not Grand Central Station, it's at least Fourteenth Street. You go there all the time." Spitzer and his lawyers used the Martin Act for all its worth, and counted on negative publicity to put pressure on their targets. But their opponents tried to influence the process in other ways. At the height of the stock analyst case, Morgan Stanley attempted to get Congress to rewrite the securities fraud laws in the middle of the stock analyst investigations, gun manufacturers lobbied for and got a congressional exemption from state lawsuits, and AIG's public relations firm tried to buy experts to speak out on its behalf. "The Chamber of Commerce and the Federalist Society play hardball, as they should," Spitzer said. "We're going to play hardball too. . . . If we have a procedural tool that cuts to our advantage and we don't use it, shame on me. I've got a client, the people of the State of New York, and they should get the same aggressive representation as Merrill or Morgan Stanley."

A second strain of criticism of Eliot Spitzer had its roots in his use of federalist theory to take on a whole host of issues that other state regulators and prosecutors had not tackled previously. In this view, Spitzer was not so much an overzealous prosecutor as an overly ambitious state politician who did not understand the limits of his role or the complexity of the issues he was wading into. "He is fundamentally trying to usurp the role of state and federal legislative and regulatory authorities," said Lisa Rickard of the Chamber of Commerce's Institute for Legal Reform. "If there are pervasive problems in a particular area there ought to be pressure on the regulators to deal with it. That pressure can come from the groups involved or from Congress. It isn't his role."

Spitzer brushed off most concerns, arguing that his office stepped in only when other regulators weren't doing their job. "There is a limit and there should be a limit" on what his office could accomplish, he said. "When you really step back, they should be doing all this in Washington." His allies pointed out that Spitzer sometimes backed out when he felt others who were better placed were going to take action. In early 2003, Spitzer's criminal prosecutors were trying to put together a case against Credit Suisse First Boston investment banker Frank Quattrone for spinning, when evidence surfaced that suggested

Quattrone had encouraged his subordinates to destroy documents during an earlier federal investigation of the same issue. Spitzer and U.S. attorney James Comey scuffled briefly over which office would bring the banker to court, as their subordinates tried to cut each other out of crucial interviews and depositions. In the end, Spitzer was the one who yielded. Then he went the extra mile, telling his lawyers to help the federal prosecutors prepare to cross-examine Quattrone by turning over the evidence they had independently dug up against the banker. (Quattrone was convicted at trial but an appeals court overturned the guilty verdict in March 2006.)

Spitzer's critics in the Federalist Society were not appeased. They argued that competition from Spitzer had corrupted the national enforcement and regulatory agencies, leading them to come down harder on business than they should. "If you've got one responsible agency and one nutcase—e.g., Spitzer—you get the good agency preempted by the nutcase. The more vigorous enforcer always calls the shots," said University of Chicago law professor Richard Epstein. "Wall Street is a national market, and the reforms Spitzer is putting in are affecting the whole country. It wasn't as though the folks in Illinois elected him as our attorney general."

Spitzer's decision to patrol areas that were normally the beat of the federal government also meant that he and his staff had to use fraud cases and enforcement settlements, rather than new regulations, to impose structural changes. That approach had several downsides: Spitzer and his attorneys generally had less expertise and experience than the federal securities regulators, so their solutions were not always practical. The deals were also struck without a public comment period, eliminating another chance to identify potential pitfalls. Finally, Spitzer's settlements affected only the particular companies where he had found wrongdoing, rather than entire industries, which limited the reach of his reforms. So the twelve investment banks that were party to the global settlement were stuck with the cost and confusion of monitoring conversations between analysts and bankers and a series of other restrictions, while their smaller competitors were left far less fettered. "We now have different rules for the big players and for the smaller players with ambitions. Our rules come from too many sources. It's not healthy," said former SEC commissioner Harvey Goldschmid, but he blamed the problem on the SEC's failure to follow up on the global settlement by promulgating industry-wide rules for stock analysts.

Spitzer's efforts to improve the quality of research available to small investors met with decidedly mixed reviews. On the one hand, there was some evidence that the impartiality of the in-house research being put out by the major banks had improved. According to *Fortune*, 11 percent of stock analyst recommendations in the fall of 2005 were "sells" and just 38 percent were "buys," compared to 65 percent "buys" and fewer than 1 percent "sells" in 2001, as the technology bubble was bursting. But it was unclear how many small investors were actually using the independent research that Spitzer and the SEC had required the investment banks to buy and make available to their clients. While Merrill clients used the reports "extensively" and 975,000 visitors had clicked on Morgan Stanley's independent research site, just 110 Credit Suisse First Boston customers accessed its site and fewer than 1 percent of the hits on the Lehman Brothers Web site were for independent research, according to reports by the independent consultants hired as part of the global settlement. The problem was particularly acute for banks that served primarily institutional investors and had relatively few individual clients. "Nobody wants this crap," one bank executive complained, noting that his firm had been chastised by the regulators because so few customers had accessed the third-party research that was available on its customer Web site.

Mutual fund experts were similarly divided about Spitzer's demands for fee cuts as part of the settlements for market timing and late trading. Critics argued that the attorney general was turning the traditional regulatory structure on its head. In 1996, after the fund industry complained that it was being regulated to death by the states, Congress passed the National Securities Markets Improvement Act and specifically eliminated the states' authority to register and regulate mutual funds and most other securities offerings. While states were still permitted to investigate and punish fraud, these critics argued that Spitzer had stretched his authority beyond reasonable limits in the fund cases. As evidence, they noted that all five SEC commissioners had agreed that fee cuts were inappropriate and had made their position plain in the statement released at the time of Spitzer's settlement with Alliance Capital Management. "Spitzer has used this antifraud authority in ways Congress never intended by extracting conditions as part of a fraud settlement," said Stuart Kaswell, a former general counsel of the Securities Industry Association, who was deeply involved in the negotiations over the 1996 act. Because of the fee cuts, "you have the national regulator that Congress has charged with primary responsibility for regulating mutual funds publicly expressing its displeasure at a state regulator's action." David Brown countered that his boss didn't pull his demands for fee cuts out of thin air. Rather, as part of their market-timing investigations, Spitzer's lawyers would also ask for information on fees. If their preliminary results suggested that there was "a discrepancy between what [fund management companies] charge retail and institutional customers for identical services," he said, Spitzer would offer the fund companies a choice—either sign a comprehensive settlement that addressed both the market timing and the fee discrepancy or face a full-blown fee investigation. Not surprisingly, every firm but Seligman opted to settle. Consumer advocates applauded the results. Industry statistics suggested that the management fees charged to small investors had dropped significantly since Spitzer took up the issue. In 2004, 2,830 funds cut their fees and 256 raised them, according to statistics from the research firm Lipper. The statistics on fee reductions marked a dramatic increase over 2003, when 622 funds cut their fees and 1,049 raised them. "It seems reasonable to assume that the overwhelming increase in fee reductions in 2004 is directly attributed to the fund scandal and the investigations brought on by the New York Attorney General's Office," said Kip Price, Lipper's head of global fiduciary review.

Conservative advocates of states' rights also argued that Spitzer's investigations and settlements were a perversion of true federalism. The original definition of federalism, according to its free-market practitioners, divided up all government responsibilities between the state and federal governments. "For each and every problem there is one and only one sovereign," explained Epstein, the Chicago law professor who was a leading intellectual in the movement. "Then you get clear accountability." Spitzer's enforcement methods, on the other hand, stemmed from a post–New Deal version of federalism that believed that the states and federal government had shared responsibilities for consumer and investor protection, among other issues. Spitzer "is the inversion of federalism," said Michael Greve, a scholar at the American Enterprise Institute. "Everything he does is designed to impose new standards on a national level. That's not true federalism."

Spitzer's response to this strain of criticism was twofold. He respectfully disagreed with those federalists—particularly the academics—who genuinely believed that the states and the federal government should not have overlapping authority. But he argued that most of the business groups that backed federalist research were simply seeking intellectual cover for their efforts to eliminate government oversight entirely. "The financing behind the [libertarian] Cato Institute and the Federalist Society is a group that doesn't want and never wanted any government enforcement of the rules," Spitzer said. "If Steve Cutler had been the one bringing these cases, they would have come up with a different argument, that the SEC was too aggressive."

To federalist critics, the other big problem with Spitzer's approach stemmed not directly from him but from the imitators he inspired. Ambitious state attorneys general had never been shy about bringing cases—political wags often said that "AG" was short for "aspiring governor." But Spitzer's successes emboldened many of them to enter the financial services and environmental protection realms as never before. Even worse, from corporate America's point of view, many of the new state cases were piggyback rides, attempts to demand their pound of flesh based on other agencies' investigations. In June 2003, for example, West Virginia attorney general Darrell McGraw sued ten Wall Street banks, alleging that they had promulgated biased stock research that violated the state's consumer-protection laws. Two months earlier, West Virginia's state auditor—who was charged with enforcing the state's securities laws—had signed on to Spitzer's global research settlement with the same ten banks and received about four million dollars. (West Virginia's top court eventually tossed out the lawsuit.) That same summer, Oklahoma attorney general Drew Edmondson filed criminal charges against former WorldCom chief executive Bernard J. Ebbers and five other former company executives, even though the Department of Justice had already cut plea bargain deals with four of them in exchange for their cooperation. Not only did the Oklahoma case threaten to make some of those cooperators reconsider, but the allegations in Oklahoma's indictment appeared to be lifted wholesale from the documents the federal prosecutors had already filed. Federal prosecutors warned that the Oklahoma case could jeopardize their prosecution of Ebbers, but Edmondson refused to back down until U.S. attorney David Kelley made a special trip to Oklahoma to negotiate with him. In the mutual fund area, California attorney general Bill Lockyer struck many in the industry as a Johnny-come-lately when he sued Edward D. Jones & Company on the same day the giant brokerage firm settled with the Justice Department and the SEC over allegations that it took secret payments to push particular mutual funds. Lockyer had participated in joint settlement talks along with federal authorities but filed his own lawsuit after deciding that the seventy-five-million-dollar penalty was too low. New Jersey got in on the act as well, filing a complaint in February 2004 alleging that the California-based mutual fund firm Pimco, which specialized in bond funds, had cut improper deals with market timers. The SEC had investigated the same allegations and found no evidence to support them, although it did bring charges against a Pimco-affiliated stock fund manager in New Jersey. New Jersey eventually dropped its charges against the bond funds.

While much of the criticism focused on the state officials' demands for remedies, such as fines or organizational changes, the SEC's Stephen Cutler argued that the problem was larger than that. If states routinely brought cases targeting conduct that the SEC had deemed lawful, he said, mutual fund firms and investment banks could no longer be sure of the rules of the road. Then, a single large state would be able override the judgments of the SEC. "Forget about the remedy. Just saying something is a violation can be a very significant issue," he said in 2005, soon after leaving the SEC for private practice.

Insurance was a more complicated question because it had traditionally been regulated by the states, and companies were more accustomed to dealing with multiple regulators. But some industry experts and even some regulators were critical of the way Spitzer had used the Marsh bid-rigging case to attack the entire system of contingent commissions, in which insurance companies paid the brokers extra depending on the services the broker provided and the volume and quality of the business the broker sent to the insurer. "The industry was painted with a very broad brush," complained Howard Mills, New York's insurance superintendent. "Spitzer said it was 'rife with corruption.' That was an overstatement and the wrong way to go. . . . Contingent commissions are legal. There are some types of contingent commissions that are good." Although Spitzer's settlements with the three largest corporate insurance brokers—Marsh, Aon, and Willis—banned the use of contingent commissions, other regulators declined to follow suit. Even Spitzer's close ally Richard Blumenthal, the attorney general of Connecticut, failed to adopt Spitzer's absolutist stance when he investigated allegations that Hilb Rogal & Hobbs (HRH)—the nation's eighth largest broker—had steered business to the insurance companies that paid it the most. In August 2005, Connecticut reached a thirty-million-dollar settlement with HRH, but the deal pointedly did not ban contingent commissions entirely. Instead, the firm renounced the payoffs when it was serving as a "broker" but simply improved the disclosure of the deals when the firm served as an "independent agent"—the bulk of its business. As a result, Aon, Willis, and Marsh found themselves operating at a competitive disadvantage, particularly when they sought to expand. "No one who can accept the commissions will want to merge with Aon, Willis, or Marsh," said Robert Hartwig, the chief economist for the Insurance Information Institute, the main trade association. "Given that contingent commissions are legal and that the questions of conflict of interest can be managed through disclosure, I find it unfortunate that these companies were forced to give up these revenue streams. The market cap that was lost was tremendous." Industry experts also argued that the finite-insurance investigation was similarly too broad and that regulators had created a cloud of uncertainty over a product that many insurance companies were using to provide their investors with more predictable returns. Companies that bought finite insurance "were giving investors what they wanted . . . a stock with smoother earnings," Hartwig said. "Now that companies are afraid to buy the policies, insurance stocks are going to be more volatile." Spitzer's lawyers—and the SEC—saw the matter differently. In their eyes, income-smoothing products were nothing more than a way to mislead the public about a firm's true results.

From corporate America's point of view, the problem of Spitzerism seemed to be spreading. Not only were Spitzer and his imitators using state powers to investigate the securities, mutual fund, and insurance industries, but they were also combining forces to go after drug manufacturers on pricing and disclosure issues and to challenge the Environmental Protection Agency's rules on everything from carbon dioxide and mercury levels to energy standards for air-conditioners. The state suits were particularly infuriating, some corporate executives said, because they came at a time when the federal government was finally controlled by Republicans who were pursuing a more cooperative and hands-off approach. "Global climate change is an international and national issue that states and localities cannot effectively address," said Bill Fang, climate issue director for the utility industry's Edison Electric Institute. "The CO_2 lawsuits . . . are improper attempts to circumvent the federal legislative process and engage in judicial legislation." Spitzer's efforts drew criticism not only from industry, but also from some Republican state officials who argued that their peers were overstepping their proper role. "Some [state officials] are forgetting that anytime you announce you are investigating an industry, you cause the stock to drop, and you have real people, hardworking people, losing money," said Virginia attorney general Jerry Kilgore, a Republican, who had organized a coalition of nine states to oppose Spitzer's challenge to the EPA's Clean Air Act revisions. "We have to be careful and take a more reasoned and slow approach."

Still, state activism had its defenders, particularly Democrats and consumer advocates who argued that state regulators and elected attorneys general were often more attuned to the needs of small investors and consumers, while their appointed federal counterparts tended to be more sympathetic to the industries they dealt with every day. "The SEC is looking at the entire national market structure. That affects its perspective. We get individual investors walking through our door and we try to get their money back for them," said Massachusetts secretary of the commonwealth Bill Galvin, a Democrat, who served as the state's securities regulator. "People may or may not vote for Spitzer and me based on our work in this area, but . . . it makes us more responsive to the needs of the investors that we see." State enforcers also won praise for moving faster than their federal counterparts. Unlike the SEC or EPA, state attorneys general did not have to get approval from higher authorities or go through a bureaucratic approval process before bringing a case. "If there's an antitrust or consumer issue in our state, we'll step forward and say, 'Hey, we see a problem—fix it,'" said Maryland attorney general Joseph Curran, a Democrat. "The states are good laboratories. Let us do our thing, and if it's a good solution, make it federal law."

The debate over Spitzer and his imitators in many ways reflected the larger fight over competition between state and federal regulators, a battle that began at least 150 years ago, when Congress overlaid a national banking system regulated by the Office of the Comptroller of the Currency on top of a state-based system. Proponents of having federal regulators "preempt" local rules argued that a single national system promoted efficiency and rational rules, making it easier for businesses to flourish and grow. Consumers benefited from national standards that ensured that everyone received a minimum level of protection. But advocates of regulatory competition argued that having multiple enforcers prevented any single regulator from falling down on the job. "There is a natural tension in federalism. The notion that there's always going to be sweetness and light is wrong," said Eugene Ludwig, a former comptroller of the currency, whose office argued and won five preemption cases. The duplication and turf battles are "sometimes maddening and it's sometimes overkill. But it tends to bubble up better results as people debate it than if you have one person who has been doing the same thing for forty years." Former SEC commissioner Harvey Goldschmid agreed. "The reality of the United States, especially when it comes to business, is that it makes sense to have several different enforcement sources with different perspectives. So that if, God forbid, the SEC is captured or, if the antitrust division is inactive, as happened in the Reagan years, there is room for state AGs and private lawyers to come in," he said. "The AG who is going to do the wrong thing is a relatively small price to pay for the overall improvement and safety valve they represent."

With Spitzer and his imitators on the horizon actively looking for securities and insurance cases, many corporations began to wish for the predictability of federal enforcement. Run by commissions and a cadre of longtime staff members, federal agencies often produced more predictable results, and they often followed up individual enforcement cases with industry-wide regulations that created a level playing field. It was not surprising, therefore, that by 2005, Spitzer's opponents had begun to see federal preemption through the courts as their best weapon for blunting the New York attorney general's attacks. The convergence of the OCC preemption case with the Seligman lawsuit claiming that Spitzer had no jurisdiction over mutual fees and with Grasso's unsuccessful effort to move his excessive compensation case to federal court was no coincidence. Spitzer's targets were no longer willing to comply with his subpoenas and wait to see what his investigators turned up. His nose for populist issues and his willingness to use the media and New York's unusual laws to apply pressure made him simply too dangerous. From business's point of view it was far better to work with the Bush administration to preempt local enforcement and to center power in Washington. "It's cyclical. If you have an activist regulator at the federal level, it doesn't leave a lot of room for states," said Roger Noll, a Stanford University economics professor who studied regulation. In some arenas, Republicans in Congress and the executive branch were more than willing to comply. The FDA intervened on behalf of drug and medical device makers in a half dozen product liability lawsuits, arguing that the FDA's approval process should protect the manufacturers from state claims that they failed to warn consumers about harmful side effects. The comptroller of the currency promulgated regulations that gave the OCC sole power to enforce state fair-lending laws. Some members of Congress began exploring the idea of a national insurance regulator that would provide uniform rules and enforcement.

Spitzer refused to be cowed. "We have been fighting preemption battles across the board with every federal agency, the SEC, the EPA, the FCC," Spitzer said in November 2005, citing a list of nearly sixty preemption cases compiled by Caitlin Halligan, who had taken over as his solicitor general when Preeta Bansal left for private practice. "We'll just keep on fighting."

12

TO DARE MIGHTY THINGS

THE TOM PETTY TUNE "I WON'T BACK DOWN" WAS BLARING THROUGH THE loudspeakers as Eliot Spitzer rose to take the microphone at the Buffalo Convention Center on December 1, 2005. Though the morning had dawned gray and forbidding, the mood inside was warm and—for 8:00 A.M. on a Thursday—boisterous. Aiming to start the 2006 election season with a bang, Assemblyman Sam Hoyt and the Erie County Democratic Committee had organized a sixty-dollar-a-plate breakfast with Spitzer and nearly half a dozen Democratic county chairmen from New York's far-western reaches. They hoped to draw five hundred loyalists; instead they had pulled in eight hundred people, making the gathering the largest political fund-raiser in Buffalo in recent memory. The ground-floor ballroom, decked with union banners, was packed to the gills as organizers scrounged around for enough scrambled eggs and sausages to feed the unexpectedly large gathering. After John Murphy ("the voice of the Buffalo Bills") and a couple of Democratic bigwigs warmed up the crowd, Spitzer took the floor.

As was often the case at these early campaign events, Spitzer was far louder than the pols that had preceded him to the lectern. Practically vibrating with enthusiasm after receiving a standing ovation, Spitzer unwound a version of his stump speech designed to hearten the party base and tap into populist themes. "Friends in labor, you are the back-bone of this economy, and we will not forget that. We will see that you get your fair share," he told the crowd, before ripping into the Republicans. "No party has done so much for so few who need so little," he said to huge applause. "The yachts of those who have contributed have grown a lot larger in the last ten years while the lifeboat for everybody else has gotten smaller and more cramped."

From the convention center, it was on to a far different setting, a one-thousand-dollar-a-head meet-and-greet at The Mansion, one of Buffalo's boutique hotels. Beside an elegant spread of French pastries and yogurt parfaits, Spitzer listened attentively to western New York businessmen who were the clients of one of Albany's influential lobbying firms. Told of a recent plant expansion at a local food-processing facility that would allow New York milk to be shipped as far as California, he asked focused questions: "How many jobs?" and "What have you encountered on the federal regulatory level? I would guess the folks from Wisconsin wouldn't be happy about this." His short speech to the small gathering was restrained and strewn with business metaphors—his high poll numbers, he said, made him "fearful that I'm an overvalued stock and have no downside risk." Spitzer's only reference to his Wall Street cases came as he argued that he would put competence above partisanship in making appointments. "The successes I have had result from a judgment I made on day one to hire the best people," he said.

By day's end, Spitzer had raised nearly $250,000 at five events and drawn coverage from a half dozen local television and radio stations. With follow-up phone calls, his campaign staff expected to double his dollar totals. Although his emphasis varied by audience, the core of his speech remained the same. He outlined a reform agenda calculated to appeal to voters beyond the New York City elites and Democratic stalwarts who could be expected to form his base. In his vision, the Empire State was teetering on the edge of economic crisis, bogged down by inefficient and wasteful government, too-high energy costs, and a failing educational system. Spitzer argued that it was time to take the drive for reform that he had unleashed on Wall Street and train it on Albany. Steering straight for the state's political center, he insisted that New

York could no longer afford to throw money at problems. "We have a government that is failing," Spitzer said at one of the Buffalo fund-raisers. "There simply is no excuse for our failure to change, to adapt, to invest. . . . A crisis is a terrible thing to waste."

A week later, Spitzer hit the hustings downstate, with a one-thousand-dollar-a-plate formal dinner for 1,500 people in Manhattan. The up-tempo event filled the New York Sheraton's largest ballroom to capacity, raised nearly five million dollars, and drew coverage from some of the city's leading gossip columnists. The *New York Post*'s Cindy Adams complained about the quality of the food and wine but opined, "Barring Nelson Rockefeller returning from Beyond to reclaim the job, Spitzer's our next governor." In the days leading up to that dinner, Spitzer's campaign staff did everything it could to give his candidacy the appearance of a juggernaut, rolling out endorsements from fire-fighters, environmentalists, thirty-five mayors, and five of the state's six Democratic county executives. (The one exception was Nassau County executive Thomas Suozzi, who was very publicly mulling a run against Spitzer in the primary, with the potential support of Ken Langone, who had sworn to avenge himself on Spitzer.)

The gubernatorial campaign still had eleven months to go, but Spitzer was leaving large footprints at a time when his opponents were still finding their way. The leading Republican candidate for governor seemed to be William F. Weld, a former governor of Massachusetts whose support in New York was unproven at best.

At the same time, Spitzer showed no sign of losing interest in the job that had brought him national fame. In the last two months of 2005, the Attorney General's Office brought a full complement of cases—forcing retailers to recall lead-containing lunch boxes, fining gas stations for price-gouging in the wake of Hurricane Katrina, and ordering a Manhattan deli called Mr. Broadway to pay three hundred thousand dollars in back wages to delivery and kitchen workers. Spitzer also spoke out against the EPA's plan to clean pollutants out of the Hudson River (an issue he had raised during the 1998 campaign) and continued to stomp around the financial services industry. The stock analyst global settlement achieved a form of closure right before Christmas, when the SEC began mailing restitution checks to 33,677 clients of the big Wall Street firms who could show they had been burned by biased research reports. Almost half the check recipients had owned one hundred shares or fewer, which suggested that they were indeed the small investors whom Spitzer had insisted he was trying to protect. The attorney general also found himself on the receiving end of some negative publicity from an unexpected source: the Jewish newspaper *The Forward* published an article questioning the way his office had handled an investigation into a small Orthodox synagogue group, the National Council of Young Israel, several years before. William Josephson, the former head of the attorney general's Charities Bureau, told the paper that the attorney general's investigation had been highly irregular and possibly tainted by the fact that some of the staff involved in the investigation had family ties to the synagogue group. Though the Charities Bureau uncovered what Spitzer's office described as "significant problems"—including allegedly improper payments and loans to top officers—Spitzer never brought a public case against the National Council of Young Israel. "There had been so many departures in the handling of this matter from standard procedures that it made it difficult to pursue this case in a straightforward fashion," Josephson told *The Forward*. Spitzer countered that his office had forced the nonprofit "to change the entire structure of their governance. . . . The capacity we had and the leverage that we had was used to maximum extent to force governance change, personnel changes."

But in terms of sheer controversy, nothing could compare to Spitzer's ongoing battle with former AIG chief executive Hank Greenberg. In late November, Spitzer's deputies acknowledged publicly what their boss had decided privately several months earlier: that the evidence would not support state criminal charges against Greenberg in connection with either his stock trading or AIG's accounting. (Greenberg attorney Robert Morvillo said the move vindicated his client's decision to take the Fifth Amendment at the April deposition.) Then Spitzer released the results of his office's second Greenberg-related investigation: the one looking into the former AIG chief's role in a series of stock transactions in 1969 and 1970 involving companies he controlled and the estate of his late boss Cornelius Vander Starr.

The probe had involved months of digging through hundreds of boxes of ancient documents—no embarrassing e-mails this time. But the end result—according to Spitzer's office—was troubling. His investigators uncovered three separate stock transactions that involved "self-dealing" by the Starr estate executors and appeared to disadvantage the estate. Spitzer's staff calculated that the Starr Foundation—the main beneficiary of the Starr estate—had received two million dollars in cash from the various stock sales, when it could have received AIG stock worth thirty million dollars. Had the foundation received and held the stock, those holdings would have been worth six billion dollars in 2005. The Spitzer team also argued that they had found a way around the statute of limitations that normally prevented the state from taking legal action against a fiduciary for actions that were more than six years old. Since Greenberg was still the chairman of the Starr Foundation, they argued, the statute of limitations had not yet begun to run.

The next question was how to bring a case. Spitzer could have amended his existing fraud complaint against Greenberg and AIG to include the allegations about the Starr estate, but instead he opted for a more unusual course of action, one that drew upon his belief in the power of public shaming. He had his staff write a thirty-page report on what they had found, and then, on December 14, he sent it to the Starr Foundation and released it to select members of the media. In his cover letter, Spitzer gave the foundation's director, Florence Davis, until the end of January to consider taking legal action against Greenberg, the chairman of her own board, to recover the money. (Though the letter didn't say so, the report did not foreclose the possibility that Spitzer's office would bring a case of its own if the Starr Foundation refused to do so.)

Davis gave Spitzer's report a chilly reception. "While the Starr Foundation respects the authority of the attorney general to supervise charitable foundations and to investigate alleged improprieties," she said in a statement, "the foundation is concerned that allegations concerning a judicial proceeding closed more than 25 years ago and the negative publicity attendant thereto may adversely affect the value of the assets of the foundation, without discernable purpose."

Greenberg was far less restrained. In a series of interviews with major newspapers and the cable channel CNBC, he blasted Spitzer for what he called "outrageous" and politically motivated allegations. "It's simple: He's running for another office," Greenberg told *The Washington Post*. "It has nothing to do with right or wrong." He also complained about Spitzer's method of dealing with the issue, telling the *New York Post*, "instead of filing charges, they are persecuting me in the press."

Greenberg's lawyers issued a thirty-four-page rejoinder, arguing that the report was Spitzer's attempt to save face after failing to bring criminal charges against Greenberg. They conceded that Greenberg and several other executors were on both sides of the transactions but argued that the estate had followed the federal law that set out rules for dealing with such apparent conflicts of interest. Not only had the transactions involved been approved by New York courts in 1979 as the federal law required, but the New York State attorney general at the time had been a party to the case and had not objected. "There is no valid claim against Mr. Greenberg concerning the settlement of C. V. Starr's estate. The Attorney General's office knows this, which is why no court action was commenced," said David Boies in early January 2006. "If they had sued in court the case would have been thrown out. The letter and 'report' were an unfair personal attack, prepared solely for PR purposes and to put pressure on Mr. Greenberg."

A group of Greenberg's prominent supporters, including former New York governor Mario Cuomo, started a public-relations campaign to defend the former AIG chief's image. "There are many people, I included, who feel a certain respect for Hank and admiration for what he's done," Cuomo told Bloomberg News.

Spitzer did not back down. "If it was a fraud and we have jurisdiction, the fact that he committed it a long time ago doesn't mean he should get away with it," he said. "The foundation should get the money back." Besides, he added, his office had a particular interest in the case because they had discovered it by going through the documents that Greenberg's legal team had removed from AIG's Bermuda offices over the Easter weekend. "Now we know what he was trying to hide from us. That's why we care," he said. (The Boies firm lawyers took umbrage at Spitzer's suggestion that they had tried to hide Starr estate information from Spitzer's office. "These allegations had nothing to do with documents from Bermuda," said Lee Wolosky. "The documents that the attorney general used as exhibits to his report demonstrate that fact.")

Spitzer also continued to spar publicly with Ken Langone over the Richard Grasso lawsuit. On December 9, Langone gave a speech at the Cato Institute in which he accused Spitzer of engaging in "vigilante publicity" and being motivated by "raw ambition for pure political gain." He also lavished praise on Spitzer's potential primary challenger Thomas Suozzi. One liberal civic group calculated that Langone's friends and associates gave more than $510,000 to Suozzi in 2005 alone. Rather than ignore the fund-raising and criticism, Spitzer responded equally hotly, telling *The New York Times* that Langone's allegations about the case were "lies, lies and more lies."

The high-profile sniping led some observers to wonder whether Spitzer, despite his success as a prosecutor, had the temperament to serve effectively as governor, a multifaceted executive job that required both administrative and conciliation skills. *The Wall Street Journal* editorial page weighed in that New Yorkers should question "whether Mr. Spitzer's habit of publicly smearing individuals while bringing no charges in court is appropriate behavior by any prosecutor, much less one running to be New York's Governor."

Even Spitzer acknowledged that the gubernatorial job he sought was quite unlike the perch he had used to such advantage for the previous seven years. "The positions are very different," he said. "This is a binary world, good and bad. That one is triage, ranking many good programs" at a time when the state already had high taxes and burgeoning debt. But he argued that his career as attorney general proved he had the courage to challenge entrenched interests and rethink popular programs. "If I stand for anything it's that I'm not going to stand here with my finger in the air wondering what's good politically," he said.

New York's political history suggests that Spitzer's combative personality could lead him in either of two potential directions. He could follow in the pugnacious path blazed by Rudolph Giuliani—the U.S. attorney turned New York City mayor who often found himself an "army of one" as he sought to revamp the city government and cut crime during eight years in office—or he could cleave to the model established by Thomas E. Dewey, the tough Manhattan prosecutor who demonstrated a talent for coalition building and had three successful terms as governor of the Empire State in the 1940s and early 1950s.

Like Giuliani, Spitzer has a history of alienating potential allies, and sometimes his blunt speaking has gotten in the way of his getting things done. In one often-told tale, Spitzer was appalled by a proposal put forward in late 2001 by the National Association of Attorneys General to spend fifty million dollars—money left over from the gigantic tobacco settlement—on staff training and perhaps a new building in Washington. So he flew out to the group's winter meeting in California specifically to urge his fellow attorneys general to oppose the program and spend the money on health care instead. But his arrival toward the end of the gathering irked his peers, who had been in California for much of the week, spending time in meetings and at social events, including outings to a comedy club and to Disneyland. Spitzer then made matters worse when he accused them not only of padding the group's budget but also of compromising its principles by accepting free admission to the amusement park and allowing a local real estate developer to sponsor their dinner. California attorney general Bill Lockyer was incensed. His staff had spent weeks setting up the events, and he knew that the Disneyland outing was a rare treat for many of the officials, who—unlike Spitzer—did not travel much and had to live on their state salaries because they were not independently wealthy.

Spitzer's performance prompted an angry exchange, according to a report in *The American Lawyer*. "You have a hell of a lot to say for someone who doesn't give enough of a fuck to show up except when you want to be disagreeable," Lockyer told him, which led to the two men screaming expletives at each other until Spitzer declared, "You want to step outside, that's fine! I grew up in the Bronx!"

"No problem," Lockyer shouted back. "I grew up in East L.A. Let's go!"

After talking in private, the two men calmed down, but Spitzer lost the vote on how to spend the tobacco money, by a tally of thirty to one. At least a few attorneys general had agreed with Spitzer's overall point, but they were so annoyed by his late arrival and his holier-than-thou attitude that they either voted against him or abstained.

Nor was the Lockyer incident an isolated one: Congresswoman Sue Kelly had complained about a high-volume exchange with Spitzer in the summer of 2003, and the SEC staff bore the scars of Spitzer's repeated criticism. Spitzer's staff only reinforced their boss's image as a hothead with their public threats to arrest people and to drag companies "through the mud." These matters became a hot political topic in December 2005 when former Goldman Sachs chairman John Whitehead published an op-ed article in *The Wall Street Journal* alleging that Spitzer had personally threatened him the previous April for defending Hank Greenberg in another op-ed piece. Whitehead called Spitzer "scary" and wrote that his notes of the conversation showed that Spitzer had said, "You will pay dearly for what you have done. You will wish you had never written that letter." Spitzer's spokesman, Darren Dopp, took issue with Whitehead's version, calling the quote from Spitzer "fabricated." But he acknowledged that Whitehead and Spitzer had had a spat. "Eliot did call him," Dopp said. "They did have a discussion. Eliot took exception to some of the things [that Whitehead had written in the April piece] and it did conclude with Eliot telling him, focus on your day job."

Even some of Spitzer's supporters said privately that they worried about how his penchant for publicly attacking and humiliating his opponents would play in Albany. While the SEC and his corporate targets had always come back to the table after a public falling-out, it was less clear whether the powerful leaders of the State Assembly and Senate would be willing to take verbal abuse from a governor. One lawyer who had worked closely with Spitzer on a number of fronts predicted that at some tough negotiating session, "He'll get frustrated and just let loose. He'll go out and publicly flatten somebody [saying] . . . this guy is the sole impediment and it's all about pork." The unanswered question, the lawyer said, was how that kind of bomb-throwing would play in the insular, backroom world of Albany. "Either the machine will flatten him, or maybe it will work. . . . He channels the populist instinct and he's got the potential to shame them."

In seven years as attorney general, Spitzer's record of getting

Albany to follow his suggestions had not been particularly impressive. His Labor Bureau chief, Patricia Smith, tried repeatedly to get a law enacted that would bar from public construction projects contractors who had been convicted of felonies related to the prevailing-wage law. She got absolutely nowhere. Though the bill passed both chambers of the legislature in both 2000 and 2001, it was vetoed by Governor Pataki. "Having a law proposed by Eliot Spitzer was like the kiss of death," Smith remembered. Finally, Smith and Spitzer's lobbyists hit on a solution—they got one of the big unions in the state, the operating engineers, to adopt the proposal as their own, and Pataki finally let the bill become law. Two other proposals on Spitzer's wish list, one that would strengthen the New York law protecting whistle-blowers from retaliation and another that would increase the civil penalties for Medicaid fraud, languished for years without passage. Part of the problem stemmed from New York State's history of secrecy. Very few battles in Albany took place out in the open, making it harder to use Spitzer's favorite tactic of public humiliation. "There are very few close votes in Albany," said William McSpedon, secretary-treasurer of the operating engineers. "All the work is done behind the scenes. No one wants to fight you on the floor."

Spitzer himself was fairly realistic about his influence in the legislature. In 1999, his aide Dan Feldman, a former state assemblyman, lobbied his boss to go after disability insurance companies that deliberately refused to pay legitimate claims from their policyholders. During his time in the legislature, Feldman had gotten the Assembly to pass a bill that would have allowed policyholders to seek punitive damages from such firms, but it was then bottled up by the Republican-controlled Senate. Feldman thought his boss should include the proposal in his legislative requests. But Spitzer was reluctant. "It's not going to enhance its chances in the Senate by having my name on it," he told Feldman. During the gubernatorial campaign, Spitzer said that he hoped the 2006 election would help change the balance of power in his favor. "I'm hoping that I will win by a sufficient margin to show that there's a mandate for reform," he said. "A governor has a lot more leverage than I do in the legislative process, and I plan to use it."

The up-and-down saga of Rudolph Giuliani's eight years as mayor of New York City serves as both a model and a cautionary tale for a potential Spitzer governorship. In some ways, Giuliani's success as mayor stemmed from his prickly and unbending nature. At a time of economic crisis, he instituted the city's first meaningful hiring freeze in years and announced plans for tax cuts, privatization of government services, and public-sector layoffs. He and Police Commissioner William Bratton tackled the city's runaway crime problem by adopting the "broken windows" theory that held that if police cracked down on low-level quality-of-life crimes such as vandalism and turnstile-jumping, more serious offenses would drop as well. Their first big effort—a campaign to rid the city of the "squeegee men" who shook down motorists at red lights under the pretext of "cleaning" their windshields with a dirty rag—was a celebrated success. Threatened with arrest, many of the squeegee men simply disappeared from the streets. Many of the others turned out to have prior arrests for serious felonies. The whole problem was gone in a month. Giuliani's calls for welfare reform dovetailed with a bipartisan drive on the national level, and his 1995 campaign to break the mob's influence over the Fulton Fish Market became a model for similar efforts around the city. The city's larger problems also began to resolve themselves: by the late 1990s, the Wall Street boom had pulled the city's economy along with it, and serious crime, which had begun to fall during the last year of the term of Giuliani's predecessor, David Dinkins, plummeted so quickly that *Time* magazine put William Bratton on its cover. In 1997, Giuliani handily won reelection with 57 percent of the vote, a very strong showing for a Republican in a Democratic city. "People didn't elect me to be a conciliator," Giuliani later told *Time*. "They wanted someone who was going to change this place. How do you expect me to change it if I don't fight with somebody? You don't change ingrained human behavior without confrontation, turmoil, anger."

But Giuliani's combative style had its limits. New Yorkers eventually got tired of his constant crusades against everything from street vendors to jaywalking, and the city's minority communities, who had endured the most aggressive side of "broken windows" policing, actively disliked him. The shooting of Amadou Diallo in February 1999 crystallized their anger. Giuliani's ceaseless wars with the city bureaucracy also took their toll—by the end of 2000, the mayor was on his third schools chancellor and his third police commissioner. The popular Bratton was gone. Many believed he had been driven out because Giuliani believed that he, rather than the police commissioner, should have graced the cover of *Time*. Prevented by term limits from seeking a third term, Giuliani briefly ran for the U.S. Senate against Hillary Clinton, but he was beset by personal problems, including prostate cancer, the collapse of his marriage, and a very public extramarital affair. Giuliani's career seemed over, but he was reborn politically after the 2001 attack on the World Trade Center. His calm demeanor and steely resolve inspired Americans looking for leadership in a time of crisis.

While Spitzer's critics often compared him to Giuliani, Spitzer himself had another paradigm in mind. He gave a series of speeches in late 2005 to explain the kind of governor he wanted to be, and in one such speech, he spoke of the state's history of "effective, visionary government" that "did great things that actually helped set the state on a path toward greater prosperity," citing three great public projects: the Erie Canal, the New York State Thruway, and the State University of New York. Two out of three were at least partially the legacy of Thomas Dewey. Dewey is now best remembered as the "little man on the wedding cake" who lost the surprisingly close 1948 presidential election to Harry S. Truman and inspired the famous "Dewey Defeats Truman" headline in the *Chicago Daily Tribune*. But his decades-long career in law enforcement and politics showed how a tough-as-nails crime fighter could make the transformation to effective governor.

Like Spitzer, Dewey won national fame early. Known as "the Gangbuster," he aggressively went after the "rackets"—organized mobs that dominated entire economic sectors, from illegal pursuits like bootlegging, loan sharking, and prostitution to bedrock industries such as restaurants and garment manufacturing. As a special prosecutor based in the same building at 120 Broadway that would later house Spitzer's Manhattan headquarters, Dewey made headlines around the country for his hard-charging attacks on New York's mobsters, including the homicidal gang known as Murder Incorporated. "If you don't think Dewey is Public Hero No. 1, listen to the applause he gets every time he is shown in a newsreel," wrote *The Philadelphia Inquirer* in 1937. But even as he put bad guys behind bars, concern grew over his methods—in one case, he held 125 witnesses incommunicado; in others he used the threat of tax prosecutions to compel cooperation. Dewey also angered civil libertarians in 1938 by opposing constitutional restrictions on wiretapping. By 1940, while serving as Manhattan district attorney, he was being taken seriously as a presidential candidate, and in 1942, at the age of forty, he became New York's first Republican governor in twenty years.

Once in Albany, Dewey opted at first for confrontation, ordering a sweeping review of the entire state government with an eye toward rooting out fraud and cutting the budget. He also demanded that the state pass a reapportionment bill for the first time in twenty-five years, telling reluctant legislators—some of whom were facing the likely loss of their seats—that failing to accede to his demands would violate the state constitution and dishonor the soldiers then fighting in World War II. After his first legislative session, he vetoed more than 20 percent of the bills that had been sent to his desk for signature. But over time, Dewey learned to work with, rather than against, the legislature and compiled an impressive record of successes. During his three terms as governor from 1942 to 1954, New York constructed the St. Lawrence power plant, built the thruway linking New York City, Albany, and Buffalo, and enacted legislation creating the state university system. The passage of New York's first-in-the-nation law banning employment discrimination in 1945 was testimony to how far Dewey had come. Rather than use his position to ram a bill through the Republican-controlled legislature, Dewey arranged for the bill, which covered bias based on race, religion, and national origin, to be sponsored by both the Republican majority leader of the Assembly and the Democratic minority leader of the Senate. "His legislative leadership was extraordinary," remembered Dewey's counsel George M. Shapiro. "He recognized with great clarity that it was not enough to merely propose a good idea. You had to persuade people to recognize it as good and to persuade an elected legislature to follow your lead." Dewey's gubernatorial career was still remembered fondly in New York decades later for combining fiscal responsibility—he cut the state's debt by one hundred million dollars—with improvements in education, health care, and transportation. In 2005, Spitzer regularly cited Dewey as a model, both for his infrastructure improvements and for his decision to revamp the state's tax code to make it more attractive for companies to choose New York as the site of their corporate headquarters.

Dewey's success in Albany made him a presidential contender: though he lost the Republican nomination to Wendell Willkie in 1940, he was the party's standard-bearer in 1944 and 1948. But on the national stage, the skills that had served him so well in New York failed to translate into victory. In 1944, he simply could not overcome the country's fondness for Franklin D. Roosevelt and its wartime loyalty to him. In 1948, Dewey was seen as the clear favorite over President Harry S. Truman, who had taken office after Roosevelt's death, but Dewey ran an aloof campaign based on vague bromides and listless speeches that did little to draw on his successes as a progressive governor in New York. Dewey's passivity allowed Truman to link him to the unpopular right-wing Republican majority in Congress and turn his law-enforcement image against him. Truman called Dewey the New Deal's "chief prosecutor," someone who would roll back the social gains achieved under FDR. Pollsters found that voters considered Dewey "dignified" and "sincere," but "Give 'em Hell Harry" came off as a fighter for the poor and voiceless. On Election Day, Truman scored a major upset, racking up an Electoral College victory of 303 to 189.

As the 2006 governor's race got under way, Spitzer argued that he, like Dewey, had learned to do his homework and build alliances to get things done. As evidence he pointed not only to the global research settlement and the many mutual fund cases that his office had brought along with the SEC, but also to a more recent bipartisan effort to defeat a controversial proposal on the November 2005 ballot that would have swung budget-making power away from the governor. Put forward by the state legislature, "Prop One," as the proposal was known, was pitched as a reform plan, but its chief effect would have been to give the legislature additional budgetary power if the state missed its official deadline for coming up with a financial plan. Prop One was seen by many prominent business groups, Republicans, and anti-tax conservatives as another step down the road to runaway spending and irresponsible taxation. Spitzer's interest in fighting the measure was obvious—if passed, it would tie the hands of the next governor and would shift power to the legislature. But several of his natural allies were among the proposal's sponsors, including the state legislature's most powerful Democrat, Assembly Speaker Sheldon Silver; some liberal good-government groups; and several unions, most prominently Local 1199 of the Service Employees International Union, a major player in New York politics.

Concerned that the pro-amendment forces were far outspending the opponents, Spitzer and his aide Rich Baum reached out to the group New Yorkers to Change Albany, a local offshoot of the national anti-tax group Americans for Limited Government. Together they plotted a strategy to get their message out in the off-year election. The anti-tax group garnered headlines by towing an eight-hundred-pound statue of a pink pig around the state. Baum and the Business Council of New York State, the largest upstate business group, raised money to fund prerecorded phone calls to every likely voter in the state, an estimated 3.75 million calls. While Spitzer recorded a message for registered Democrats, the coalition recruited Governor George Pataki—who had also come out against the measure—and Rudolph Giuliani to tape messages for Republicans and independents. Although the anti–Prop One coalition spent only $355,000, compared to $1.28 million for the initiative's proponents, the measure was defeated by a nearly two-to-one margin. Coalition members also came out impressed by one another. "It was a really professional group that was really committed to communicating with the voters," said Marshall Stocker, a spokesman for New Yorkers to Change Albany. And when *The Wall Street Journal* editorial page criticized Spitzer for not doing more to stop the amendment, Business Council president Daniel Walsh begged to differ. "Mr. Spitzer was integral to our success," he wrote in a letter to the editor. "Mr. Spitzer spoke out early and often against the amendment. He also worked actively with us to arrange and attend coalition events around the state. He reached out to editorial boards, which ended up unanimously opposed to the amendment. And for months, he and his allies worked behind the scenes with us to strengthen the opposition to the amendment—and to dissuade some of its potential supporters." Indeed, Spitzer would later say that his efforts to defeat Prop One demonstrated his ability to work effectively with his ideological and political opponents when they shared a goal.

In running for governor of New York, Spitzer knew he was seeking to fill some very large shoes. The executive mansion in Albany had long been considered a springboard to higher office. In the twentieth century alone, two of the state's former chief executives had won the White House (Theodore and Franklin Roosevelt); two more had won a major party's nomination for president but lost in general elections (Alfred E. Smith and Thomas Dewey); and more recently, Nelson Rockefeller and Mario Cuomo had each been touted as serious presidential contenders. All six men—to one degree or another—shared the state's Progressive values and saw New York as a model for the country. Theodore Roosevelt began his attacks on corporate monopolies in New York; FDR used his stint as governor to pass sweeping protections for labor and to experiment with public works projects as a form of relief in the early days of the Great Depression. As Spitzer sought to follow in their footsteps, Democrats around the country were watching closely. His Wall Street investigations and dynamic presence had already made him a household name far beyond New York. But it remained an open question whether he could use the state as a laboratory for his ideas and a path to even greater prominence. "Spitzerism: Is a Prosecutor's Zeal What the Democrats Need?" ran a headline in *The New York Times Magazine* in October 2005.

For himself, Eliot Spitzer publicly professed not to be looking beyond Albany, but his supporters and even his campaign rhetoric suggested a higher ultimate goal. As the 2006 campaign year dawned, he had taken to closing many of his speeches with a warning about the difficulties ahead and a quote from Theodore Roosevelt: "Far better is it to dare mighty things, to win glorious triumphs, even though checkered by failure . . . than to rank with those poor spirits who neither enjoy nor suffer much, because they live in a gray twilight that knows not victory nor defeat."

EPILOGUE

IN THE FIRST MONTHS OF 2006, WALL STREET WAS BOOMING—THE DOW
Jones Industrial Average had climbed past 11,000 and several key indexes were approaching five-year highs. Many of the investment banks
were reporting huge profits. At 120 Broadway, Eliot Spitzer was tying
up loose ends and gearing up for the governor's race. His chief of staff
Rich Baum, who had run the 1998 campaign, left the state payroll and
joined the Spitzer 2006 campaign full-time. By all appearances, things
were going well. Spitzer had already raised more than nineteen million
dollars, which was more than ten times the amount any of his Republican rivals had on hand. His major contributors included hedge fund
managers, wealthy investors, and a swarm of Albany lobbyists with a
history of giving mostly to incumbents. A potential rival, billionaire
Thomas Golisano (who had run three times on the Independence Party
line), announced that he would sit out the 2006 campaign, and a Siena
Research Institute Poll showed Spitzer with a favorable opinion rating
of about 50 percent among Democrats, Republicans, and independents,
as well as every major ethnic and religious group, men and women alike.

Considered a prohibitive favorite, Spitzer began flexing his political
muscles. In late January, he announced that he wanted state senate minority leader David A. Paterson to be his running mate, even though

Paterson had not entered the race for lieutenant governor, and several other candidates had already declared their interest in seeking the position. Paterson, an African American from Harlem, had a record as a reformer and was respected by both parties. "It's a statement about the values I hope to bring to governing," Spitzer explained in an interview. "He's smart, funny, understands government, and he speaks for a constituency that needs to be part of state government."

But the choice initially angered some top black Democrats who were already on record favoring another candidate, Leecia Eve of Buffalo. Representative Charles Rangel gave voice to that group's anger when he bitterly told *The New York Times*, "When Eliot Spitzer, the world's smartest man, is telling me that he has picked his candidate and knows that his candidate can win, who am I to question the world's smartest man?" Spitzer got his way. Eve and two other declared candidates pulled out of the lieutenant governor's race within days, clearing the field for Paterson. Rangel took a little longer to come around, but on February 25, he too endorsed the Spitzer-Paterson ticket.

Spitzer's people saw the spat as entirely positive—their boss had picked a candidate that he believed would inspire African-American voters to turn out but had also demonstrated his independence from the black political establishment. Others, more critical, said it reinforced their view that Spitzer was too enamored of his own brilliance and unwilling to work with others. The choice of Paterson, who represented Harlem in the state senate, also meant the likely Democratic ticket could well be vulnerable to charges that it was too liberal, too heavily weighted toward New York City, and too enmeshed in the current political system to bring real reform to Albany.

Thomas Suozzi sensed an opportunity. The Nassau County executive was an Italian-American Catholic suburbanite in a state loaded with all three. He also had a history of taking on the Democratic Party elders—he had defeated an establishment candidate in the 2001 Democratic primary for county executive and later launched a "fix Albany" crusade that openly criticized state legislators of both parties. After months of speculation, Suozzi officially declared his candidacy for governor at an upbeat February 25 rally in his hometown of Glen Cove, where he had served as mayor from 1994 to 2001. "I'm trying to bring democracy back to the Democratic Party," he explained in an interview. "I can do it because I've done it before."

Unlike the known Republican candidates, Suozzi had a sizeable war chest—he had transferred more than three million dollars from his successful 2005 reelection campaign and had raised an additional $1.7 million before declaring his candidacy, including the more than $500,000 put together by friends and associates of Ken Langone, in fulfillment of Langone's pledge to bankroll a worthy challenger to Spitzer in 2006. Suozzi's January fund-raising report also revealed he had received substantial donations from executives at First American Corporation, one of the state's largest title insurance firms, at a time when Spitzer's office was probing the title insurance industry. "It's the way people Spitzer has gone after are getting back at him," said Richard Kirsch, the executive director of Citizen Action, a liberal group that endorsed Spitzer and was seeking campaign finance reform. "Suozzi is letting himself be used as a tool." Suozzi disagreed, arguing that the donations were perfectly appropriate, especially when compared with the millions Spitzer was raising from lobbyists and trial lawyers. "The only thing [Langone] is looking for is for me to win and for me to continue doing the good job I have done in Nassau County," Suozzi said. "He's not looking for something from state government." And the money was certainly coming in handy. Suozzi's campaign began airing television commercials in early March—the same week as Spitzer. It was clear that Spitzer was in for a serious fight, and Langone said he was just getting started. "New York State desperately needs an environment that's conducive for business and this guy [Spitzer] hasn't got it. He's a fraud and he knows it," Langone said. "Suozzi has got a fabulous message: clean up Albany. . . . I hope and trust the people of New York recognize how inimical to their interest Eliot Spitzer is."

Langone's lawyers were also sparring with Spitzer's staff in the courtroom as the Grasso executive compensation case moved closer to trial. Langone's lawyer, Gary Naftalis—who had also represented Eddie Stern—was seeking sanctions against Spitzer's office for what he said was a failure to comply with a court order requiring Spitzer's office to specify more clearly the evidence against Langone. At the same time, Grasso's lawyers weighed in, asking the judge to let them take testimony directly from Spitzer, a highly unusual step for this kind of fraud case. Avi Schick, who was still handling the Grasso case for Spitzer's office, fought both requests and fired a shot of his own—he asked for copies of a SEC confidential deposition in which Grasso refused to answer requests about his own conduct as a regulator on the grounds that the answers might incriminate him. Charles Ramos, the judge overseeing the case, complained, "You're having a war, and I'm the civilian caught in the crossfire," Ramos said. "I've got 350 other cases. I can't spend my life on this case."

The judge had a point, and for their part, Spitzer and his staff had plenty of other fish to fry. On February 9, after months of feuding, Spitzer's office, the Justice Department, and the SEC combined forces to negotiate a settlement with AIG. The insurance giant agreed to pay a total of $1.64 billion to settle a whole series of allegations including bid-rigging, accounting fraud, and a scheme to systematically cheat states of taxes on workers' compensation premiums. The settlement was the largest of its kind, dwarfing both the Marsh & McLennan deal and the global research settlement. True to form, Spitzer again insisted that the company issue a statement in which it publicly expressed remorse. AIG complied, stating that it "regrets and apologizes for the conduct that led to the action brought by the New York Attorney General and the New York Superintendent of Insurance and to today's settlement. Providing incorrect information to the investing public and to regulators was wrong." AIG also specifically acknowledged that the company had "improperly recorded" the reinsurance deal that Hank Greenberg had negotiated with Gen Re president Ronald Ferguson in the fall of 2000.

Even so, Greenberg pointedly refused to join the settlement negotiated by his former company. "We have already debunked many of the allegations settled today by AIG in a white paper issued last summer," his spokesman, Howard Opinsky, said. "The suggestion . . . that Mr. Greenberg may have been involved in any wrongdoing is false. We are confident that when the debate moves from the newspaper to the courts Mr. Greenberg will be vindicated." But Greenberg was also facing pressure from another direction. That same month, a federal grand jury in Virginia handed up criminal fraud indictments against Ferguson, two other Gen Re officials, and the former head of reinsurance at AIG. All of the counts were based on that same controversial reinsurance transaction from 2000. Officials familiar with the case conceded privately that they did not have enough evidence to seek charges against Greenberg, but they insisted that their investigation was continuing.

Spitzer viewed the settlement and the federal criminal indictments as an affirmation of his May 2005 civil case against Greenberg, which had drawn so much public criticism and increasingly looked like it would drag on past the gubernatorial election. "The beauty of having the SEC and the Department of Justice on board embracing the facts is [that] it's absolute validation of what we are doing," he said. "It puts a lie to all the crap that this is a personal vendetta of Eliot Spitzer against the Greenberg family."

A month later, Spitzer was at it again, unveiling a two-hundred-fifty-million-dollar civil fraud complaint against the nation's largest tax preparer, H&R Block. The lawsuit alleged that H&R Block had defrauded hundreds of thousands of its clients by encouraging them to invest their tax refunds in individual retirement accounts (IRAs) without disclosing the high fees that would cause most small investors to lose money. David Brown's Investment Protection Bureau had been working on the case since January 2005, when an H&R Block tax preparer had griped about being forced to sell a lousy product in a forum where the information was sure to get to Spitzer's office. The "Express IRA" offered only one investment choice—a money market savings account that often paid small investors less interest than the company charged in fees. Brown and Spitzer jumped on the tip immediately. The Express IRA program had more than five hundred thousand customers, who were typically relatively poor, with annual incomes under thirty thousand dollars, and often saving for the very first time. They were exactly the kind of investors that Spitzer had come into office pledging to protect. Brown handed the matter to James Park, newly arrived from the high-priced firm of Wachtell, Lipton, Rosen and Katz. The bureau chief heard almost nothing until September, when Park dropped a complete draft of a complaint on his desk. "He'd done an entire soup to nuts investigation," said Brown, remembering his surprise.

According to the lawsuit Spitzer eventually filed, 85 percent of Express IRA customers paid more in fees than they received in interest.

The losses were worst for the more than half of the customers who put in the minimum three hundred dollar investment: 99 percent of them lost money, according to a review Spitzer's office did of those who had opened accounts in 2002. Further investigation uncovered an internal e-mail from a district manager addressed to CEO Mark A. Ernst saying that many customers were losing money and expressed concern that "clients won't be happy seeing thier [*sic*] investments decreasing not increasing." But, according to Spitzer, the company failed to act on these concerns and continued to market the Express IRA program as "a better way to save."

"H&R Block misled investors about the fees. This is a blatant violation of law," Spitzer said in an interview. "The outrageous nature of this misrepresentation is magnified by the fact that the most vulnerable members of our society were being ripped off."

H&R Block had spent months trying to convince Spitzer not to take them on, arguing that their program was one of the few options available to low- and moderate-income customers who were trying to get into the habit of saving. Ernst even flew to Albany in early March 2006 to meet with Spitzer in a last-ditch effort to avoid a lawsuit. But the two sides were simply too far apart: Spitzer's staff calculated that the firm's customers had lost more than twenty-five million dollars and wanted all that money repaid. H&R Block countered that the program was basically a good one and that Spitzer's calculations far exaggerated the losses. From the company's perspective, any tally should include the immediate tax savings that resulted from setting up an IRA. When viewed that way, it would later argue publicly, 78 percent of Express IRA customers ended up ahead. Spitzer was unimpressed. "If you don't make these people whole, I will sue you within a week," he warned.

When Spitzer went to court on March 15, the company fired back immediately, announcing that it had enlisted former state attorney general Robert Abrams to defend its product in court. "Make no mistake—we believe in the Express IRA program," Ernst said in a statement released minutes after Spitzer announced his case. "We've helped 590,000 clients begin saving for their future, and more than 40 percent of them had never saved before." Ernst also employed another time-honored tactic for fighting Spitzer: he submitted an op-ed piece to *The Wall Street Journal* that dripped with outrage and contempt for the New York state attorney general. "This suit is an unfair attack on a good product that plays a key role in our mission to help lower- and middle-income Americans start saving for retirement," Ernst wrote. Outside investors were dubious: H&R Block's stock dropped more than 6 percent the day Spitzer's lawsuit was announced. It looked as if Spitzer might be in for another protracted court fight.

At the same time, Spitzer's office remained hard at work, probing alleged violations of Internet privacy rules as well as claims of improper kickbacks in the title insurance industry and several other matters that had not yet become public. Environmental Bureau chief Peter Lehner was still pushing polluters to mend their ways and in mid-March he scored one of the office's biggest victories, as a federal appeals court in Washington ruled in favor of Spitzer's second—and more substantial—challenge to the Bush administration's effort to rewrite the Clean Air Act's rules for power plant modernization. The unanimous decision in favor of a multistate coalition that Spitzer and Lehner had put together was immensely gratifying, particularly after the partial loss the previous fall in the first of the two lawsuits. Here, the court found that the Environmental Protection Agency had ignored Congress's clear intent when it redefined the rules for power-plant upgrades to allow many facilities to avoid installing state-of-the-art pollution controls. The EPA's interpretation would fly "only in a Humpty Dumpty world," wrote Judge Judith W. Rogers, adding dryly, "We decline to adopt such a worldview." The opinion even garnered the support of a recent Bush appointee, Judge Janice Rogers Brown, who had faced serious opposition from liberal groups that feared she would limit the scope of worker and environmental protection laws. "The fact that you have a unanimous court with her [Brown] signing on shows how egregious what the EPA was trying to do and how right we were," Spitzer exulted. "It's the capstone of seven years of work."

There were other signs that Spitzer's work would continue, even as he prepared to move on. The SEC was still pursuing the AIG and Gen Re executives implicated in the reinsurance deal and bringing cases against brokers that had helped hedge funds engage in market-timing. The state insurance commissioners, meanwhile, were cracking down on the insurance companies that had been implicated in the Marsh bid-rigging scheme and forcing them to make restitution to their customers. But not all of Spitzer's efforts had succeeded. The fights with OCC over minority lending, the illegal guns case, and the failed effort to get the EPA to regulate carbon dioxide were obvious losses, and his adversaries were growing more skilled at using the media in their efforts to push back.

Yet all in all, his vision of state-based progressivism had caught on more than he could have hoped when he took office. "We were able to plant some seeds that are now growing," he observed. "What may have begun as a lonely fight now has some people standing with us. . . . There are others who are going to step up to the plate."

NOTES

The vast majority of the material in this book was derived from on-the-record interviews, publicly available documents, and published reports. Where that was the case, I have noted the source of direct quotations in the notes. I have also tried to make clear in the text whether the quotations were contemporaneous or based on someone's recollection at a later date.

Careful readers will note that not every quotation can be found in the endnotes. In some cases, that is because the speakers asked not to be identified, and I have respected their requests. Where the speakers are identified, but the source is not, I have confirmed the account with at least two direct eyewitnesses (or, in the case of telephone conversations, with parties to the call) or with one direct witness and someone who was told of the conversation at the time it occurred. There were also a few instances where the participants and witnesses did not agree about what was said. I have tried to make that clear by presenting both sides.

Finally, most of the major players in this account spoke to me either directly or through a spokesman or an attorney. But, to my regret, there were a few important exceptions, most notably former New York Stock Exchange chairman Richard A. Grasso and former Citigroup stock analyst Jack Grubman. I have done my best to represent their points of view by quoting from interviews they gave to other members of the media.

Chapter 1. When Markets Need to Be Tamed

2   *You just don't understand the insurance business:* Description of the meeting based on the recollections of Spitzer and three other people who attended.

2   *some core ethical behavior is necessary:* Author's interview with Eliot Spitzer, New York, N.Y., Sept. 19, 2005.

3   *no apparent controls:* Author's interview with David D. Brown IV, New York, N.Y., Sept. 15, 2005.

3   *I'm going to refuse to negotiate:* Author's interview with Eliot Spitzer, New York, N.Y., Sept. 19, 2005.

4   *so terribly wrong:* Eliot Spitzer, speech to lawyers being sworn in to the New York Bar, New York, April 19, 2004.

5   *The market does not survive:* Eliot Spitzer, speech to the annual Investorside conference, New York, April 13, 2005.

5   *The firebrand politician William Jennings Bryan:* Description of Bryan based on Michael Kazin, *The Populist Persuasion* (New York: Cornell University Press, 1995), p. 37.

6   *egregious and unacceptable:* Brooke A. Masters and Jeffrey H. Birnbaum, "A Run for the Money; Spitzer's Sparring with Wall Street Doesn't Hinder Fundraising for His Gubernatorial Campaign," *Washington Post*, April 7, 2005, p. E01.

7   *have a populist air:* Author's interview with Eliot Spitzer, New York, N.Y., Feb. 12, 2004.

7   *the market needs to be tamed:* Author's interview with Eliot Spitzer, New York, N.Y., Feb. 12, 2004.

7   *New York's proud progressive tradition:* Eliot Spitzer, speech, Sheraton New York, Dec. 9, 2004.

7   *the Progressive solution was reform, not revolution:* This description of the Progressives draws on Franklin Foer, "The Joy of Federalism," *New York Times Book Review*, March 6, 2005, p. 12.

8   *government as a supporter of free markets:* Eliot Spitzer and Andrew G. Celli, Jr., "Bull Run," *The New Republic*, March 22, 2004, p. 18.

8   *perverse joy:* Author's interview with Andrew G. Celli, Jr., New York, N.Y., Sept. 12, 2005.

8   *traction right now:* Author's interview with Eliot Spitzer, New York, N.Y., Sept. 19, 2005.

9   *Theodore Roosevelt is remembered fondly today:* This description of T.R. draws on Edmund Morris, *The Rise of Theodore Roosevelt* (New York: Coward Mc-Cann & Geoghegan Inc., 1979), p. 179.

10   *Government must now interfere:* Theodore Roosevelt, *An Autobiography* (New York: Macmillan, 1913), available online at bartleby.com.

10   *Wall Street is paralyzed* and *Are you going to attack:* Nathan Miller, *Theodore Roosevelt: A Life* (New York: William Morrow and Co., 1992), pp. 368–69, citing Joseph B. Bishop, "Theodore Roosevelt and His Times" (New York: Scribner's, 1930), vol. 1, pp. 184–85.

11   *amazing and reckless robbery:* Gates letter to Rockefeller, Aug. 9, 1907, quoted

in Ron Chernow, *Titan: The Life of John D Rockefeller, Sr.* (New York: Random House, 1998), p. 542.

11   *where the bodies were buried:* Author's interview with Alan Dershowitz, New York, N.Y., May 2004.

12   *best of disinfectants:* Louis D. Brandeis, "Other People's Money and How the Bankers Use It," first published in *Harper's Weekly*, Dec. 20, 1913. Spitzer cited this quotation in three separate conversations with the author over the course of two years.

12   *customers as fee generators:* Author's interview with Eliot Spitzer, New York, N.Y., Feb. 12, 2004.

12   *extraordinary wastefulness:* Louis D. Brandeis, "The Greatest Life Insurance Wrong," *The Independent* (Boston), Dec. 20, 1906, pp. 1475–80. Reprinted in Brandeis, *The Curse of Bigness: Miscellaneous Papers of Louis D. Brandeis*, ed. Osmond K. Fraenkel (New York: Viking, 1934), p. 20.

13   *Curse of Bigness:* Brandeis, "Other People's Money."

13   *Brandeis's economic theory:* This description of Brandeis's career draws on Thomas K. McCraw, *Prophets of Regulation* (Cambridge, Mass.: Belknap Press, 1984), pp. 112–14.

13   *meddlesome interference: Lochner v. New York*, 198 U.S. 45 (1905).

13   *strength and vigor of the race: Muller v. Oregon*, 208 U.S. 412 (1908).

14   *a little knot of men:* Henry Higginson, letter to Henry Cabot Lodge, Feb. 13, 1916, Henry Cabot Lodge Collected Papers, Massachusetts Historical Society, Boston.

14   *He has not the confidence:* "Contend Brandeis Is Unfit," *New York Times*, Feb. 13, 1916, p. 16.

14   *the federal system: New State Ice Co. v. Liebmann*, 285 U.S. 262 (1932).

15   *They didn't really expect:* Author's interview with Lloyd Constantine, New York, N.Y., April 18, 2005.

16   *single biggest mistake:* Arthur Levitt with Paula Dwyer, "Take on the Street," (New York: Pantheon Books, 2002), p. 11.

16   *The federal pullback also picked up steam:* Statistics drawn from Jeffrey Rosen, "Can Bush Deliver a Conservative Supreme Court?" *New York Times*, Nov. 14, 2004, section 4, p. 1. Recently, the Court has shied away from opportunities to strike down major environmental and health and safety laws, such as the Endangered Species Act, but many of the key votes have been close, and the two Bush appointees could change the balance of power.

17   *had been on the job fewer than three years:* U.S. General Accounting Office, "Report to Congress: SEC Operations," Washington, D.C., March 2002, p. 25. (The number of complaints grew by 100 percent, but the enforcement staff grew by just 16 percent. The number of corporate filings grew by 60 percent, but the staff time devoted to reviewing them by 29 percent—p. 13. At the SEC, for example, turnover was 33 percent between 1998 and 2000—p. 25.)

17   *Collectively we are a much stronger adversary:* Author's telephone interview with Joseph Curran, Jr., New York, N.Y., May 18, 2005.

17   *what RiteAid does in Lisbon Falls:* Brooke A. Masters, "States Flex Prosecutorial Muscle; Attorneys General Move into What Was Once Federal Territory," *Washington Post*, Jan. 12, 2005, p. A01.

18   *The timing was perfect:* Author's interview with Lloyd Constantine, New York, N.Y., April 18, 2005.

19   *There should be a law:* Author's interview with Robert G. Morvillo, New York, N.Y., June 14, 2005.

19   *a needless harm:* Author's interview with Howard Mills, New York, N.Y., Nov. 20, 2005.

20   *A proliferation of conflicting state rules:* Masters, "States Flex Prosecutorial Muscle," p. A01

20   *Imagine 50:* Stan Luxenberg, "Imagine 50 Eliot Spitzers," Registered Rep Online, Sept. 9, 2005.

20   *intellectually consistent view:* Author's interviews with Eliot Spitzer, New York, N.Y., May 23, 2005, and November 17, 2005.

20   *There will always be apologists:* Eliot Spitzer, press conference, New York, N.Y., Sept. 15, 2005.

20   *the very highest levels:* Eliot Spitzer, press conference, New York, N.Y., Oct. 14, 2004.

Chapter 2.   A Man in a Hurry

22   *Spitzer family lore:* Author's telephone interview with Daniel Spitzer, April 12, 2005.

22   *Jerry Stiller:* Anne said that the Spitzer children made fun of her Stiller tales until Eliot met Stiller at an event shortly after being elected attorney general. When Eliot mentioned his mother's maiden name, Stiller instantly recognized it. "It was a Tom Sawyer thing, falling in love just from looking at her," Stiller remembered. Author's interview with Anne Spitzer, New York, N.Y., May 26, 2005; author's telephone interview with Jerry Stiller, June 10, 2005.

22   *The practice of engineering:* Author's interview with Bernard Spitzer, New York, N.Y., May 26, 2005.

23   *Curiosity, commitment:* Ibid.

23   *It would take two people:* Author's interview with Anne Spitzer, New York, N.Y., May 26, 2005.

23   *what happens when you borrow:* Author's interview with Eliot Spitzer, New York, N.Y., April 12, 2005.

24   *He didn't realize his own rights:* Author's interview with Bernard Spitzer, New York, N.Y., May 26, 2005.

24   *His eyes would gleam:* Author's telephone interview with Daniel Spitzer, May 12, 2005.

24   *exclusive beach club:* Beach Point Club in Mamaroneck, N.Y., is almost 100 percent Jewish and white. Eliot Spitzer resigned from the club before running for office, but his parents continued to be members. Author's interviews with Eliot Spitzer, New York, N.Y., Feb. 12, 2004, and Herbert Nass, New York, N.Y., June 6, 2005.

24   *Go to school:* Author's telephone interview with Daniel Spitzer, May 12, 2005.

25   *I don't think Eliot's B.S.'d:* Author's telephone interview with Daniel Spitzer, May 12, 2005.

25   *I used to study harder:* Author's telephone interview with Bill Taylor, April 11, 2005.

25   *If it takes more than thirty minutes:* Author's telephone interview with Anne Spitzer, June 2, 2005.

25   *His visage:* Author's interview with Jason Brown, New York, N.Y., May 25, 2005.

26   *number one player:* Eliot Spitzer on WNBC, Channel 4, Dec. 7, 2003, right before McEnroe headlined a fund-raiser for his campaign.

26   *Eliot and Emily volunteered:* In 2004, Meyer reentered politics, running for state senate in Connecticut, and Spitzer campaigned and helped raise money for him. This time Meyer won. Author's telephone interview with Ed Meyer, May 18, 2005.

26   *tried marijuana:* Author's telephone interviews with Eliot Spitzer, April 12, 2005, and May 23, 2005. Asked during the 1998 campaign if he had inhaled, Spitzer replied, "Absolutely. With pride, at the time." John Kaher, "Attorney General Hopefuls Admit Pot Use," *Times Union* (Albany), Sept. 5, 1998, p. B2.

26   *very serious guy:* Author's telephone interview with Elena Kagan, May 7, 2004.

27   *Economics 101:* Author's telephone interview with William Bowen, May 11, 2005.

27   *spaghetti-eating contest:* Mayer won by finishing seven bowls' worth, he and spectators agree. The contest made the front page of the *Daily Princetonian* student newspaper. Author's telephone interview with Carl Mayer, May 27, 2005.

27   *good roughage:* Author's interview with Jason Brown, New York, N.Y., May 25, 2005.

27   *didn't even know he was running:* Author's interview with Anne Spitzer, New York, N.Y., May 26, 2005.

27   *pushing the deadline:* Author's telephone interview with Carl Mayer, May 19, 2005.

27   *organization person:* Author's telephone interview with William Bowen, May 11, 2005.

27   *reading the riot act:* Author's telephone interview with Bill Taylor, April 11, 2005.

28   *Bruce Caputo:* Caputo later became infamous for having falsely claimed during his 1982 Senate campaign that he had served in Vietnam. Caputo declined to comment, May 18, 2005.

28   *He tried so hard:* Author's interview with Anne Spitzer, New York, N.Y., May 26, 2005.

28   *did you have to be on welfare:* Author's telephone interview with Daniel Spitzer, May 12, 2005.

28   *a really tense time:* Author's telephone interview with Bill Taylor, April 11, 2005.

29   *an easy question:* Author's interview with Eliot Spitzer, New York, N.Y., April 12, 2005.

29   *on his way to making his mark:* Author's telephone interview with Miles Kahler, April 18, 2005.

29   *Wow:* Author's telephone interview with Anne-Marie Slaughter, May 20, 2005.

29   *very steady:* Author's telephone interview with Runa Alam, May 31, 2005.

29   *create an environment:* Eliot Spitzer, "Revolutions in Post-Stalin Eastern Europe: A Study of Soviet Reactions," a thesis presented to Princeton University, 1981.

30   *Mom, I don't write my exams:* Author's telephone interview with Anne Spitzer, June 2, 2005.

30   *Sleazeville, USA:* Author's telephone interview with Alan Dershowitz, May 27, 2005.

30   *the library guy:* Author's telephone interview with Alan Dershowitz, April 2004. Part of the interview is quoted in Brooke A. Masters, "Eliot Spitzer Spoils for a Fight," *Washington Post,* May 31, 2004, p. A01.

31   *I can lick you:* Author's interview with Lloyd Constantine, New York, N.Y., April 18, 2005.

31   *such a brilliant guy:* Author's telephone interview with Nadine Muskatel Tung, Aug. 8, 2005.

32   *Who are you?:* Author's interview with Silda Wall, New York, N.Y., May 12, 2004.

32   *This is my house:* Author's interview with Eliot Spitzer, New York, N.Y., April 12, 2005.

32   *paged through the entire face book:* Author's interview with Eliot Spitzer, New York, N.Y., April 12, 2005.

32   *didn't have a chance:* Author's telephone interview with Cliff Sloan, May 16, 2005.

32   *I learned something there:* Author's interview with Eliot Spitzer, New York, N.Y., April 12, 2005.

33   *nice legs:* Author's interview with Anne and Bernard Spitzer, New York, N.Y., May 26, 2005.

33   *what the law is for:* Author's interview with Eliot Spitzer, New York, N.Y., Feb. 12, 2004.

33   *like a steam engine:* Author's telephone interview with Robert Sweet, May 24, 2005.

34   *I'm going to kill you:* Author's telephone interview with Emily Spitzer, May 17, 2005.

34   *seemed even more lame:* William Taylor, e-mail to author, May 27, 2005.

35   *Eliot was the star:* Author's telephone interview with Michael G. Cherkasky, April 2004. Five months later, Cherkasky would find himself at the other end of Spitzer's lance during an insurance investigation. Part of the interview is quoted in Masters, "Eliot Spitzer Spoils for a Fight."

35   *the garment industry was a great place to start:* This description of the Gambino case draws on Ralph Blumenthal, "When the Mob Delivered the Goods," *New York Times Magazine,* July 26, 1992, p. 23.

36   *police investigators broke into:* Description of the bugging operation from Peter Robison and Eric Moskowitz, "Cherkasky Says Spitzer Friendship Won't Help at Marsh," Bloomberg News, Dec. 7, 2004.

36   *overriding sense of fear:* Description of the tapes' contents based on Gay Jervey, "Waltzing with the Wise Guys," *The American Lawyer,* May 1992, p. 84.

36   *mob tax:* Emily Sachar, "Gambino Jury told of Sales 'Enforcers,'" *Newsday* (New York), February 5, 1992, p. 20.

36   *young Eliot Ness:* Author's telephone interview with Gerald Shargel, May 18, 2005.

37   *Aren't the wiseguys laughing:* Jervey, "Waltzing with the Wise Guys," p. 84.

37   *Yes, we gave up jail:* Ralph Blumenthal, "Gambinos to Quit Trucking Business in a Plea Bargain," *New York Times*, Feb. 27, 1992, p. A1.

37   *We might have gotten a bigger headline:* Masters, "Eliot Spitzer Spoils for a Fight."

38   *If this is truly a dream of his:* Author's interview with Silda Wall, New York, N.Y., July 6, 2005.

38   *You're not going to win:* Author's interview with Lloyd Constantine, New York, N.Y., April 18, 2005.

38   *how articulate he was:* Author's interview with Bernard Spitzer, New York, N.Y., May 26, 2005.

38   *New York is an add-on:* Author's telephone interview with Steven Alschuler, May 23, 2005.

39   *almost contemptuous:* Kevin Sack, "4 Candidates: Crime Issue May Not Rule in This Race," *New York Times*, Sept. 5, 1994, p. 19.

39   *I voted for you:* Author's interview with Silda Wall, New York, N.Y., May 12, 2004.

40   *did Eliot dress the girls today?:* Ibid.

41   *thanked Spitzer from the ring:* Tom Wheatley, "A Real Knockout," *St. Louis Post-Dispatch*, July 24, 1997, p. 2D.

41   *what he had to do to win:* Author's interview with George Fox, Greenwich, Conn., May 31, 2005.

41   *truly interested:* Author's interview with Rich Baum, New York, N.Y., April 21, 2005.

42   *I shot ninety-eight spots:* Author's interview with Hank Sheinkopf, New York, N.Y., June 6, 2005.

42   *gonna get killed:* Sridhar Pappu, "The Crusader: Eliot Spitzer, the Attorney General of New York," *The Atlantic Monthly* 294, no. 3, Oct. 1, 2004, p. 108.

43   *Shame on you, Dennis:* Douglas Feiden, "Mud Flies in Attorney General Debate," *Daily News* (New York), Oct. 24, 1998, p. 7.

43   *ask the bandito:* Alan Finder, "Hispanic Civic Leaders Assail Vacco over Remarks," *New York Times*, Oct. 29, 1998, p. B1.

43   *It was just brutal:* Author's interview with Rich Baum, New York, N.Y., April 21, 2005.

43   *you will say anything:* Feiden, "Mud Flies," p. 7.

44   *unfit to serve:* Lara Jakes, "Koppell Withdraws Spitzer Endorsement," *Times Union* (Albany), Oct. 29, 1998, p. B2. Koppell had filed a legal complaint about Spitzer's spending during the primary, which was dismissed, and another primary rival, Evan Davis, complained, "Spitzer thinks great family wealth entitles him to great advantage. He doesn't fight for the interest of communities—he tries to buy them." Greg Birnbaum, "Spitzer Trying to 'Buy' AG Race: Foes," *New York Post*, Sept. 13, 1998, p. 26.

44   *It was stupid:* Joel Siegel, "Spitzer Lent 8M to AG Campaign; Ethical Woes in
     Huge Loan," *Daily News* (New York), Dec. 26, 1998, p. 59.

44   *flabbergasted:* Author's interview with Bernard Spitzer, New York, N.Y., May
     26, 2005.

44   *the temptation is to skip an endorsement:* "Eliot Spitzer for Attorney General,"
     New York Times, Oct. 29, 1998, p. A30.

44   *He would eventually pay off the 1994 loan*: Spitzer came up with the four million
     dollars by selling municipal bonds at a three-thousand-dollar loss. "Eliot
     Spitzer Pays a Big Debt," *Daily News* (New York), December 6, 2004, p. 34,
     and Elizabeth Benjamin, "Pataki, Spitzer Release Tax Returns," *Times Union*
     (Albany), April 16, 2005, p. B3.

45   *I threw up on my shirt:* Monte R. Young, "Election 98 / Spitzer Has Edge in
     Tight AG Race," *Newsday* (New York), Nov. 4, 1998, p. A55.

45   *a variety of claims:* Richard Perez-Pena, "Political Memo; Whiff of Red Her-
     ring in Strategy for Vacco," *New York Times,* Nov. 29, 1998, p. 52.

45   *I've done a lot of recounts:* Author's telephone interview with Marty Connor,
     May 24, 2005.

45   *it fell upon me as a leader:* Robert J. McCarthy and Tom Precious, "Vacco
     Wishes Spitzer Well as Next Attorney General; Emotion-Laced Speech
     Cites Accomplishments," *Buffalo News,* Dec. 15, 1998, p. 1B.

Chapter 3.   An Exciting Time to Be a New Yorker

46   *Today is pure fun:* Tracy Tully, "Gov Takes Oath for 2nd Term; Pataki's Opti-
     mistic at Subdued Ceremony," *Daily News,* Jan. 2, 1999, p. 5.

46   *1,775 staff members:* Author's telephone interview with Marc Violette, May 5,
     2005. According to the National Association of Attorneys General, New
     York is one of four states with more than five hundred lawyers on the payroll,
     and the AG's budget is third among all states.

47   *accidental attorney general:* Charles Gasparino, *Blood on the Street* (New York:
     Free Press, 2005), p. 214. The nickname never gained wide currency, in part
     because Spitzer soon proved to be extremely hardworking.

47   *disappointing start:* "The Ethical Challenge to Eliot Spitzer," *New York Post,*
     Jan. 10, 1999, p. 78.

48   *extremely proud:* Author's interview with David Axinn, New York, N.Y., Oct.
     6, 2005.

48   *I've got to do it:* Eliot Spitzer on WNBC-TV, July 20, 2003.

48   *refused to defend:* This brief history of recusals draws on Wayne Barrett,
     "Why Did Spitzer Defend Pataki," *Village Voice,* July 8, 2003, p. 24.

48   *objecting violently:* Author's interview with Michael Rebell, New York, N.Y.,
     Sept. 20, 2005.

48   *false but time-honored tradition:* Author's telephone interview with Pamela
     Jones Harbour, April 28, 2005.

49   *As a former criminal prosecutor:* Author's interview with Michele Hirshman,
     New York, N.Y., May 3, 2005.

50   *An equally obscure 1926 court case:* "Court Adds Scope to Stock Fraud Act,"
     New York Times, March 20, 1926, p. 12.

50   *proving "intent to defraud":* This brief discussion of the history of the Martin Act is indebted to Nicholas Thompson, "The Sword of Spitzer," *Legal Affairs*, May–June 2004.

50   *This guy is great:* Author's interview with Michele Hirshman, New York, N.Y., May 5, 2005; Dietrich Snell, e-mail to author, Aug. 9, 2005.

50   *economic discrimination:* Author's interview with Andrew G. Celli, Jr., New York, N.Y., Sept. 12, 2005.

51   *loans in black neighborhoods* and *Do these guys have it?:* Author's interview with Andrew G. Celli, Jr., New York, N.Y., Sept. 12, 2005.

51–52 *Swiss cheese agreement:* Randy Kennedy, "Spitzer Sues Lender after It Makes a Deal with Banking Regulators," *New York Times*, Aug. 21, 1999, p. B1. Author's interview with Eliot Spitzer, New York, N.Y., Sept. 19, 2005.

52   *rolling their eyes:* Author's interview with Eliot Spitzer, New York, N.Y., May 23, 2005.

53   *up to the states:* Eliot Spitzer, speech to the Federalist Society, Washington, D.C., June 22, 1999. Transcript available on the Federalist Society Web site, www.fed-soc.org.

53   *aghast:* One version is in James Traub, "The Attorney General Goes to War," *New York Times Magazine*, July 16, 2002, p. 12.

53   *paying very much attention:* Federalist Society vice president Leonard Leo called Spitzer's version a "distortion [that] has been very unfortunate and frustrating. . . . To characterize the theme of the talk as [federalism] is a bit of a stretch. . . . The questions don't focus at all on that." Leonard Leo, e-mails to author, May 12, 2005, and May 23, 2005. Searches of online databases found no media coverage of Spitzer's participation in the event.

54   *blocked the EPA's efforts:* The Supreme Court later overturned the soot ruling, returning authority to the EPA, and the EPA eventually shifted to a system that allows utilities to trade credits for nitrogen oxide emissions.

54   *a majority of Congress hated us:* Author's telephone interview with Carol Browner, May 5, 2005.

54   *interested in pushing hard:* Author's interview with Peter Lehner, New York, N.Y., May 25, 2005.

55   *I had to be careful:* Author's telephone interview with Carol Browner, May 5, 2005.

55–56 *New York could park every car:* Author's interview with Peter Lehner, New York, N.Y., May 25, 2005.

56   *I hate to tell you:* Author's telephone interview with Bruce Buckheit, May 10, 2005. Browner didn't get any heads-up at all.

56   *Air pollution simply knows no boundaries:* Jesse J. Holland, "N.Y. Attorney General Threatens to Sue Companies over Acid Rain," Associated Press state and local wire, Sept. 15, 1999.

56   *We needed to pull the EPA along:* Author's interview with Eliot Spitzer, May 5, 2005.

56   *naturally we disagree:* Dan Fagin and Liam Pleven, "Aiming for Clean Air / Spitzer: Midwest Power Plants Violate Fed Pollution Law," *Newsday* (New York), Sept. 15, 1999, p. A7.

56   *effort in the Northeast to blame their problems with air quality:* Holland, "N.Y. Attorney General Threatens to Sue."

57   *not nice playing inside the sandbox:* Author's telephone interview with Bruce Buckheit, May 10, 2005.

57   *forty lawyers:* Author's interview with Peter Lehner, New York, N.Y., April 7, 2005.

57   *Eliot Spitzer in the mix:* Author's telephone interview with Carol Browner, May 5, 2005.

58   *The SEC has plenty of power:* Tamara Loomis, "Martin Act: The New York Securities Statute Has Made Headlines Before," *New York Law Journal*, Nov. 14, 2002, p. 5.

58   *we moved right in:* Author's interview with Michele Hirshman, New York, N.Y., April 21, 2005.

58   *fraudulent financial plan:* Office of New York State Attorney General Eliot Spitzer, "$1 Million Recovered for Upstate Dairy Farmers," press release, July 23, 1999.

58   *thrilled to have this offer:* Lara Jakes, "Insurer Settles with Farmers Who Lost Investments," *Times Union* (Albany), June 24, 1999, p. B2.

58   *handing real checks to real people:* Author's telephone interview with Eric Dinallo, Oct. 25, 2005.

59–60   *whistle past the graveyard* through *Courts are about remedies:* Author's interview with Andrew G. Celli, Jr., New York, N.Y., Sept. 12, 2005.

60   *We don't bring cases if we don't think there's a remedy:* Author's interview with Eliot Spitzer, New York, N.Y., Feb. 12, 2004.

60   *lighter fines and fewer cases:* Fines on employers during the first nine years of Governor Pataki's tenure averaged 8 percent of recovered wages, two-thirds less than in 1994, the last year Democrat Mario Cuomo held the governorship. Jordon Rau, "A Fight for Fair Pay; State Labor Agency's Reinforcement of Rules Requiring Proper Wage for Workers Has Waned during Pataki's Tenure," *Newsday* (New York), April 11, 2004, p. A6.

60–61   *looking to get out* through *we have to make the marketplace work:* Author's interview with Patricia Smith, New York, N.Y., April 7, 2005.

61–62   *we were naïve:* Andrew Jacobs, "Walkers Make a Tentative Stand; African Deliverymen Complain, Gently, of a Tough Job," *New York Times*, November 10, 1999, p. B1.

62   *Employees are not to be excluded: Martino v. Michigan Window Cleaning Co.*, 327 U.S. 173 (1946).

63   *He gave them a number:* Author's interview with Patricia Smith, New York, N.Y., April 7, 2005.

63   *head and shoulders above:* Author's telephone interview with Catherine Ruckelshaus, April 11, 2005.

64   *the ATF would release a study:* Richard Simon, "Clinton Cracks Down on 1,020 Gun Dealers," *Los Angeles Times*, Feb. 5, 2000, p. A14.

64   *a Philadelphia-area study:* David Kairys, "A Philadelphia Story," *Legal Affairs*, May–June 2003.

64   *a broad-based assault:* Author's interview with Carl Mayer, New York, N.Y., May 19, 2005.

65   *Pope doubted that this victory would withstand appeal:* As it turned out, Pope was right. Although the Brooklyn jury bought the argument at trial, the New York Court of Appeals ruled that gun manufacturers had no special duty to

the victims to make sure that their distributors and third-party retailers kept the guns out of the hands of criminals. *Hamilton v. Beretta,* Court of Appeals of New York, April 26, 2001, 96 N.Y.2d 222.

65 *Eliot's was it:* Author's telephone interview with David Kairys, May 9, 2005.

65 *an aggressive theory:* Author's interviews with Peter Pope, New York, N.Y., April 7, 2005, and May 23, 2005.

66 *bankruptcy lawyers knocking at your door:* Paul Jannuzzo, appearance on CNN, March 31, 2000.

66 *very very close:* Author's interview with Peter Pope, New York, N.Y., April 7, 2005.

66 *hailed the talks as historic:* Fox Butterfield, "Safety and Crime at Heart of Talk on Gun Lawsuits," *New York Times,* Oct. 3, 1999, p. A1.

66 *He didn't have the juice to do it:* Author's interview with Lawrence Keane, Mamaroneck, N.Y., May 11, 2005.

66 *everyone at one table:* Andrew Cuomo, news conference, Washington, D.C., Nov. 8, 1999.

67 *lush government contracts:* Geoff Metcalf, "Gun Maker Stands Up to Clinton," WorldNetDaily, April 19, 2000.

67–68 *the company will cut off dealers:* Transcript of Clinton's announcement from the Oval Office, March 17, 2000. Author's interview with Peter Pope, New York, N.Y., May 23, 2005.

68 *squeeze them like a pincers:* Eliot Spitzer, March 22, 2000, press conference at HUD announcing the buying coalition.

68 *illegal attempt:* Robert Delfay, president of the National Shooting Sports Foundation, quoted in David Lightman, "Gun-Makers Fight Back with Lawsuits," *Hartford Courant,* April 27, 2000, p. A24.

68 *coalition members had begun backing down:* Steve Pardo, "Safe Gun Pledge Loses Bite," *Detroit News,* May 4, 2000, p. 3C.

68 *voluntarily withdraw its lawsuit:* Spitzer's people said that the industry knew they were going to lose a motion to dismiss; industry representatives said that they were going to lose because the communities had dropped their plans to favor Smith & Wesson—"we were a victim of our own success," said Lawrence Keane. Author's interview with Lawrence Keane, Mamaroneck, N.Y., May 11, 2005.

69 *turn a blind eye: People v. Sturm, Ruger & Co.,* original complaint, June 26, 2000, p. 17.

69 *lawful non-defective products: People v. Sturm, Ruger & Co.,* Justice York's decision, August 10, 2001, p. 25.

69 *Blumenthal considered it:* Author's interview with Richard Blumenthal, Hartford, Conn., May 16, 2005.

69 *we didn't have a case:* Ibid.

69 *All he wants is a press conference:* Author's interview with Lawrence Keane, Mamaroneck, N.Y., May 11, 2005. Boston, one of the few plaintiffs to get its hands on gun industry documents, ended up dismissing its case voluntarily and saying in a statement, "The City acknowledges that the members of the Industry and firearms trade associations are genuinely concerned with and are committed to, the safe, legal and responsible sale and use of their products."

69   *other regulators are going to get into the game:* Author's interview with Peter Pope, New York, N.Y., May 23, 2005.

70   *just another pretty face:* Author's telephone interview with Elisa Barnes, April 18, 2005.

70   *more skilled at putting the lawsuit together first:* Author's interview with Michele Hirshman, New York, N.Y., May 3, 2005.

70   *an exciting time to be a New Yorker:* Eliot Spitzer, Law Day speech, May 1, 2000. Most newspaper coverage of the event focused on another speaker, Court of Appeals chief judge Judith S. Kaye, and only briefly mentioned Spitzer.

71   *The coins were real:* Greg Farrell, "Six Face Charges in Rare-Coin Scam That Made $25M," *USA Today,* May 25, 2001, p. 2B.

71   *first felony conviction of a sweatshop operator:* Bob Port, "Chinatown Sweatshop Owner Guilty," *Daily News* (New York), March 9, 2001, p. 22.

71   *an obscure law* through *You have to settle:* Author's telephone interview with John Catsimatidis, April 11, 2005.

71   *affirmative cases . . . had more than tripled:* Statistics provided by Patricia Smith, April 26, 2005.

72   *redefined what attorney generals do:* Steven Greenhouse, "Waging War from Wall Street to Corner Grocery; Beyond the High Profile Cases, Spitzer Helps Low Wage Workers," *New York Times,* Jan. 21, 2004, p. B1.

72   *vulnerable parties and easy prey:* Author's telephone interview with Eliot Spitzer, May 5, 2005.

Chapter 4.   A Shocking Betrayal of Trust

73   *eruption coming right at us:* Yancey Roy, "Spitzer Watched Horror from Office Window," *Poughkeepsie Journal,* Sept. 15, 2001, p. 2A.

74   *Try to give:* Martin Mgbua, "Kin Told to Be Wary of Scams," *Daily News,* Sept. 22, 2001, p. 28.

74   *we have jurisdiction over charities:* Author's telephone interview with Eliot Spitzer, Aug. 30, 2005.

74   *People will not come:* Katharine Q. Seelye, with Diana B. Henriques, "Red Cross President Quits, Saying That the Board Left Her No Other Choice," *New York Times,* Oct. 27, 2001, p. B9.

74   *The logic of the database:* Author's telephone interview with Eliot Spitzer, Aug. 30, 2005.

75   *Those who gave to the Red Cross:* Reuters, "Red Cross Still Could Face Legal Action, Spitzer Warns," *Newsday,* Nov. 9, 2001, p. A57.

75   *personally very discomforted:* Jacqueline L. Salmon and Lena H. Sun, "Embattled Red Cross Rethinks Aid Fund; Plan to Set Aside Donations Decried," *Washington Post,* Nov. 9, 2001, p. A1.

75   *utterly charming:* Monica Langley, "The Enforcer: As His Ambitions Expand, Spitzer Draws More Controversy," *Wall Street Journal,* Dec. 11, 2003, p. A1.

77   *When analysts recommend these stocks* and *It was just one of many investigations:* John Cassidy, "The Investigation, How Eliot Spitzer Humbled Wall Street,"

The New Yorker, April 7, 2003, p. 54. Although it was published before the final settlement, this article is the first really comprehensive look at the research analyst investigation.

77   *It's the most obvious trade:* Author's interview with Bruce Topman, New York, N.Y., June 20, 2005.

78–79   *I've been waiting for someone to call me:* Author's interview with Jacob Zamansky, New York, N.Y., June 6, 2005.

79   *What's so interesting* and *Nothin:* Exchange quoted in "In Re: *Spitzer v. Merrill Lynch,* Affidavit in Support of an Application of General Business Law Section 354," April 8, 2001, p. 25.

79–80   *whore for f-ing management:* Kirsten Campbell to Henry Blodget, Nov. 16, 2000, quoted in "In Re: *Spitzer v. Merrill Lynch,* Affidavit in Support of an Application of General Business Law Section 354," April 8, 2001, p. 26.

80   *I don't think I've downgraded* and *Beautiful fuk em:* Exchange quoted in "In Re: *Spitzer v. Merrill Lynch,* Affidavit in Support of an Application of General Business Law Section 354," April 8, 2001, pp. 30–31.

80   *We really started to make the case:* Author's interview with Bruce Topman, New York, N.Y., June 20, 2005.

81   *powder keg* and *I'm getting killed* and *bad smell:* Blodget's e-mails quoted in "In Re: *Spitzer v. Merrill Lynch,* Affidavit in Support of an Application of General Business Law Section 354," April 8, 2001, pp. 32–35.

82   *one of his best* and *sort of poking fun:* Deposition of Henry Blodget, "In Re: Investigation Regarding Research Recommendations and Reports Respecting Securities," Aug. 1 to 8, 2001.

82–83   *Cases ought to be brought:* Author's interview with Eliot Spitzer, New York, N.Y., Feb. 12, 2004.

83   *Get me the damn e-mails:* "Heard on the Street: Wall Street Has an Unlikely New Cop: Spitzer—State Office, Used to Policing Junk Mail, Finds Fertile Ground in Stock Research," *Wall Street Journal,* April 25, 2002, p. C1.

83   *You could spend a whole day:* Author's interview with Gary Connor, New York, N.Y., June 20, 2005.

84   *just start calling the stocks:* Quoted in "In Re: *Spitzer v. Merrill Lynch,* Affidavit in Support of an Application of General Business Law Section 354," April 8, 2001, p. 19.

84   *I had been a defense attorney:* Author's interview with Roger Waldman, New York, N.Y., June 28, 2005.

85   *in hindsight, I was a moron:* Henry Blodget, updated disclosure statement, posted Tuesday, Dec. 14, 2004, at 5:11 A.M. PT, Slate.com.

86   *He's way beyond where we are:* Author's telephone interview with Robert Morvillo, Aug. 10, 2005.

86   *we are not as bad as our competitors:* Eliot Spitzer, speech to Investorside conference, New York, N.Y., April 13, 2005.

86   *He had clearly made up his mind:* Author's telephone interview with Robert Morvillo, Aug. 10, 2005.

86   *The meetings were real:* Author's interview with Dietrich Snell, New York, N.Y., June 27, 2005.

87   *They're far too sophisticated:* Author's telephone interview with David Becker, July 19, 2005.

87   *kinder and gentler:* Harvey Pitt, speech before the American Institute of Certified Public Accountants governing council, Oct. 22, 2001.

87   *You have a huge problem:* Author's interview with Harvey Pitt, New York, N.Y., June 28, 2005.

88   *Are you about to do something:* Author's telephone interview with William Baker, July 11, 2005.

88   *We wanted what you normally get:* Author's telephone interview with Robert Morvillo, Aug. 10, 2005.

89   *I will not seal* and *In a case of structural impact:* Author's interview with Eliot Spitzer, New York, N.Y., July 11, 2005.

89   *We always communicated on his terms:* Author's interview with Robert Morvillo, New York, N.Y., June 14, 2005.

89   *except on the merits:* Author's interview with Beth Golden, New York, N.Y., June 29, 2005.

89   *I had no choice:* Eliot Spitzer, speech to the National Press Club, Washington, D.C., Jan. 31, 2005.

89   *I said to David:* Author's interview with Eliot Spitzer, New York, N.Y., July 11, 2005.

90   *It was time to pull the trigger:* Ibid.

90   *We file nothing before it's time:* Author's telephone interview with Michele Hirshman, Oct. 7, 2005.

90   *I'm always worried:* Author's interview with Eliot Spitzer, New York, N.Y., Feb. 12, 2004.

91   *This could be my end:* Author's telephone interview with Michael Cherkasky, April 2004.

92   *shocking betrayal of trust:* Office of New York State Attorney General, "Merrill Lynch Stock Rating System Found Biased by Undisclosed Conflicts of Interest," press release, April 8, 2002.

92   *Fundamentals [were] horrible* and *such a piece of crap:* "In Re: *Spitzer v. Merrill Lynch,* Affidavit in Support of an Application of General Business Law Section 354," April 8, 2001, pp. 11, 13, 21.

93   *We were lulled:* Author's telephone interview with Robert Morvillo, Aug. 10, 2005.

93   *there is no basis:* Patrick McGeehan, "Merrill Lynch under Attack as Giving Out Tainted Advice," *New York Times,* April 9, 2002, pp. A1, C1.

93   *I would have strung them up:* Author's interview with Harvey Pitt, New York, N.Y., June 28, 2005.

94   *interesting for twenty-four hours:* Author's interview with Eliot Spitzer, New York, N.Y., July 11, 2005.

95   *At the end of the day:* Charles Gasparino, "New York Attorney General Turns Up Heat on Wall Street—His Probe of Research Analysts, Conflicts of Interest Is Forcing Brokerage Firms to Make Changes," *Wall Street Journal,* April 10, 2002, p. C1.

95   *We weren't racing:* Author's telephone interview with Harvey Pitt, Aug. 18, 2005.

95   *That speaks volumes:* Author's telephone interview with Stuart Kaswell, June 30, 2005.

95   *Am I Don Quixote:* Author's interview with Eliot Spitzer, New York, N.Y., Feb. 12, 2004.

95   *Wall Street's Inquisitor:* Joshua Chaffin, "Wall Street's Inquisitor: Man in the News Eliot Spitzer," *Financial Times*, April 13, 2002, p. 11.

95   *Prosecutor in the Spotlight:* Ben White and Robert O'Harrow, Jr., "Wall Street Probe Puts Prosecutor in the Spotlight," *Washington Post*, April 24, 2002, p. A1.

96   *maybe thirty seconds of bristling:* Author's telephone interview with David Becker, July 19, 2005.

97   *The banks won't go for it:* Eliot Spitzer, speech to Investorside conference, New York, April 13, 2005.

97   *utterly false:* David Becker e-mail to author, Aug. 12, 2005.

97   *I didn't care if the banks liked it:* Author's telephone interview with Mary Schapiro, Aug. 10, 2005.

97   *It didn't make sense:* Author's telephone interview with Stephen Cutler, Aug. 8, 2005.

98   *Hi, I'm Eliot Spitzer:* Author's interview with Beth Golden, New York, N.Y., June 29, 2005.

98   *The SEC is one of one:* Author's interview with Harvey Pitt, New York, N.Y., June 28, 2005, and telephone interview Aug. 18, 2005.

98   *We'd like to work with you:* Author's interview with Harvey Pitt, New York, N.Y., June 28, 2005.

98   *I was trying to be very very helpful:* Author's telephone interview with Harvey Pitt, Aug. 18, 2005.

98   *not as smart as he thinks he is:* Author's interview with Harvey Pitt, New York, N.Y., June 28, 2005.

98–99 *He had internalized the defenses:* Author's interview with Eliot Spitzer, New York, N.Y., July 11, 2005.

99   *may be criminal:* Judith Burns, "NY AG Spitzer: Wall Street Is 'Corrupt,' May Be 'Criminal,'" Dow Jones Newswires, April 24, 2002.

99   *This is a consequence of federalism:* "Wall Street Has an Unlikely New Cop: Spitzer," *Wall Street Journal*, April 25, 2002, p. C1.

99   *very distressing and disappointing:* Patrick McGeehan, "Merrill Chief Is Apologetic over Analysts, One Dismissed," *New York Times*, April 27, 2002, p. C1.

100   *a good first step:* Ibid.

100   *game over at that point:* Author's interview with Eliot Spitzer, New York, N.Y., Feb. 12, 2004.

100   *a case we're going to lose:* Author's telephone interview with Beth Golden, Nov. 14, 2004.

100   *Some small piece of me:* Author's interview with Eliot Spitzer, New York, N.Y., April 12, 2005.

100   *The single question:* Tom Perrotta, "Spitzer Urges Panel to Reinstate Gun Suit; Manufacturers' Liability for Nuisance Questioned," *New York Law Journal*, May 13, 2002, p. 1.

100–101 *North Pole:* Perrotta, "Spitzer Urges Panel," p. 1.

101   *The legislative and executive branches: People v. Sturm, Ruger & Co.*, 761 N.Y.S.2d 192; 2003 N.Y. App. Div.; June 24, 2003.

101   *I always suspected we would lose:* Author's interview with Eliot Spitzer, New York, N.Y., April 12, 2005.

101 *Wall Street is totally corrupt:* Charles Gasparino, "Big Board Chairman Offers Help to Quickly Resolve Merrill Case," *Wall Street Journal,* May 6, 2002, p. C3.

102 *You can't do that right:* Author's interview with Eliot Spitzer, New York, N.Y., July 11, 2005.

102 *Merrill Lynch is setting a new standard:* Ben White, "Merrill Lynch to Pay Fine, Tighten Rules on Analysts," *Washington Post,* May 22, 2002, p. A1.

Chapter 5.   Going Global

104 *out the window:* Author's telephone interview with Stephen Cutler, Aug. 8, 2005.

104 *I remember thinking, whoa:* Author's interview with Roger Waldman, New York, N.Y., June 28, 2005.

105 *not a single substantive contribution:* "U.S. Rep. Baker Urges SEC to Take Lead in Analysts' Inquiry," Dow Jones Newswire, April 30, 2002.

105 *failed to elicit:* Office of New York State Attorney General, "Spitzer Responds to Rep. Richard Baker's Letter to the SEC," press release, April 30, 2002.

105 *legislation at the federal level:* Robert Schmidt, "States Battle Wall Street over Securities Beat: Lawmakers Lobbied: Brokerages Want Power Centered with One Federal Watchdog," *National Post,* June 18, 2002, FP4.

106 *perversion of American law:* Charles Gasparino, "Cleaning Up Wall Street: Morgan Stanley Goes to Washington—Firm Quietly Seeks to Fend Off States Regulating the Industry; Spitzer Criticizes the Move," *Wall Street Journal,* June 21, 2002, p. C1.

106 *Not good enough:* Author's interview with Harvey Pitt, New York, N.Y., June 28, 2005.

106 *There has been a void:* Transcript of the Senate Consumer Affairs Subcommittee of the Senate Commerce, Science and Transportation Committee Hearing on Corporate Governance, June 26, 2002.

106 *a whipping boy:* Author's interview with Harvey Pitt, New York, N.Y., June 28, 2005.

106 *lethargic, lazy, and inattentive:* Author's interview with Eliot Spitzer, New York, N.Y., July 18, 2005.

106 *Every American should be outraged:* Eliot Spitzer, statement on "Bush Administration Proposal to Cut the Clean Air Act," June 13, 2002.

106–7 *when the federal agencies are failing the public:* Author's interview with Eliot Spitzer, New York, N.Y., July 18, 2005.

107 *asleep at the switch:* Michael Gormley, "Spitzer: SEC 'Asleep at Switch,'" Associated Press Wire, July 25, 2002.

107 *people like him:* Author's telephone interview with Christine Bruenn, Aug. 17, 2005.

108 *we support our banking clients too well:* Walter Hamilton, "Salomon to Pay $5 Million to Settle Grubman Allegations," *Los Angeles Times,* Sept. 24, 2002, p. 1.

108 *a possibility we explored:* Author's telephone interview with Harvey Pitt, Aug. 18, 2005.

108   *for the benefit of the markets:* Charles Gasparino, "Pitt and Spitzer Butted Heads to Overhaul Wall Street Research," *Wall Street Journal,* Oct. 31, 2002, p. A1.

109   *not a harmless corporate perk:* Washington Post Staff Writer, "Suit Seeks IPO Profits from Five Executives," *Washington Post,* October 1, 2002, p. A1.

110   *enormous distortion of capital:* Author's interview with Eliot Spitzer, New York, N.Y., July 11, 2005.

110   *a Manhattan judge found him liable:* Office of the New York Attorney General Eliot Spitzer, "Court Finds Telecom Exec Liable in Stock Spinning Case," press release, Feb. 13, 2006.

111   *either you're in:* Author's telephone interview with Christine Bruenn, Aug. 17, 2005.

111   *speedy and coordinated:* "SEC, NY Attorney General, NYSE, NASD, NASAA Reach Agreement on Reforming Wall Street Practices," SEC press release no. 2002-144, Oct. 3, 2002.

111–12 *I did not know then:* Eliot Spitzer speech to Investorside conference, New York, April 13, 2005.

112   *I put my foot down:* Author's interview with Harvey Pitt, New York, N.Y., June 28, 2005.

112   *we got rid of the Soviet Union:* Author's telephone interview with Harvey Goldschmid, July 6, 2005.

113   *something of a brake:* Stephen Cutler e-mail to author, Sept. 13, 2005.

113   *Sometimes there's sheer frustration:* Author's telephone interview with Eliot Spitzer, Aug. 19, 2005.

114   *What Eliot brought to the table:* Author's telephone interview with Christine Bruenn, Aug. 17, 2005.

115   *in* The Wall Street Journal *the next day:* Charles Gasparino and Randall Smith, "Deals & Deal Makers: Wall Street's Cost to End Inquiry to Be Known Soon," *Wall Street Journal,* Nov. 1, 2002, p. C5.

115   *really solid evidence of abuses:* Author's telephone interview with Lori Richards, July 20, 2005.

116   *these folks don't work for you:* Author's telephone interview with Christine Bruenn, Aug. 17, 2005.

116   *compared Meeker's record:* Gasparino, *Blood on the Street* (New York: Free Press, 2005), pp. 264–65.

116   *without e-mails showing a disconnect:* Author's telephone interview with Roger Waldman, Aug. 29, 2005.

118   *played him like a fiddle:* E-mail quoted in *Securities and Exchange Commission v. Citigroup Global Markets,* complaint filed April 28, 2002.

118   *ticking time bomb:* Author's interview with Beth Golden, New York, N.Y., June 29, 2005.

118   *AT&T and the 92nd Street Y: Securities and Exchange Commission v. Citigroup Global Markets,* complaint filed April 28, 2002.

119   *very appreciative:* Ibid.

119   *completely baseless:* Ben White, "Weill's Biggest Crisis; Citigroup Chief Called to Account for Conflicts in His Empire," *Washington Post,* Nov. 14, 2002, p. E1.

119   *denied that Spitzer's people were the source:* Gasparino, *Blood on the Street,* p. 296.

120   *take a fresh look:* Sanford Weill, memo to company executives quoted in

Charles Gasparino, "Grubman Boast: AT&T Upgrade Had an Altogether Different Goal," *Wall Street Journal*, Nov. 13, 2002, p. A1.

120 *His basic worldview:* Author's interview with John Savarese, New York, N.Y., Aug. 9, 2005.

120 *We had Grubman pretty good:* Author's interview with Bruce Topman, New York, N.Y., June 20, 2005.

121 *Steve tried to make sure:* Author's telephone interview with Barry Goldsmith, July 11, 2005.

122 *lackluster performances:* Eliot Spitzer, speech to the *Institutional Investor* Dinner, New York, N.Y., Nov. 12, 2002.

122 *flaming asshole:* Author's interview with Rich Baum, New York, N.Y., April 21, 2005, and telephone interview with Avi Schick, Nov. 18, 2004.

122 *why he is so successful:* Author's telephone interview with Avi Schick, Nov. 18, 2004.

123 *I have a way with words:* Susanne Craig, "Morgan Stanley Taps Regulators to Rehab Image," *Wall Street Journal*, June 21, 2004, p. C1.

124 *never be able to disprove:* Author's telephone interview with Eliot Spitzer, Aug. 19, 2005.

124 *Look, there's no case here:* Ibid.

124 *We made our own decision:* Author's telephone interview with Mary Schapiro, Aug. 10, 2005.

126 *investors get a fair shake:* Transcript of press conference announcing the global settlement, Dec. 20, 2002.

126 *placement of commas:* Author's interview with Beth Golden, New York, N.Y., June 29, 2005.

126 *could have a huge impact:* Author's telephone interview with Stephen Cutler, Aug. 22, 2005.

127 *Blodget's report on GoTo.com was "materially misleading":* Securities and Exchange Commission v. Henry McKelvey Blodget, complaint filed April 28, 2002.

127 *His 1999 AT&T upgrade was labeled "misleading":* Securities and Exchange Commission v. Jack Benjamin Grubman, complaint filed April 28, 2002.

128 *we're all on the same team:* Author's telephone interview with Lori Richards, July 20, 2005.

128 *Dear Chairman Powell:* Transcript of the SEC Historical Society's Fourth Annual Meeting, Wednesday, June 4, 2003.

129 *Market structure remains in the providence [sic]:* Transcript of the House Financial Services Committee Subcommittee on Capital Markets markup of HR 2179, the Securities Fraud Deterrence and Investor Restitution Act of 2003, July 10, 2003.

129 *Groundhog Day:* Jenny Anderson, "Spitzer Victory—House Nemesis Shelves Bill to Limit Policing Powers," *New York Post*, July 25, 2002, p. 39.

130 *I think we'll lose:* Author's telephone interviews with Bill Galvin, June 30, 2005, and Barney Frank, June 27, 2005.

130 *Sue, do you realize what you have done?:* Author's interview with Rich Baum, New York, N.Y., June 27, 2005.

130 *He was firm:* Author's interview with Rich Baum, New York, N.Y., June 27, 2005; Rich Baum e-mail to author, Aug. 25, 2005.

131   *stand up loudly and clearly reject this amendment:* Landon Thomas, Jr., "States Intent on Regulating, Look at Morgan," *New York Times,* July 15, 2003, p. C1.

131   *The SEC must be supreme:* Brooke A. Masters and Ben White, "Donaldson Backs SEC Supremacy Bill," *Washington Post,* July 15, 2003, p. E1.

131   *I had to go to war with them:* Author's interview with Eliot Spitzer, New York, N.Y., July 11, 2005.

132   *he has made real inroads in uncovering corporate corruption:* E.J. Dionne, "Defending States' Rights—Except on Wall Street," *Washington Post,* July 22, 2003, p. A17.

132   *not pleased:* Ben White and Brooke A. Masters, "Bill to Limit State Probes of Wall Street Delayed," *Washington Post,* July 25, 2003, p. E1.

132   *I would kindly caution opponents:* Randall Smith and Deborah Solomon, "State Level Stock Cops Retain Power," *Wall Street Journal,* July 25, 2003, p. C1.

Chapter 6.   Betting Today on Yesterday's Horse Races

133   *You're from Wall Street* through *the savings for consumers are enormous:* Author's interview with David D. Brown IV, New York, N.Y., June 9, 2005.

133–34 *This is the next logical step:* Author's interview with Eliot Spitzer, New York, N.Y., July 18, 2005.

134   *mutual fund shareholders being overcharged to the tune of $9 billion-plus:* John Freeman and Stewart Brown, "Mutual Fund Advisory Fees: The Cost of Conflicts of Interest," *Journal of Corporation Law* (Spring 2001): 672. The industry lobbying group the Investment Company Institute disputed the methodology and conclusions of this article.

134   *This Is News?:* Tom Lauricella, "This Is News? Fund Fees Are Too High, Study Says," *Wall Street Journal,* Aug. 27, 2001, p. C1.

134–35 *something very genuinely amiss in the mutual fund world:* Author's interview with Eliot Spitzer, New York, N.Y., July 18, 2005.

135   *a failure to disclose to investors:* Author's telephone interview with David Brown, Aug. 15, 2005.

135   *I think you should investigate mutual funds:* Author's interviews with David Brown, New York, N.Y., June 9, 2005, and Noreen Harrington, New York, N.Y., June 13, 2005.

135   *Who would trade at an old price:* Author's telephone interview with David Brown, Aug. 15, 2005.

136   *I'm that woman who was calling you about mutual funds:* Author's interview with Noreen Harrington, New York, N.Y., June 13, 2005.

136   *That doesn't look like a nut to me:* Author's interview with Roger Waldman, New York, N.Y., June 28, 2005.

137   *Canary had $400 million in assets:* Edward J. Stern, letter to investors in Canary Capital Partners LLC, Jan. 5, 2002.

137–38 *We just picked off this fund* through *I thought it was a Goldman issue:* Author's interview with Noreen Harrington, New York, N.Y., June 13, 2005.

138   *We go back door through some of them:* Ibid.

139   *amicably terminate their relationship:* Marcia Vickers, "Dynasty in Distress," *BusinessWeek,* February 9, 2004, p. 62.

139   *Money isn't created:* Author's interview with Noreen Harrington, New York, N.Y., June 13, 2005.

139   *Don't do it* through *I don't want people to think we're all crooks:* Ibid.

141   *I think you need a lawyer, too* through *Spitzer has a reputation for doing the right thing:* Author's telephone interview with James Nesfield, June 14, 2005, and interviews with David Brown, New York, N.Y., June 9, 2005, and June 27, 2005.

142   *Spitzer's team learned later: State of New York v. Canary Capital Partners LLC et al.,* Sept. 4, 2003, complaint, pp. 32–33.

142   *STC received a 1 percent fee: People v. Grant Seeger,* felony complaint filed Nov. 23, 2003, p. 5. The top two officers of STC pleaded guilty to criminal charges in August 2005 and received five years' probation each.

143   *I didn't make the yuppie cut:* Author's telephone interview with James Nesfield, June 15, 2005.

143   *I can't help you with that:* Author's telephone interview with David Brown, July 8, 2005.

144   *stepping up and saying, it is real:* Ibid.

145   *the broker would put the other order tickets into the wastebasket: State of New York v. Canary Capital Partners LLC et al.,* Sept. 4, 2003, complaint, p. 23.

145   *Are you sure we can trade until 9 P.M.:* Author's telephone interview with Andrew Goodwin, July 6, 2005.

145   *I have an expert SEC lawyer:* Ibid.

145   *We didn't want to attract the attention of the SEC:* Author's interview with David Brown, New York, N.Y., June 9, 2005.

146   *I wasn't aware of any of this corruption* through *Don't filter it:* Marcia Vickers, "Dynasty in Distress," *BusinessWeek,* Feb. 9, 2002, p. 62.

146   *This wasn't going away:* Author's interview with Gary Naftalis, New York, N.Y., Aug. 11, 2005.

147   *a little bit earlier than Matt specified:* Edward J. Stern, letter to Theodore C. Sihpol III, May 1, 2001, *State of New York v. Canary Capital Partners LLC et al.,* Sept. 4, 2003, complaint, exhibits, p. 12.

148   *nice insurance:* Edward J. Stern, testimony at the trial of *People v. Theodore Sihpol,* May 17, 2005, transcript p. 2014.

148   *having to dig stuff out of him:* Author's interview with David Brown, New York, N.Y., June 27, 2005.

148   *There were moments over the summer:* Author's interview with Eliot Spitzer, New York, N.Y., July 18, 2005.

148   *I was so afraid we'd missed something:* Author's telephone interview with David Brown, July 8, 2005.

149   *This could be bigger than the research analysts:* Author's telephone interview with Beth Golden, Nov. 18, 2004.

149   *lead with the late trading:* Author's interview with David Brown, New York, N.Y., June 27, 2005.

150   *Eddie felt strongly:* Author's interview with Gary Naftalis, New York, N.Y., Aug. 11, 2005.

150   *That was my one week of vacation:* Ibid.

150–51 *I thought we were going to have to sue them:* Author's telephone interview with David Brown, Aug. 15, 2005.

151 *it was more important to get this done:* Author's interview with Bruce Topman, New York, N.Y., June 20, 2005.

152 *You end up with an accepted base of facts:* Author's interview with Eliot Spitzer, New York, N.Y., July 18, 2005.

152 *That's the way the criminal justice system works:* Ibid.

152 *The mutual-fund industry operates on a double standard:* Mark T. Kuiper, "NY Atty Gen'l Spitzer: Mutl Fnd Trading Abuses Widespread," Market News International, Sept. 4, 2003.

Chapter 7.   Two Sets of Rules

153 *Just wait:* Author's telephone interview with Matthew Fink, Nov. 11, 2005.

153–54 *We should all be outraged:* Richard Baker, "Baker Commends Spitzer Mutual Fund Investigation," Sept. 3, 2003, press release.

154 *this is the worst day of my professional life:* Author's telephone interview with Stephen Cutler, Aug. 22, 2005.

154 *The FBI, in all my years as a state prosecutor, has never called us:* Author's interview with Eliot Spitzer, New York, N.Y., July 18, 2005.

155 *We've done what we can do:* Author's interview with Eliot Spitzer, New York, N.Y., Feb. 12, 2004.

155 *God bless Eliot Spitzer:* Stephen Cutler, press conference, U.S. Attorney's Office, New York, Sept. 4, 2003.

155 *I would have done it differently:* Author's telephone interview with Stephen Cutler, Aug. 22, 2005.

155 *we wanted to do an industry-wide investigation:* Author's telephone interview with Lori Richards, Sept. 2, 2005.

155 *one-quarter of the brokers:* Brooke A. Masters, "SEC Finds Illegal Fund Trading; Survey Discloses After-Hours Deals," *Washington Post*, Nov. 3, 2003, p. A1.

156 *Get on this immediately:* Author's telephone interview with Stephen Cutler, Aug. 22, 2005.

156 *hard feelings:* Author's telephone interview with Christine Bruenn, Aug. 17, 2005.

157 *preparing and time-stamping order tickets:* "In the Matter of Theodore Charles Sihpol III," SEC Administrative Proceeding File No. 3-11261, Oct. 12, 2005, p. 5.

157 *ever-widening reach* and *Whether it is the tip of the iceberg:* Brooke A. Masters, "Mutual Fund Abuses Alleged in Two Cases; Charges on 'Timing'; a Fine for Sales Incentives," *Washington Post*, Sept. 17, 2003, p. E1.

159 *you have to forfeit a worthy defense:* Author's interview with Stanley Arkin, New York, N.Y., June 28, 2005.

159 *We only have the leverage that we have:* Author's telephone interview with David Brown, Aug. 29, 2005.

159 *you are probably holding them right now:* Author's interview with David Brown, New York, N.Y., July 14, 2005.

159 *I didn't invent it:* Author's interview with Eliot Spitzer, New York, N.Y., July 18, 2005.

161   *Maybe I should have taken the deal:* Ibid.

161–62 *two sets of rules:* Jenny Anderson, "Strong Medicine—Mutual Fund Chief Cheated Own Investors: Gov't," *New York Post,* Oct. 30, 2003, p. 35. Spitzer and his investigators gave similar interviews to several major newspapers on October 29.

162   *Heads should roll:* Riva D. Atlas, "Spitzer Vows Legal Action against Head of Fund Family," *New York Times,* Oct. 30, 2002, p. C1.

162   *the use of the public bludgeon:* Author's interview with Stanley Arkin, New York, N.Y., June 18, 2005.

162   *I'm not going to apologize for that:* Author's interview with Eliot Spitzer, New York, N.Y., July 28, 2005.

162   *I'll be damned if I'm going to come this far:* Author's interview with David Brown, New York, N.Y., June 9, 2005.

163   *We are not adequately protecting the tens of millions:* Transcript, hearing of the House Financial Services Committee's Subcommittee on Capital Markets, Nov. 4, 2003.

163   *I don't think they're following you:* Author's telephone interviews with William Galvin, June 30, 2005, and in April 2004.

163   *Look, I couldn't. It wasn't your case:* Author's telephone interview with Stephen Cutler, Aug. 22, 2005.

164   *This is not intended to be an industry template:* Brooke A. Masters, "States, SEC Split Again in Attack on Investment Abuses; Spitzer Critical of Settlement with Putnam," *Washington Post,* Nov. 15, 2003, p. E1.

164   *left the money open:* Author's telephone interview with Stephen Cutler, Aug. 22, 2005.

164   *This document is not a settlement with me:* Brooke A. Masters, "Putnam, SEC Settle as State Fumes; Mass. Probe Continues into Mutual Fund's Trades," *Washington Post,* Nov. 14, 2003, p. E1.

164   *handle a house closing:* Masters, "States, SEC Split Again."

164   *has the capacity to issue rules:* Eliot Spitzer, speech to the SEC Historical Society, Washington, D.C., June 4, 2003.

165   *you put a little Band-Aid on it:* Gretchen Morgenson, "Market Watch; Slapping Wrists as the Fund Scandal Spreads," *New York Times,* Nov. 16, 2003, section 3, p. 1.

165   *But it was fun:* Author's telephone interview with Eliot Spitzer, Aug. 19, 2005.

165   *the highest regard for you:* Author's interview with David Brown, New York, N.Y., July 14, 2005.

166   *My office and the SEC have worked together:* Transcript, hearing of the Senate Banking Housing and Urban Affairs Committee, Nov. 20, 2003.

166   *You don't cheat people who have trusted you:* Brooke A. Masters, "Mutual Fund Firm Founders Accused of Fraud," *Washington Post,* Nov. 21, 2003, p. A1.

166   *Bruce Calvert is okay with this:* Brooke A. Masters, "Alliance Struggles to Settle with Regulators; Size of Firm, Weight of Evidence May Make Deal a Model for Other Money-Management Firms," *Washington Post,* Dec. 12, 2003, p. E1.

167   *It is our intention to settle this:* Author's interview with David Brown, New York, N.Y., July 14, 2005.

167   *800-pound gorilla:* Monica Langley, "The Enforcer: As His Ambitions Expand, Spitzer Draws More Controversy—In Latest Move, He Pushes Fund

Giant to Cut Fees; New Clash With the SEC—Eyeing Drugs and Annuities," *Wall Street Journal,* Dec. 11, 2003, p. 1.

167 *The SEC should not serve as a fee setter:* Brooke A. Masters, "Alliance Capital to Reduce Fees," *Washington Post,* Dec. 17, 2003, p. E1.

167 *we don't think this is a high enough number:* Author's telephone interview with Stephen Cutler, Aug. 24, 2005.

167–68 *an unregulated market does not safeguard certain core American values:* Eliot Spitzer and Andrew Celli, Jr., "Bull Run," *New Republic,* March 22, 2004, p. 18.

168 *It was me that prevented you from getting information:* Author's telephone interview with Stephen Cutler, Aug. 22, 2005.

168 *a mutual fund has failed to look out for its investors:* Masters, "Alliance Capital to Reduce Fees."

169 *These directors clearly failed to protect the interest of investors:* Office of New York State Attorney General, "Spitzer, S.E.C. Reach Largest Mutual Fund Settlement Ever," press release, March 15, 2004.

169 *We kept trying to cooperate:* Author's telephone interview with Harvey Goldschmid, July 6, 2005.

170 *farm boy from the wheat fields of North Dakota: State of New York v. Strong Financial Corp et al.,* verified complaint, May 20, 2004.

170 *Employees had to pull their cars:* Robert Mullins, "Profile: Richard Strong—Strong Funds," *Business Journal-Milwaukee,* Oct. 23, 1998, p. S32.

170 *we are turning over every rock:* Kathleen Gallagher, "Strong Chief Says Inquiry Comes as a Surprise," *Milwaukee Journal-Sentinel,* Sept. 6, 2003, p. 1D.

171 *He timed his own fucking fund:* Author's interview with David Brown, New York, N.Y., July 14, 2005.

172 *Dick Strong didn't do anything terrible:* Author's interview with Stanley Arkin, New York, N.Y., June 28, 2005.

172 *It's not such a costly price to pay:* Ibid.

172–73 *aggressive application of the Martin Act:* Dennis Vacco, "Martin Act Martinet," *Wall Street Journal,* April 12, 2004, p. A18.

173 *I'll take the blame:* Author's interview with Eliot Spitzer, New York, N.Y., July 18, 2005.

Chapter 8. Simply Too Much

175 *It's simply too much:* Eliot Spitzer, press conference announcing his lawsuit against Richard Grasso, New York, May 24, 2004.

175 *smacks of politics:* Richard A. Grasso, "My Vindication Will Come in a Courtroom," *Wall Street Journal,* May 25, 2004, p. A16.

175 *I like it when people push back:* Brooke A. Masters, "Eliot Spitzer Spoils for a Fight; Opponents Blast Unusual Tactics of N.Y. Attorney General," *Washington Post,* May 31, 2004, p. A1.

176 *a consummate diplomat:* Transcript of the press conference announcing the global settlement, New York Stock Exchange, New York, December 20, 2002.

176 *the right time:* Charles Gasparino and Randall Smith, "Behind Weill's Almost Directorship at NYSE," *Wall Street Journal,* March 25, 2003, p. C1.

176–77 *apoplectic* through *It would have been ridiculous to invite me:* Author's telephone interview with Eliot Spitzer, Aug. 19, 2005.

177   *doubts about the veracity of Dick Grasso:* Ibid.

177   *a gross misjudgment and a violation of trust:* Patrick McGeehan, "Weill Declines Board Seat on N.Y.S.E.," *New York Times*, March 24, 2003, p. D3.

178   *When Sandy Weill was informed of the comments:* Rachel Kipp, "Weill Withdraws Name from NYSE Nominees," AP Online, March 23, 2003.

178   *If you're going to set standards for other people:* Patrick McGeehan, "S.E.C. Asks That Exchanges Review Their Governance," *New York Times*, March 27, 2003, p. C8.

178   *a friend who has been a tireless campaigner:* Susan Harrigan, "Amid Controversy, Spitzer, Grasso 'Remain Friends,' " *Newsday*, April 8, 2003, p. A63.

178   *great friend:* Transcript of the press conference announcing the final global settlement, SEC, Washington, D.C., April 28, 2003.

179   *"spectacular" job:* Charles Gasparino, Kate Kelly, and Susanne Craig, "Grasso Is NYSE's $10 Million Man—Chairman's 2002 Pay Package Came Amid a Slump in Stocks and the Big Board's Earnings," *Wall Street Journal*, May 7, 2003, p. C1.

179   *a straw poll on the contract had come out in favor of it by eleven to seven:* Dan K. Webb, "Report to the New York Stock Exchange on Investigation Relating to the Compensation of Richard A. Grasso," Dec. 15, 2003, p. 88.

179   *the board is very pleased with the leadership he has provided:* Landon Thomas, Jr., "Big Board Chief Will Get a $140 Million Package," *New York Times*, Aug. 28, 2003, p. 1.

180   *raises serious questions regarding the effectiveness:* Ben White, "SEC Chairman Assails NYSE on Grasso Pay; Exchange's Practices Questioned," *Washington Post*, Sept. 3, 2003, p. E1.

180   *I've put this issue behind me* and *Dick was and is the right leader:* Ben White, "Grasso to Give Up Extra $48 Million; NYSE Had Been Quiet about Payment," *Washington Post*, Sept. 10, 2003, p. E1.

181   *we don't tag along and cause trouble:* Author's telephone interview with Eliot Spitzer, Aug. 19, 2005.

181   *the tide has turned:* The most detailed description of the events leading up to Grasso's ouster is in Susanne Craig, Ianthe Jeanne Dugan, Kate Kelly, and Laurie P. Cohen, "Taking Stock: As End Neared, Grasso Held On in Hopes Pay Furor Would Ebb—CEO Misread Depth of Anger on Floor, Insiders Say; Support from Giuliani—'I Didn't Offer to Resign,' " *Wall Street Journal*, Sept. 26, 2003, p. A1.

181   *I should submit my resignation:* Webb, "Report to the New York Stock Exchange," pp. 95–96.

181–82 *This is about the integrity of the Exchange* through *Well, the board has voted you out:* Susanne Craig, Ianthe Jeanne Dugan, Kate Kelly, and Laurie P. Cohen, "Taking Stock," p. A1.

182   *For the past 36 years, I have had the honor and privilege:* Ben White, "NYSE Ousts Grasso as Chairman; Size of Pay Package Drew Wide Criticism," *Washington Post*, Sept. 18, 2003, p. A1.

182–83 *Webb's report, which was completed on December 15, 2003,* through *None of the other compensation committee members . . . corrected McCall at the meeting:* Webb, "Report to the New York Stock Exchange."

183   *The truth will set Carl free:* Author's telephone interview with William
       Wachtell, March 21, 2006.

183   *The Webb report does not take issue with Dick Grasso* through *Dick Grasso was*
       worth a great deal to the NYSE: Thor Valdmanis, "Report Calls Grasso's Pay
       'Grossly Excessive,'" *USA Today,* Feb. 3, 2003, p. 3B, and Ben White, "Pay
       Raised Eyebrows Early On; NYSE Disagreed over Grasso in '98," *Washing-*
       ton Post, Feb. 3, 2005, p. E3.

183   *it lacked a "smoking gun":* Ben White, "Study Finds Weak Case against
       Grasso; N.Y. Attorney General, SEC Not Optimistic about Legal Action,"
       Washington Post, Jan. 10, 2004, p. E1.

183   *under no compulsion to do anything: People of the State of New York v. Richard A.*
       Grasso, Kenneth Langone and The New York Stock Exchange Inc., videotaped
       deposition of John Reed, Feb. 17, 2006, p. 66.

184   *Generally, when we bring actions involving nonprofits:* Author's telephone inter-
       view with Michele Hirshman, Nov. 23, 2005.

185   *was able to piece together that they were the good guys:* Ibid.

185   *disaster! The new members were shocked: People of the State of New York v. Richard*
       A. Grasso, Kenneth Langone and The New York Stock Exchange, complaint filed
       May 24, 2003.

185   *no brainer* and *essentially a done deal:* Dan K. Webb, "Report to the New York
       Stock Exchange," p. 67.

186   *significantly erode the retention value of the pension:* Vedder Price report to the
       New York Stock Exchange Human Resources Policy and Compensation
       Committee, Oct. 3, 2002, pp. 13–18.

186   *Ashen later conceded that the board minutes were "inaccurate":* In Re Investigation
       by Eliot Spitzer of Matters Relating to the New York Stock Exchange, Assur-
       ance of Discontinuance, Exhibit A, "Frank Ashen's Statement of Facts," May
       23, 2004, p. 8.

186   *Bob Stucker reported to Schrempp and the comp committee that such cash-out plans*
       were "rare": Vedder Price report to the New York Stock Exchange Human
       Resources Policy and Compensation Committee, Feb. 6, 2003, p. 12.

186   *Vedder Price also submitted a third report:* Webb, "Report to the New York
       Stock Exchange," p. 76.

187   *the Ashen convention:* In Re Investigation by Eliot Spitzer of Matters Relating
       to the New York Stock Exchange, Assurance of Discontinuance, Exhibit A,
       "Mercer's Statement of Facts," May 19, 2004, p. 3.

189   *I felt this was not the way the NYSE conducts business:* In Re Investigation by Eliot
       Spitzer of Matters Relating to the New York Stock Exchange, Assurance of
       Discontinuance, Exhibit A, "Frank Ashen's Statement of Facts," May 23,
       2004, pp. 12–13.

190   *We want people to sit on the boards of not-for-profits:* Author's telephone interview
       with Eliot Spitzer, Aug. 19, 2005.

190   *a photo composite that purported to show Grasso and Langone in bed together:* Jenny
       Anderson, "KISS MY GRASSO!—Imus Tells Tale of NYSE Boss' Shrug at
       Critics," *New York Post,* May 30, 2003, p. 43.

190–91 *Other directors had told Dan Webb's investigators that McCall had not told them*
       through *you can proceed as you see fit:* Webb, "Report to the New York Stock
       Exchange," p. 77.

191   *hatchet job and somebody lied:* William Wachtell, at a hearing of *People v. Grasso et al.*, Manhattan Supreme Court, March 16, 2006.

192   *My hesitancy was reported immediately: People of the State of New York v. Richard A. Grasso, Kenneth Langone and The New York Stock Exchange,* complaint filed May 24, 2003, pp. 7–8.

192   *I said, "This is crazy":* Author's telephone interview with Eliot Spitzer, Aug. 19, 2005.

192   *The alternative was to do nothing:* Author's interview with Michele Hirshman, New York, N.Y., Oct. 5, 2005.

193   *We would have acted the same if this was the NYSE, the Botanical Gardens:* Author's telephone interview with Eliot Spitzer, Aug. 19, 2005.

193   *But what we've got is exponentially more powerful:* Ibid.

193   *Eliot Spitzer really had no choice but to sue:* "Chasing Mr. Grasso's Millions," *New York Times,* May 26, 2004, p. 22.

193   *McCall's status as a prominent New York Democrat who could help Mr. Spitzer:* "Spitzer v. Grasso," *Wall Street Journal,* May 25, 2004, p. A16.

193–94 *Tom already has his problems in the party:* Patrick D. Healy and Bruce Lambert, "Nassau Leader Considers Run against Spitzer, Pleasing G.O.P.," *New York Times,* June 2, 2005, p. B1.

194   *Mr. Ashen recognizes in hindsight that certain mistakes were made:* Bruce Yannett, statement on behalf of Frank Ashen, May 24, 2004.

194   *totally offensive: People of the State of New York v. Richard A. Grasso, Kenneth Langone and the New York Stock Exchange Inc.,* videotaped deposition of Gerald Levin, Sept. 9, 2005, p. 314.

195   *If some of the directors were surprised, that's a reflection on their own lack of diligence:* Jim McCarthy, e-mail to author, Nov. 16, 2005.

195   *It was very clear that it was $8,050,000: People of the State of New York v. Richard A. Grasso, Kenneth Langone and The New York Stock Exchange Inc.,* videotaped deposition of Gerald Levin, Sept. 8, 2005, p. 191.

196   *Paulson's spokesman said that the only person:* Author's telephone interview with Lucas van Praag, Nov. 21, 2005.

196   *That is false . . . Grasso was terrific:* Author's interview with Harvey Pitt, New York, N.Y., June 28, 2005.

196   *September 9, we gave this man a rousing round of applause, and eight days later we fired him:* Author's interview with Kenneth Langone, New York, N.Y., July 19, 2005.

197   *Poke around that and see what emerges:* Author's telephone interview with Eliot Spitzer, Aug. 30, 2005.

198   *the company owns that data. They can do what they want:* Author's telephone interview with Rose Firestein, Aug. 24, 2005.

198   *manage the dissemination of these data:* Wayne Kondro, "Drug Company Experts Advised Staff to Withhold Data about SSRI Use in Children," *Canadian Medical Association Journal,* March 2, 2004.

198   *We knew we were onto something:* Author's interview with Joe Baker, New York, N.Y., Aug. 23, 2005.

199   *The point of the lawsuit is to ensure that there is complete information:* Gardiner Harris, "Spitzer Sues a Drug Maker, Saying It Hid Negative Data," *New York Times,* June 3, 2004, p. A1.

199   *acted responsibly in conducting clinical studies:* "GlaxoSmithKline Issues Statement in Response to a Lawsuit Filed Today by New York Attorney General Elliot Spitzer," press release, Philadelphia, June 2, 2004.

199   *we had good law on our side:* Author's interview with Joe Baker, New York, N.Y., Aug. 23, 2005.

199   *The remedy is so easy: honest disclosure:* Author's telephone interview with Eliot Spitzer, Aug. 30, 2005.

200   *The spirit of these agencies has been eaten away:* Author's interviews with Eliot Spitzer, New York, N.Y., May 23, 2005, and July 11, 2005.

200   *campaign of disparagement and defamation:* Ben White, "Grasso Sues NYSE, Reed for $50 Million; Ex-Chairman Also Offers Rebuttal to Spitzer," *Washington Post*, July 21, 2003, p. E1.

200   *I'm not going to stop until I win:* Charles Gasparino, *Blood on the Street* (New York: Free Press, 2005), p. 317.

200   *I made honest decisions that were thoroughly researched:* Kimberly A. Strassel, "Mr. Grasso's Money," *Wall Street Journal*, Aug. 13, 2004, p. A14.

Chapter 9.   The Concrete Club

201–2   *Huh?* through *This looks real:* Author's interview with David Brown IV, New York, N.Y., Sept. 15, 2005.

202   *I've sent you a subpoena* through *I'll explain it to you:* Ibid.

204   *it's a pay-to-play arrangement:* Author's interview with David Brown, New York, N.Y., Sept. 22, 2005.

204   *bells and whistles go off:* Author's interview with Maria Filipakis, New York, N.Y., Oct. 5, 2005.

204   *We found all kinds of e-mails:* Author's interview with Matthew Gaul, New York, N.Y., Sept. 19, 2005.

205   *Find me the disgruntled broker:* Author's interview with David Brown, New York, N.Y., Sept. 22, 2005.

205   *oh no, no, no, this is not just about disclosure:* Author's interview with Maria Filipakis, New York, N.Y., Oct. 5, 2005.

205   *Going forward we are going to push Zurich: People of New York v. Aon Corp.*, complaint filed March 4, 2005, p. 9.

206   *There was a real arrogance there:* Author's interview with David Brown, New York, N.Y., Sept. 22, 2005.

206   *There is going to be accountability:* Ibid.

207   *it's apples to apples* through *Doesn't this increase the cost of insurance:* Author's interview with Matthew Gaul, New York, N.Y., Sept. 19, 2005.

207–8   *throwing the quote: People of the State of New York v. Marsh & McLennan Companies Inc. and Marsh Inc.*, complaint filed Oct. 14, 2004, p. 24.

208   *These guys are really in trouble:* Author's interview with David Brown, New York, N.Y., Sept. 22, 2005.

208   *Hint, hint: People of the State of New York v. Marsh & McLennan Companies Inc. and Marsh Inc.*, complaint filed Oct. 14, 2004, p. 25.

208   *Oh my god:* Kate Kelly, "In Spitzer's Office, Hours of Drudgery, Moments of 'Gotcha!'—Interns Pore Over Documents to Find 'Hot' E-Mails; Paydirt on Bid-Rigging," *Wall Street Journal,* Oct. 27, 2004, p. A1.

208   *reasonably competitive but will not be a winner: People of the State of New York v. Marsh & McLennan Companies Inc. and Marsh Inc.,* complaint filed Oct. 14, 2004, p. 26.

208   *Unbelievable Marsh document:* Author's interview with David Brown, New York, N.Y., Sept. 22, 2005.

209   *buy yourself a toothbrush:* Author's interview with Maria Filipakis, New York, N.Y., Oct. 5, 2005.

209   *We knew there was something there:* Author's interview with Maria Filipakis, New York, N.Y., Oct. 13, 2005.

209   *the deadline was not negotiable:* Author's interview with Matthew Gaul, New York, N.Y., Sept. 19, 2005.

210   *This was not a real opportunity: People of the State of New York v. Marsh & McLennan Companies Inc. and Marsh Inc.,* complaint filed Oct. 14, 2004, p. 17.

210   *I do not want to hear you are not doing "B" quotes: People of the State of New York v. Marsh & McLennan Companies Inc. and Marsh Inc.,* complaint filed Oct. 14, 2004, p. 19.

210–11 *cartel-like behavior:* Monica Langley and Theo Francis, "Risky Business: Insurers Reel from Spitzer's Strike—Subpoena on Bid-Rigging Spurred Rush to Admit Collusion with Broker—Fallout for a Family Dynasty," *Wall Street Journal,* Oct. 18, 2004, p. A1. Pope quote corrected to reflect memories of those involved.

212   *There was a major criminal conspiracy:* Author's interview with David Brown, New York, N.Y., Sept. 22, 2005.

212   *Just focus on Marsh:* Ibid.

212–13 *this office is super cautious:* Author's interview with Michael Berlin, New York, N.Y., Oct. 5, 2005.

213   *We've got a real crisis* through *a practice for seventy years:* Author's telephone interview with Michael Cherkasky, Nov. 18, 2005.

214   *there was not a meeting of the minds:* Author's interview with Michele Hirshman, New York, N.Y., Oct. 5, 2005.

215   *They did the opposite of the what you would expect:* Author's interview with Eliot Spitzer, New York, N.Y., Sept. 19, 2005.

215   *This stuff isn't that complicated:* Ibid.

215   *no reasonable justification:* Eliot Spitzer press conference, New York, N.Y., Sept. 15, 2005.

215–16 *The company is not entitled to a settlement:* Author's interview with Eliot Spitzer, New York, N.Y., Sept. 19, 2005.

216   *To do it at a press conference was unusual:* Author's interview with Michele Hirshman, New York, N.Y., Oct. 5, 2005.

216   *it hits the nail on the head:* Author's interview with David Brown, New York, N.Y., Sept. 15, 2005.

216   *Moody's warned that the credit ratings:* "Insurers Reel Friday on Spitzer's Probe," AFX.Com, Oct. 15, 2005.

216   *the market had spoken:* Author's interview with David Brown, New York, N.Y., Oct. 20, 2005.

217   *Spitzer is not persuadable:* Author's telephone interview with Michael Cherkasky, Nov. 18, 2005.

217   *Eliot was so far out on a limb:* Author's interview with Richard Beattie, New York, N.Y., Sept. 8, 2005.

217–18 *I was rigid on that point:* Author's telephone interview with Eliot Spitzer, Oct. 24, 2005.

218   *We could not afford it:* Author's telephone interview with Michael Cherkasky, Nov. 18, 2005.

218–19 *the "Eliot and Mike show"* through *Will this work:* Ibid.

219   *This is a fundamental shift:* Brooke A. Masters, "Marsh Replaces CEO in Wake of Charges; Firm Implicated in Insurance Investigation," *Washington Post,* Oct. 26, 2004, p. E1.

219   *Spitzer is building his political career by collecting trophies:* "Editorial," *Chief Executive,* vol. 204, Dec. 2004, p. 72.

219   *Normally, the prosecutor's role:* Ann Davis, Kara Scannell, and Charles Forelle, "CEOs Grumble at Spitzer Style," *Wall Street Journal,* Oct. 26, 2004, p. C1.

219   *They had a major crisis with clients and the market:* Author's telephone interview with Eliot Spitzer, Oct. 24, 2005.

Chapter 10.   Foot Faults

220   *to re-energize state government:* Eliot Spitzer, speech, Sheraton New York, N.Y., Dec. 9, 2004.

221   *remarkable turnabout:* Patrick O'Gilfoil Healy, "Spitzer, in a Shift, Will Yield Inquiries to U.S. Regulators," *New York Times,* Dec. 25, 2004, p. A1.

221   *If there's one thing I guard jealously:* Author's telephone interview with Eliot Spitzer, Nov. 28, 2005.

221   *the* Times *agreed to run both a correction and a corrective article:* "Spitzer Says He Won't Drop Any Inquiries Begun by State," *New York Times,* Dec. 26, 2004, p. 46.

221   *This wasn't an effort to squeeze the last penny out of the rock:* Author's telephone interview with Eliot Spitzer, Oct. 24, 2005.

222   *I never scream and I hardly ever curse:* Author's telephone interview with Michael Cherkasky, Nov. 18, 2005.

222   *somebody needed to rise above it:* Author's telephone interview with Eliot Spitzer, Oct. 24, 2005.

222   *Everybody was frustrated:* Author's telephone interview with Dietrich Snell, Nov. 1, 2005.

222   *It turned out there wasn't that big a gap:* Author's telephone interview with Michael Cherkasky, Nov. 18, 2005.

223   *So everyone is going to be back here at 8 a.m.:* Kathleen Day and Brooke A. Masters, "Insurance Broker Will Pay Back Customers; Marsh to Create $850 Million Fund to Settle Charges," *Washington Post,* Feb. 1, 2005, p. E1.

223–34 *Aon officials explained the move as a way to "make it up to" Zurich: People of New York v. Aon Corp.,* complaint filed March 4, 2005, p. 13.

224 *Ryan [was] willing to put his personal credibility:* Ibid., p. 27.

224 *he couldn't remember a goddamn thing:* Author's interview with David Axinn, New York, N.Y., Oct. 6, 2005.

225 *It's not true:* Ibid. and telephone interview with Lloyd Constantine, Oct. 10, 2005.

226 *That's pretty good:* Author's interview with David Axinn, New York, N.Y., Oct. 6, 2005.

226 *the more we looked into it the clearer it got:* Author's telephone interview with Dietrich Snell, Nov. 1, 2005.

226 *I feel like I failed:* Author's telephone interview with Lloyd Constantine, Oct. 10, 2005.

227 *We did not pull any punches:* Author's telephone interview with Eliot Spitzer, Oct. 24, 2005.

227 *selling a telecommunications firm called Brightpoint a "purported 'insurance' product":* "SEC Charges American International Group and Others in Brightpoint Securities Fraud," SEC press release 2003-111, Sept. 11, 2003.

228 *We're going to back off this one out of comity:* Author's interview with David Brown, New York, N.Y., Oct. 13, 2005.

228 *Finite insurance was the drug of choice:* Ibid.

228 *The issues with finite insurance seemed "inchoate":* Author's telephone interview with Dietrich Snell, Nov. 1, 2005.

228 *Is this ever going to be a case:* Author's interview with David Brown, New York, N.Y., Oct. 13, 2005.

229 *You didn't want us to know about it:* Author's telephone interview with Maria Filipakis, Nov. 28, 2005.

230 *Mr. Greenberg never requested nor intended to participate in any sham transactions:* Author's telephone interview with Howard Opinsky, Nov. 30, 2005.

230 *AIG's publicly reported loss reserves at that time:* Memorandum re: American International Group Inc. *Form 10-K for the fiscal year ended December 31, 2004,* July 26, 2005, p. 17.

230 *They did it the right way:* Author's interview with David Brown, New York, N.Y., Oct. 13, 2005.

230 *Get the subpoenas out:* Ibid.

230 *I can't believe this. Look at this:* Ibid.

231 *look at foot faults and make them into a murder charge:* Devin Leonard and Peter Elkind, "All I Want in Life Is an Unfair Advantage," *Fortune,* Aug. 8, 2005, p. 76.

231 *these aren't just foot faults:* Ibid.

231 *Are we working together or not:* Author's telephone interview with David Brown, Nov. 23, 2005.

232 *These are fact patterns that revolve around him:* Author's telephone interview with Eliot Spitzer, Oct. 24, 2005.

232 *I want you to be a little bit more aggressive:* People of the State of New York v. American International Group Inc. et al., complaint filed May 26, 2005, p. 3.

233 *Stock repurchase programs are commonly employed:* Author's telephone interview with Howard Opinsky, Nov. 30, 2005.

233 *We think our books are clean:* Author's interview with Matthew Gaul, New York, N.Y., Oct. 13, 2005.

233 *you don't really interview Mr. Greenberg:* Author's interviews with Matthew Gaul and Maria Filipakis, New York, N.Y., Oct. 13, 2005.

234 *We're not putting off our deposition:* Author's interview with David Brown, New York, N.Y., Oct. 13, 2005.

234 *It certainly was not a consultative process:* Author's telephone interview with Lee Wolosky, Jan. 24, 2006.

235 *I was trying to get a sense from Eliot how serious it was:* Author's interview with Richard Beattie, New York, N.Y., May 25, 2005.

235–36 *There was no ambiguity that this was risk free:* Author's interview with Eliot Spitzer, New York, N.Y., April 12, 2005.

236 *I had told him he made a mistake with Jeffrey:* Author's interview with Richard Beattie, New York, N.Y., May 25, 2005.

236–37 *In one oft-described incident:* Monica Langley, "Palace Coup: After a 37-Year Reign at AIG, Chief's Last Tumultuous Days—Faced with Indictment Threat, Directors Move Quickly against Mr. Greenberg—Hopes Dashed for Soft Landing," *Wall Street Journal,* April 1, 2005, p. A1.

237 *We are here to represent the shareholders:* Author's interview with Frank Zarb, New York, N.Y., Nov. 1, 2005.

238 *This company's being run by a bunch of lawyers:* Richard Beattie's contemporaneous notes of the conversation.

238 *I felt for him:* Author's interview with Frank Zarb, New York, N.Y., Nov. 1, 2005.

238 *Nobody in that room had a complaint:* Ibid.

238 *The board did the right thing:* Author's telephone interview with Richard Beattie, Nov. 15, 2005.

238 *I've always called him Mr. Greenberg:* Ibid.

239 *She was frantic:* Author's interview with Maria Filipakis, New York, N.Y., Oct. 13, 2005.

239 *the consequences for the company do get much more severe:* Author's telephone interview with Eliot Spitzer, Oct. 24, 2005.

239–40 *In retrospect it's clear:* Author's interview with Howard Opinsky, Jan. 24, 2006.

240 *I'm going to indict the company:* Author's interview with Richard Beattie, New York, N.Y., Sept. 8, 2005.

240 *Any suggestion that there was any impropriety:* David Boies' e-mail to author, "David Boies Quotes in Response to Spitzer Book," Jan. 23, 2006.

240 *Good morning, Happy Easter:* Author's interview with Frank Zarb, New York, N.Y., Nov. 1, 2005.

240–41 *intention to retire:* "M.R. Greenberg to Retire," Business Wire, March 28, 2005.

241 *the wise actions of the AIG board:* Carrie Johnson, "Greenberg to Resign as AIG Chairman; Company, Ex-CEO under Pressure from Multiple Investigations," *Washington Post,* March 29, 2005, p. E1.

241 *He is the man who built the greatest insurance company:* Author's telephone interview with Edward E. Matthews, Nov. 21, 2005.

241 *That company was a black box, run with an iron fist:* Eliot Spitzer on *This Week with George Stephanopoulos,* ABC News, April 10, 2005.

241–42 *Mr. Spitzer has gone too far:* John C. Whitehead, "Mr. Spitzer Has Gone Too Far," *Wall Street Journal,* April 22, 2005, p. A12.

242   *it's now a war between us:* John C. Whitehead, "Scary," *Wall Street Journal,* Dec. 22, 2005, p. A14.

242   *embellished and false:* Joseph A. Giannone, "Former Goldman Head Says Spitzer Made Threats," Reuters News, Dec. 22, 2005.

242   *appear to have been structured:* AIG, "AIG Delays 10-K Filing to Finish Review," press release issued March 30, 2005.

242   *The facts speak for themselves:* Author's telephone interview with Eliot Spitzer, Oct. 24, 2005.

242   *Why not get on with it and indict the man:* "So Indict Him Then," *Wall Street Journal,* April 13, 2005, p. A18.

243   *I didn't want him to think I was gloating:* Author's interview with Eliot Spitzer, New York, N.Y., April 12, 2005.

243   *same answer:* Author's interview with David Brown, New York, N.Y., Oct. 13, 2005.

243   *inaccurate and ridiculous:* Dean Starkman and Carrie Johnson, "Loss of Coordination; Spitzer and Federal Officials Pursuing Insurance Probe Separately," *Washington Post,* July 19, 2005, p. E1.

244   *We wanted to get our facts out first:* Author's interview with David Brown, New York, N.Y., Oct. 13, 2005.

244   *I didn't notice them banging down the door:* Author's telephone interview with Eliot Spitzer, Oct. 24, 2005.

245   *AIG makes millions of dollars illegally each year: People of the State of New York v. American International Group Inc. et al.,* May 26, 2005, complaint, pp. 27–29.

246   *Being here at night is part of the job:* Author's telephone interview with Eliot Spitzer, Oct. 24, 2005.

246   *One of the cool things about working for Eliot:* Author's interview with David Brown, New York, N.Y., Oct. 13, 2005.

247   *many of the restatement items appear exaggerated or unnecessary:* Memorandum re: American International Group Inc. *Form 10-K for the fiscal year ended December 31, 2004,* July 26, 2005, pp. 10–11.

247   *never a man who worked on details:* Author's telephone interview with Edward E. Matthews, Nov. 21, 2005.

248   *notable increase in [the] net worth:* Office of the New York State Attorney General, "Report on Breaches of Fiduciary Duty by the Executors of the Estate of Cornelius Vander Starr," Dec. 14, 2005, exhibit 4, pp. 2–3.

248   *On October 31, 1969:* Ibid., pp. 13–15.

249   *Any suggestion that Mr. Greenberg somehow cheated:* David Boies, "David Boies Quotes in Response to Spitzer Book," Jan. 23, 2006.

249   *This is very interesting:* Author's telephone interview with David Brown, Dec. 19, 2005.

Chapter 11.   The Limits of Spitzerism

250   *The OCC is threatened with irreparable harm: Office of the Comptroller of the Currency v. Eliot Spitzer,* complaint filed June 16, 2005, Southern District of New York, p. 5.

251   *If they want to enforce state consumer protection:* Author's telephone interview with Thomas Conway, Oct. 3, 2005.

251   *The Attorney General cannot enforce fair lending laws:* Office of the Comptroller of the Currency v. Eliot Spitzer, Opinion and Order, Oct. 12, 2005, pp. 3, 39–40.

251–52 *Congress said who they wanted to deal with fees:* Author's interview with Daniel A. Pollack, New York, N.Y., Oct. 12, 2005.

252   *we are at least entitled to look:* Author's interview with David Brown, New York, N.Y., Oct. 20, 2005.

252   *shackled to this man in perpetuity:* Author's interview with Daniel Pollack, New York, N.Y., Oct. 12, 2005.

252   *stopping the attorney general of the state from trying to patrol:* "Standing Up to Spitzer," *New York Sun,* Sept. 7, 2005, p. 6.

252   *Spitzer's Waterloo:* Dan Dorfman, "Seligman Lawsuit Could Become Spitzer's Waterloo," *New York Sun,* Sept. 14, 2005, p. 6.

253   *a gun full of blanks:* Marc Humber, "GOP Jumps on Spitzer Court Defeat," Associated Press, June 11, 2005.

253   *There are so many unsolved crimes in the state of New York:* Author's interview with Harvey Pitt, New York, N.Y., June 28, 2005.

253   *You have bigger fish to fry:* Joseph Nocera, "Maybe Let This Big Fish off the Hook," *New York Times,* Nov. 26, 2005, p. C1.

253   *put a spike through Langone's heart:* Charles Gasparino, "Wall Street: This Case Is Personal," *Newsweek,* Sept. 27, 2004, p. 8.

253   *baby, it buys a lot of bombers:* Author's interview with Kenneth Langone, New York, N.Y., July 19, 2005.

254   *Of the six directors deposed thus far:* Kenneth Langone, "Boondoggle of a Case," *Wall Street Journal,* Sept. 30, 2005, p. A10.

254   *I have nothing but disdain for this man:* Author's interview with Kenneth Langone, New York, N.Y., July 19, 2005.

254   *We think the case has gotten stronger:* Eliot Spitzer at the Citizens Budget Commission, New York, N.Y., Oct. 13, 2005.

255   *Cases presenting political questions are consigned to the political branches:* State of Connecticut v. American Electric Power Company, 2005 U.S. Dist. LEXIS 19964, Sept. 15, 2005.

255   *They want to throw us back to the way it was two hundred years ago:* Eliot Spitzer, speech to the Eleanor Roosevelt Legacy Committee, New York, N.Y., Oct. 17, 2005.

255   *the whole evolution of rights that has been so central:* Author's telephone interview with Eliot Spitzer, Oct. 21, 2005.

256   *He has too much power and no accountability:* Author's telephone interview with Lisa Rickard, Oct. 6, 2005.

256   *a kind of overkill, a kind of overzealousness:* Suzanne Daley, "In 2 Mayoral Debates, Missing Evidence," *New York Times,* Nov. 6, 1989, p. B7.

257   *Because they should be:* Clifford May, "Lauder Runs Race Unlike Any Other," *New York Times,* Sept. 9, 1989, p. 1.

257   *This decision begs the question:* Jenny Anderson, "In Rarity, Spitzer Drops Case," *New York Times,* Nov. 22, 2005, p. C1.

258   *Pick your medicine:* Author's telephone interview with Eliot Spitzer, Nov. 28, 2005.

258   *Eliot lends a speed and violence to this process:* Steve Fishman, "Inside Eliot's Army," *New York,* Jan. 10, 2005.

259   *That one bothers me more than everything else:* Author's interview with Eliot Spitzer, New York, N.Y., July 18, 2005.

259   *undermine [Spitzer's] ongoing efforts to raise the business ethics of Wall Street:* Dennis Vacco, "Statement of Former New York State Attorney General Dennis C. Vacco Regarding Thursday's Announcement on Theodore Sihpol," U.S. Newswire, July 7, 2005.

261   *Seligman stumbled but picked itself up:* Author's interview with Daniel Pollack, New York, N.Y., Oct. 12, 2005.

261   *We simply want to investigate potential fraud:* Author's interview with David Brown, New York, N.Y., Oct. 20, 2005.

262   *It is in and of itself a good thing to have speedy enforcement:* Ibid.

262   *Frontier justice wasn't all bad:* Author's interview with Stanley Arkin, New York, N.Y., June 28, 2005.

262   *What Eliot has done very successfully is outsource his work:* Author's interview with Richard Beattie, New York, N.Y., May 25, 2005.

263   *The big guys can buy their way out with him:* Author's interview with Jacob Zamansky, New York, N.Y., June 6, 2005.

263   *unprofessional* and *dishonest: People v. Edward Coughlin*, SCI 6133-04, sentencing hearing, Sept. 29, 2005, p. 15. Yates later apologized for his language but reiterated that the prosecutor's claim was "wrong."

263   *When we are doing triage, it just happens:* Author's telephone interview with Eliot Spitzer, Nov. 28, 2005.

263–64 *We start in the middle because that's where the evidence takes us:* Ibid.

264   *it was all very professional:* Author's interview with Gary Naftalis, New York, N.Y., Aug. 11, 2005.

264   *Where have we been wrong on the facts:* Author's telephone interview with Eliot Spitzer, Nov. 28, 2005.

264   *But he hasn't drilled a dry hole yet:* Author's interview with James Tierney, New York, N.Y., June 6, 2005.

264–65 *That office wasn't even a stop on the railroad for the white-collar bar:* Author's interview with Mark Pomerantz, New York, N.Y., Nov. 21, 2005.

265   *We're going to play hardball too:* Author's interviews with Eliot Spitzer, New York, N.Y., Sept. 19, 2005, and Oct. 28, 2005.

265   *He is fundamentally trying to usurp:* Author's telephone interview with Lisa Rickard, Oct. 6, 2005.

265   *There is a limit and there should be a limit:* Author's interview with Eliot Spitzer, New York, N.Y., Nov. 17, 2005.

266   *Spitzer and U.S. attorney James Comey scuffled briefly:* Chris Nolan, "Spitzer Aiming a Criminal Probe at Quattrone," *New York Post*, May 12, 2003. Available at Spot-On.com.

266   *If you've got one responsible agency and one nutcase:* Author's telephone interview with Richard A. Epstein, Nov. 15, 2005.

266   *We now have different rules for the big players:* Author's telephone interview with Harvey Goldschmid, Nov. 7, 2005.

267   *According to Fortune, 11 percent of stock analyst recommendations:* Geoffrey Colvin, "Lawman's Legacy," *Fortune*, Nov. 28, 2005, p. 96.

267   *Merrill clients used the reports "extensively" through fewer than 1 percent of the hits on the Lehman Brothers Web site:* Judith Burns, " 'Independent' Stock Research Hasn't Been Must-See," *Wall Street Journal*, Nov. 26, 2005, p. B3.

268   *Spitzer has used this antifraud authority in ways Congress never intended:* Author's telephone interview with Stuart Kaswell, June 30, 2005.

268   *a discrepancy between what [funds management companies] charge retail and institutional customers:* Author's telephone interview with David Brown, Nov. 23, 2005.

268   *In 2004, 2,830 funds cut their fees:* Lipper, *Directors Analytic Data* 2003, p. 49; Lipper, *Directors Analytic Data* 2005, New York: Lipper Analytic Services, 2005, p. 51.

268   *the overwhelming increase in fee reductions:* "Lipper Releases Unparalleled Management Fee Benchmarking Guide," press release, Dec. 14, 2005.

269   *the inversion of federalism:* Author's telephone interview with Michael Greve, Nov. 1, 2005.

269   *a group that doesn't want and never wanted any government enforcement:* Author's telephone interview with Eliot Spitzer, Nov. 28, 2005.

270   *Forget about the remedy:* Author's telephone interview with Stephen Cutler, Aug. 22, 2005.

271   *an overstatement and the wrong way to go:* Author's interview with Howard Mills, New York, N.Y., Sept. 20, 2005.

271   *No one who can accept the commissions will want to merge with Aon, Willis, or Marsh:* Author's telephone interview with Robert Hartwig, Sept. 14, 2005.

271   *were giving investors what they wanted:* Ibid.

272   *improper attempts to circumvent the federal legislative process:* Brooke A. Masters, "States Flex Prosecutorial Muscle; Attorneys General Move into What Was Once Federal Territory," *Washington Post,* Jan. 12, 2005, p. A1.

272   *you cause the stock to drop, and you have real people, hardworking people, losing money:* Ibid.

272   *The SEC is looking at the entire national market structure:* Brooke A. Masters, "States, SEC Split Again in Attack on Investment Abuses; Spitzer Critical of Settlement with Putnam," *Washington Post,* Nov. 15, 2003, p. E1.

273   *Hey, we see a problem—fix it:* Author's telephone interview with Joseph Curran, May 18, 2005.

273   *It tends to bubble up better results as people debate it:* Author's telephone interview with Eugene Ludwig, Oct. 11, 2005.

273   *it makes sense to have several different enforcement sources:* Author's telephone interview with Harvey Goldschmid, Nov. 7, 2005.

274   *It's cyclical:* Masters, "States Flex Prosecutorial Muscle," p. A1.

274   *We'll just keep on fighting:* Author's interview with Eliot Spitzer, New York, N.Y., Nov. 17, 2005.

Chapter 12.   To Dare Mighty Things

276   *Friends in labor, you are the backbone:* Eliot Spitzer, speech to the Erie County Democratic Club, Buffalo, N.Y., Dec. 1, 2005.

276   *I'm an overvalued stock:* Eliot Spitzer, remarks at a fund-raiser at The Mansion, Buffalo, N.Y., Dec. 1, 2005.

277   *A crisis is a terrible thing to waste:* Eliot Spitzer, speech to Women for Spitzer luncheon, Buffalo, N.Y., Dec. 1, 2005.

277 *Barring Nelson Rockefeller returning from Beyond:* Cindy Adams, "New Book Conjuring Quite a Controversy," *New York Post,* Dec. 9, 2005, p. 18.

277 *the SEC began mailing restitution checks:* Greg Farrell, "Checks for Faulty Stock Research Go Out," *USA Today,* Dec. 22, 2005, p. B1.

278 *it made it difficult to pursue this case in a straightforward fashion:* Nathaniel Popper, "Probe of Shul Group Had N.Y. Crimebuster's Office in Tangles," *Forward,* Dec. 9, 2005.

278 *the evidence would not support state criminal charges:* Ian McDonald and Leslie Scism, "AIG's Ex Chief Clears a Hurdle but Faces More," *Wall Street Journal,* Nov. 25, 2005, p. C1.

278 *vindicated his client's decision:* Author's telephone interview with Robert G. Morvillo, Jan. 9, 2006.

279 *self-dealing:* Office of the New York State Attorney General, "Report on Breaches of Fiduciary Duty by the Executors of the Estate of Cornelius Vander Starr," Dec. 14, 2005, p. 1.

279 *the Starr Foundation . . . had received two million dollars in cash:* Ibid., pp. 17–18.

279 *the statute of limitations had not yet begun to run:* Eliot Spitzer, letter to Florence A. Davis, Dec. 14, 2005, p. 3.

279 *While the Starr Foundation respects the authority of the attorney general:* Gretchen Morgenson, "Report Says Ex-A.I.G. Chief Defrauded Foundation 35 Years Ago," *New York Times,* Dec. 15, 2005, p. C1.

280 *He's running for another office:* Dean Starkman, "Greenberg Opens Attack on Spitzer, Allegations," *Washington Post,* Dec. 16, 2005, p. D1.

280 *persecuting me in the press:* Roddy Boyd, "Spitzing Mad," *New York Post,* Dec. 16, 2005, p. 49.

280 *There is no valid claim:* David Boies, "David Boies Quotes in Response to Spitzer Book," Jan. 23, 2006.

280 *feel a certain respect for Hank and admiration:* Jesse Westbrook, "Former Governor Leads List of Greenberg Allies; Ex-AIG Chief Is Signing Up Supporters," Bloomberg News, Dec. 20, 2005.

280 *the fact that he committed it a long time ago doesn't mean he should get away with it:* Author's telephone interview with Eliot Spitzer, Dec. 20, 2005.

281 *nothing to do with documents from Bermuda:* Author's telephone interview with Lee Wolosky, Jan. 24, 2006.

281 *raw ambition for pure political gain:* Michael Cooper, "Spitzer Target Gets Even by Supporting an Opponent," *New York Times,* Dec. 10, 2005, p. B3.

281 *One liberal civic group:* Patrick D. Healy, "Group Criticizes Donations to Suozzi Linked to a Spitzer Target," *New York Times,* Jan. 20, 2006, p. B7.

281 *lies, lies and more lies:* Michael Cooper, "Spitzer Target Gets Even by Supporting an Opponent."

281 *Spitzer's habit of publicly smearing individuals while bringing no charges in court:* "Spitzer's Turkey," *Wall Street Journal,* Dec. 22, 2005, p. A14.

281 *The positions are very different:* Author's telephone interview with Eliot Spitzer, Nov. 28, 2005.

281 *I'm not going to stand here with my finger in the air:* Author's interview with Eliot Spitzer, New York, N.Y., Sept. 19, 2005.

281 *army of one:* Andrew Kirtzman, *Rudy Giuliani: Emperor of the City,* New York: Harper Paperbacks, 2001, p. 78.

282 *You want to step outside:* Matt Fleischer-Black, "Independent Means," *American Lawyer,* Oct. 1, 2002.

283 *You will pay dearly for what you have done:* John C. Whitehead, "Scary," *Wall Street Journal,* Dec. 22, 2005, p. A14.

283 *focus on your day job:* Jonathan D. Glater, "Executive's Article Revives Feud with Prosecutor," *New York Times,* Dec. 23, 2005, p. C4.

284 *Having a law proposed by Eliot Spitzer was like the kiss of death:* Author's interview with Patricia Smith, New York, N.Y., April 7, 2005.

284 *There are very few close votes in Albany:* Author's telephone interview with William McSpedon, Nov. 16, 2005.

284 *It's not going to enhance its chances in the Senate by having my name on it:* Author's interview with Dan Feldman, New York, N.Y., Sept. 27, 2005.

284 *A governor has a lot more leverage than I do:* Author's telephone interview with Eliot Spitzer, Nov. 28, 2005.

285 *a campaign to rid the city of the "squeegee men":* Fred Siegel, *The Prince of the City* (San Francisco: Encounter Books, 2005), pp. 102–3.

285 *How do you expect me to change it if I don't fight with somebody:* Eric Pooley, "Mayor of the World," *Time,* Dec. 31, 2001, p. 40.

286 *great things that actually helped set the state on a path toward greater prosperity:* Eliot Spitzer, speech at the Rockefeller Institute of Government, Nov. 21, 2005.

286–87 *If you don't think Dewey is Public Hero No. 1:* Quoted in Richard Norton Smith, *Thomas E. Dewey and His Times* (New York: Simon and Schuster, 1982), p. 216. Smith's book is the most definitive account to date of Dewey's life and career.

287 *he vetoed more than 20 percent of the bills:* Ibid., p. 374.

287 *it was not enough to merely propose a good idea:* George M. Shapiro, "Gov. Thomas E. Dewey's Legislative Leadership," in *Memories of Thomas E. Dewey,* ed. Gerald Benjamin (Albany: Nelson A. Rockefeller Institute of Government, 1991), pp. 39, 48–49.

289 *It was a really professional group:* Author's telephone interview with Marshall Stocker, Nov. 25, 2005.

289–90 *Mr. Spitzer was integral to our success:* Daniel B. Walsh, "Spitzer Helped to Defeat Legislature's Power Grab," *Wall Street Journal,* Nov. 12, 2005, p. A7.

290 *What the Democrats Need:* Noam Scheiber, "Spitzerism: Is a Prosecutor's Zeal What the Democrats Need?" *New York Times Magazine,* Oct. 2, 2005, p. 78.

290 *Far better is it to dare mighty things:* Eliot Spitzer quoting Theodore Roosevelt, Women for Spitzer luncheon, Buffalo, N.Y., Dec. 1, 2005, also Gala Dinner, New York, N.Y., Dec. 7, 2005.

Epilogue

291 *Spitzer had already raised more than nineteen million dollars:* Spitzer 2006, "2006 January Periodic Report," filed with the New York State Board of Elections, Summary page.

291 *Siena Research Institute Poll:* Siena Research Institute, "Spitzer and Clinton Remain in Solid Positions," press release, Jan. 30, 2006.

292   *It's a statement about the values I hope to bring:* Author's interview with Eliot Spitzer, New York, N.Y., Feb. 28, 2006.

292   *When Eliot Spitzer, the world's smartest man:* Patrick D. Healy, "Spitzer Names Harlem Senator to His Ticket," *New York Times,* Jan. 24, 2006, p. B1.

292–93 *trying to bring democracy back:* Author's telephone interview with Thomas R. Suozzi, March 1, 2006.

293   *Suozzi is letting himself be used as a tool:* Brooke A. Masters, "One Fight Leads to Another," *Washington Post,* March 8, 2006, p. D01.

293   *He's not looking for something from state government:* Brooke A. Masters, "Spitzer Foes Giving to Rival in Primary; Former NYSE Director Has Taken On Spitzer in His Gubernatorial Bid," *Washington Post,* March 8, 2006, p. D01.

293   *He's a fraud:* Author's telephone interview with Kenneth Langone, March 2, 2006.

294   *You're having a war:* Brooke A. Masters, "Grasso Took the Fifth in SEC Trading Probe," *Washington Post,* March 17, 2006, p. D01.

294   *regrets and apologizes:* "Agreement Between the Attorney General of the State of New York and American International Group, Inc.," Jan. 18, 2006, Exhibit 1, p. 46.

294   *improperly recorded:* American International Group Inc., *Form 8-K filed with the Securities and Exchange Commission,* Feb. 9, 2006, Exhibit 10.1, "Agreement with the DOJ," p. 1.

294   *Mr. Greenberg will be vindicated:* Howard Opinsky's e-mail statement to the press, "Statement from Howard Opinsky," Feb. 9, 2006.

295   *it's absolute validation of what we are doing:* Author's telephone interview with Eliot Spitzer, Feb. 8, 2006. *People of the State of New York v. H&R Block Inc.,* et al., complaint filed March 15, 2006.

295   *soup to nuts investigation:* Author's telephone interview with David Brown, March 17, 2006.

295–96 *85 percent* through *99 percent of them lost money: People of the State of New York v. H&R Block Inc., et al.,* complaint filed March 15, 2006, pp. 3–4.

296   *clients won't be happy:* Ibid., pp. 4–5.

296   *a better way to save:* Ibid., p. 13.

296   *blatant violation of law:* Author's telephone interview with Eliot Spitzer, March 14, 2006.

296   *78 percent:* Brooke A. Masters, "H&R Block Accused of Defrauding Customers; Firm Misled about Fees on IRAs, Civil Suit Charges," *Washington Post,* March 16, 2006, p. D01.

296   *I will sue you within a week:* Author's telephone interview with David Brown, March 17, 2006.

296   *we believe in the Express IRA:* Brooke A. Masters, "H&R Block Accused of Defrauding Customers; Firm Misled about Fees on IRAs, Civil Suit Charges," *Washington Post,* March 16, 2006, p. D01.

297   *unfair attack:* Mark A. Ernst, "Unfair Attack," *Wall Street Journal,* March 17, 2006, p. A12.

297   *Humpty Dumpty world: State of New York, et al. v. Environmental Protection Agency,* 2006 U.S. App. LEXIS 6598, March 17, 2006.

297   *how egregious:* Author's telephone interview with Eliot Spitzer, March 20, 2006.

297 *bringing cases against brokers:* Under Chairman Christopher Cox and Enforcement director Linda Chatman Thomsen, the SEC charged Bear Stearns with facilitating late trading and helping hedge funds evade rules against market-timing. The March 16, 2006, settlement required the brokerage firm to pay two-hundred-fifty-million dollars to mutual funds that were the subject of the trades. "SEC Settles Fraud Charges with Bear Stearns for Late Trading and Market Timing Violations," SEC press release, March 16, 2006.

297–98 *cracking down on the insurance companies:* On March 20, 2006, Zurich American forged two separate settlements with attorneys general and insurance commissioners from a total of thirteen states, including New York. The firm did not admit wrongdoing but agreed to pay up to $325 million in penalties to customers who alleged they overpaid for insurance because of bid-rigging. National Association of Insurance Commissioners, "NAIC Task Force Announces Insurer Bid-Rigging Settlement," press release, March 20, 2006. Zurich American, "Zurich Announces Settlement with Authorities in New York, Connecticut and Illinois," press release, March 27, 2006.

298 *We were able to plant some seeds:* Author's telephone interview with Eliot Spitzer, March 20, 2006.

ACKNOWLEDGMENTS

Writing a biography of a living figure who still has much of his career in front of him is always a daunting task, but Eliot Spitzer made my work much easier. He was candid and accessible, and encouraged his family and friends to be equally open. More to the point, he demanded no concessions and attached no strings to his cooperation. The conclusions and analysis in this book are mine alone.

So many current and former members of Spitzer's staff talked to me and dug through their files that I am afraid to list them, lest I leave someone out. But there are a few who deserve individual thanks because they sat down with me so many times: David Brown, Matt Gaul, and Maria Filipakis in the Investment Protection Bureau; Peter Pope in the Criminal Division; Michele Hirshman, Dieter Snell, Rich Baum, and Marlene Turner in the executive office; and former staffers Beth Golden and Andrew Celli, Jr. Communications director Darren Dopp fielded phone calls from me almost daily and smoothed the way with just about everyone.

I am equally grateful to my many sources who stood outside Spitzer's circle of friends and staff. Thank you for believing me when I said I wanted to write the truth and be fair. Many of you have asked not to be identified, and I have honored those requests. But I would like to acknowledge a few people whose advice and information were invaluable: former SEC commissioners Harvey Goldschmid and Harvey Pitt; Mary Schapiro and Barry Goldsmith, who were at NASD; former Maine attorney general James Tierney; Maine commissioner of professional and financial regulation Christine Bruenn; and New York lawyers Stanley Arkin, Richard Beattie, Robert Morvillo, Gary Naftalis, and John Savarese.

I am first and foremost a *Washington Post* reporter, and this work grew directly out of my wonderful beat on that paper's financial staff. Jill Dutt and Martha Hamilton gave me the freedom to delve into Spitzer's investigations. Some of the articles that resulted are cited here. They and other *Post* executives were also exceedingly gracious about giving me the time off I needed to turn what I had learned into this book.

Eliot Spitzer's career has drawn more than a little press coverage. In places, I have supplemented my interviews with the published work of other reporters to capture the flavor of what he and others were saying at the time of specific events. They are credited in the notes, but I would like to single out two *Washington Post* colleagues: Carrie Johnson, for generously covering for me when I had too much for one person to do, and Ben White, for sharing the wisdom he had gained covering Wall Street.

My agent Gail Ross was the first person to recognize that there was a market for a Spitzer biography. Without her perspicacity, this book would not exist. My editor Paul Golob at Times Books helped shape this into what I hope is a tale that will appeal to readers who are not legal or financial junkies. His obsession with baseball also proved surprisingly relevant. Copy editor Jenna Dolan asked smart questions. Mark Fowler also kept me out of trouble with his friendly but thorough legal review. Terri Rupar has saved me from embarrassment many times with her smart fact-checking over the years.

The Progressive Era references in this book owe much to Brian Balogh, who served as my undergraduate thesis adviser more than fifteen years ago and who has continued to encourage my interest in history. My parents, Jon and Rosemary Masters, and my brother, Blake, have always cheered on my endeavors, and my in-laws, Joe and Jill

Farry, have been more supportive than any daughter-in-law could ever hope for.

Finally, no one—and no working mother in particular—is an island. My husband, John Farry, makes my career possible and has been a source of support and strength. My children, Andrew and Eleanor, bring joy to my life. I love all three of you more than I could ever express.

INDEX

ABOUT THE AUTHOR

BROOKE A. MASTERS is a staff writer for *The Washington Post*, based in New York, where she writes about financial services and white-collar crime. She has reported on the trials of Martha Stewart, Frank Quattrone, and Bernard Ebbers. In her sixteen years at the *Post*, she has also covered criminal justice, education, and politics. A graduate of Harvard University and the London School of Economics, she lives in Mamaroneck, New York, with her husband and two children.